COLLECTED PAPERS ON EPISTEMOLOGY, PHILOSOPHY OF SCIENCE AND HISTORY OF PHILOSOPHY

VOLUME II

SYNTHESE LIBRARY

MONOGRAPHS ON EPISTEMOLOGY,

LOGIC, METHODOLOGY, PHILOSOPHY OF SCIENCE,

SOCIOLOGY OF SCIENCE AND OF KNOWLEDGE

AND ON THE MATHEMATICAL METHODS OF

SOCIAL AND BEHAVIORAL SCIENCES

VOLUME 91

WOLFGANG STEGMÜLLER

COLLECTED PAPERS ON EPISTEMOLOGY, PHILOSOPHY OF SCIENCE AND HISTORY OF PHILOSOPHY

VOLUME II

D. REIDEL PUBLISHING COMPANY

DORDRECHT-HOLLAND / BOSTON-U.S.A.

Library of Congress Cataloging in Publication Data

Stegmüller, Wolfgang.
Collected papers on epistemology, philosophy of science and history of philosophy.

(Synthese library; v. 91)
Translated from German.
Includes bibliographies and index.
1. Philosophy — Addresses, essays, lectures.
B29.S73 100 76-51547
ISBN-13: 978-94-010-1134-1 e-ISBN-13: 978-94-010-1132-7
DOI: 10.1007/978-94-010-1132-7

This Collection translated in part by B. Martini;
partly revised by W. Wohlhueter

Published by D. Reidel Publishing Company,
P.O. Box 17, Dordrecht, Holland

Sold and distributed in the U.S.A., Canada, and Mexico
by D. Reidel Publishing Company, Inc.
Lincoln Building, 160 Old Derby Street, Hingham,
Mass. 02043, U.S.A.

TABLE OF CONTENTS

VOLUME II

TABLE OF CONTENTS OF VOLUME I

PREFACE

These two volumes contain all of my articles published between 1956 and 1975 which might be of interest to readers in the English-speaking world.

The first three essays in Vol. 1 deal with historical themes. In each case I have attempted a rational reconstruction which, as far as possible, meets contemporary standards of exactness. In *The Problem of Universals Then and Now* some ideas of W.V. Quine and N. Goodman are used to create a modern sketch of the history of the debate on universals beginning with Plato and ending with Hao Wang's System Σ.

The second article concerns Kant's Philosophy of Science. By analyzing his position vis-à-vis I. Newton, Christian Wolff, and D. Hume, it is shown that for Kant the very notion of empirical knowledge was beset with a fundamental logical difficulty. In his metaphysics of experience Kant offered a solution differing from all prior as well as subsequent attempts aimed at the problem of establishing a scientific theory.

The last of the three historical papers utilizes some concepts of modern logic to give a precise account of Wittgenstein's so-called *Picture Theory of Meaning*. E. Stenius' interpretation of this theory is taken as an intuitive starting point while an intensional variant of Tarski's concept of a relational system furnishes a technical instrument. The concepts of model world and of logical space, together with those of homomorphism and isomorphism between model worlds and between logical spaces, form the conceptual basis of the reconstruction.

In the first purely systematic article of Vol. I, H. Reichenbach's Philosophy of Quantum Mechanics serves as a point of departure for describing the Reductionistic Program of Phenomenalism. The seemingly insurmountable difficulties blocking a realization of this program are discussed in detail. To these belongs in particular a threefold infinite regress.

The second systematic essay deals with the logical connection between the problem of ontological commitment and the analytic-synthetic dichotomy. It is shown that Carnap's attempt to make the discussions about ontological positions superfluous by distinguishing between external questions and internal questions either leads to a highly controversial conception or presupposes a precise definition of 'analytical statement'. A critical discussion of the pros and cons of the use of the concept of analyticity follows.

Vol. II begins with *The So-Called Circle of Understanding*. Six different meanings of the phrase 'hermeneutic circle' are distinguished. Of these, two are discussed in detail: the 'confirmation dilemma' and the 'dilemma of separating background knowledge and facts'. In order to illustrate the seriousness of the difficulty involved here, two case studies are cited: a dispute among Germanists about the correct interpretation of the famous poem by Walther von der Vogelweide about dreams of love and the astrophysical riddle of Quasars.

In the next two papers, *'The Problem of Causality'* and *Explanation, Prediction, Scientific Systematization and Non-Explanatory Information*. The Hempel-Oppenheim scheme of scientific explanation is used to construct at least a partial explication of concepts like 'cause', 'law of causality', 'causal explanation' and 'general principle of causality' as well as to discuss the question of the structural uniformity of explanation and prediction. Some of these results are partly outdated by two of my more recent books: *Wissenschaftliche Erklärung und Begründung* (Berlin-Heidelberg-New York, 1969), in particular Ch. VI, and *Personelle und statistische Wahrscheinlichkeit*, second half, *Statistisches Schliessen – Statistische Begründung – Statistische Analyse,* in particular Part IV.

In the essays *The Problem of Induction: Hume's Challenge and the Contemporary Answers* and *Carnap's Normative Theory of Inductive Probability* I take a new and novel approach to modern attempts at coping with Hume's challenge concerning induction. It is argued that the basic problem of induction must either be characterized as unsolvable or as having a trivial negative solution only. The basis for a rational discussion must consist of what I call the successor problems to induction. They fall into two main classes: those belonging to the realm of theoretical reason and those belonging to the domain of practical reason. Only a relatively small part of human rationality has to do with theoretical reasoning; the rest embraces rational decision and rational behavior. In my opinion, the objections against Carnap's idea of an inductive logic put forward by W. Salmon force us to reinterpret Carnap's project as belonging to the second domain. This demand for a decision-theoretic reinterpretation of Carnap's inductive logic is also illustrated by an imaginary dialogue between D. Hume and R. Carnap. Should this result be accepted, the Carnap-Popper debate proves, in retrospect, to be pointless, since Popper's program is exclusively concerned with theoretical reasoning.

The articles *Logical Understanding and the Dynamics of Theories* and *Structures and Dynamics of Theories* try, roughly speaking, to dispense with certain irrational elements thought to be inherent in the progress of science according to a widely-held notion stemming from Thomas S. Kuhn. The first essay contains a sketch of the material treated in detail in my book *The Structure and Dynamics of Theories* (New York, 1976). First, the structuralistic or non-statement view of theories as developed by J.D. Sneed is described. Then, by distinguishing between theories, the empirical claims of theories, and acts of holding a theory, a simple solution to the Kuhn-Popper controversy is given. Furthermore, I indicate how the difficulties created by Kuhn's problem of the 'incommensurability of theories' may be overcome with a new, presumably still to be modified, concept of reduction introduced by Sneed; this concept permits a comparison of theories with completely different theoretical superstructures. The second of these papers makes an additional concession to Kuhn's so-called subjectivism. Whereas both the previous paper and the book mentioned first introduce an objective concept of a theory which is then used to define 'holding a theory', the concept of holding a theory is now introduced independently without the help of a previously defined notion of a theory. Intuitively, this method appears circular without actually being so, namely, that a theory comes into existence only by virtue of the existence of persons holding it.

In the *historically* earliest of my articles on *Language and Logic* I describe several philosophical pitfalls created by logical connectives, variables, quantifiers, and modal operators.

The last contribution deals with the 'game-theoretical models of logical systems' stemming from Paul Lorenzen and Kuno Lorenz. These bring two *prima facie* quite different disciplines into close contact, which yields several new and interesting insights. It turns out, e.g. that the whole difference between classical and intuitionistic logic, in game-theoretical form, reduces to the question of whether repetitions of defence moves are permitted or not. And it is for just this reason that Lorenzen's fundamental philosophical thesis to the effect that intuitionistic logic alone represents 'true' logic appears to be ill-founded. For there is no cogent, convincing reason for preferring one set of defence rules to another.

Several of these essays, in particular the earlier ones, originated in the effort to promote and to enhance the understanding of the methods of analytical philosophy, to which I had tried to gain access only by 'solipsistic solitariness'. At the time of writing the earlier papers, the works of the Vienna

Circle were almost forgotten in German-speaking areas and modern analytic philosophy was practically unknown. I therefore chose partly historical subjects in order to demonstrate by way of example how this method could be brought into fruitful contact with the German historical tradition. In the later articles, the main endeavor was to achieve new systematic results. But even there my driving motive was to contribute to mutual understanding and to reciprocate stimulation and intellectual fertilization.

The number of philosophers whose publications have stimulated me and for which I am grateful is very large. Above all, I feel especially indebted to W.V. Quine, N. Goodman, H. Scholz, A. Tarski, R. Carnap and the other members of the Vienna Circle as well as such closely-related thinkers as H. Reichenbach and in later years J.D. Sneed and T.S. Kuhn.

Finally, I wish to thank the translators for the successful completion of their by no means easy labors.

University of Munich
December 1976

WOLFGANG STEGMÜLLER

ACKNOWLEDGEMENTS

The publishers wish to thank the following publishers and editors for permission to include the respective chapters in this volume.

Wissenschaftliche Buchgesellschaft, Darmstadt, the copyright holders of the original German, for Chapter 2, which is a translation of 'Das Problem der Kausalität', in E. Topitsch (ed.), *Probleme der Wissenschaftstheorie. Festschrift für Victor Kraft,* Springer 1960, pp. 171-190; and for Chapter 8, which is a translation of 'Sprache und Logik', *Studium Generale* 9 (1956), pp. 57-77.

The editor of *Ratio* and Wissenschaftliche Buchgesellschaft for Chapter 3, which originally appeared in the English edition of *Ratio* 8 (1966), pp. 1-24.

F. Vieweg und Sohn, Wiesbaden, the copyright holders of the original German, for Chapter 4, which is a translation of 'Das Problem der Induktion: Humes Herausforderung und moderne Antworten', in H. Lenk (ed.), *Neue Aspekte der Wissenschaftstheorie,* Vieweg 1971, pp. 13-74.

North-Holland Publishing Company, Amsterdam, for Chapter 5, which originally appeared in P. Suppes *et al.* (eds.), *Logic, Methodology and Philosophy of Science* Vol. 4, North-Holland 1973, pp. 501-513.

The editor of the *Notre Dame Journal of Formal Logic,* for Chapter 9, which originally appeared in the *Notre Dame Journal of Formal Logic* 5, No. 2, (April 1964), pp. 81-112.

CHAPTER 1

THE SO-CALLED CIRCLE OF UNDERSTANDING

If you pass by a construction site, you will often notice some people standing around with nothing to do. Hasty West Europeans will typically shake their finger – at least in spirit – and mutter a few words about the declining work morale in times of a construction boom. This is a typical case of *prejudice*. In point of truth, the case is quite different. Although no friend of 'real' definitions purporting to exhibit the essence of entities, if I were asked for the *essence of human planning* I would answer: 'there must always be someone waiting for something'. Prejudices are very often difficult to eradicate.. This can be seen in our example and is exemplified on a higher level and to a much greater extent in states with a centralised economy. For several decades Marxists – but not just Marxists – have waged a dogged and hopeless fight against the truth that planning failures constitute an integral part of planning. Nevertheless, Marxist Utopians seem to this very day to remain blind to this truth.

Prejudices block the *road of inquiry* in everyday life as well as in science, at any rate if understood in the sense we usually mean when we speak of prejudices. But now the question arises whether there are not *certain kinds of prejudices* which are (1) *insurmountable*, and (2) *are not to be judged negatively at all* since they reflect a basic feature of the human mind, that is, a 'prejudice-structure', so to speak, of human understanding. Ever since the hermeneuticist Ast used the metaphor, later taken over by Schleiermacher (and dubbed by him 'hermeneutic principle'),[1] 'Just as the whole is understood in terms of the individual, so also the individual can only be understood in terms of the whole', one is inclined to answer both questions in the affirmative. Today it is maintained, particularly by an appeal to Heidegger, that this circle has an *ontologically positive sense*,[2] and that the essential subjectivity involved here is a distinctive and delimiting feature of the arts and humanities (*Geisteswissenschaften*) as opposed to the 'objective natural sciences'.

We have been, and are, often reminded by the opponents of Hermeneutics of the dubious historical background of the hermeneutic theories of understanding; for example, that they are of theological origin and hence simply amount to a secularized theology, that they originated in the Christian idea that man is distinguished from all the rest of creation by virtue of his immortal soul, and that subsequently the Cartesian myth and/or the Hegelian metaphysics of the spirit have also entered into hermeneutic thinking. All of these things will not be taken into account here for they concern only the *genesis* and this *never* decides over the *validity* or *invalidity* of a philosophical position.

I will limit myself entirely to the phenomenon of the hermeneutic circle. *For the circle of understanding seems to be the rational core which is left after all the irrational factors are eliminated from the thesis of the distinctive or special place of the humanities (Geisteswissenschaften) vis-à-vis the natural sciences.* Even this, however, may not be especially important, for it may well be doubted whether such a sub-division of the sciences is at all philosophically important. But that is exactly what the hermeneuticists claim: the difference in content necessitates a difference in method. In particular, since the analytic theory of science fails to pay attention to the circle of understanding, it is not applicable to the humanities (*Geisteswissenschaften*).

Before such a sweeping claim can be critically examined, two questions about meaning must be answered: what is really *meant* by the *hermeneutic circle* and what is meant by saying that it *cannot be eliminated*.

In discussing these questions I will try to avoid any appeal to hermeneutics. I will use the expressions 'hermeneutic' or 'understanding' only as incomplete linguistic symbols within the context of 'hermeneutic circle' or 'circle of understanding' that is, only as linguistic tools to designate a *phenomenon that is yet to be explained*. As a justification for disregarding the hermeneutic literature in this way I can only cite the fact that, in my opinion, absolutely everything is wrong with the usual designation 'the circle of the understanding': the *definite article* is inappropriate because we are not dealing here with *one* specific and sharply circumscribed phenomenon; the expression '*understanding*' is also out of place because the 'circle of understanding' is not anything peculiar to any form of understanding; and even the use of the word 'circle' is mistaken because the 'circle of understanding' does not involve a circle at all. To be sure, this designation has in *one* of its meanings something to do with the *mistaken impression that there exists a circle*. In so far as this is the case, one must confine himself to explaining how it is that this impression arises and why it is possibly miscontrued as a correct impression. It will become clear that at the root of this impression lies a genuine problem.

Although the following discussion should make no mention of hermeneutics, I nonetheless want to mention at the outset a number of difficulties that a logician encounters when he attempts to deal with the hermeneutic literature.

(1) First of all there is the *pictorial-metaphorical* language used by all hermeneuticists. There is nothing objectionable at all about the use of pictures per se as long as those who resort to them are also aware that they are talking in metaphors. Unfortunately, this is almost never the case here: pictures are used and it is *mistakenly thought* that one is working with precise concepts.

(2) It must also be pointed out that the *distinction between object- and meta-level* is blurred. I mention briefly one example: E. Staiger in his essay 'The Art of Interpretation' has given an interpretation of Mörike's poem 'Die Lampe'. There has subsequently arisen an argument over it between him and Heidegger which has spilled over into an exchange of letters that has been published. The poem in question closes with the line: '*Was aber schön ist, seelig scheint es in ihm selbst*'. In order to convey most clearly how his interpretation departs from that of Staiger, Heidegger makes a very reasonable suggestion: he translates into Latin the phrase '*selig scheint es in ihm selbst*' in two different ways. This suggestion may be considered reasonable in view of the fact that the Romans often expressed themselves much more clearly and unambiguously than we do in German (as holds for the case at hand). Heidegger starts out with the observation that Staiger's interpretation of the expression '*seelig scheint es in ihm selbst*' means: '*felix in se ipso (esse) videtur*'. *Seelig* is here construed predicatively and '*in sich selbst*' ('*in se ipso*') as belonging to '*seelig*' ('*felix*'). Heidegger, on the other hand, espouses the view – by appealing among other things to the 'in the air' Hegelian aesthetics – that the last line must be read in such a way that the '*in ihm selbst*' belongs to '*scheint*' and *not* to '*seelig*' and that '*scheinen*' is to be construed in the sense of shining; the correct translation would thus read: '*feliciter lucet in eo ipso*'. The reply from Staiger contains, among other things, the astonishing objection that Heidegger is being pedantic with concepts: "You seem to me, quite contrary to your own convictions, to insist too much on concepts and to overlook the floating, flowing, shy, cautious ... iridescent quality of poetic language, such as Morike has developed."[3] He succumbs here to the logical error that a poem composed in such a language can only be talked *about* in a floating, flowing, iridescent language. This error quite evidently goes counter to Staiger's own reassurance that interpretation must be something quite different than 'paraphrasing in prose'. Obviously a scientist *can* and *must* talk in clear concepts about Morike's poem and he furthermore may take a clear stand or he must simply leave it alone. What Heidegger has done is simply to

compare two competing hypotheses of interpretation; he has attempted to clarify how the content of these hypotheses differs by translating them into Latin and he has given his reasons for preferring the second hypothesis.

(3) The next and particularly important point is the *unclearness surrounding the status of the key hermeneutic concepts*, that is, concepts such as *understanding*, *prejudice*, *preconception*. Let us consider for example the expression 'prejudice'. One is here confronted by the following alternatives:

First alternative: The word is *taken from everyday language*. This cannot be; for Gadamer and others differentiate very explicitly prejudice in the negative sense from *positive prejudice*. In everyday life, however, this word is used *only* in the negative sense, that is, it occurs together with 'against' and not together with 'for'. I very often hear expressions such as: 'N.N. has a prejudice *against* the Americans, *against* the Jews, or *against* the Germans'. But I have yet to hear an expression such as: 'N.N. has a prejudice *for* the Eskimos, *for* the Italians, or a prejudice *for* the Japanese'.

Second possibility: The expression is introduced as a *terminus technicus* by means of an explicit definition. It *sounds* indeed *like* an everyday word, but yet is not *synonymous* with it as may be seen from the definition. Unfortunately such a definition is nowhere to be found.

Third possibility: One might advocate the view that we are dealing with a *theoretical concept* which, like many basic physical concepts, does not admit of a sharp definition. To such a suggestion I can only reply with a Latin sentence, which possesses a negative reputation in so far as it has *not* been uttered by *any* scholastic philosopher nor by *any* modern philosopher, even though it *ought* to have been uttered long before: '*termini sine theoria nihil valent*'. *What theory?*

(4) Yet another key hermeneutic concept is the expression 'understanding'. Even today the juxtaposition of *understanding* and *explanation* which originated with Dilthey seems to play as big a role as ever. It is supposed to characterize as well as cement the antithesis between the natural sciences and the humanities (*Natur- und Geisteswissenschaften*). Of all the epistemological dichotomies which I am familiar with, such as 'analytic-synthetic', 'a priori-empirical', 'descriptive-normative', all of which prove more or less useful in *certain contexts*, Dilthey's juxtaposition is *by far the most fruitless*. The grounds for this are of a logico-linguistic nature and concern both of the words used by Dilthey. In the first place the expression 'understanding' is so ambiguous that I am almost inclined to give an expression of Wittgenstein I (the author of the *Tractatus Logico-Philosophicus*) an ironical twist and say: 'understanding fills the entire logical space'. It is hard to conceive of a scien-

tific activity with respect to which one might not use the word 'understand' in a number of ways, all of them perfectly adequate. Thus, it is indeed correct to emphasize that it is the business of literary scientists and historians to *understand* texts (to *construe them with understanding*), to strive to *understand* the motives and character traits of historical personalities, to seek to *understand* the norms and values of cultures. Such remarks are, however, quite comparable to similar statements about the activity of mathematicians and physicists. A student of both of these disciplines must above all attempt to *understand* the basic concepts of mathematics and physics. He must later go on to *understand* theorems, theories, and hypotheses. And to do that it will again become necessary that he learns to *understand* the proofs given for the theorems and the reasons given for the hypotheses. This parallel does not show that mathematics and physics are *also* 'to be interpreted hermeneutically' but that the word 'understand' in view of its numerous meanings and shades of meaning is of no help if our aim is to gain information about the nature of the individual sciences and their relation to each other. If one wants to draw distinctions and recognize differences, then one should not use as a 'key word' an expression out of which one can squeeze *some* meaning for *any* situation.

The situation is actually even worse, for the word 'explain' is also unfortunately an extraordinarily ambiguous word. Thus it is indeed quite true that natural scientists often use the so-called subsumption model of explanation and say for example: 'The Galilean law of gravitation and the Keplerian laws can at least be approximatively explained by the Newtonian theory.' But one can again cite other uses of the word 'explain' and by means of them describe the activity of interpretation. Thus, for example, a linguist *explains* to us the meaning of words of a language which is not familiar to us; or a Sinologist *explains* to his audience the meaning of a Chinese poem. Hence, *either* the two expressions 'understand' and 'explain' designate completely *disparate* concepts, as for example in: 'understanding a text – explanation of the laws of gravity' in which case the juxtaposition is just as uninteresting and fruitless as in other cases of disparate concepts: we don't after all expect any fundamental insight from the juxtaposition of concepts such as 'prime number' and 'parrot'. Or the meanings overlap. Then the *question aiming at understanding* can be formulated in such a way that it becomes a *question calling for an explanation* as we had occasion to see, for example, in the three cases where someone *does not understand and would like to have explained* a concept, a theory, or a proof. It is just like the case where we are dealing with the analysis of the function of an automaton. Someone may ask, for example: '*I do not understand* the copy and translation mechanism of the genetic code. Can somebody *explain* this mechanism to me?' Even in the question and answer game of moral objections and justifications the two meanings become intertwined, so that if someone says to another: '*I do not understand*, how you could possibly have done something like that. Can you *explain* your action to me? '

(5) I personally find the following very disturbing: contemporary hermeneuticists reassure us often and gladly that they have *completely freed* themselves from the *psychologism* of Schleiermacher and the young Dilthey. Yet, *in the same breath*, they use expressions which cannot be construed in any way but psychologically. Thus there is talk for example of *acts* of understanding or of *achieving* understanding, and the like. I know of only very few indeed unimportant meanings of the word 'understand' which lend to such expressions a semblance of meaning.

For the most part, they are simply ungrammatical (*sprachwidgrig*). In order to *understand* how it came to this, we have to refer to a tradition quite different from that of Schleiermacher-Dilthey: many, if not most, of today's hermeneuticists are somehow under the influence of Heidegger or phenomenology and are thus intellectual great-grandchildren of F. Brentano, whose *doctrine of intentionality* is still quite influential. Brentano has explained what he meant with much greater clarity and plainness than any of his followers: The intentional acts (of perceiving, judging, wanting, etc.) are acts of *psychic activity*, that is, of what *I would call the second invisible man within the visible man*. Brentano's philosophy of consciousness is *a variant* of the opposite theory which formed Wittgenstein's point of reference for demarcating his own philosophy of mind. (What comes to mind are Wittgensteinian expressions such as language gives us the illusion of a bodily process and as we find none, we invent an invisible mind; for 'thinking' and 'perceiving' have the same grammar as 'running'.)

(6) The biggest difficulty concerns the question of the analyses of examples. As long as we are not dealing with the interpretation of religious texts, and thus with hermeneutics in the theological sense, we unfortunately have to say: *such analyses of examples* are completely non-existent. One would nevertheless expect that authors who write extensive works and long essays on hermeneutics or on the distinction between scientific and intellectual knowledge would show through concrete examples taken from history or from the history of literature how a humanist (*Geisteswissenschaftler*) as opposed to a natural scientist (*Naturwissenschaftler*) *formulates* his hypotheses, how he establishes *logical relationships between them, how he supports the*

theses he espouses, and how he *defends them against the criticism and attacks of colleagues who think otherwise.* In this respect there doubtlessly exists a gap between the natural philosophy and theory of so-called 'scientific knowledge', on the one hand, and hermeneutics on the other hand. Whereas there one at least makes an attempt at illustrating abstract considerations by examples and clarifying – be it via simplified models, be it via an analysis of present scientific theories and their applications – the equivalent of this is altogether missing here.

Let us now turn to the real issue. I will distinguish between various meanings of the expression 'hermeneutic circle' without, however, making any claim to completeness. In each of these meanings we are dealing with a particular form of a

dilemma:

(I) *The dilemma of interpreting one's own language*;
(II) *The dilemma of interpreting a foreign language*;
(III) *the problem of the theoretical circle*;
(IV) *the dilemma of the perspective of the observer*;
(V) *the dilemma of confirmation*;
(VI) *a dilemma in the distinction between background knowledge and facts*

The first four types of problems will be treated briefly, whereas the last two will be treated in greater detail.

To prevent any misunderstanding, let me expressly point out that in this list I have intentionally taken into account only the interpretations of 'hermeneutic circle' which involve certain kinds of *difficulties* for the sciences in question. There doubtlessly exist still other versions which are *harmless* in that what is there attempted is to call attention in a metaphorical way to a more or less interesting phenomenon which does not lead to any special scientific difficulty and which furthermore does not contain anything specific to liberal arts research. One might here cite as an example a feature of what Carnap calls *concept explication.* One is dealing here with a typical case where an *intuitive 'preconception'* is furnished with an explicans so that one can then say that what is thereby obtained does not abandon or solve the original preconception but constitutes an *elaboration* of it. In contrast to Carnap who regarded this process as a straightforward linear progression from the vague to the precise, I would be more inclined to view an explication of a concept as a process involving multiple negative feedback, for the success of an explication will depend on a frequent return to the intuitive starting point and revisions of it.[4] One might try to depict this process with the picture of a *spiral*, wherein the ascent serves as a measure of the growth in understanding gained by means of the explication. Perhaps something like this was what one or the other hermeneuticist had in mind by the 'circle of understanding'.

The picture of the '*hermeneutic spiral*' is applicable whenever there occurs a *growth* in understanding, but *not without considerable effort*. There are no grounds for supposing that this picture is appropriate only in the case of certain kinds of liberal arts' research. In particular, it is *likewise* applicable *to metatheoretical interpretations*, even to those which refer to *scientific* theories. For, contrary to a very widespread opinion, it must be emphasized that we are still only at the beginning of a deeper understanding of scientific theories. The picture is thus applicable in a variety of ways. It must, nevertheless, not be overlooked that in all of these applications it is still *only a picture*.

Let us now return, however, to the difficulties we have enumerated. Some of them, namely (I) and (II) are to be found only in disciplines which have been traditionally called the Humanities, where they *may* appear, but need not. Others, as for example (IV) and (V), are presumably not limited to certain branches of science. Finally, the last difficulty (VI) occurs only in sciences of a certain formal type. But these sciences need not be any of the Humanities.

(I) *The dilemma of interpreting one's own language*: construed abstractly this problem – which crops up only in certain cases – can be formulated in the following way: *in order to interpret a particular text formulated in the language of the interpreter, one must start out with an assumption about the intention of the author* – I will call this assumption the underlying hypothesis – *which upon further reading may turn out to be false*. Should, indeed, the underlying hypothesis be contradicted in the course of the study, it must then be replaced by a better one; but here one encounters the following problem: *the correct underlying hypothesis could only be gained by a successful study of just that text which itself can be meaningfully construed only by reference to this underlying hypothesis which is not yet available.*

So as to illustrate what here looks like a complicated state of affairs, let me cite a particularly up-to-date example: the *Philosophical Investigations* of L. Wittgenstein. Although this masterpiece of German prose contains not a single technical expression, reading it proves to be extraordinarily difficult. What accounts for this?

Wittgenstein develops his ideas very often in the form of a dialogue with an imaginary opponent whose views he cites directly and to which he then replies. Most readers will experience, I suppose, much the same thing I experienced in my first reading of it: everything Wittgenstein's opponent says seems to be right, whereas Wittgenstein's replies seem partly incomprehensible, partly absurd. This impression becomes quite strong, particularly in those places where Wittgenstein argues heatedly against the view that it is possible to refer to private sensations via language. At a later stage the reader realizes that his difficulties in understanding might rest on the fact that Wittgenstein is presenting a theory of the meaning of linguistic expressions which radically departs from the commonly accepted conception. Wittgenstein links the concept 'meaning of a word' directly with 'use of a word'. The reader is not aware of this connection. With this we have already arrived at the crux of the difficulty which I have called the dilemma of interpreting one's own language. *In order to be able to read the Philosophical Investigations with real understanding the reader must be acquainted with Wittgenstein's theory of meaning. But there is no other way of learning this theory except by understanding this very book*. This is a genuine difficulty. It has the following formal structure:

'In order to understand *A*, one must first know *B*;
to gain knowledge of *B*, one must first understand *A*'.

As we have just said, this indeed constitutes a genuine difficulty; nevertheless it is not a *circle*, but rather a *dilemma*. The difficulty is surely not in principle insurmountable. Mutually competing hypotheses of interpretation may be tested on the basis of various criteria: inner consistency, accord with as many texts as possible, logical connection and coherence of the components of interpretation, agreement with other information about the author, etc. If at the end, after the elimination of inadequate hypotheses several possibilities still remain open, this may (but need not) be the result of missing information. In any event, it does *not* lie in the nature of the case. By the expression 'if several possibilities lie open, then this need not be due to missing information' I wanted to allude to the thesis that one can understand an author not only better than he himself does, but that this 'better understanding' is possible in various ways.

If the hermeneuticists advocating the thesis of the indestructability of the hermeneutic circle mean that *this dilemma cannot be overcome*, then what might be inferred from this is not that there exists something which pertains specifically to the kind of knowledge obtainable in the Humanities, but simply that all disciplines which are affected by this dilemma should just fold up since theirs is a hopeless undertaking.

Instead of setting out from the radical alternative: 'the dilemma can always be overcome – the dilemma can never be overcome' one should undertake specific investigations in every concrete individual case. Two possibilities may here result: *either* one arrives at a solution despite the difficulty (in our example: at a theory of Wittgenstein's doctrine of meaning). Then the dilemma is overcome and no longer exists. *Or* again the dilemma persists with the available information. One must then, at least temporarily, abandon the hope of arriving at a usable theory (in our example: to be able to read the book with understanding), and one can only hope that some day in the future a way out of the impasse will be found through new empirical evidence or through luck, accident, and new insights.

(II) *The dilemma of interpreting a foreign language*: Similar, though, in one important respect quite different, is another difficulty. Its formal structure is analogous to that of the former case. It differs from case (I) in that the text to be interpreted is written not in the language of the interpreter but *in a foreign language*, possibly even in a language which is no longer spoken on this planet. Perhaps a difficulty of this structure crops up more often in the latter case than in the former, i.e. we may perhaps have to deal much more often with *this* kind of dilemma of interpretation. Habermas seems to have this difficulty in mind when he talks about the phenomenon of the hermeneutic circle (cf. '*Knowledge and Interest*', p. 214). His line of thought is roughly as follows: if an interpreter wants to interpret texts of the past epochs, then the life-style of that age is not given independently of the texts, for this life-style is irretrievably past. So, *it is alleged*, a circle is involved: *from the texts handed down, the interpreter must infer the life-style of that era; but he needs, on the other hand, a knowledge of this life-style in order to understand the language of that era.*

Here too we are not dealing with a *circle* but with a *dilemma*. This dilemma is however not as great as one might be led to believe by the above observation. First of all, it is simply not true that there exists an historical access to a past life-style only through texts. One can also gain interesting information about man's behaviour in the past through his art and other findings. Second, the claim that what is here called the life-style of past epochs is irretrievably lost is likewise incorrect. Old customs, such as, for example, marriage customs, have often maintained themselves to this very day. An ethnologist who studies today's customs can quite well supply the historian with knowledge about particular social patterns of behavior of the past.

I nevertheless don't want to dwell any further on this type of difficulty represented by (I) and (II). For even though this dilemma appears as a dilemma of *interpretation* only in the interpretation-oriented Humanities, the difficulties of the *said formal structure* are not at all limited to research in the Humanities. Difficulties of this type may well crop up, in principle, in *all* of the sciences. (Thus, for example, a basic difficulty involving the Quasar phenomenon, which will be mentioned later, might be put into a form which has exactly the same structure as that of the interpretation dilemma, namely, 'In order to interpret the Quasar phenomenon satisfactorily one must have available the correct cosmological model. But an adequate cosmological hypothesis cannot be had as long as no correct interpretation of the Quasar phenomenon has been found.')

(III) *The problem of the theoretical circle*: the so-called *theoretical function concepts* and their somewhat mysterious nature have played quite an important role in the meta-scientific discussions of these past few years. While there has been for a long time no agreement as to how these concepts are to be distinguished, new investigations, especially those of J.D. Sneed, have suggested the idea of characterizing these concepts in terms of the role they play in the application of a theory. They assume here quite a remarkable role, for the values of these functions are *measured in a theory-dependent way*. Roughly speaking, this means that in order to determine *whether such a concept holds* in a particular case, *one must already have successful applications of this theory.* Here there indeed arises the danger of a circle, indeed a genuine, that is, vicious circle. To escape this danger, Sneed draws quite drastic consequences, for example, the following: a theory may *not* be construed as a system of statements.

The grounds for citing this point in the present context, are that here too, a *circle of understanding* is involved in so far as understanding a theoretical term presupposes an 'understanding' of the theory in which this term occurs.

But for exactly the same reason as before, it does not seem appropriate to go into more details *in the present context*. It *may* well be that we have here a situation which is somewhat *analogous* to that which various hermeneuticists had in mind. But the problem in question crops up wherever certain kinds of theoretical concepts are used. Perhaps it comes up *only* in physics, possibly in the other natural sciences, but at any rate *not exclusively* in the Arts and Humanities. Hence, however interesting the problem may in itself be, it will, nevertheless, not be considered as belonging to the present context by all of the philosophers who are willing to subsume under the concept 'hermeneutic circle' only those phenomena which are potential candidates for demarcating the Humanities (or some of them) from the natural sciences.

(IV) *The dilemma of the perspective of the observer*: By an observer is here meant the historian or the interpreter and the *thesis that the hermeneutic circle is unavoidable* is put on a par with the assertion that this perspective cannot be done away with. A stand in regard to this thesis depends upon what exactly it means.

(1) A possible interpretation and indeed a very radical one is the following: every interpretation of a text and every construal of human action requires a *preconception* (*Vorverständnis*). And the interpreter can 'never completely escape' this preconception since it involves certain presuppositions ('prejudices') which not only have not de facto been tested but *which he in principle cannot test.* He thus makes, tacitly or expressly, a series of hypothetical assumptions which he cannot in principle put to the test and from which he simply cannot free himself *since* he is incapable of testing them.

I can only point out two things here: first the hermeneuticist who asserts something like this would have to carry the burden of proof for such thesis. Second, I have not the slightest idea what such a proof is supposed to look like.

If this radical thesis may nevertheless seem plausible to some, it may be due either to confusing the concepts 'actually not proved' with 'not provable in principle', or of mistakenly inferring from the premise that in all reasoning and interpretation one must make some presuppositions – for without them one could not even begin to reason – the claim that there exist unprovable presuppositions. (This inference is mistaken since the following two propositions are perfectly compatible with each other and can thus both be right: (a) one cannot simultaneously drop or doubt all presuppositions; (b) every one of these presuppositions can be subjected to critique and be consequently open to revision.)

(2) What might be meant by the so-called perspective is something like what T.S. Kuhn has called a 'paradigm'. An exact analysis of this view would demand a detailed discussion of his concept of science, something which cannot be done here. I must thus limit myself to some brief comments. In the view of the Popperian and other rationalist critics, Kuhn's unprecedented main idea is said to relegate the natural sciences to a completely irrational position (and might lead one to believe with Lakatos that Kuhn is replacing the philosophy of science with applied mass psychology). Both forms of scientific endeavor described by Kuhn seem to be characterized by the predo-

minance of a non-rational attitude: the *normal scientist* uses his paradigm theory only as an instrument for solving puzzles, yet he never subjects it to a critical test but holds on to it uncritically (like a narrow-minded dogmatist). And *in times of scientific revolutions* a new theory is not invented because the old one has failed the test of experience (was empirically falsified); rather *the new theory dislodges the old one directly* and this process does not rely on arguments but rather on conversion experiences, persuasions, propaganda.

It seems to me that Kuhn's analyses and historical illustrations represent the greatest challenge made so far to contemporary philosophy of science. I find this challenge particularly great in view of the fact that I am convinced that Kuhn is quite correct in his main theses. Hence I also don't believe that one can meet his challenge by resorting to 'rationalistic polemics' as practiced by the Popperians. Rather, it behooves us to provide a rational reconstruction of Kuhn's concepts of *normal science* as well as of the phenomenon of the *direct dislodgment of a theory by an alternate theory*. This is, in fact, possible. One must, however, be prepared *to abandon certain models of rational scientific behavior*. It seems to me, namely, that Kuhn has done for the theory of science exactly the opposite of what the critics accuse him of: he has not pointed out the irrationality in the behaviour of scientists, *but discovered new dimensions of scientific rationality*.

First of all, the concept of scientific rationality should not be connected to concepts like that of strict proof and corroboration (or confirmation). The rational reconstruction of the concept of normal science comes about, for example, through *explication of a concept of holding a theory*, according to which persons have one and the same theory and yet may associate with it the *most divergent convictions and hypotheses*. If we bear this in mind, many of Kuhn's provocative comments become not only understandable but even justifiable, as for example, the assertion that the only sort of theory rejection to which counterexamples can lead, is the rejection of *science as a profession*: for failure to match experience does not reflect *on the theory*, but rather on the *person* holding it; or as Kuhn says: the inability to find solutions for difficulties (anomalies) *discredits only the scientist and not the theory*.[5]

My main reason for not dwelling on this point any longer is again the same as before; namely, if what is supposed to be understood by the hermeneutic circle is the 'impossibility of escaping from preconception' and if this is, in turn, supposed to represent something analogous to what I have just called 'holding a theory in the sense of Kuhn', then the hermeneutic circle would not constitute anything peculiar to the Humanities and typical of them alone; rather, one would here be dealing with something which so far has only been precisely explicated for the exact natural sciences and might be transferred at best secondarily to the case of the Humanities. Furthermore, the word 'circle' would here be used at best in a metaphorical sense.

I want now to go on to the two other possible interpretations (V) and (VI) of the hermeneutic circle and discuss both of them simultaneously since they are so closely connected.

Once again we are dealing with certain kinds of difficulties which I will label '*confirmation-dilemma*' [Problem (V)] and 'the problem of the distinction between background and factual knowledge' [Problem (VI)].

My reasons for concentrating principally on these last two issues, especially on (VI), are the following: first of all, only problem (VI) contains a dilemma which affects *historical* knowledge alone. Secondly, this is the only interpretation in which the phenomenon to be analyzed is connected with the *impression of a genuine circle*. Third, it will become apparent that talk of the unresolvability of the hermeneutic circle is here not only meaningful but indeed correct, *for this last dilemma actually cannot be eliminated*. For the sake of greater perspicacity, I will briefly elucidate the difficulties by means of two examples; one from Germanic Literature, the other from astrophysics.

The first example is taken from a detailed case-study which may be found in the book by Heide Göttner: *Logic of Interpretation*.[6] It deals with a discussion between the two German philologists, Wapnewski and Hahn, over the correct rendering of the poem by Walther von der Vogelweide (74, 20). This song of Dream-love (*Lied von der Traumliebe*) is given in an English translation (based on a modern German translation by Gerhard Hahn).

(I) 'Take, my love, this garland' I once said to a beautiful young maiden, 'You are the festive crown of the dance, when you are adorned with these beautiful flowers. Were I to have a precious crown I would bestow it upon you. Of that you can rest assured, for I mean it with all my heart.'

(II) You are so beautiful that I would like to offer you the most beautiful garland of flowers that I possess: I know where there are many red and white flowers – out there in yonder meadow. There where they all bloom in splendor and the birds sing shall we together pluck them.'

(III) She accepted what I offered her in the true manner of a young maiden. She blushed – just like the rose next to the lily. Bashfulness showed in her bright eyes. Yet, she responded with a beautiful bow. That was my reward. If I receive more I will keep it for myself.

(IV) It seemed to me as if I had never been so happy as then: blossoms from the tree rained down upon us onto the grass. I couldn't help but laugh from pure joy. But as I was so richly blessed – in dream, day broke and I awoke.

(V) This encounter forces me this summer to look deeply into the eyes of all young maidens. Perhaps I shall find 'her', and then will I be free of all sorrowful thoughts. Maybe she is among these dancers? My ladies be so good to lift up your hats a bit. Oh, would that I see her with her glorious crown standing before me!!

This poem which is handed down to us in three handwritten manuscripts constitutes a problem in so far as the reader is not able to grasp the overall sense. Since the individual phrases as well as the individual stanzas form understandable units, the problem of the connection of meaning amounts to the *question of the correct sequence of stanzas.* At any rate, this is the common assumption of both interpreters which I here adopt.

Many literary scholars were agreed that the last two stanzas of the manuscript were to be switched around, that is, *d* must come after *e*, so that not the Dream-motive and the Awakening, but rather the search for the young maiden comes at the end. This *communis opinio* has already been taken into account above. The following discussion will always refer, therefore, to the text so revised.

The poem seems to be a Dance-song (*Tanzlied*). In the first verse, the knight invites his young maiden to accept 'this bouquet' together with his compliments. The lady, surprisingly enough, gives no reply. Instead the knight starts again in the second verse, i.e., he goes on singing her praises and mentions a – new? – crown of flowers, 'the best that he possesses'. Seemingly this bouquet does not yet exist; for he wants, with her, to pick the white and red flowers for the bouquet far from the place of the dance. Only now does she accept. It is not clear what 'reward' ('*lôn*') refers to in this verse. In the fourth verse the bliss of love (*Liebeswonne*) turns out to be a dream-fantasy (*Traumgaukelei*). According to the fifth and final verse, the consequence should be that the poet, in the course of the summer, must look all the girls in the eye in order to find 'her' again.

Given the assumption we made at the beginning, the problem is limited to the correct sequence of the second and third verses. Two hypotheses have been offered here. The *first interpretation*, which originates with Wapnewski, may be analysed schematically into four sub-hypotheses: the two basic hypotheses H_1 and H_2 which serve as auxiliary hypotheses for the main hypotheses H_3 and H_4.

H_1 says that in the second verse it is not the same person who is speaking as in the first. Verse I is a gentleman's verse; verse II on the other hand is a lady's verse: in the first verse it is the courting knight who is speaking, in the second, the courted lady.

H_2 says that verse *c* comes before verse *b*; the sequence between the second and third verses must thus be reversed. This reversal-hypothesis H_2 is *simply* an immediate consequence of the first hypothesis. But Wapnewski, however, does not support it by such an inference, but instead cites independent proofs in favour of his conjectures H_1 and H_2.

H_3 is the real *hypothesis of interpretation* which restores the missing overall sense. It consists of the construal proposed by Wapnewski and it can best be rendered in his own words:

I. *Nemt frowes* (a): the knight offers a beautiful young girl, as is the custom, a bouquet of flowers which she is supposed to carry at the dance. He would rather crown her head with jewels, so he pleads.

II. *Sie nam* (c): she accepts and with a gesture which expresses her inner nobility. The white cheeks turn red ... her eyes are cast down in happiness and modesty ... she bows thankfully ... if more favour were shown him, he would know how to secretly guard it.

III. *Ir sît* (b): Now she answers: the knight is also beautiful. She too would like to give him a bouquet ... the most beautiful that she has kept she will give him. Far from here, in the meadow by the singing of birds they will pick flowers and she will present him the bouquet.

IV. *Mich dûhte* (e): He is filled with sublime joy; and the blossoms flutter down. At this instant ... a transformation occurs; the excess of joy has brought him to laughter and the laughter has awakened him! This circumstance shows that Walther has not really become 'untrue to his word' when he promised to keep the secret: ... for the whole encounter was only a dream.

V. *Mir ist* (d): In the 'waking state' now the poet is still forced to act as a slave of his dreamt happiness (*Traumglücks*): he searches the whole summer through for his beloved. Perhaps he shall find her among the girls dancing before him? They may lift their crowns of flowers; what if he were to find her under the precious bouquet (*kranzschmuck*) (and with this the poem returns, in the final line, literally as well as metaphorically to the Dreamworld of the first verse).'

'The second fundamental hypothesis H_4 is a *literary-historical hypothesis* which deals with the literary-historical arrangement of the poem. After very subtle investigations, which we cannot here go into, Wapnewski arrives at the conclusion that this poem is a *pastoral* poem. In his view, Walther's *Lied* contains all of the characteristics of this genre: 'The encounter of a young man and a girl which leads to a union of love. The setting is free nature; and the time of year is obviously spring. The social statures of the two are quite different; that of the young man is high (knight) whereas that of the girl is low (country-girl). The hero of the adventure is identical with the teller of the story (*I*-form). The story comprises at its core an erotic dialogue.'

(Whether an investigator directs his attention mainly to H_3 or to H_4 depends on whether he is interested in the interpretation as such or as in the case of Wapnewski, above all in the historical classification.) Should H_4 prove correct, it would amount to a rather interesting literary-historical discovery. Contrary to earlier views, one would have to acknowledge that Walther von der Vogelweide was not only familiar with pastoral poetry, but even tried to introduce it for the first time into Germany.

The second interpretation stems from G. Hahn. I will label it the *counter-interpretation* to Wapnewski's version. Corresponding to Wapnewski's 4 hypotheses we have here 4 counter-hypotheses, viz. $CH_1, ..., CH_4$, with CH_3 representing the counter-interpretation in the narrower sense. This counter-interpretation rests on a thorough-going critique of Wapnewski's hypotheses. Hahn, too, brings forward a line of independent arguments concerning H_1 and H_2 which, however, contrary to those of Wapnewski, are not grounds in support of these hypotheses, but rather cast doubt on their correctness. As concerns hypothesis H_4 Hahn, quite apart from the indirect criticism already manifest in the doubts cast on the basic-hypotheses H_1 and H_2, also raises quite direct doubts about Wapnewski's classification of Walther's song, in particular the following: (1) in all other pastoral-poems the difference in status (in the present case between knight and country-girl) is very emphatically stressed. In the case of Walther's poem one must at best read between the lines; it is not expressly stressed. (2) Walther's poem contains motifs which are foreign to the pastoral form, viz. the dance motif and the dream motif.

If these criticisms are considered to be justified then Wapnewski's interpretation hypothesis H_3 will also break down; the rejection of H_1 and H_2 already renders the interpretation hypothesis H_3 questionable, since both of these hypotheses H_1 and H_2 form the basis upon which it rests. Since according to Wapnewski, the literary-historical hypothesis H_4 is a consequence of H_3, the critique against H_4 will further undermine the interpretation hypothesis H_3 and indeed quite independently of the previous critique.

The most decisive point of difference in Hahn's interpretation boils down to the following: *in verse b, the courtier continues his plea with waxing intensity*. In order to follow this thought through consistently to the end, Hahn must suppose that in the poem no less than three bouquets are in question: The only *real* one is the bouquet of flowers offered to the young maiden in verse *a*; *unreal* is the crown of jewels which the courtier would so gladly give; *potential*, left open to future decision, is the 'very best of veils' ('*aller beste schapel*') in verse b.

As this example shows, we find ourselves in a rather remarkable position: even after the evaluations of all the findings as well as of all the available philological and textual analyses of these findings, after bringing in all the literary-historical and cultural history, as well as after a thorough analysis of the meanings of the symbols in the expressions and phrases employed in the poem; and finally after having undertaken a comparison with the rest of Walther's works and indeed with all of the German and non-German lyric poetry and much more as well – yet even after the evaluation of all this we seem to be faced by a *dilemma of confirmation: every argument in favor of Wapnewski's hypothesis can be matched by a counter-argument that supports Hahn's alternative hypothesis*.

The following question now comes to mind: does the hermeneutic circle perhaps mean this dilemma of confirmation, or better still: the consequence that results from it; i.e., *that in the final analysis the decision in favor of the one or the other interpretation must be determined by the subjective feeling of the interpreter instead of by objective criteria?*

It is argued, for example, that in the natural sciences, an analogous dilemma cannot arise. And in this lies the *objectivity of scientific knowledge*: Placed in a similar situation the natural researcher would think up an *experimentum crucis*, the outcome of which would result in a falsification of the one and consequently an unambiguous decision in favor of the other hypothesis.

Things are not, however, that simple. Even if for the moment we accept the really problematic concept of the *experimentum crucis*, we must nevertheless bear in mind that we surely cannot force decisions between competing alternative hypotheses *by means of experiments* in *all* of the natural sciences. A science which, like history, must remain content with the given facts, is *astronomy*. (It can never become an experimental science, since heavenly bodies cannot be shifted. Our second illustration, which *in its formal structure exhibits a certain parallel to the example from German philology*, is also chosen from this discipline.

As is well known even to many who are not themselves astronomers, there have occurred many more exciting things in this discipline the past 12 years than in all of the previous 150 years. One of the most sensational discoveries has been the *Quasars*. A brief introduction may elucidate the significance of this discovery:

If one were to imagine that the sun would be removed from our planetary system and shifted to the position of one of the closest stars, then the incoming radio waves on the earth would be weaker by the magnitude of roughly 100 billion and hence impossible to trace. It therefore created quite a stir in professional circles when in 1963 live tiny stars were discovered within a short span of time, stars of the 13th stellar magnitude, which could be identified with radio-sources already known. They were given the name 'Quasars' which is an abbreviation for 'quasi-stellar radio-sources'. Beside the fact that they emitted *intensive radio waves,* they also constituted a puzzle for researchers on yet another ground: the light was sufficiently strong to be dissected as usual into its rainbow colors. As is well known, every chemical element has its characteristic lines, which lie in a very specific place in the spectrum. The Quasar-spectra were not, however, interpretable in this way. To be sure, one had some leads that these luminous objects were surrounded by gas; but still this gas seemed to be totally unknown. Only several years later did it become apparent that the gas in question was nothing else but the most frequent element in the universe: hydrogen. There was one very simple reason for the initial failure to recognize the hydrogen lines: these lines did not occur where one would expect them, but were instead shifted quite far toward the red end of the spectrum.

This *extremely strong red shift* gave the astronomers quite a headache. And it is at this point that the formal analogy to Walther's example also begins. Just as there, the *presupposed background knowledge* – I will speak of it as the *underlying hypothesis of the overall sense of the context* – together with other accepted knowledge permits only two possible interpretations, so in the present case the *available physical background knowledge* – or as we may also call it: the *underlying physical hypothesis* – permits only two interpretations. In a nutshell, this underlying hypothesis says: *red shifts can only arise in two ways*.

Both of these alternatives must be briefly considered just as we did in the example from poetry:

(1) *alternative*: it may well be that the light from these sources must cross a very strong gravitational field and in so doing lose energy; and red light is poorer in energy than blue light.

The evaluation of this first possibility rests on an hypothesis which has actually been verified in 1967: the hypothesis of the existence of so-called *neutron-stars*. Thus the first alternative-hypothesis involved the assumption *that a Quasar is a neutron-star (hypothesis of local gravitation)*. The 'light's struggle against a gravitational field' which had been made responsible for the strong red shift, did as a matter of fact occur here. For these stars have a tremendous density: a cm^3 possesses a density on the magnitude of a billion tons.

But there immediately arose considerable doubts. Two decisive difficulties were: neutron stars have a diameter of ca.10 kms. But since Quasars are seen as stars of stellar magnitude 13, they could *be at most 0.3 light-years away from us*. Hence they would still be practically within our planetary system and would disturb the orbits of the planets to such an extent that these disturbances could be ascertained not just by means of today's precise instruments but would have been quite easily noticed even by Kepler in the 17th century. Secondly, the position of the Quasars in the heavens remains completely unchanged during the whole revolution of the earth around the sun. From this it may be inferred *that they must be at least 6000 light-years away from us*.

(2) *alternative*: the only possibility that still remains asserts that the red shift of the hydrogen lines in the spectrum occasioned by the Quasars is the result of the so-called *doppler effect*. Accordingly, the Quasars would have, relative to the earth, an extraordinarily high velocity which, in some cases, approaches the speed of light.

But now from this velocity together with the relative stable position of the

Quasars in the heavens during the revolution of the earth around the sun, it can be inferred that even the Quasar closest to us must be two billion light-years away (*cosmological hypothesis*).

The physico-astronomical background knowledge thus forces us to set up the alternative: *either quasars are at the very most 0.3 light years away or they are at the very least 2 billion light years away.*

What consitutes a big problem for this latter alternative is *the brightness of the Quasars at these vast distances.* This can only be explained by claiming that the Quasars possess a *huge mass,* which next occasioned the supposition that we might here be dealing with '*super-galaxies*' having a large magnitude, perhaps even 100 to several 100 times that of a medium galaxy such as our Milky Way. This line of thought would also accord with the law of the universal expansion of the universe, according to which a galaxy retreats from the earth all the faster, the further away it happens to be.

Unfortunately this conjecture soon broke down too. Independent of each other, American and Russian astronomers arrived at the conclusion, via an analysis of available charts of the stars' brightness, that between the years 1896 and 1963 the brightness of Quasar 3 C 273 has changed by the stellar magnitude of 0.7. Later investigations yielded brightness shifts of even a few days. If it happened to be a Milky Way or indeed a super-galaxy, light would take at least 100,000 years or several 100,000 years to cross the Quasar's diameter and hence the brightness fluctuations would be observable only within such vast time-spaces. One seemed therefore forced to accept the conclusion that the Quasars could be cosmic bodies with a diameter of at most a few light-days.

One can well understand why this result presented such a tremendous challenge to astronomy. It had been previously supposed that there were only two kinds of cosmic objects: *stars and galaxies*. One seemed now confronted with the fact that the Quasars formed a *third category of cosmic objects* totally unknown so far, which thus failed to fit into the existing astronomical world-view. Relative to our planetary system such a body would be extra-ordinarily big. Measured against the size of a Milky Way, on the other hand, it would be quite small (its diameter amounts to ca. 1/16,000,000 the diameter of our galaxy). And it is exactly here that the problem for the cosmological hypothesis advanced as the second alternative lies: *the idea of a compact body with a diameter of only a few light-days possessing a much bigger mass than our Milky Way with its ca. 150 billion suns, that is to say, 4,000 to 10,000 billion solar masses, is something which shatters all 'physical perceptions',* which 'boggles the mind' so to say. Let's consider once again in what

way the two examples are parallel:
(1) In *both* cases the so-called facts (*There*: the three available manuscripts; *Here*: a line-spectrum) are *interpreted in the light of background knowledge that is accepted and unquestioned* (There: the poem available in three manuscripts stems from Walther von der Vogelweide; Here: the light originates from a Quasar which not only is visible but is furthermore identical with a particular source of inconceivably great radiation.)
(2) The additional background knowledge adduced produces in each case a *split into two alternative-hypotheses* (There: the two mutually competing hypotheses of interpretation of the poem; Here: the local Gravitation hypothesis as opposed to the Cosmological hypothesis).
(3) An examination of both alternative hypotheses leads us into difficulties: *both hypotheses seem to be undermined*. We fall into a *confirmation dilemma*. (The differences that exist are only concerned with aspects which are without relevance for our problem. It is likewise of no consequence, of course, that in the further course of the discussion there no longer exists any other parallel in the two cases).

Is there nevertheless still a difference? It seems to me that the difference between the two cases lies in the following: *in the astronomical case one can distinguish sharply between background knowledge and facts, while in the literary-historical case one cannot*. In the literary-historical example one has *no sharp criterion* to distinguish, on the one hand, between the hypothetical components in the data of observation and the theoretical background knowledge, on the other hand. In the example from astronomy a boundary line can be drawn since the background knowledge consists of general law-hypotheses. In the example from old German philology, on the other hand, *no nontrivial laws* were used at all. That is where the difference lies and not in the antithesis between that 'which one can understand' and that 'which one cannot understand' – whatever this may exactly mean.

In the case of the complicated example from Astronomy it would be very difficult to carry out in detail the distinction in question. It can be more easily illustrated by the example of the *testing of simple statistical hypotheses.* Suppose that two persons are arguing as to whether a given coin is loaded or not. Let E be the result of the observation of n tosses of the coin. The background knowledge consists for example in the assumption that we are dealing with independent tosses having a constant probability (technically speaking: the background knowledge involves the supposition that there is a binomial distribution). This background knowledge can be packed into a statement which can again be called the underlying hypotheses O. *Of course both components E and O can be clearly separated without much effort. O* simply amounts to the claim that in order to calculate the probabilities one must apply the known statistical formula of binomial distribution; *E,* on the other hand, consists of a report of the outcome of *n* tosses of this coin.

In the historical case, and quite generally in all cases where no hypothetically postulated laws of the science are used, this clear-cut demarcation between hypothetical components in the facts and background knowledge is no longer possible. Just as in the field of statistics, let us call the hypothesis which is at issue, the *null-hypothesis*. We can then say that in both cases one can argue about the correctness of the null-hypothesis. But only in natural science and in statistics can the agreement required for making sense of this argument *be dissected into two acts*.

(a) Achieving agreement over the facts *E*;

(b) achieving agreement over the background knowledge *O*.

In the case of natural science we can thus distinguish between *three* components: the null-hypothesis H_0, *O* and *E*; in the case of the arts and history, on the other hand, *O* and *E* merge together, and we can only distinguish between H_0 on the one hand, and *O* and *E merged to OE,* on the other hand.

Remarkable is not *the* circumstance that the facts are hypothetical! In *this* respect there exists no difference whatsoever between the two cases. There is today wide reaching agreement that the assumption of naive Empiricism to the effect that we have such a thing as uninterpreted data of experience must be abandoned. And there is absolutely nothing strange at all about this. What is remarkable is rather that in the historical case no clear dividing line can be drawn between hypothetical facts, on the one hand, and background knowledge, on the other hand. Let us, for example, try to draw such a dividing line in the example of Walther's poem and say exactly what *the facts are*!! Do the facts consist in having available *three literary pieces*, namely, the three copies of the manuscripts we have mentioned? Or do they consist in having available three *pieces of literature originating ca. 1300*? Or do they consist in the fact that there are three copies originating ca. 1300 *of a poem written by Walther von der Vogelweide*? Or are we to include among facts the *communis opinio* presupposed in the discussion of this example and say that we have here a poem in three copies stemming from Walther von der Vogelweide whereby *in the original, E comes before D*? Whichever of these alternatives we may happen to choose the decision would be *completely arbitrary*. And this means nothing else but that every attempt to set up a boundary line between what is a *fact* and what is *imported background knowledge* amounts to an arbitrary decision.

Since the historian then does not 'activate' *nomological knowledge* at all in his evaluation, it cannot be said that the already available facts are 'evaluated in the light of the available background knowledge'. For *what* are here the facts of observation will only be *determined* by the whole background knowledge acquired through years or perhaps decades of painstaking work. Let me, at this point, resort to metaphor: in the facts *qua facts* his background knowledge 'shines' into the literary historian's face: he is incapable of separating it from the hypothetical components in the factual knowledge. That is the reason why agreement about the so-called facts is also much harder to reach here than in the case of natural science; for the two kinds of discussions, those which lead to agreement of type (a) and those which lead to agreement of type (b), *cannot even be methodically separated here*.

This, it seems to me, is the truth which very often lies behind the thesis of the indispensability of the so-called hermeneutic circle. On the basis of this analysis it will now also become *psychologically understandable* why the method of interpretation '*seems like a circle*' to the philosopher who reflects on it: already in his description of the facts '*the interpreter extracts from this description his background knowledge hidden in their construal*'!

In the example from natural science, on the other hand, there can be no question that what *is seen in the spectral apparatus* can be agreed upon only if there has been agreement about the natural laws to be accepted (e.g., the wave-theory of light, the general theory of relativity, etc.) whereas in the case of Walther there is *no sharp line of demarcation between* 'what is on paper' and 'what was Walther's intention'.

I have intentionally expressed myself cautiously when I said that it is 'psychologically understandable' why the literary method of interpretation '*seems* somehow circular'. Fortunately it is simply a matter of *mere appearance*. If it were to amount to something more than that, it would constitute a logical catastrophe for the historical sciences: the *hermeneutic* circle would then really be *vicious*. Fortunately this is not how things are. And so the historical sciences have also the same chance of survival as the law-governed sciences.[9]

Finally I want to try to offer a possible explanation (completely independent of the discussion so far) for the fact that the 'circle of understanding' not only stirred up quite strong emotions but also for the fact that it has been viewed as a positive distinguishing characteristic of the humanistic disciplines. It seems to me that Wittgenstein's remark about S. Freud can be applied to the present case by way of a paraphrase (and perhaps with even greater justification than in the case chosen by Wittgenstein). *The theory of the hermeneutic circle has the magnetic pull of mythology*. Its wide appeal consists in the fact that it supplies a *kind of tragic model* for the scientific activity of the philosophers and historians reflecting on it. To many of us philosophers and humanists our inability to clearly separate facts and hypotheses has occasionally come to be felt as something that is burdensome and troublesome in our work as well as in our discussions with our colleagues. And in situations in which this inseparability comes persistently to the fore, some of us may secretly have wished: 'Had I only become a natural scientist!! Then I could at least have stated clearly: "Here are the facts and here are the hypotheses available for the explanation of these facts" '. Caught in such a mental state where we succumb to an inferiority complex with respect to the 'objective' and 'precise' natural sciences, it is then perhaps an immense relief to be told by a hermeneuticist that there exists in the mental life of a historian or philosopher something like the form of a tragedy, which one then learns that Heidegger has succeeded in 'anchoring ontologically' in the anxiety-structure of human existence: man as an imitative creature full of prejudice can only come to understand what he has already previously invested via an act of preconception.

Instead of seeking refuge in such a mythology, one must throw light on the real difficulties which lie behind the expression 'circle of understanding'. As the previous analysis has shown, we have here several heterogeneous difficulties. And as a more extensive and more exact analysis would show, *all* sciences are to a greater or lesser extent potentially threatened by these difficulties.

NOTES

[1] Schleiermacher, *Akademiereden* V, p. 141.

[2] H. Gadamer, *Vom Zirkel des Verstehens*, p. 27.

[3] E. Staiger, *Die Kunst der Interpretation*, p. 39.

[4] Cf. W. Stegmüller, *Problems and Results of the Theory of Science*, Section 4 of the introduction of Volume II/2, and Volume IV/2, p. 25.

[5] For details about the logical reconstruction of Kuhn's concept of science cf. W. Stegmüller, *The Structure and Dynamics of Theories*, Berlin-Heidelberg-New York 1973.

[6] Munich, 1973.

[7] There is even a place-constancy during the ten years since the discovery of the first Quasars.

[8] For a more exact logical analysis cf. W. Stegmüller, *Personalistic and Statistical Probability*, part III: The Logical Foundations of Statistical Inference, 1973.

[9] A more detailed analysis of the foregoing examples as well as an investigation as to whether and in what sense the dilemma here discussed is *paradigmatic for certain branches of science* or whether, in point of fact, we are here dealing at most with *gradual distinctions*, will soon be forthcoming in an article of mine.

CHAPTER 2

'THE PROBLEM OF CAUSALITY'

When the English philosopher B. Russell was put in prison during World War I as a result of his pacifist speeches, he wrote his *Introduction to the Philosophy of Mathematics*. In it he discussed, among other things, the definite article 'the' as well as descriptions of the form 'the so-and-so' remarking that the questions connected with this article would absorb his interest even if he were drawing his last breath and not just spending some time in prison. Nowadays, anyone familiar with modern logic knows that the theory of the definite article presents no small difficulty.

Less attention, however, is given to the fact that the definite article not only exhibits logically intractable features, but also possesses a characteristic pertinent to the field of ethics. It is doubly distressing that this characteristic is of a negative nature and that the definite article has made philosophers the main target of its untoward behaviour. This negative feature consists, in short, of the fact that wherever the definite article is used we get the impression that we are simply talking about just one object. The person who speaks of *the* victor at Jena or *the* discoverer of America is letting us know that he is referring to only one single human being in each case. And the person who has learned to speak of *the* problem so-and-so thinks, at least at first, that *just one problem* is involved here.

The history of philosophy provides us with notable examples of what can happen because of this. Thus, for example, it is notorious how philosophers love to speak about *the* One. Repeated use of this expression has given philosophers ever since Parmenides the fundamental 'insight' that there can only be one single Unity and that an explanation must be given for the apparent multiplicity in the world. Thus, it becomes apparent that a misconstrual of the definite article can give rise to metaphysical systems. But, to stay with the problem of *the One*, when we further consider that monistic and pantheistic doctrines of unity have tended to interpret social relationships as some kind of totality and this, in turn, has led to a philosophical justification of dictatorships, it will become clear that the definite article, besides playing a prolific role in metaphysics, may also, under certain circumstances, stimulate considerable political activity.

The title of this essay is 'The Problem of Causality'. The pair of quotation marks with which I have surrounded it serve to signal that we must be on our guard here. It might turn out that there are a whole series of different questions hiding under this one comprehensive title. In any case we should not succumb at the very outset to the suggestive force of the definite article and assume that we have here only a single question requiring philosophical discussion.

There is yet another reason why it is absolutely necessary to be on one's guard respecting philosophical reflections on causality. For while all the rest of the problems of natural philosophy are sure to be treated in an atmosphere of cold factuality and strict objectivity, questions about causality have always tended to stir up passions. For these questions are not just important from the point of view of natural philosophy; they also affect the ideological, religious and ethical concerns of human beings in a most vital way. Hence we always find the exponents and opponents of a particular point of view talking past each other in a most curious manner. The person who, for example, asserts the unlimited validity of causality supports his case, for the most part, with scientific arguments, or at least with the philosophical belief that every event in the world can be subsumed under a natural law. The opponents of such a conception, on the other hand, do not, as a rule, set out from an opposing *philosophical* point of view, but focus instead on the *ethically* relevant factors in the human sphere; they believe that in the world of consciousness there exist processes that are the product of free acts or decisions; for otherwise, so they argue, the concept of responsible action would be destroyed. From this it is then but a short step to a reconciliation via a dualistic theory according to which the principle 'every event has a cause' enjoys unlimited validity in the world of appearances while the conscious self belongs to a different world, a world of freedom in which it is released from the straitjacket of causality.

In what follows, I will try my best to avoid such a split-level discussion by putting aside all ethical and religio-philosophical questions that might be involved in this problem. By doing so I do not, of course, mean to deny that such problems exist or that they may be important.

Let's first ask ourselves how we come to have a notion such as that of causality. We can readily point to two different things: first, certain laws are designated in science as *causal laws*. It is said, for example, that the laws of classical mechanics possess a causal character whereas the laws of quantum mechanics are not causal laws. But secondly, in philosophy we also speak of the general causal law which may roughly be formulated as follows: 'Every event has a cause,' or 'Every becoming is brought about.' For the sake of a clear terminological distinction, let's avoid the expression 'law' in this latter case and speak, instead, of the *general principle of causality*. One of our tasks will be to clarify the relationship between these two concepts: causal law and the principle of causality.

Already at this point we can make *one* important determination: the expression 'causal law' can be used in the plural. We can speak of causal *laws*. This means that we have here a type concept intended to delineate a certain characteristic or group of characteristics belonging to certain natural laws: causal laws are natural laws possessing still other characteristics. The expression 'principle of causality' on the other hand is only used in the singular. Here the definite article is, in fact, appropriate: one may speak of *the* principle of causality.

I would like to point out yet a third class of sentences in which causality plays a role. We come across them very often in our everyday life. They are primarily those sentences containing 'since' or 'because', that is, expressions of the following form: 'the forest was ravaged *because* of an avalanche' or 'the car swerved off the road *because* of a blow-out' or 'John died *because* he took belladonna.' Here we are dealing with singular causal judgments in which, as is sometimes said, individual causal connections are described. These singular causal judgments mark the initial stage of what might be called a scientific causal explanation (briefly: causal explanation). In other words, there are three things at issue here:

Causal law

Causal explanation

Principle of causality

Our task will consist above all in attempting to analyze these three concepts as well as the relationship that obtains between them. Had we asked a traditional philosopher how he would define these three concepts, we would, I suppose, have received in all three cases an answer in which one and the same concept recurs in the following typical form: he would have started with the concept of *cause* and would have tried to reduce everything else to this concept. And so we would be told, for example, that causal laws are those laws which have as their content *cause-effect connections*; that a causal explanation of an event consists in giving the *cause* of the event in question; the principle of causality would finally be formulated in the way I have already indicated: 'every event has a *cause*.' This kind of answer might be characterized schematically by writing next to the three expressions cited above the abbreviation 'C' in place of the word 'cause':

C – Causal law

C – Causal explanation

C – Principle of causality

But it is exactly this way of operating with the causal concept that is unsatisfactory in all of these answers. This concept stems from the vague language of everyday life where it is undoubtedly quite useful, for it serves adequately all the practical purposes of our everyday language; but it cannot serve as the point of departure for a philosophical concept explication. Suppose a house caves in as a result of removing a prop in the course of construction work being done in the basement. It will then be said that the house collapsed because that prop had been removed. And since such a because-statement is equivalent to a singular causal assertion, it might also be stated as follows: the removal of that prop was the *cause* of the collapse of the house. It becomes immediately clear now that despite the removal of that prop the house would still not have collapsed had it had a different structure. If, for example, the structure of the house had been such that the prop was not necessary to maintain its stability, then nothing would have happened. Thus, if we designate the removal of that prop as the cause of the collapse, this is basically a very one-sided description of the situation. Such an act must actually have coincided with quite a large number of other factors to bring about the said effect; and yet all these other factors were not taken into account at all.

In all other similar cases we can observe the same thing. Whenever a certain event takes place there is, as a rule, quite a large number of conditions involved. Out of this complex of conditions we pick out, more or less arbitrarily, one condition and designate it as the cause. The question as to which motives guide us in such a choice is not an epistemological but a psychological one. It seems very doubtful whether a general answer can be given to such a question. The choice of motives may be different depending on the situation: sometimes we simply designate as the cause of an event the conditions that catch our eye, or those which strike us as unusual (whereas the other conditions are less conspicuous since they have already been observed often), or, finally, those which immediately preceded the event (whereas the other conditions have obtained for a longer period of time).

These observations should suffice to show that we cannot expect to achieve the desired clarification by means of this pre-scientific concept of cause. Nor does it help to proclaim the concept of cause (or the cause-effect relationship) an a priori category as Kant did; for Kant never explained what he meant by a cause so that the question as to whether or not it is something a priori cannot even be discussed. Theoretically it might indeed be conceivable to render this concept of cause precise in such a way that it could be used to explicate the three other causal concepts. I do not, however, know of any definition of the concept of cause which might really be considered satisfactory and yet does not presuppose the clarification of those other concepts (or at least the first two of them). The following considerations will make it even clearer that there is not the slightest prospect of elucidating causality in terms of the concept of cause (or its correlate: the concept of effect).

And so we are now confronted with the task of freeing ourselves of the inexact expression 'cause' altogether, and hence of answering the questions of what a *causal law* is, what constitutes a *causal explanation*, and how the general *principle of causality* is to be formulated without making use of this expression. It will then become apparent that the concept of cause can, as a matter of fact, be made more precise; but this will prove to be merely a side-effect of the explication of the concept of causal explanation so that the concepts 'cause' and 'effect' are no longer of any particular importance.

When a scientist compiles law-like regularities his central concern is to devise conceptual tools that will enable him to make prognoses and explanations; let us then start with the concept of causal explanation. Before we can say what a causal explanation is, we must first know what is meant by a *scientific explanation in general*, whether it be causal or non-causal. Once we have answered this preliminary question, we can separate the causal explanations from the rest by virtue of the fact that in the former case only causal laws are used. A clarification of the concept of causal law must, therefore, precede the explication of the concept of causal explanation.

It must be noted here that the concept of a causal law is in no way related to that of explanation as such. For one may well discuss the question of what constitutes a causal law without tackling the problem of what constitutes a scientific explanation; and conversely, the concept of scientific explanation can generally be explicated without bringing in the question of causal law. Only if our aim is to explicate what a *causal* explanation is, do we need the one as well as the other. We thus obtain the following schema in which the arrows indicate the sequence that the explication of the concepts in question must follow (the concepts which are not connected by arrows are independent of each other):

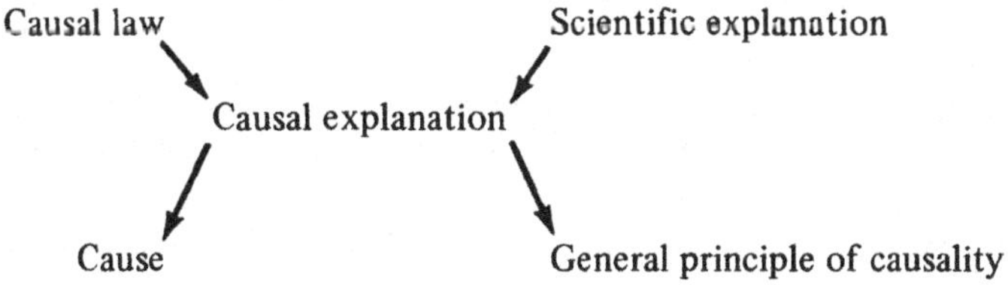

The meaning of the two upper arrows follows directly from what we have just said. The lower left arrow is supposed to convey the fact that the concept of cause is, as we have already said, simply a side-effect obtained from the concept of causal explanation. And the lower right arrow is supposed to indicate that we will subsequently formulate the general principle of causality with the help of the concept of causal explanation. In other words, this principle is not to be characterized from the point of view of the object but rather from the viewpoint of the knowledgeable scientist.

Let's start then with the concept of explanation. The expression 'explanation' is used in various different contexts. Thus, for example, one speaks of explaining to someone the meaning of an expression. I am not, however, referring to cases of this kind. I am thinking solely of cases where one speaks of *the explanation of events*.[1] Such explanations are quite distinct from pure *descriptions*. With a description one answers the question 'what is the case?' or 'what was the case?' while explanations answer the question '*why* is this the case?' or '*why* was this the case?' It becomes clear here that every explanation of a phenomenon or event E contains two quite distinct classes of statements: the statements in the one class describe the conditions which have been realized prior to or simultaneously with the event to be explained. Let's call these the antecedent conditions $A_1, ..., A_k$. The statements in the other class have for their content certain general law-like regularities $L_1, ...,$ L_r.[2] This may be illustrated by means of an example: we want to explain why the part of the oar that lies in the water appears to be bent upward to the man sitting in the rowboat. In this particular case the explanation is given by citing relevant regularities and antecedent conditions. The regularities would include, for example, the laws of the refraction of light and the claim that water is an optically denser medium than air; the antecedent conditions, on the other hand, would include, for example, statements to the effect that a part of the oar lies in the water while the rest is in the air, that the oar is actually a straight piece of wood, that this oar is being viewed from the boat, i.e., from just above the surface of the water, etc.

It can thus be seen that at least the natural scientist interprets a question such as 'why does such a phenomenon occur?' to mean 'On the basis of what laws and by virtue of what antecedent conditions does the phenomenon occur?' The explanation then consists in showing that the sentence *E is logically deduced from the sentences* $A_l, \ldots, A_k, L_l, \ldots, L_r$. Let that which is to be explained be called the *explanandum* and let the series of statements necessary for the deduction of the explanandum be called the *explanans*; we can thus set up the following schema which is, in principle, applicable to any scientific explanation:

$$\left.\begin{array}{ll} A_l, \ldots, A_k & \text{Antecedent Conditions} \\ L_l, \ldots, L_r & \text{General Law-Statements} \end{array}\right\} \quad \text{Explanans}$$
$$\begin{array}{ll} \hline E & \text{Explanandum} \end{array}$$

The horizontal bar indicates that E is deducible from the statements above it. This schema formed the basis of Hempel and Oppenheim's analysis of the concept of scientific explanation.[3]

The statements belonging to the explanans must satisfy a number of adequacy conditions if this schema is not to admit pseudo-explanations; they must, in particular, possess an empirical content and they must contain at least one law-statement. As Hempel and Oppenheim have shown, a precise formulation of these adequacy conditions involves certain difficulties; let us here, however, not concern ourselves with these technical details and presume, instead, that we have succeeded in explicating the concept of explanation in a satisfactory way.[4] Toward the end of our discussion we will return again to a particular problem that arises in connection with this.

Thus, supposing we have given an explication of the concept of scientific explanation, we can then define the concept of causal explanation in accordance with our schema by simply adding the following requirement: *the law-statements* $L_l, \ldots, L_r$ *must represent causal laws*. But nothing will be gained by this characterization unless we now define the concept of causal law. It may well be hopeless to look for a single characteristic that will enable us to demarcate causal laws from other laws. In order to discern all the essential properties of causal laws, one must classify law-statements from the most divergent points of view.[5] Here I would like to expressly add that the observations that follow will be of a provisional nature as all of the concepts involved are themselves in need of more precise explication.

We can first classify laws as deterministic or statistical depending on their type. *Deterministic regularities* enable us to give a positive explanation or make a positive prediction of individual events, or, to put it more exactly, of certain features (characteristics) of these events.[6] *Statistical regularities*, on the other hand, permit predictions of individual aspects of events only with a certain probability. If one wants to provide an exact explication for the concept of a deterministic physical law, one must, it seems, take care to construe the concept of determinism in such a strict way that it applies not just to the law-concept but also to the concept of state (of affairs). The reason for this is that, for example, even the laws of quantum mechanics can be formulated as deterministic laws as is shown, say, by wave mechanics operating with differential equations. If, nevertheless, using these laws one cannot definitely infer future states in respect to their individual characteristics, but only the probability of such states, then this is due to a change in the very concept of state within quantum mechanics. For there, namely, the states themselves are determined only probabilistically, which is why the regularities of quantum physics can be thought of as deterministic laws linking present with future probabilities.[7] In view of the fact that the statistical components of the law concept can be 'shifted' to the state concept, it becomes necessary to construe the determinism concept in such a way that it encompasses not only the laws themselves but also the states described by the antecedent conditions; in other words, the concept of probability should not enter into the deterministic concept of state of affairs. This is just one of the problems connected with the concept of determinism. The concept of a closed system presents yet another problem, which, however, cannot be discussed here.

In any event, the concept of determinism must be included as a feature of the concept of a causal law; for if you wanted to include even statistical laws in the class of causal laws, the whole controversy as to whether or not the laws of modern physics can be construed causally would become pointless. The property of determinism is not at all sufficient to characterize causal laws. To accomplish this, it is necessary to consider still other aspects.

Beside classifying laws according to types, we can also differentiate them by the kind of concepts that appear in them. The simplest kind of concept, one which we encounter most often in our everyday life, is the *qualitative* or *classificatory concept.* It serves to arrange things or processes into mutually exclusive groups. The laws formulated with the help of such concepts might be called *qualitative laws.* Examples of such would be, say, 'friction produces heat,' 'thick lead plates are not penetrable by X-rays,' 'recessions arise as a result of mismanaging capital.' A higher kind of concept consists of so-called *comparative* or *topological* concepts, i.e., those which are applied whenever comparisons are made. In everyday life such concepts are commonly reflected in the comparative form of the adjective, that is, either with the help of the expressions 'more' and 'less' or via such expressions as 'warmer', 'bigger', 'longer', 'shorter', and so on. The descriptions obtained by means of these concepts are substantially more precise than those made possible by qualitative concepts. The laws in which such concepts occur are called *topological laws*. The following are examples: 'the greater the distance between two masses, the less their mutual attraction' or 'the higher the temperature, the greater the speed of chemical reactions.'

But the most precise kind of concept available to us is the *quantitative* or *metric* concept. It characterizes things and events by means of numerical values. Most physical concepts are of this kind, as for example, the concepts of duration, temperature, length, velocity, volume, etc. Laws that take into account the functional relationships between such quantities are called *quantitative laws*. Any physical law may serve as an example. When one speaks of causal laws, it is always tacitly assumed that one means quantitative laws.

Laws can further be subdivided, depending on their form, into *succession* and *concurrence laws*. The former concern sequences of events whereas the latter assert the simultaneous occurrence, that is, the coexistence of properties of things. If, for example, one lists the physical and chemical properties of substances, this amounts to setting up certain concurrence laws. Causal laws belong, of course, to the first type. In any event, it is presupposed here that a clear distinction between these two kinds of laws is always possible. Doubt about such a claim has justifiably been raised.[8] Should, for example, a disposition predicate occur in a law statement, it seems this statement may be formulated as a succession law as well as a concurrence law. The sentence 'sugar is soluble in water' seems to express a concurrence law. For what it says is that the properties of sugar always appear together with the property of solubility in water. But if, on the other hand, the sentence is restated as follows: 'every time a piece of sugar is put in water, it dissolves', then it seems to involve a law of succession.

Laws can further be divided according to their level into *macro-laws* and *micro-laws*. A typical example of such a distinction is provided by thermodynamics. Classical thermodynamics was a macro-theory whose basic concepts, e.g., 'temperature,' 'pressure,' 'volume,' belong to the physical macroworld and hence are all, in principle, open to observation. The laws of this theory were macro-laws which, however, were deducible from the principles of the kinetic theory of heat or statistical thermodynamics. But since in the latter the concept of heat is reducible to molecular motion, what we have here is a micro-theory with micro-laws. An analogous distinction can also be found in other fields including sociology and economics. There exists today a general tendency of reducing macro-regularities to micro-laws. Hence we may also include the property of being a micro-law as one of the characteristics of the concept of causal law. When this characteristic is linked to the one mentioned earlier according to which we are dealing with quantitative laws, then a somewhat more precise reason can be given for the fact that in formulating physical laws one no longer works with the concepts of cause and effect: the cause-effect terminology seems to be adequate only for qualitative regularities at the macro-level. Once the transition to physical micro-concepts is made, we have moved out of the sphere of everyday life and sensory perception; consequently, many of our everyday concepts are no longer applicable, in particular the concept of cause. If, furthermore, the laws are formulated in a purely quantitative language, then we have completely given up thinking in terms of cause and effect. In lieu of statements about cause-effect relations we now have statements about functional relations between exactly measurable quantities, that is, statements in a mathematical form.

Apropos to the differentiation of laws into macro- and micro-laws, it must nevertheless be borne in mind that just as in the case of the distinction between laws of succession and concurrence, one is not dealing with an absolute distinction that can be fixed once and for all by an exact definition. It is, instead, a relative distinction as witnessed by the fact that in a given case it may prove useful on methodological grounds to distinguish more than two levels.

Beside the characteristics we have mentioned up to this point, there seem to be still other features that must be included in the concept of causal law. These features will be discussed here only briefly. First, one should mention the *homogeneity and isotropy of space and time*. The former refers to the purely relational character of space and time, that is, the fact that the particular place and the particular time at which an event occurs does not affect the properties of this event. The isotropy of space refers to the fact that for the propagation of processes it makes no difference what directions these propagations take.

A further characteristic of causal laws is that all of them satisfy the 'principle of nearby action.' This implies specifically that the speed of propagation of processes has an upper limit and also that the propagation of physical force fields, for example, is spatio-temporally continuous.

Another aspect concerns a property of the functions which in the presence of quantitative laws determine the dependencies between the quantities connected by the law, namely, the idea that all natural laws can be represented by means of functions which are *continuous from a mathematical point of view*. As Feigl points out, this requirement might be viewed as the modern version of the old principle *'natura non facit saltus'*; a principle which in Leibniz's philosophy took on the form of a metaphysical principle in its own right, i.e., the *'lex continui.'* As is well known, this principle has become very questionable in the light of modern theories of the atomic structure of matter.

One may finally cite the existence of certain *physical principles of conservation*. This can be viewed, on the other hand, as the modern correlate to the principle of the conservation of matter, which for Kant still constituted a metaphysical presupposition of empirical knowledge, and it may also, on the other hand, perhaps be considered an abstract and very remote cousin of the medieval principle *'causa aequat effectum.'*

Still others might be added to the features we have already mentioned. But since with these the concept of a causal law has already reached such a high level of complexity, let us confine ourselves to them. For faced with the question 'what are causal laws?' we must, in accordance with them, give the following answer: *causal laws are quantitative, deterministic, nearby action, succession micro-laws formulated by means of continuous mathematical functions in relation to a homogeneous, isotropic spatio-temporal continuum governed by certain principles of conservation.* Apropos to this concept, three more observations are in order:

(1) The complexity of the concept of a causal law ought to have conclusively demonstrated that any attempt to introduce the three causal concepts we discussed (i.e., causal law, causal explanation, and the principle of causality) via initially defined concepts of cause and effect is totally hopeless.

(2) Among the characteristics mentioned so far, there is one missing which in earlier times was often considered to be the principle feature of causality, namely, *necessity*. It was D. Hume's great achievement to have banished the concept of necessity from the concept of cause. As regards this point (but *only* this point) Hume's analysis of the concept of cause can be accepted.[9] The concept of causal necessity is nothing but a last remnant of an animistic world-view; for when it is here claimed that one state of the world causally effects another, the necessity is construed in the sense of compulsion, that is, of a psychic force with which we are acquainted from our own experience; the course of nature is pictured metaphorically as each world state of affairs exerting a force on the text.

(3) Every conceptual analysis contains conventional features, that is, it rests,

at least in part, on stipulations. As can be seen from the above definition, the conventional component is particularly strong in the concept of a causal law.

One can debate, for example, whether all the characteristics that have been mentioned are to be included in the concept of the causal law. It is, for example, theoretically conceivable that in some world the character of the physical processes depended upon the spatial direction that these took; or the nature of an event might depend in such a world on the spatio-temporal locus where the event takes place; to put it in mathematical language: the variables of space and time would be explicitly inserted into the functions by means of which the natural laws are mathematically formulated. If in such an extraordinary world laws which satisfy the rest of the conditions included in our concept of a causal law hold, then one would still probably say that such a world is governed by causal laws. This could be taken as a sign that the homogeneity and isotropy of space and time do not represent essential features of the concept of causal law.

Faced with this situation, one can only raise the question as to whether there are not some features that *must* concur if we are to speak meaningfully of causal laws. As a matter of fact, three of the features we have mentioned seem to constitute such a 'minimal concept' of a causal law: only *quantitative, deterministic, nearby-action laws* can be designated as causal laws. As we have already seen, the inclusion of the concept of determinism needs no further justification. That such laws must be nearby-action laws follows from the fact that with the assumption of infinitely fast propagations of physical processes, one can no longer speak of laws concerning sequences of events; but surely only those laws which refer to events that succeed each other temporally should be called causal law. That 'quantitative' has to be included can easily be made clear with an example. Suppose the *qualitative* law that mercury expands when heated holds in some world, but that it would not be possible to put this law into a quantitative form, since one and the same mercury column when subjected to the same heat (keeping all the other conditions constant) would at one time expand, say, 1 cm while at another time 15 cm. We would not be inclined to call the laws of such a world, which cannot be quantitatively formulated, causal laws.

As far as our problem is concerned, the important point is that *the conventional aspect of the concept of causal law also affects the concepts of causal explanation and the principle of causality.* For depending on whether one takes the weakest concept of causal law as characterized by the three minimal conditions of a narrower concept resulting from the addition of some further features like homogeneity of space etc., the expression 'causal explanation' and – what is especially of philosophical importance – the general principle of causality acquire a different meaning.

Let's leave now the concept of causal law and turn to the other causal concepts. Supposing we have a satisfactory explication of the concept of causal law, we can readily say what constitutes an *adequate causal explanation of an event*: it is when we have an explanation which satisfies all the adequacy conditions (not explicated here) of a scientific explanation and also satisfies the additional condition that the law statements used in the explanans are causal laws.

As was mentioned earlier, even the concept of cause can now be defined in retrospect: assuming there exists an adequate causal explanation for an event E, the cause of E may be taken as the totality of antecedent conditions which occur in the explanans of E. But it seems doubtful, however, whether the concept of cause so construed is of any theoretical or practical significance.

But what about the general principle of causality? Here the original formulation: 'every event has a cause' is replaced by: '*for every event there is an adequate causal explanation*.' Thus, this principle too has been reduced to the two concepts of causal law and scientific explanation.

Up to now we have concerned ourselves solely with questions of concept explication. Questions of existence and problems of validity have not been raised; that is, questions such as whether causal laws exist and whether the principle of causality holds. Before making some further observations about these questions, I must here emphasize something which, while it is indeed well recognized nowadays, is still easily overlooked in discussions of causal problems: all the law statements that one works with in the various sciences are merely hypothetical suppositions. We are never in a position to verify even a single law statement in a definitive way, regardless of whether or not it is causal laws that are involved. Consequently, hypothetical components also lie hidden in every causal explanation, namely, in the law statements which were earlier designated as L_l, ..., L_r in our schema of explanation. And so the fact that an explanation is adequate is not at all to be construed to mean that the hypothetical aspect has been banished from it.

When we now try to put together all the questions that can be raised in connection with causality, we arrive at the following seven problems:

(1) What is a causal law?
(2) What is a causal explanation?
(3) What is the general principle of causality?
(4) What is meant by a cause?

(5) Are there causal laws?
(6) Are all the laws in the world causal laws?
(7) Is the general principle of causality valid? [10]

We have only concerned ourselves with the first four questions and only these seem to be philosophical questions. The answers to questions (5) and (7) must be left to the natural scientist; for they involve empirical problems which cannot – after the model of Diogenes in the barrel – be decided by mere reflection. It is for this reason that there is no philosophical problem of determinism, if what is understood by it is the question of whether the world is governed by deterministic laws. But if, for a moment, we take as our basis what the scientist has to say with regard to these problems, we only get negative answers: the fifth question and, eo ipso, also the sixth question would be answered negatively. With regard to the seventh question, a physicist of today would not only deny that there exists an adequate causal explanation for every event, but he would presumably make the even stronger claim that there is *no* scientifically valid causal explanation for any event whatsoever. These answers, dismaying to every causality fanatic, are unavoidable as long as we take the narrow concept of causal law we have earlier defined. If, on the contrary, we resort to a wider concept, then we might perhaps get a positive answer to the fifth question, since there exist laws on the physical micro-level that can be designated as causal. The answers to the last two questions, however, would still remain negative (although the 'strong negation' of 7 just mentioned no longer holds).

The answer to the last question may draw protest from philosophical quarters. It has always been claimed that the validity of the general principle of causality is a basic presupposition of empirical knowledge. In his *Analytical Theory of Knowledge* A. Pap has attempted to give some sense to this claim – always presupposing that causal laws can be found.[11] He uses the following illustration: when someone is fishing in a pond, his belief that there are fish in this pond is a presupposition for his action. And every single fish that is caught is a further empirical confirmation of that presupposition. We can likewise say that belief in a general principle of causality is a 'pragmatic presupposition' of the action of any scientist who is searching for causal laws. And just as in the case of the fisherman, every single causal law found in science would then constitute a further empirical confirmation of the general principle of causality. Such a characterization of it in terms of a pragmatic presupposition for scientific activity would thus be consonant with its empirical content.

Quite apart from the problematic assumption of the existence of causal laws, the illustration of the fisherman is deficient in one important respect: in the various sciences one cannot, in principle, simply 'find' causal laws in the way that the lucky fisherman finds fish in his pond. The reason for this is that such laws involve hypothetical suppositions. This leads us to a most important point: the principle of causality as we construe it, runs as follows: 'for *every* event *there is* an adequate causal explanation.' In the original version it was formulated as: 'for *every* event *there is* a cause.' And so we are here dealing with a combined universal and existential statement. But since, as is well known, universal sentences are not verifiable while existential sentences are not falsifiable, the general principle of causality can be neither the one nor the other. The non-verifiability of the principle of causality is also shared by all the other natural laws. But whereas these latter are, as a rule, at least refutable on the basis of observations, there is nothing whatsoever in the world that can refute the principle of causality. This fact places the principle of causality very close to the logical tautologies, and this is perhaps why it has often been viewed as an a priori valid sentence.

One can picture the situation even more clearly if the above example of the fisherman is modified in such a way that the belief of the fisherman – which is supposed to be the presupposition for his action – can only be expressed as a combined universal and existential statement. One must then imagine that the fisherman stands before an unlimited number of ponds and that he enjoys an unlimited lifespan. In his search for fish, he moves from pond to pond for all eternity. The underlying belief that guides him in all this is 'in *every* pond of this interminable series *there are* fish.' He can never prove such a statement, for no matter how long he searches he has nevertheless tried his luck in only a finite number of ponds, whereas a potentially infinite number of unsearched ponds still lies before him. This belief of his cannot be definitively refuted by any observation either: if after an extensive search in one of the ponds he has failed to catch any fish, he will indeed be inclined to believe that there are no fish in the pond; but his partners – should there be any in such a metaphysical world – would be more inclined to infer something about his capacities as a fisherman.[12]

It might now be asked whether there is not a principle representing a generalization of the principle of causality which is actually presupposed, at least in a pragmatic sense, in all of the empirical sciences (with the restrictions mentioned in the last footnote)? In fact, there actually is such a principle. Just as we formulated the general principle of causality by means of the concept of an adequate causal explanation, we can likewise set up an entirely analogous formal principle if we eliminate the expression 'causal' and work exclusively with the general concept of an adequate explanation. The principle then reads as follows: *for every event there is an adequate scientific explanation*. This principle might be called the *general principle of explanation* or the *general law-principle*.

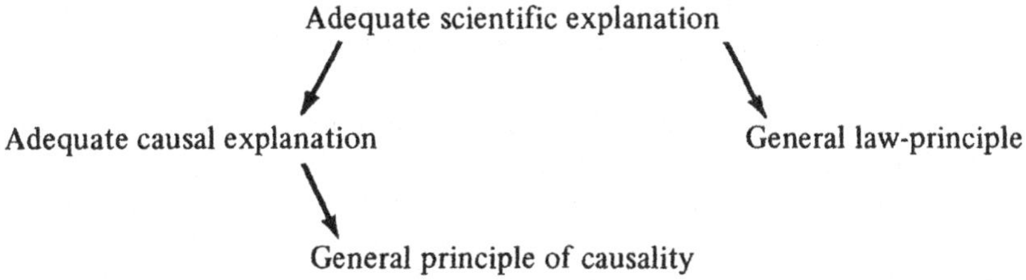

This general law-principle is accepted as valid in a pragmatic sense by almost all scientists who really aim at knowledge via laws; and it is also this law which is indirectly confirmed by every special law that is directly confirmed, or to be more exact, by every special hypothetical law that is directly and positively confirmed whether or not it be of a causal nature. If, on the other hand, one tries to interpret this principle as a logical presupposition for all the sciences which aim at knowledge via laws, then such a claim would amount to a tautology or it would not be able to stand up to stricter criticism. The former would be the case if the thesis is construed as saying: 'the general law-principle must hold if we are to find a scientific explanation in terms of laws for everything in the world'; the latter would be the case if it were claimed that the general law-principle must hold in order for there to be nomothetic sciences. That such a claim is mistaken can be seen from the fact that laws can be found in the world even if *not all* events can be subsumed under laws.

We must finally mention, at least briefly, one obvious problem: we have talked continually about laws and events. But what are laws and what are events? There is little doubt that we are dealing here with concepts in need of explication. As regards the concept of law, it is above all Nelson Goodman [13] who has shown us by way of a penetrating analysis that, up to now, the attempts to define this concept have all failed. He has, at the same time provided us with some positive leads towards an explication of this concept. It is to be hoped that along this or some other line a final clarification can eventually be achieved.

The failure of the attempts made so far to define the concept of law indicates at the same time that the task of clarifying the concept of an event is just the reverse side of this problem. Thus, just as, for example, an identification of law-like statements with unlimited universal sentences must be viewed as inadequate, so, for exactly the same reasons, statements that talk about events cannot be identified with singular statements. There seems to be no other possibility left but to construe the expression 'event' in as wide a sense as possible and subsume under it all that is not law-like. The import of this for the above analyses is that *the explanandum E must be supposed to be a non-law-like-statement.*

Both of the still unresolved problems have now been reduced to the question of the law-likeness of statements. A solution to this problem must be assumed if we are to give a precise meaning to the concepts of causal law and scientific explanation as well as the concepts of causal explanation and the general principle of causality (or the general law-principle). What the exact solution will look like is not known at this time. The importance of this question can also be seen from the fact that other problems of the modern philosophy of science also require for their final solution a knowledge of the criteria by means of which laws are distinguished from non-laws. The problem of counterfactual conditionals and the problem of induction form a particularly important part of this complex of problems.

NOTES

[1] Thus we also expressly omit from our analysis the case of the explanation of laws which is itself very important. It is without relevance for us because we are steering towards the concept of *causal* explanation and this concept is only applicable to processes and events.

[2] In what follows the symbols 'E', 'A_i' ($l \leqslant i \leqslant k$), '$L_j$' ($l \leqslant j \leqslant r$) will not usually be taken to designate phenomena, events, conditions, and regularities 'in the world,' but rather the appropriate linguistic objects which have all of this as their content; that is, '*Li*' designates law-statements, '*E*' designates the *sentence* which describes the event or phenomenon to be explained, etc. This stipulation serves merely to avoid unnecessary complications in the formulations that follow.

[3] C.G. Hempel and P. Oppenheim, 'The Logic of Explanation'. *Philosophy of Science* 15 (1948); reprinted in H. Feigl and M. Brodbeck, *Reading in the Philosophy of Science*, New York 1953, pp. 319 – 352.

[4] It must be expressly pointed out that the attempts towards an explication are restricted to the case where the language of first order predicate logic suffices for the formulation of the explanans and the explanandum.

[5] Most of the following observations concerning the concept of causal law were inspired by H. Feigl's essay, *Notes on Causality* which appeared in H. Feigl and M. Brodbeck, *Readings in the Philosophy of Science*, New York 1953, pp. 408 – 418.

[6] When we speak of the explanation of events this is, of course, always an inaccurate manner of speaking: for no event can be explained in respect of all its properties – to which belong all of the spatio-temporal relations to all the other events of the universe –

but only in respect of certain features which, depending on the situation, appear in need of an explanation.

[7] In matrix-mechanics one works with so-called *state* vectors. Even these determine only the probability of specific individual states.

[8] Cf. A. Pap, *Analytische Erkenntnistheorie*, Vienna 1955, p. 129.

[9] Strangely enough, one keeps hearing that D. Hume took a skeptical position with regard to the question of causality and that he 'denies causality.' This is not the case at all; indeed, Hume seems to have been the first philosopher who saw that the *meaning* of the expression '*A* is the cause of *B*' must be explained, that is, that one must say *what is meant by it*. Hume's explication can be construed in such a way that it translates the expression '*A* is the cause of *B*' into the expression 'an event of type *A* is *regularly followed* by an event of type *B*' (and not, for example, '... is necessarily followed by ...').

[10] The seventh question does not have the same meaning as the one preceding it. For it may well be the case that all of the laws in the world are causal laws, but that there also exist events which cannot be subsumed under any law and are, therefore, not explainable. In such a world the causal principle would, of course, not be valid.

[11] *Loc. cit.*, p. 138f.

[12] Incidentally, the belief of the fisherman has been formulated too strongly here. That it appear sensible to the fisherman to go on and search for fish in ever new ponds, he does not need to believe that there are fish in every pond, but only that in the succession of ponds he will *always* come across another one that contains fish. It might analogously be said that the causal principle does not constitute a presupposition of the scientist's search for causal laws even in the pragmatic sense. The scientist must only believe that one will always come across causal laws in the world (or in his special field of research), but not that all laws are causal laws nor even that everything in the world can be subsumed under laws.

[13] *Fact, Fiction and Forecast*, Cambridge, Mass. 1955. Cf. also my discussion of this book in *Kant Studien*, 50 (1958 – 59), 363 – 390.

CHAPTER 3

EXPLANATION, PREDICTION, SCIENTIFIC SYSTEMATIZATION AND NON-EXPLANATORY INFORMATION*

1. INTRODUCTION

In the course of the discussion of an unimportant question important features may come to light. This certainly was the case in the dispute over the problem of similarity or dissimilarity between explanation and prediction; it gave us new insights into the enormous varieties of possible applications of scientific theories to concrete events, though the question itself does not seem to be a very important one. Strangely enough, this very question has not been settled up to now. This is partly due to the vagueness and ambiguity of four classes of terms used in this dispute: (1) the terms 'explanation' and 'prediction' themselves; (2) expressions such as 'structural similarity' and 'structural divergence' which are used in the formulation of the thesis and counterthesis in question; (3) the distinction between what is 'given' and what is 'provided later'; (4) the difference between 'reasons of belief' and 'grounds of events'. With respect to (1) and (2) an attempt will be made to give an explication; (3) will be settled by a simple decision; as far as (4) is concerned no suggestion will be made how to explicate these concepts, but in Section 3 an argument will be based on this intuitive distinction.

In the next section it will be argued that the dispute on the similarity thesis in its present form is unsolvable in the sense that it can neither be shown that it is true nor that it is wrong. Several conventions will be introduced; under certain of these conventions the similarity thesis becomes provable while other conventions imply the counterthesis. By means of intuitive arguments it will be shown that none of these classes of conventions are unreasonable, at least if we restrict ourselves to the arguments that have been put forward in the past. In Section 3 an additional argument will be considered which has the effect that it seems more plausible to accept the counterthesis. A more systematic approach is suggested in Section 4 where all expressions like 'explanation', 'prediction,' 'retrodiction', etc., are avoided completely. In the fifth section it will be shown that even the most general concept of scientific systematization is insufficient, since there are important applications of laws and theories to concrete situations which cannot be subsumed under this heading. Applications of theories of this kind will be called non-explanatory information. A seeming paradox produced in N. Rescher's article [7] will be solved with the help of this concept.

In order not to burden the following discussions with obsolete material we briefly anticipate two items which have been pointed out by I. Scheffler and about which we suppose that there is now general agreement. First, the predicates 'is an explanation' and 'is a prediction', as used in everyday discourse, have a different range; the latter predicate is applied to certain statement-utterances, the former is applied to concrete arguments only (at least if one agrees that one has to consider a 'because-sentence' as a rudimentary argument, i.e. as something which *is intended* as an argument). Therefore only the comparison between explanations and *rational* or *scientific* predictions is of interest. Secondly, there are of course more specializations of scientific systematization than explanation and prediction. A systematic survey will be given in Section 4. For the moment we mention only three possibilities, in addition to those given by Scheffler.

(1) As has been shown in [7], it may be essential for an explanation to be successful that the 'antecedent event' be split up into two parts, the one being earlier and the other later than the 'explanandum event'.

(2) Suppose the antecedent event is earlier than the explanandum event, the latter being later and the former not later than the time of the deduction (i.e. the systematization utterance); within this deduction the explanandum sentence is given first and the antecedent and laws provided afterwards. If it should be objected that such a situation is impossible, then a simple description of it in everyday terms shows that it is not: the case in question could be called 'rationalization of a previously irrational prediction' (but this characterization suggests in a misleading way the idea that an irrational prediction is compared with a rational one which actually is not the case).

(3) All three components of the deduction – the antecedent, the laws and the explanandum – may be given. This seems to be a triviality, but in general it is not because of Church's theorem. Such a case may arise within a classwork in astronomy; it could therefore be called 'solution of an exercise in deductive-nomological (or statistical) systematization'.

In view of the great varieties of scientific systematizations we have to make up our minds whether the similarity thesis is to be applied to explanations and predictions only or to all types of systematizations. It will turn out that this makes a certain difference.

As an introduction to the next section some remarks on the vagueness and the ambiguity of the term 'explanation', as distinct from 'prediction', seem to be pertinent here. The phenomenon in question has a trivial and a non-trivial aspect. The *trivial* aspect is this: 'explanation' has, besides its use in contexts like 'explanation of events' (where it is used in a manner similar to the expression 'prediction'), at least four connotations to which there is no analogue in the case of the term 'prediction'. Namely, we speak of (1) explanations of laws or theories; (2) explanation of the functioning of a system (e.g. of the working of a machine or, e.g. of the self-regulating behaviour of 'teleological' systems);[1] (3) explanations of the meaning of a word or of the import of something; (4) explanation in the sense of (moral) justification (e.g. in contexts like 'explain, why you have done this!'). In all these cases it makes no sense to speak of prediction.

The *non-trivial* aspect concerns the vagueness of the concept of explanation in the narrow sense of 'explanation of events'. It is not the *fact* that such a vagueness exists which is important here but rather that there exists, so to speak, 'a structural divergence with respect to the vagueness of these two words "explanation" and "prediction" '. Both have a core meaning where their use is almost completely clear to us and besides this, unclear borderline cases. But the range of the latter seems to be much wider in the case of explanation than in the case of prediction. We therefore hesitate when asked whether (in the non-statistical case) an inductive argument suffices for an explanation or whether there can be an attempt to explain something that 'could have happened', whereas we do not always hesitate to speak of rational predictions when the argument presented is non-deductive or the predictive statements are false. This fact is used in the next section for the formulation of conventions 1 and 2.

2. ON POSSIBLE CONVENTIONS GOVERNING THE USE OF 'EXPLANATION' AND 'PREDICTION'

After having pointed out differences between explanations and predictions Scheffler concludes: 'Such divergence is surely structural, in any natural sense of the word' ([9], p. 46). But as long as these 'natural senses' are not made precise one cannot expect to settle the matter at issue.

It seems to be advisable first to define the positive case, 'structural similarity', and then to identify 'structural divergence' in a second step with 'structural similarity not holding'. It will turn out that the definition has to be different depending on whether we define these predicates with reference to explanation and prediction only or with reference to all kinds of scientific systematization. As in [9] we refer to the antecedent and explanandum events by '*a*' and '*b*', whereas capital letters are reserved to designate utterances (or inscriptions) involved in the argument. '*A*' designates the antecedent statement, '*T*' the theory- (or law-) statement, '*B*' the explanandum statement; the whole deduction, again interpreted as an event and not as a shape, will be referred to by '*D*'.

The expression '*pragmatic circumstances*' is to cover two items: (a) the temporal relation between the occurrence of *D* on the one side and of *a* and *b* on the other side (in Section 4 it will be called the *pragmatic time relation*); (b) the *pragmatic relation of givenness*, i.e. the specification of those constituents of *D* which are given first (e.g. *A* and *T*) and of those which are provided later (e.g. *B*). (Some remarks on the possible definitions of 'given' will be made later; here we take it as a familiar distinction.)

We now say that there is a *structural similarity between explanation and prediction* if (1) to each explanation D_1 there exists at least one possible prediction D'_1 such that D_1 and D'_1 differ from each other with respect to the pragmatic circumstances only; and (2) to each prediction D_2 there exists at least one possible explanation D'_2 such that D_2 and D'_2 differ from each other with respect to the pragmatic circumstances only. The occurrence of 'possible' obviously makes this definition an intensional one. This apparently cannot be avoided in view of the fact that explanations and predictions are events.

The natural generalization of this definition to the case of arbitrary scientific systematizations would seem to consist in a replacement of the definiens by 'to each type of scientific systematization[2] *D* there exists for each other type at least one possible scientific systematization *D'* such that *D* and *D'* differ from each other with respect to the pragmatic circumstances only'. But this would not do, as can be seen from the fact that under such a definition the thesis of structural divergence would become trivially true, since for any prediction the temporal relation between *a* and *b* is opposite to the temporal relation between these two events in the case of a retrodiction. Therefore, there always exists a structural divergence between these two types of scientific systematizations. Calling the time relation in question the ontological time relation (*vide* Section 4) we would therefore have to replace the last clause of the definiens by 'with respect to the pragmatic circumstances or the ontological time relation only'. For the sake of simplicity we shall for the rest of this section refer only to the special case of explanation and prediction.

Three arguments against the similarity thesis have to be considered. The first says that more truth value distributions are allowed in the case of predictions than in the case of explanations; in a rational prediction the prediction utterance itself may be false while a scientific explanation even in case of falsity must consist in a rational attempt to explain a *fact* (i.e. something described in a *true* statement). We call this argument the *truth value argument*. Hempel introduced the concept of *potential explanation* as a generalization of 'explanation of facts' which by definition includes arguments with false conclusions. So we have to consider two possible conventions:

Convention 1*a*. The term 'explanation' may be applied only to arguments with true conclusions.

Convention 1*b*. The term 'explanation' may be used in such a way that it covers all cases of potential explanations (including those with false conclusions).

There is no need for considering similar conventions in the case of predictions as we can take for granted the general agreement upon the fact that arguments with false conclusions may be rational predictions.

The opponents of the similarity thesis seem to believe that only convention 1a is a reasonable one. It is hardly possible to substantiate this claim. *First*, the case of a potential explanation with false conclusions is just one of the borderline cases which are not covered by the normal use of the word. So why not include it into the extended use of 'explanation'? This inclusion does not in any way impair the core meaning of the term. *Secondly*, it seems that one can successfully support convention 1b with the help of a 'mental experiment'. Suppose a historian or a scientist *Y* makes great efforts to explain a certain historical event. It later turns out that this event never took place. But if *Y*'s information that it did, as well as the laws and theories which he used in his attempt, were highly confirmed at this time then we would not call this attempt an irrational one. We are therefore entitled to say that *Y* made a rational attempt to explain something. And the concept of potential explanation is just the technical equivalent of this intuitive notion 'rational attempt to explain something'.

Whether we include a case of this kind in the extension of 'potential explanation' or not depends on whether we allow the word 'possible' to occur twice or only once in the definition of this concept. Is this always to be a possible explanation of something that actually took place or can it be a possible explanation of something that *could have taken place*? The example given shows that it is not completely unreasonable to make a choice in favour of the second alternative.

Of course, such a choice is made by fiat. The other alternative could have been chosen as well. We therefore come to the conclusion that both conventions are reasonable ones. But this amounts to saying that the truth value argument breaks down.

Perhaps the most expedient approach would consist in choosing the following way out. Instead of using only *one* concept of explanation we could introduce three different concepts: (a) the concept of a *correct* or *true* explanation of a *fact*; (b) the concept of a rational *attempt* of explaining a *fact*; (c) the concept of a rational *attempt* of explaining *something* (namely either a fact or a mere possible state of affairs). (a) corresponds to the original conditions of adequacy of Hempel and Oppenheim; (c) corresponds to Hempel's concept of a potential explanation; (b) corresponds to the concept of a potential explanation with the restriction added that convention 1a should hold of this concept.

According to the second objection against the similarity thesis a rational explanation must always contain laws whereas a rational prediction need not. The latter can be a non-statistical inductive argument (i.e. an argument whose premises contain not even statistical laws). In terms of Carnap's theory of inductive probability such predictions would be cases of 'instance confirmation'. This objection need not be considered separately because its validity depends on the question of the admissibility of non-statistical inductive arguments as arguments of the explanatory type.

So we come to the third and final argument. Rational predictions include cases of non-statistical inductive reasoning whereas rational explanations can be inductive in character only if statistical laws occur among the premises. On pp. 31ff. of [9] Scheffler reports on an example given by Hempel in [4] which would be an inductive explanation of this type using no statistical laws. On p. 38 Scheffler suggests a different account. One additional premise is added and 16 premises of the original argument are dropped. The addition of the new premise transforms the argument into a deductive one while the 16 premises dropped constitute an inductive basis for the acceptance of the new premise. The original argument is thereby split up into two completely different procedures: a confirmatory argument in favour of some of the explanans statements and the explanation proper, the latter being now of the deductive-nomological type.

The general procedure is this: to an inductive argument so many lawlike premises are added that a purely deductive transition from the explanans to the explanandum is made possible. Therefore certain singular premises become unnecessary. But these premises can now in a new and independent procedure be interpreted as a supporting inductive evidence for the new lawlike principles.

It is certainly true that this transformation *can* be made. What is at stake is the question *whether it has to be made* in order to avoid getting an 'unnatural' construction of the term 'explanation'. Again the answer seems to be: No. As in the truth value case we encounter here borderline cases where the normal use of the word does not guide us to give a clear answer. Therefore a decision has to be made by fiat. And whatever the naturalness of the suggestion of Scheffler may be (e.g. to get a concept which is not time-relative) the following aspects can be brought forward in favour of Hempel's original account:

(1) If in principle we accept Hempel's account of statistical explanation then we are forced to include inductive arguments within the class of explanations if we do not want to withdraw the term 'explanation' from statistical arguments altogether.[3] But then it may seem more natural to include other kinds of inductive arguments as well, instead of excluding them.

(2) It cannot be taken for granted that the transformation is always practicable. Even if we accept the supposition that a suitable deductive-nomological explanation of the kind required can always be found, it is not at all clear that the new explanans must in all cases be highly confirmed by the original premises. Whether this will be the case or not may depend on how certain problems of the theory of confirmation have to be solved. If, for example, the new premise is a general law, then on the basis of Carnap's theory it would have the zero confirmation, no matter what kind of evidence is used for it.

(3) Finally it may turn out that all or at least most of the so-called deductive-nomological explanations are in truth inductive and not deductive arguments, in view of the difficulty which has been pointed out by Canfield and Lehrer in [1].[4]

So it seems that we can accept either one of the following two conventions:

Convention 2a. It is permissible to apply the term 'explanation' to inductive arguments only if they are of the statistical type.

Convention 2b. Besides its application to arguments of the statistical and the deductive-nomological type the term 'explanation' may be applied to non-statistical inductive arguments.

We leave the question open whether the inductive arguments admitted by convention 2b but excluded by convention 2a have to satisfy additional requirements of adequacy in order to be called explanations.

Suppose we accept conventions 1b and 2b. The ontological time relation is the same in the case of explanations as in the case of predictions. Therefore to each prediction a possible explanatory argument can be constructed (and vice versa) such that both differ only with respect to the pragmatic circumstances. So by definition there is a structural similarity between explanation and prediction, provided that no further arguments can be given. If on the other hand one of the other three possible combinations of the conventions are chosen (e.g. convention 1a and convention 2b, etc.) then the thesis of structural divergence becomes provable.

It has therefore been shown that under suitable conventions, none of which can be considered as unreasonable, the thesis of structural similarity as well as the counterthesis can be proved. In the case of the thesis the procedure consisted simply of these three steps: (a) pointing out certain ambiguities in the term 'rational explanation'; (b) introducing a concept of potential explanation co-extensive with prediction, apart from the pragmatic circumstances; (c) showing that this concept is not quite artificial but can be considered as one possible explication of the intuitive concept of a rational explanation.

3. AN ADDITIONAL ARGUMENT OF PLAUSIBILITY IN FAVOUR OF THE COUNTERTHESIS

The foregoing result is based on the supposition that no further arguments can be offered in favour of one of the two theses. Such an argument will now be produced. It uses a conceptual distinction which has been emphasized by Scheffler in the course of his discussion of the similarity thesis, namely the distinction between *grounds for an event* and *reasons* or *grounds for a belief*. It largely coincides with a similar distinction made in traditional philosophy, e.g. with what in the German philosophical tradition had been called '*Seinsgründe*' and '*Vernunftgründe*'. This distinction was not included in the meditations of Section 2 for the following reason: As far as we use inductive arguments we can give only grounds for a belief and not grounds for an event.

Therefore if we accept inductive explanatory arguments we cannot avoid admitting explanatory 'premises' (evidence) which do not give us grounds for the event described in the explanandum statement. But we should expect that at least explanations of the deductive-nomological type always give us such grounds and Scheffler apparently thinks that they do. But this is not so, as will be shown with the help of a counter-example.[5] The concept of deductive-nomological systematization is compatible with both 'kinds of grounds'. This for the first time is a really disturbing element, speaking against the acceptance of the similarity thesis.

First, we make a few remarks about the intuitive distinction in question. It seems that it can best be clarified with the help of a simple dialogue game. The game consists of two players, *X* (the proponent) and *Y* (the opponent). The first move always consists of an assertion made by *X*. *Y* is allowed to make a challenge in order to determine the degree of rationality of *X*'s assertions. The challenge is always formulated by means of the one-word question: 'Why?'. *X* has to react 'properly' to this challenge, i.e. to give a rational answer. It is presupposed that standards are formulated with the help of which we can find out whether the counter-reaction to the opponents' challenge is acceptable, i.e. whether it is a proper or correct answer. Every time *X* gives a proper answer he wins; otherwise *Y* is the winner. Suppose now that *X* decides to make predictions of the kind '*z* will happen at time *t*' whereby *t* is later than the time of this utterance. In this case the opponent's why-question can be interpreted in a twofold way. It can mean either: (1) Why will *z* happen at *t*? or (2) Why *do you believe that z* will happen at *t*? With respect to both interpretations a satisfactory answer to the question can in principle be given; so in both cases *X*'s prediction would become a *rational* prediction. All rational reactions to the challenge in interpretation (1) are rational reactions to the challenge in interpretation (2), *but not* vice versa. This is most easily seen if one changes the pragmatic time circumstances so that *t* is earlier than the time of *X*'s utterance (which thereby of course ceases to be a prediction). Answering (1) means answering the question why *z* happened at *t* while answering (2) means giving an answer to the question: Why do you believe that *x* happened at *t*? For a rational answer to this question it suffices to give inductive evidence in favour of the truth of an historical description.

Up to now we have only illustrated Scheffler's point. If one decides that with respect to past events only rational answers to why-questions in interpretation (1) should be called explanations, then we automatically would have made a decision in favour of the counter thesis. The thesis of structural similarity could still be defended along the lines of the previous section.

But a new difficulty arises *if X presents a deductive-nomological argument satisfying all the further requirements of 'rational explanation' which gives a rational answer to the why-question in interpretation (2) only.*

The most striking examples of rational reactions to questions of type (2) which normally are not at the same time considered as answers to questions of the type (1) are those where we justify our assertions by reference to reliable testimony of experts. So let us take an example of this kind. Suppose I predict an eclipse of the sun at a future time *t* and when asked why I do believe in this event I answer: 'I was told that this will happen by *n* professional astronomers.' Under these circumstances one would certainly call my belief in the event in question a rational belief; and if nothing else is provided the argument is an inductive one. But in principle it is possible to expand this argument into a deductive-nomological prediction.

We first introduce a new complex predicate 'person of type *C*' which includes, among others, mental properties such as: being a person skilled in applied mathematics, having a profound physical knowledge, having many years' practical experience in astronomy, etc., and, besides this, moral traits like: being an honest person, never lying in matters of one's own profession, etc. We can assume that all these characteristics are empirical properties. Then the following *non-statistical law* may be highly confirmed and even be true: 'Whenever at least 10 astronomers of type *C* predict an event in the universe (or, more specifically, in our planetary system) then this event will take place' (3). This statement together with the information '12 astronomers of type *C* predicted an eclipse for the future time *t*' (4) makes it possible for me to predict this eclipse by deriving the prediction *logically* from (3) and (4); it therefore is of the deductive-nomological type.

Suppose now that the pragmatic circumstances become the same as those of an explanation while the argument remains unchanged. We furthermore presuppose that *a* is earlier than *b*. It should be noticed that the time of *a* in the present case includes the time interval within which the predictions of our 12 astronomers have been made. This whole interval precedes by assumption the time of *b* (the eclipse). If we accept the similarity thesis we would have to classify this argument as an explanation of the deductive-nomological type. If we further agree that at least explanations of the deductive-nomological type answer questions of the kind 'why did *x* happen?' then this would in the present case commit us to the acceptance of a mythical theory on the magic powers of astronomers. As the days of the old Babylonians have definitely gone, one may reasonably doubt the expediency of such an attitude.[6]

The reason why this result is more disturbing than the analogous situation in the case of the inductive argument is this: a non-statistical inductive argument can and must be considered as something incomplete which *because of its incompleteness* gives grounds for a belief only, instead of giving grounds for an event. The incompleteness is so to speak our excuse for the fact that at the moment nothing more than reasons for acceptance can be given. But if the argument is 'completed' by making it a perfect logical derivation of the deductive kind then this subterfuge is no longer possible; we can improve the situation only by *replacing* the argument which we feel is an unhappy one by *another* argument that satisfies us, but we cannot improve the argument itself by trying to get new information which we could use as additional premises. It therefore seems that arguments satisfying all the requirements of deductive-nomological explanations (including the pragmatic circumstances and the ontological time relation characteristic for explanations), providing no more than 'reasons for a belief' which are not 'grounds for an event', exhibit a definite and insurmountable gap between explanation and prediction. The similarity thesis can still be upheld but apparently only at the cost of interfering seriously with the core meaning of the concept of explanation.

This result, of course, is based on two assumptions that have been made tacitly: that there are deductive-nomological explanations at all and that the distinction between reasons for a belief and grounds for an event can be made precise. We must leave the question open whether an affirmative answer can be given. But let us suppose for the moment that it can and that a satisfactory explication of the two different types of 'grounds' has been given. Then the foregoing considerations would give us a reasonable motive for the acceptance of a new requirement of adequacy. In distinction to the other conditions of adequacy it would not hold for *all* scientific systematizations but only for the deductive-nomological systematizations of the explanatory type (by requiring that they have to give grounds for the explanandum event). One effect of this procedure would be that there exist scientific systematizations – call them *quasi-explanations* – resembling deductive-nomological explanations in all respects, except for the fact that they are no explanations (because they are 'explanatory arguments' corresponding to deductive-nomological predictions which give reasons but not grounds for events).

Incidentally it should be mentioned that there is a certain similarity between our example and the one given by Hempel in [5], end of Section 4, which Hempel attributes to S. Bromberger. In this example the height of a flagpole standing vertically on level ground is determined with the help of measurements of angle and distance on the ground-level. The argument is a deductive-nomological argument satisfying all the conditions of adequacy. Nevertheless, we would not say that the height of the flagpole had been explained. This example does not look artificial as every case of a deduction based upon the law (3) does. In both cases we would normally hesitate to speak of an explanation. It seems to be Hempel's conjecture that cases of this kind can arise only if the argument is not of the causal type, i.e. if the laws involved are not laws of succession (see last paragraph of Section 4 in [5]). This would not hold for our example as apparently (3) *is* 'a law of succession'. But it is just this similarity which may cause additional doubts of the possible success of an explication of the difference between 'reasons for belief' and 'grounds for events'. In the negative case, i.e. if the explication should turn out to be impossible, we should drop the intuitive idea that an explanation has to give an answer to a question of the kind 'Why did x happen?'

4. A SYSTEMATIC APPROACH

In view of the results of Sections 2 and 3 it might seem to be expedient not to start with familiar terms 'explanation', 'prediction', 'retrodiction' and the like. We should rather choose a systematic approach in which we free ourselves entirely from these terms.

A possible approach of such a kind is the following one: we start with a most general concept of scientific systematizations, including deductive-nomological ones as well as statistical ones and non-statistical inductive systematizations. Next we try to compile the various respects in which scientific systematizations can diverge, thereby getting a list in which these respects are distinguished by numbers. A specific systematization is obtained by picking out one item from each subcase of the list and combining it with the items chosen from the other subcases. As it will turn out we will get in this way many more possibilities than could be named by familiar terms like 'explanation', etc. After having finished the list we can come back to our familiar words and ask which specific combination would *normally* be called an explanation or a prediction or a retrodiction. But the answer to this question will have no systematic import and will not exclude the alternative that either more or fewer possibilities are named by the same expressions.

In order to avoid a misunderstanding we emphasize two points. First, the conditions of adequacy for scientific systematizations are supposed to be satisfied in all the cases considered, no matter how they have to be formulated precisely. So we shall of course not distinguish between those cases where the criterion for law-likeness is fulfilled and those where it is not; for arguments of the latter kind – if they pretend to use laws – are not proper instances of scientific systematizations. Secondly, it will be assumed that the cases accepted by most authors exist, though this may be denied by some philosophers, e.g. with respect to deductive-nomological systematizations. We now start with our list:

I. With respect to *the distribution of truth values* three possibilities can arise: (a) both the conjunction of the premises and the conclusion are true; (b) the conjunction of the premises is false and the conclusion is true; (e) both the conjunction of the premises as well as the conclusion are false. All the premises (singular and law-like ones, if the latter occur at all) are thereby put together. Of course, the singular premises can be separated from the rest so that we get a more subtle subdivision with three subcases in each of (b) and (c). Such a refined classification may be of relevance, e.g. for a detailed account of the differences between a scientific and an historical explanation. In the case of a false scientific explanation it is in general the lawlike sentences which are partly wrong whereas the falsity of the singular premises would in most cases be considered as a kind of carelessness on the part of the scientist. In the case of a false historical explanation the situation will often be of the opposite kind. Because of the hypothetical character of all assumptions about the past, a false explanation will presumably contain false singular premises while the.laws used are taken from other fields of inquiry (or from everyday experience) and, due to their raw character, are mostly true.

II. With respect to the *laws* we can again distinguish three cases: (a) only deterministic laws are used; (b) some of the laws used are statistical laws; (c) no laws are used at all. For special investigations it may be of interest to distinguish within (b) between the 'mixed' case where both deterministic and statistical laws are used in the premises of the argument and the 'pure' case where all the laws are statistical hypotheses. Case (c) has to be taken into account no matter what attitude is accepted with respect to the similarity thesis because there is general agreement upon the fact that inductive arguments which do not use lawlike premises at all can be used for rational predictions.

III. With respect to *the logical character of the argument* there are two possibilities: (a) the argument is a logical deduction; (b) the argument belongs to inductive reasoning. If the statistical systematizations were the only inductive arguments we would have to consider, then this distinction would be extensionally identical with the distinction between II (a) and (b).

IV. Two different time relations have to be considered. We first distinguish subcases with respect to the time relation between the antecedent event

a and the explanandum event b. In default of a better designation we speak of *the ontological time relation*. Four different possibilities can arise: (a) $a < b$; (b) $b < a$ (c) $a = b$; (d) $a_1 < b < a_2$. Here '<' designates the relation 'earlier than' and '=' the relation 'simultaneous with'. Case (d) concerns the 'temporally dispersed' systematizations whose importance has been pointed out by Rescher in [7]. Systematizations of type (a) will be called *predictive arguments*, systematizations of type (b) *retrodictive arguments*. In the other two cases we could speak of timeless and temporally mixed arguments. All rational predictions are predictive arguments but not all predictive arguments are predictions. Actually most of those systematizations which normally are called 'explanations' are predictive arguments as well. We notice explicitly that this fourfold distinction presupposes a solution of the puzzle of aboutness to which Hempel has drawn our attention (*vide* end of Section 6 in [5]).

V. By *pragmatic time relation* we understand the temporal relation between the time of the formulation of the argument-event and the two events a and b. With respect to this relation three main cases can arise (here we use the letter 'D' and in what follows the letters 'A', 'B' and 'T' in the same sense as in section 2: (a) $a \leqslant b \leqslant D$; (b) $b < a < D$; (c) $a < D < b$. The possibility '$a = D$' in (b) and (c) was excluded because in the strict sense of the word it cannot hold in any serious case of scientific systematization.

The importance of a sharp distinction between the two time relations becomes clear if we compare explanations and predictions (in the 'normal' use of these terms). The ontological time relation is the same because both are predictive arguments; but with respect to the pragmatic time relation they differ; (a) applies to explanations, (c) applies to predictions.

For simplicity the analogy to IV (d) was omitted here; it would constitute an intermediate possibility between (a) and (b).

VI. It was not necessary to analyse the internal stucture of D in V in order to distinguish between the two cases of pragmatic time relation. We encounter a different pragmatic aspect of scientific systematizations when we ask which components of D are given first and which ones are provided or derived later. Here, of course, a differentiation within D becomes necessary. As in Section 2, we call this *the pragmatic relation of givenness*. We have two possible cases:

(a) A and T are given first, B is derived afterwards.

(b) B is given first, A and T are provided later.

The logically possible but, despite its non-triviality, unimportant case 'A, B and T given', mentioned in the introduction, was omitted here. As in V all three components have to be taken as concrete utterances or inscriptions in order to be able to provide them with a time index. Following Scheffler we can refer to systematizations of type (a) by the name '*positing*' and to systematizations of type (b) by the term '*substantiating*'.

The distinction between these two cases (a) and (b) has originally been used by Hempel and Oppenheim to single out explanations and predictions from the class of scientific systematizations. It can still be considered as an important differentiation, corresponding to an intuitive distinction made in everyday and scientific discourse. The somewhat unhappy situation about this distinction is the need for a use of the term '*given*' which is certainly ambiguous in several ways.[7] Does the phrase 'B is given to person X at time t' mean that X uttered B at t or that he uttered it and B is true or that he uttered B and believed in its truth or that besides these last two conditions a third one must be fulfilled, namely that X's belief in B was 'justified' in a pragmatic sense of justification yet to be made precise? Or does it mean that B was 'justifiably assertable' by X at that time? We give only a hint to show that an explication of this latter concept need not be too easy. An irrational prediction may be uttered by X at time t; this prediction may be true as well as justified in the sense that a justification *could be given* for it by deriving it from well-established premises either logically or with the help of an acceptable inductive argument; X's prediction is nevertheless not 'justifiably assertable by X' as he himself did not get it on the basis of a rational argument but by means of a mythical theory. One could finally make the additional requirement that the utterance B has to be made in a certain context, e.g. as component of a challenge 'why B?'. Similar difficulties arise if we ask for the precise meaning of a phrase like 'A was *provided later*.' Thinking again in terms of contexts we possibly have to take into account the *reaction* to the challenge 'why B?'. Further ambiguities emerge with respect to 'the theory (or the law) T was provided later.' It can mean that X runs through the list of laws known to him until he finds a suitable one; or it can mean that he addresses himself to qualified experts providing him with the theory needed or even that this theory was *discovered* later.[8]

In order to prevent us from getting an enormous variety of different concepts most of which will either again turn out to be more or less vague or very unwieldly to handle we follow the suggestion of P. Patel and reduce all these possibilities to one: we simply decide to take the bar time relation within the D-utterance as criterion. VI (b), for example, is to be interpreted only in the sense that within the concrete D-utterance in question the event B preceded the two events A and L temporally.

VII. As it turned out that the difference between (a) arguments giving *grounds for an event*, and (b) arguments giving *reasons for a belief* is virtually independent of the question whether the argument is deductive or inductive (in the sense at least that nomological-deductive arguments, too, can give only reasons for a belief) we have to list these two possibilities separately. We thereby tacitly presupposed that this distinction could be upheld.

Even if we take into account that II and III together give only three possible cases and that various other possible combinations will have to be excluded as well, we still get a number of different kinds of scientific systematizations largely exceeding 100. It therefore seems to be pointless to look for special names for all of them. We rather refer to them by expressions like 'a I (a), II (a), III (a), IV (b), V (b), VI (b), VII (b), VIII (b) – systematization.'

If we go back to the usual expressions it will in most cases turn out that they cover several types of systematizations if the latter are described by reference to our list in the way indicated. This holds especially in the case of the terms 'explanation' and 'prediction'. If we decide to accept a use of these terms which comes as close as possible to the 'normal' use (thereby neglecting all problematic borderline cases) then the term 'explanation' would presumably cover one of the following 6 possibilities:

I (a) or (b); II (a) or (b); III (a) or (b); IV (a) or (c); V (a); VI (b); VII (a),

while under the heading 'prediction' one of the following 29 (or 48?) combinations would be subsumed:

I (a) or (b) or (c); II (a) or (b) or (c); III (a) or (b); IV (a) (or (c)?); V (c); VI (a); VII (a) or (b).

So an explanation may (but of course need not) differ from a prediction up to a maximum of five (or even six) respects: in a 'normal explanation' the explanandum sentence must be true, in a prediction it need not be true; in an explanatory argument at least one law must be used, in a prediction this need not be the case; the pragmatic time relation of an explanation is of the type $b < D$, the pragmatic time relation of a prediction is of the type $D < b$; an explanation is always a case of substantiation, whereas predicting means positing something; an explanatory argument has to give grounds for an event, for a predictive argument it is sufficient to provide reasons for a belief. For a possible sixth respect of deviation see the remark at the end of this section. To the common features of explanations and predictions belongs the fact that both are predictive arguments. This distinguishes them from retrodictions. We do not fill in the list for retrodictions but mention only in passing that the term 'retrodiction' is ambiguous too; it includes, for example, instances of positing as well as instances of substantiating. We call them retrodictions of the first and the second kind.

Remark 4.1. If certain scientific systematizations exhibiting features IV (c) or IV (d) are called explanations then this would again give rise to a differentiation between explanation and prediction. This time the non-pragmatic extension of 'explanation' would be wider than that of 'prediction'. But it seems to be advisable not to call arguments with the ontological time structure IV (d) 'explanations' as this term is normally not used to include partially retrodictive arguments. And as far as IV (c) is concerned we can still decide to apply the term 'prediction' if the systematization is a case of positing (notice that this pragmatic relation of givenness in our interpretation is only another kind of pragmatic time relation; it is even a 'purely pragmatic' one').

5. NON-EXPLANATORY INFORMATION

Apart from some occasional critical remarks the foregoing considerations were based on the assumption that the schema of scientific systematization is correct in principle. There has been ample criticism of this conception of scientific systematization and it has been suggested by various authors that a different account of scientific systematizations should be given. The following remarks too are intended as a criticism of the notion of scientific systematization, but as a criticism of a different sort. It is not the *correctness* of the schema of scientific systematization which will be called into question; it is rather the idea of its *sufficiency* that will be briefly commented upon, i.e. the hypothesis that this schema covers all types of applications of laws and theories to concrete situations in order to get a certain amount of knowledge about them.

An example taken from Rescher's discussion of DS systems (discrete state systems) will serve to illustrate the salient point (*vide* [7], especially pp. 335f.). For those readers who are not familiar with Rescher's article we give a brief characterization of DS systems. These are physical systems which are at every moment in exactly one state out of a list of possible states: S_1, S_2, ... Every such state remains unchanged for a certain interval which may be arbitrarily small or large. So a discrete time parameter can be chosen. The succession of states is governed by deterministic or probabilistic laws. A deterministic law says that a state of kind S_i is always followed by a state of kind S_j. A probabilistic law says that to a state of kind S_i there follows a state of kind S_j with statistical probability P_{ij}. The behaviour of such a system can be completely described with the help of a matrix of the transition probabilities. Here the symbols S_i at the beginning of each row designate the initial state. The symbols S_j on top of each column designate the state with respect to which the transition is considered. The numbers within the matrix indicate the transition probabilities. If the transition law is deterministic then in each row there is a number 1 at one place and zeros elsewhere. In the case of a probabilistic law there are different numbers in each line whose sum equals 1.

For the proof of (T 6.2) a DS system containing three different states is considered whose matrix is the following one:

	S_1	S_2	S_3
S_1	0	.5	.5
S_2	0	.1	.9
S_3	.1	0	.9

Even if the complete history of the system with the exception of one unknown state at time t is given, e.g.:

... $S_3 S_1 - S_3 S_1$ ... (the blank representing this unknown state at t),

we may be unable 'to fill in the blank', even probabilistically. Neither a deductive explanation nor what Rescher calls a strong or a weak probabilistic explanation of this unknown state can be given. (Here it should be noticed that the word 'explanation' is used by Rescher in basically the same sense as our expression 'scientific systematization'). From this Rescher draws the conclusion that the occurrence of this state lies 'outside the range of scientific rationalization' and he gives Aristotle credit for the conception of such states of affairs ('accidents') whose occurrence lies outside the reach of scientific explanation. He says: 'This circumstance strongly suggests that *scientific understanding* is not necessarily to be construed in terms of an ability to predict or even to explain the specific phenomena. It would seem to be more appropriate to think of 'scientific understanding' in terms of a grasp of the general laws governing the structure of events'.[9]

It seems to us that Rescher has drawn our attention to a really important point which apparently has been overlooked by the other authors. But nevertheless the interpretation he has given of this fact is somewhat misleading.

From his analysis we get the impression that in the case of a complete knowledge of the laws governing a system we would always face only a twofold dichotomy, namely: either we can apply the known laws to all situations *in the way of 'explanatory' arguments* or we cannot apply them to *explain* certain situations or states. In the latter case these states lie beyond the reach of scientific systematization and therefore 'outside the range of scientific rationalization'.

Now it is certainly true that the concept of scientific explanation (or scientific systematization), if construed in one of the usual ways, cannot be applied to the situation described in Rescher's example. But from this it does not at all follow that we do not have *scientific information* about the given DS system at time t. The information we *do* have about this 'possible state' (and which is placed at our disposal only by the laws contained in the matrix of the system) is this: (1) state S_1 cannot be realized at time t; (2) the system exhibits at t one of the two states S_2 or S_1, the probabilities for the realization of these two states being equal. Since it cannot be subsumed under one of the specializations of the concept of scientific systematization, we call this type of knowledge *non-explanatory information*. By 'scientific systematization' we hereby understand an argument which under suitable pragmatic circumstances would become an explanation, a retrodiction or a prediction (of the deductive kind or of one of the two probabilistic kinds), or, more systematically, an argument which exhibits the features of an admissible combination of subcases from I – VII of Section 4. It is obvious that similar kinds of information can be obtained in all of the other cases of discrete state systems where probabilistic or deductive explanatory arguments become impossible. We must therefore reject this alternative as incomplete: '*Either* we can give a scientific account of concrete events (phenomena, situations), then this account must be one type of scientific systematization; *or* we can get only a grasp of the general laws governing the structure of the events without being able to apply them to these concrete events (phenomena, situations).' There are important applications of theories and laws to concrete events of a different type which do not fall under the general heading of 'scientific systematization'. Such events of which we can give an account by means of non-explanatory information only, do *not* lie outside the range of scientific rationalization though they definitely lie beyond the reach of scientific systematization.

That the knowledge in question is a *particular knowledge* related to special events is furthermore shown by its influence upon human actions. It can have the same effect on practical decisions as scientific predictions; for knowing that certain possibilities are ruled out and that the remaining ones are of equal probabilities can in principle be of analogous importance for the practical life as predictions mentioning only one future event. That non-explanatory information exhibits a kind of *rational knowledge* follows simply from the fact that we can obtain this knowledge about a particular space-time region of the world only by first grasping the general principles governing the course of events. This distinguishes it clearly from all irrational pseudoknowledge about the future. So we cannot help but recognize it as a kind of scientific rationalization.

If this idea of non-explanatory information is accepted, then the paradoxical aspect of Rescher's observations, namely that 'despite the fact that, in the systems considered, we have a *complete knowledge* of the functioning of the system ... we can neither predict nor retrodict nor even explain certain occurrences', [10] disappears. Our inability to explain a situation does not exclude our ability to get the best detailed information about this very situation that can be obtained on the basis of the prevailing laws. One could say that the apparent paradoxical impression is caused only by the use of the *philosophical* theory of explanation. A statistician, not familiar with the philosophical attempts to make this concept of explanation precise, will presumably find no essential difference between the special case described with respect to the given DS system and those cases where the state symbol before the blank differs from S_1 or that behind the blank differs from S_3 or where only the symbol before or behind the blank is given. The reason for this lies simply in the fact that he will in the latter case give an account of the situation in principally the same way as in the former case: by giving a list containing the 'possible' and the 'impossible' states and the transition probabilities for the possible states. And he will not even later be disturbed if he learns that some of his accounts can be classified as deductive or strong or weak probabilistic explanations, while some others cannot. He will perhaps react by pointing out that the concept of scientific explanation (systematization) implies an artificial narrowing down of the *possible* kinds of applications of theories and laws to *special* kinds of applications.

For all these reasons it seems to the present author, his esteem and respect for Aristotle notwithstanding, that presumably Rescher's defence of Aristotle's theory of the 'accidents' has to be withdrawn, at least if Aristotle's account is reconstrued not only in terms of missing explanatory knowledge, but in terms of missing informatory knowledge (despite a complete knowledge of the governing laws). Whenever the functioning of a system is known completely, the theory can be applied to all relevant situations; some of these applications will turn out to be explanatory, some will not, but will give us non-explanatory information.

As the most general notion, including all kinds of applications of theories, we use the concept '*scientific rationalization*', consisting of scientific systematization and non-explanatory information as sub-cases. The latter concept could in principle motivate *an extension of the use of 'prediction' beyond the domain of scientific systematizations*. This fact reveals a new ambiguity in the term 'prediction' which has not been noted before. It need not be a concrete event that is predicted; it may be a complex situation, including 'impossible' states and a distribution of equal probabilities among the remaining ones. If, for example, in Rescher's example we are given the matrix and the state S_1 at the present time t and nothing else, then we can *predict* in this new sense of prediction that at time $t + 1$ exactly one of the two states S_2 or S_3 will be realized, each of them with equal probability. If we further decide – as would seem to be natural – not to extend the use of 'explanation' beyond the domain of scientific systematizations, then we get again the result *that 'prediction' has a wider range of application than 'explanation'*. This would not mean that we have obtained a 'structural divergence' between two kinds of scientific systematizations; but rather that one of the two names, originally introduced to designate certain kinds of scientific systematizations, was, in addition to this, used to characterize information falling outside the range of scientific systematizations, while no similar extension of the use of the term 'explanation' had been open to us.

In all the considerations of this section we tacitly accepted Rescher's presupposition that the explanandum statements of our *object language* are always atomic statements of the form 'the state of the DS system at time t equals S_i.' The non-explanatory information must then be expressed within the *metalanguage*. Now we could think of increasing considerably the expressive means of the object language so that the truth-functional connections between these atomic sentences and simple probabilistic statements are admitted as *singular* sentences. In this case our information could be formulated and established within the object language itself. But then our informative utterance would be interpretable as explanandum utterance. This reflection shows that the question whether scientific rationalization goes beyond scientific systematization depends finally on linguistic conventions, namely on the expressive strength of the object language and its relation to the expressive strength of the metalanguage.

Remark 5.1. Rescher's concept of discrete state system could be used to clarify the essential aspect of example (1) in Section 3. This example will presumably be that part of the foregoing reflections which are most likely subject to criticism. It will perhaps either be argued that a statement like this is no lawlike principle or that, if it is, it is obviously not true and cannot, therefore, be accepted as an empirical hypothesis. Such a criticism would miss the point. What matters is only this: suppose we are given a physical system S governed by deterministic laws of succession and besides this a second system, called 'information center $J(X)$' (X being a variable ranging over the domain of systems of the type of S). This second system makes predictions about future states of S if it is supplied with the laws and the present state of S, call it then $J(S)$. If the predictions are made quick enough and the future time about which predictions are made is far ahead enough, then the 'prediction utterance' is an event E_1, which precedes the predicted event E_2 in such a way that E_1 is deterministically followed by E_2. In this situation a statement describing E_2 can be obtained from an analogous statement about E_1 with the help of an argument satisfying all requirements set up for deductive nomological systematizations. Yet we will only call earlier states of S 'grounds for the event E_2' but not states of J such as E_1; for J can be removed without affecting the processes of S.

An example of this kind would be, for example a 'discrete information system' J assigned to a deterministic DS system S which works in the following way: J is provided with the matrix characteristic for S and therefore with all the laws governing S. It further has two switchkeys. If both of them are turned on, then J 'observes' the momentary state st(t) of S and if simultaneously the second one is set on number n ($n \leqslant N$ for an N characteristic for J) then J predicts state st($t + n$) at a time, say, not exceeding $t + [n/10]$. (This prediction could be made by showing the number indices of the predicted state or, if the number of the states is not too large, by coloured lights flashing on a panel, different colours assigned to different states, etc.) We then have a deterministic law that can roughly be described in the following way: 'Whenever J predicts at t_0 for the later time t that st(t) $=S_j$ in S then the DS system S will exhibit state S_j at time t'. But despite this law we will certainly refuse to say that the law plus the prediction made by J at t answers the question why the system S exhibited S_j at t, i.e. that these two items together give us grounds for the event which consists of the realization of state S_j at t in S. For otherwise we would have to say, like in the astronomer's example, that S exhibited the physical state S_j at t because it had been predicted that it would.

NOTES

* I wish to express my thanks to professor Carl G. Hempel for his stimulating critical remarks on the first draft of this paper.

1 Explanations of this type can certainly not be reduced to explanations of events and/ or explanations of laws because they normally include a great amount of 'mere descriptions'.

2 It is here presupposed that there are clear-cut boundary lines between the various kinds of systematizations such as explanation, prediction and retrodiction (or retrodiction of the first and of the second type (*vide* Section 4)).

3 Such a decision would have the paradoxical consequence that nothing could be explained with the help of the principles of quantum mechanics.

4 Even in such cases as an astronomer's prediction of an eclipse, where the scientist has a clear feeling of producing a deductive argument, it can happen that a yet unknown celestial body of big size moves rapidly towards our planetary system, thereby thwarting all the astronomer's precalculations. This difficulty can certainly not be overcome by requiring that the law statement or the theory satisfy what the two authors quoted call the 'completeness condition.' The only possible solution seems to be to add an additional premise making the tacit assumption of the physicist that the system is a *closed* system explicit. The problem is how the closeness property has to be formulated in precise terms.

5 In order not to do Scheffler an injustice it should be pointed out that at one place (*vide* [9], p. 49, example (5) and the remarks about it on top of p. 50) he mentions a deductive-nomological argument which gives only grounds for the acceptance of something without providing an explanation. But this is a case of retrodiction which is excluded from our present discussion.

6 This drastic example has been chosen in order to emphasize the salient point. We could have chosen instead arbitrary cases of two kinds of laws satisfying the following conditions. The first one is a 'causal law' of the kind 'all *A* are *B*'. The second one is an 'indicator law' describing symptoms *F* which are sufficient for the occurrence of *A*. Together these two laws enable the deductive-nomological transition from the occurrence of an *F* to the occurrence of a *B* though it could not be claimed that in this argument grounds for the event *B* have been given. The causal law need not even be known. It is sufficient if a strict law is available which makes the transition from symptoms of the kind *F* to events of the kind *B* generally possible. Of this kind, for example, is the barometer example discussed in A. Grünbaum's book, *Philosophical Problems of Space and Time*, New York 1963, pp. 309ff.

7 The difficulties connected with the use of the term 'given' have been pointed out by P. Patel in [6], p. 7ff. We follow Patel in some of the possible suggestions made in the text.

8 For some special purposes it may be useful to distinguish between predictions made for the first time (because based on a theory just propounded) and *routine-predictions* which in distinction to the *first-time-predictions* are based on principles often used in the past.

9 [7], p. 335.

10 [7], p. 335.

BIBLIOGRAPHY

[1] Canfield, J. and Lehrer, K., 'A Note on Prediction and Deduction', *Philosophy of Science* 28 (1961), 204 – 8.

[2] Grünbaum, A., 'Temporally Asymmetric Principles, Parity between Explanation and Prediction, and Mechanism Versus Teleology', *Philosophy of Science* 29 (1962), 146 – 70.

[3] Hempel, C.G. and Oppenheim, P., 'Studies in the Logic of Explanation', *Philosophy of Science* 15 (1948), 135 – 75.

[4] Hempel, C.G., 'The Theoretician's Dilemma', in Feigl, Herbert, Scriven, Michael and Maxwell, Grover (eds.), *Minnesota Studies in the Philosophy of Science*, University of Minnesota Press, Minneapolis, 1958, II.

[5] Hempel, C.G., 'Deductive-Nomological Versus Statistical Explanation, in Feigl, Herbert and Maxwell, G. (eds.), *Minnesota Studies in the Philosophy of Science*, III.

[6] Patel, P., 'Logische und methodologische Probleme der wissenschaftlichen Erklärung. Eine kritische Übersicht über die neueste Entwicklung in den U.S.A.', Doctoral dissertation, München 1964.

[7] Rescher, N., 'Discrete State Systems, Markov Chains, and Problems in the Theory of Scientific Explanation and Prediction', *Philosophy of Science* 30 (1963), 325 – 45.

[8] Scheffler, I., 'Explanation, Prediction and Abstraction', *The British Journal for the Philosophy of Science* 7 (1957), 293 – 309.

[9] Scheffler, I., *The Anatomy of Inquiry, Philosophical Studies in the Theory of Science*, New York 1963.

CHAPTER 4

THE PROBLEM OF INDUCTION: HUME'S CHALLENGE AND THE CONTEMPORARY ANSWERS

1. INTRODUCTION

Every new scientific discovery and every additional philosophical essay on induction seems to further confirm C. D. Broad's claim that *induction is the triumph of science and the disgrace of philosophy*. Since at least the latter part of the statement is not to be doubted, this essay, too, promises to contribute its share to increasing the philosophic scandal.

But is the first part of Broad's thesis also true? May it not simply be a philosophical myth that it is the so-called *inductive method* which is responsible for scientific progress? And may it not be the case that this myth has become so firmly entrenched in our minds just because, unlike most other myths, it is espoused not only by professional philosophers but by both philosophers and philosophically minded scientists alike?

What I plan to say about this topic departs so radically from what has come to be expected in an essay of this nature – whether pro or con – that, given the short space allotted me here, I cannot hope to make myself well understood let alone find agreement. If I did eventually succumb to the pressure of the publisher and compress the material into slogans it was because I consoled myself with the hope of soon being able to write more about these matters in the projected series of essays on the philosophy of science.

The framework of the essay is built around three well known names: the *problem* is first described on the basis of a reconstruction of *Hume's* thinking. *The discussion of possible responses* to this problem draws upon the views of the two most prominent exponents of 'deductivism' and 'inductivism': *Karl Popper* and *Rudolf Carnap*.

To facilitate reading, perhaps even to arouse a measure of curiosity in the reader, I will mention in advance a few of the most important theses which will later be presented and defended:

(1) In order to correctly assess the meaning and significance of Hume's *problem of induction* it must first be formulated quite generally as has been

done, for example, by Wesley Salmon. This means that it must not be prematurely narrowed down to particular forms of 'non-demonstrative inference' such as, for example, induction by enumeration; for in the case of *any* specialization there lurks the potential danger of being accused of failing to take sufficient notice of such and such non-demonstrative inference; one is then told that *true* induction lies in the very kinds of inference he happened to neglect!

(2) This problem of induction is non-existent. It must today be replaced by two quite different *successor problems*; one belongs to the domain of *theoretical reason*, the other to the domain of *practical reason*.

(3) Within the domain of theoretical reasoning the *deductivism* advocated by Popper is presumably right, at least as far as deterministic hypotheses are concerned.

(4) Yet the deductivists, especially Popper and his followers, have so far failed to provide us with an explication of the deductive concept of confirmation. This will become evident upon examining a key concept of Popper's theory, namely, his concept of corroboration.

(5) The *intuitive* concept of corroboration provides an excellent example of the mistakes and superfluous discussions that ensue if a concept explication is omitted: such an omission is responsible for W. Salmon's mistake of construing the Popperian corroboration as a *non-demonstrative type of inference* and claiming that the concept of induction simply re-enters Popper's theory under a new name. The partly futile, partly unnecessary attempts of, for example, I. Lakatos to come to terms with Salmon's argument constitute a second stage of the fruitless discussion.

(6) The 'successor problem' to the problem of induction consists from a theoretical point of view of the problem of *proving the adequacy of a deductive concept of confirmation* and not in finding some kind of 'justification of inductive inference.'

(7) This problem is by its very nature a *normative* problem.

(8) *Statistical hypotheses* constitute a very problematic special case. The application of Popper's theory of corroboration to this case is not something trivial; the concept of *rational refutation* which is here necessary is not simply a 'natural' generalization of the concept of falsification but represents something fundamentally different. Even here, however, the non-inductivist successor problem is somewhat analogous to the deterministic case since no probability of hypothesis is to be ascribed to hypotheses of probability.

(9) There is no point of contact whatever between the theories of Popper and Carnap. The contrary view – held even by these two thinkers themselves

– is the result of Carnap's mistaken idea that his theory is a theory of *partial logical implication*, that it deals with *inductive logic* or that it constitutes an *inductive theory of the confirmation of scientific hypotheses*. All this, however, is incorrect. Popper's theory of corroboration has to do with the *theoretical appraisal (evaluation) of unverifiable hypotheses*. Carnap's theory, on the other hand, is concerned with *setting up norms for human decisions involving risk*.

(10) Popper's theory is intended to be a *metatheory of theories*, whereas Carnap's theory is a *metatheory of practice*. Popper's observations belong to the domain of 'theoretical reason' whereas Carnap's investigations pertain to the domain of 'practical reason.'

(11) There are compelling reasons for a decision-theoretical reinterpretation of Carnap's project. A *theoretical* interpretation produces a threefold dilemma: (a) it does not lead to any formal inconsistency (as has been claimed by Popper) but rather to a *material inconsistency*; (b) it leads to a *circle* with respect to the concept of partial implication; (c) it leads to the *unsolvability of Hume's problem*.

(12) All of these difficulties disappear once Carnap's project is construed as an attempt at establishing a *logical foundation for a normative decision theory*.

(13) Via such a reinterpretation *scientific hypotheses no longer belong to the domain of objects of Carnap's theory*: this is because in decision theory one considers only hypotheses upon which one can *meaningfully* bet. One cannot, however, meaningfully bet on scientific theories (for betting only makes sense in cases where one can ascertain the *outcome of the bet*; but this is ruled out in the case of scientific theories).

(14) Carnap's real opponents are not the deductivists, i.e., the Popperians, but rather the subjective probability theoreticians. For in contrast to Carnap, they do not care to make the transition from manifest belief predicates to the deeper lying dispositional structures as is done in science.

(15) The concept of *inductive reasoning* obtains a sharply circumscribed and reasonable sense in Carnap's domain of rational decisions involving risk: it is concerned with the *subjectivist probabilistic considerations* upon which such decisions are based.

(16) For this area there also exists a *successor problem* to Hume's problem of induction. It runs as follows: how can you justify the norms that someone acting rationally under risk *ought* to follow in his subjective probabilistic considerations?

Both of the *successor problems* (or classes of problems) to Hume's problem of induction are consequently problems of the justification of norms. In the one case we are dealing with *norms for the theoretical appraisal of scientific hypotheses* and in the other case we are dealing *with norms for rational action involving risk*.

(17) Carnap's so-called inductive logic seemed to be plagued with three serious shortcomings: the null-confirmations of laws, the lack of rules of acceptance and rejection, and the lack of rationality criteria for singling out exactly one *C*-function. The decision-theoretic reinterpretation of Carnap's investigations shows that these shortcomings are *only apparent* and are, indeed, perfectly *desirable consequences* of his system.

2. THE HUMEAN CHALLENGE

Two observations form the basis of Hume's formulation of the problem of induction, namely:

(1) *All of our knowledge about the real world must somehow be based on what we perceive and observe* (formulated negatively: we cannot arrive at a knowledge of the nature of the world by means of pure logical reasoning alone);

(2) *We nevertheless think we are in possession of much more factual knowledge than we could have acquired through our sense experience.*

From this there immediately arises the first and *general* form of the problem: how can we justify or support our *conviction* that this *alleged* knowledge of ours is really knowledge?

It is extremely important at this point not to overlook the fact that this question does not involve a *problem of discovery* but only a *problem of justification*. It does not matter in the least how I have arrived at the alleged knowledge cited in (2). The answer to the question of justification alone is decisive.

Since this is not a question of logical demonstration, justification can only proceed by way of *arguments* whose premises contain the observation-knowledge mentioned in (1) but whose conclusions, on the other hand, express knowledge, mentioned in (2), which goes beyond the observations. The problem thus boils down to the question of *what kinds of arguments lead from the observed to the unobserved*?

There are only two possibilities:

(a) The first possibility would involve arguments based on inferences which Hume calls *demonstrative inferences*. We have a *demonstrative infer-*

ence in Hume's sense if and only if, to use current terminology, *a purely logical consequence relation* obtains. The logical consequence relation has two formal features: first, the content of the conclusion does not go beyond the content of the premises; logical inferences do not augment the content. By analogy to well known Kantian terminology we may express this briefly by saying *demonstrative inferences are not ampliative inferences*. Second, if there is a logical consequence relation, the truth of the premises is transferred to the conclusion as long as the premises are true. This fact is expressed by saying *demonstrative inferences are truth-preserving*.

Let us now add to our two initial observations yet another premise that has never been questioned or disputed:

(3) *The content of statements which express our alleged knowledge of the unobserved is not included in the content of our knowledge of the observed.*

It can now be readily seen that we are not capable of mastering the task we have set ourselves by resorting to logical inference: since logical inferences are not ampliative inferences, knowledge of things unobserved would be logically derivable from knowledge of things observed only if, contrary to (3), the content of the former would be included in the content of the latter.

(b) Thus the kind of arguments we are looking for cannot simply rest on demonstrative inferences alone. On what kind of inferences then? Philosophers claim that so-called inductive inferences would have to assume this role. Due to the above reasons, they would have to involve ampliative inferences. Are there any such inferences? Of course! One need just pick out a *logically invalid inference* in which the conclusion possesses a stronger content than the conjunction of premises!

But that, of course, is not what the inductivists have in mind. Invalid logical inferences are worthless; but inductive inferences should not be worthless. The feature of *augmenting the content* is indeed a necessary but still not a sufficient condition for the kind of inference we are looking for. In order for it to augment *our knowledge* (and not, for example, simply our superstitions) it must, furthermore, be *truth-preserving*, just like demonstrative inference. This is the *Humean problem of induction: are there truth-preserving ampliative inferences*?

It must be noted that in this question no reference is made to *any particular* so-called 'inductive rule' or 'inductive method'.

Hume's answer to this question is: *no, there is no such thing*. Either an inference is correct – and then it is indeed truth-preserving, but does not augment the content – or it augments the content, but then there is no guarantee that the conclusion is true even if all of the premises are true.

The most impressive illustration of this can be seen by looking at the relation between the past and the future. All of our observational knowledge refers to past events. Non-tautological assertions about what will take place are not included in the content of statements about the past. Thus, if they are to constitute *knowledge*, they could only be derived from our knowledge about the past by means of correct, i.e., truth-preserving, ampliative inferences; but since there are no such inferences we have no knowledge about future events. The future *could* be completely different from the past.

Since the class of inferences which qualify as potential candidates for inductive inferences must be contained in the class of ampliative inferences, Hume's conclusion constitutes a clear refutation of any form of inductivism, *regardless of how a particular rule of induction may be defined*.

A way out of this dilemma might be found if we could rely on a non-logical principle, that is, a *synthetic principle about the world* such as, for example, the *principle of uniformity* which states that regularities which have been observed in the past will also hold in the future. But the difficulty reappears immediately, however, as soon as we ask ourselves how we are to justify such a principle. *We certainly cannot prove it logically*; for it would then be superfluous as an additional premise and whatever would have been gained by it could also have been gained without it, viz. by truth-preserving ampliative inferences; but this is logically impossible. If, however, we wanted to *justify it inductively*, we would obviously end up in an *infinite regress*. Thus, such a principle would simply have to be *asserted dogmatically*. But with such blind dogmatism we would move *outside the pale of science*: that is, we would be on the same level as those who do not argue their point but, instead, simply assert it.

In conjunction with this last point it must be noted that the predicate 'dogmatism' is ascribed not just to one *particular* suggestion, but to an infinite class of such candidates.

There is not just one possible principle of induction but an infinite class of them which, furthermore, is completely unsurveyable.

A magic word that is often thrown in at this point of the discussion is the word 'probable'. Inductive inferences, so it is claimed, are simply *probability inferences*. We must give up the requirement of finding truth-preserving ampliative inferences. Instead of truth we have to remain content with probability (and bear in mind here that we may very well go wrong and that what is probable may at times not occur).

But, according to Hume, even this idea won't get us very far; for either we construe the expression 'probable' in the *sense of frequency* and then the more probable is what has so far (sic!) occurred more often, in which case we are faced with exactly the same difficulty as before, for *how do we know that past frequency distributions will also hold in the future*? In order to arrive at such knowledge we must again have at our disposal a truth-preserving ampliative inference for which we have just searched in vain. Or again, we interpret the word 'probable' *in some other sense* and then it becomes unexplainable why we should expect the more probable to be realized than the improbable.

The significance and force of Hume's argument has again and again been underestimated. Even today it still is underestimated for the most part. Hume's thought is, for example, often misconstrued as having merely shown that it cannot be proved that every inductive inference with true premises also has a true conclusion.[1] As W. Salmon correctly points out,[2] Hume has, however, shown much more than this; namely, that we cannot even prove that *any inductive inference with true premises ever has a true conclusion*, regardless of how the rule of induction is characterized.

Hume's position is completely skeptical: *there is no extrapolation of knowledge from the observed to the unobserved. In particular, it is a human illusion to believe that we can gain knowledge about the future*.

By way of conclusion let's consider a particularly drastic example. It should, above all, serve to show the *strange kinds of inductive rules* we must envisage, when we speak quite generally of inductive inferences. Second, we want to criticize by means of it one possible type of solution which resorts to a method nowadays particularly fashionable in English-speaking countries: the *ordinary language approach.*

Let us refer to the person whom we want to consider as the anti-inductivist. This expression should not suggest, for example, that he rejects induction – for in such a case he would be a Humean – but instead that he uses a *rule of induction* which would actually be rejected as absurd by all of us. We are, nevertheless, dealing with a precise rule. Let's call it the anti-induction rule.[3] It is a potential candidate for a non-demonstrative rule of inference. In the everyday non-quantitative, qualitative manner of speaking, the rule may be formulated as follows: the future occurrence of an event is all the less probable the more often it has occurred until now, and so much more probable the less often it has occurred so far. Put in a more precise quantitative form, the rule says: if in the initial n-member segment of a series the characteristic C has been observed m times, then it is to be expected that the relative frequency of the members with the characteristic C in the entire series corresponds to $1 - m/n$.[4] In other words, if, for example, our anti-inductivist has drawn 10 balls from an urn and seven are black and three white, he will reckon with a probability of 7/10 that the next ball he draws will be white; if he has drawn 1000 balls and 999 of them were black and one white, then he figures the probability that a white ball will turn up in his next draw at 999/1000, etc.

How can the anti-inductivist be dissuaded from his view? His conviction *that the rule he follows is a true rule of induction cannot*, at any rate, *be logically refuted*. One can try to make him abandon his position by resorting to 'persuasive arguments'. Let's suppose, however, that admonitions beginning with the words: 'but have you gone mad ...!' will leave him unmoved and will not make him change his mind. May one perhaps succeed with a pragmatic argument? No, even that won't do, for every such argument is circular. (According to *our* rule of induction it may well be that following his rule, since it was not successful *so far*, will not be successful in the future; but on the basis of exactly the same experience he will according to *his* rule conclude that he will be successful.) One cannot even tell him that his method *precludes learning from experience.* For he certainly does *learn* from experience in the sense that he constantly keeps revising his judgments of probability on the basis of varying observations in accordance with a fixed rule. At this point the philosopher of ordinary language will butt in and say: 'but such a form of learning from experience is *not reasonable*.' The ordinary language philosopher will furthermore try to prove that the anti-inductive behaviour ought not to be called rational.

The anti-inductivist will remain *completely unmoved* by all of these attempts. The fact that everybody else uses criteria of rationality which exclude his rule, *is for him not at all a proof that he himself is irrational but only goes to show that these other persons are stupid* This fictitious example illustrates quite clearly, incidentally, the failure of ordinary language arguments in cases where problems of validity are concerned.

To prevent any misunderstanding: no anti-inductivist propaganda is being urged here. Probability theoreticians of the most divergent backgrounds, such as H. Reichenbach and R. Carnap, might bring forward cogent objections against the rule of the anti-inductivist.[5] What I wanted to say was simply this: one cannot dismiss the case of the anti-inductivist by simply referring to how people talk, in particular, to how they use the words 'rational', 'reasonable', 'confirming data', etc.

3. DEDUCTIVISM: K. POPPER

3.1. *Intuitive Sketch*

The Humean challenge, which apparently has first been fully grasped in this century, has split modern philosophers of science into two camps. To one faction[6] belong the '*inductivists*', i.e., those who believe that despite all the difficulties one can set up either a *rule of induction* which can be defended against attacks and criticisms or that one may succeed in developing a *theory of the inductive confirmation of scientific hypotheses*. R. Carnap was originally an exponent of this latter view and today there are a number of scholars attempting to realize the Carnapian project in a more or less modified form.

The other party is comprised of '*deductivists*', namely, Popper and his followers. Popper takes the view that the difficulties pointed out by Hume are insurmountable. According to him, Hume has conclusively proved that there can be no rational justification of induction and, furthermore, that the concept of inductive inference is a pseudo-concept: induction is an illusion.

This negative posture applies whether induction is construed as a method of discovering hypotheses or as a *method of justification* for already available hypotheses. Deductivists and inductivists alike, in particular Popper and Carnap, agree today that there are no inductive discovery procedures.[7] The divergence in views emerges only with regard to the second point. According to Popper, Hume's argument also constitutes a refutation of the claim that there is an inductive method of justification for hypotheses; according to Carnap,[8] on the other hand, such a method of justification can be developed by means of the inductive logic he devised.

In view of modern scientific hypotheses, progress, and enormous success, we cannot abide, says Popper, by these two negative observations. Even if there is no induction, there must, nevertheless, be a method by means of which scientific hypotheses can be tested so that in virtue of the test's results they can either be rejected or at least provisionally accepted.

Scientific law-hypotheses have the structure of unlimited universal sentences. They are, therefore, not empirically verifiable since the experiential basis at our disposal is, and will always, remain finite. Down to the very end of time mankind cannot definitively establish the truth of even a single scientific hypothesis. If the expression 'knowledge' is taken in the sense of definitive knowledge (*episteme* in contrast to *doxa*) then there is no knowledge in the empirical sciences: '*We do not know; we simply guess*.'[9]

But how then are empirico-scientific conjectures to be distinguished from metaphysical ones? The answer is that all empirical conjectures or hypotheses can be subjected to a *strict empirical test.* It is not inductive rules, however, that are used in this test, but only rules of deductive logic. To be sure, an unlimited universal hypothesis cannot be derived from any number of singular statements; it can, however, be refuted by particular facts. The *potential empirical falsifiability* or empirical refutability is thus the sole criterion by which empirical hypotheses are demarcated from metaphysical conjectures. '*It must be possible for an (empirical) scientific system to be refuted by experience.*' [10] The schema for testing is always the same: one derives prognoses from the hypothesis to be tested and the appropriate initial conditions. If the prediction fails to materialize, then the hypothesis is *effectively falsified* (more exactly, it is falsified *relative to the acknowledged basis*). The only rule of inference that is needed here is the deductive rule of *modus tollens*. If what is predicted does take place, one usually says that the test has *turned out positive*. This manner of speaking tends to create misunderstanding for it suggests we have here found a *positive instance that supports the hypothesis*; such an idea then leads immediately to the further idea that given an increasing number of these positive instances the hypothesis will be *increasingly supported and confirmed*.

Popper rejects such a line of thought: the so-called positive outcome of a test is in fact nothing else but an unsuccessful attempt at falsification; we have not succeeded, he says, in contradicting the hypothesis; we have failed in our attempt at having the hypothesis falsified by experience. (Various qualifications which apply here will be considered in the course of our discussion.)

But a problem crops up here: even when a hypothesis about some domain of objects has been empirically refuted we are still left with a vast number of possible unfalsified hypotheses. This overabundance is overwhelming. So as to draw a line of demarcation Popper introduces the concept of *corroboration*, which, in turn, rests essentially on the concept of *content*.

The unfalsified hypotheses do not all lie on the same plane: they differ as regards their empirical content. *The empirical content* of a theory is determined by the class of basic sentences which the theory precludes, i.e., by the class of possibilities for its falsification or its potential falsifiers. The greater this class is, that is, the greater the content, the lesser the logical probability of the theory. Popper's strategy is: in every empirical scientific field of research we should pick out from among the competing theories those with *the greatest empirical content*, that is, those *with the greatest number of potential falsifiers, viz. the most risky* or *the most logically improbable*; not for the sake of accepting them, but rather so as *to subject them to a strict test* (or more exactly, to the strictest possible test). If it fails to stand up to the test, then it is rejected. If, on the other hand, it withstands the test, then it has been *corroborated* and can provisionally be accepted.

Later on we will discuss W. Salmon's thesis according to which one must distinguish between two phases, or better, two aspects of the Popperian theory of testing. As long as only attempts at refutation, falsification and retention of unfalsified hypotheses are at issue, deductive logic is actually sufficient. But this no longer holds the moment the concept of corroboration is introduced. For here we attribute a positive characteristic to a hypothesis which has more content than the relevant basic sentences. No deductive logic is capable of such a feat. The concept of corroboration introduces a distinction that cannot be justified deductively. In short: the concept of corroboration amounts to nothing but a variant of a 'non-demonstrative rule of inference'; namely, *the Popperian variant of induction*.

Various thinkers closely associated with Popper have taken this objection quite seriously; Lakatos is one of them and he tries to meet this difficulty by introducing, in [*Changes*] p. 390, the concept of acceptability$_3$, for the description of which he relies on the Popperian concept of verisimilitude.

In my opinion, however, Salmon's objection rests on a mistake. I will try to point it out. Although Salmon's argument is wrong, it is psychologically *understandable* how it arose in the first place: Popper as well as his followers have failed to provide us with a sharp characterization of the concept of corroboration and so one might actually get the impression that hidden behind it lies something like a non-logical, that is, ampliative inference rule. I find myself, therefore, in the strange position of having to defend Popper's intention against W. Salmon *as well as* Lakatos. My comments on Salmon will be of a polemical nature. My comments on acceptability$_3$ boil down to two claims: first, the introduction of this concept is *superfluous* as soon as Salmon's difficulty disappears. Secondly, even were it not superfluous I still fail to comprehend how one can possibly regard the concept of verisimilitude as the Popperian analogue to the principle of induction. I don't want to make any polemical remarks about this last point; I only wish to present my reasons for failing to understand.

As a matter of fact the Popperian theory, just like *every* theory of corroboration and confirmation, is faced with what I call *the theoretical successor problem to the problem of induction*. This problem must be clearly seen lest we look for a solution in places where it is impossible to find one. Its solution does not lie, for example, in attempting to construct a 'Popperian analogue to the principle of induction' – for example in terms of the concept of acceptability$_3$ – it consists, rather in a *proof of the adequacy of the concept of deductive confirmation or corroboration* which must be sharply defined.

3.2. *Details and Discussion*

(I) *A few clarifying comments*. In the foregoing intuitive sketch we have described Popper's alternative solution to the so-called problem of induction but have left aside the rest of his theoretical observations concerning science. Is this permissible, or must one also bring into the discussion at least his stand with regard to the *problem of the empirical basis* as well as his proposal with regard to the *demarcation line between empirical science and metaphysics*? The omission of both of these points needs to be justified. This is very simple: it is quite possible that someone is willing to accept Popper's thesis of the conventionalist basis and yet be unwilling to accept deductivism; and conversely, it is quite possible that someone is willing to accept deductivism and yet not willing to believe in absolutely certain basic sentences. This means that it is permissible to discuss the positions in these two problem areas independently of each other. Something quite similar holds in the case of the demarcation problem (about which I will make a few comments later on).

It is, however, important not to overlook a consequence of Popper's metatheoretical characterization of the basic sentences: *falsification does not imply falsity*. Even a correct theory can be effectively falsified.

Misinterpretations and misunderstandings resulted from *Popper's rejection of the concept of the probability of hypotheses*. It is an incontrovertible fact (which I have ascertained time and again) that empirical scientists talk about the probability of hypotheses.[11] Does Popper want to deny such a fact or does he wish to claim that scientists are talking nonsense when they speak of the probability of hypotheses? Neither. The facts are again quite simple: in the use of the word 'probability' two linguistic trends have developed independently of each other. Mathematicians, especially in the theory of measurement and statistics, use the word in a sharply circumscribed technical sense.[12] Empirical scientists, on the other hand, use the expression in its pre-scientific, intuitive sense. It is not at all self-evident that the precise form of this latter concept would have the formal characteristics of the former, that is, that the concept of the probability of hypotheses, if rendered precise, would satisfy the rules of the mathematical calculus of probability. Popper is convinced that this is not the case.

He has clearly and repeatedly emphasized this point, e.g., in [*L.F.*], new appendices IX, p. 344. Particularly interesting is the polemical remark against Carnap that one finds there: whereas Carnap acknowledges only two interpretations of 'probability', namely, *inductive probability* and *statistical probability*, both of which represent interpretations of the mathematical probability calculus, there is in addition, according to Popper, yet a third concept that must be distinguished, namely, *degree of corroboration*. If, to be brief, we earmark with italics those probabilities which satisfy the rules of the probability calculus and call them *probabilities*, then Popper's thesis reads as follows: there are probabilities which are not *probabilities*. To these belongs especially the concept of the probability of hypotheses. As a non-quantitative concept it is to be explicated by the *deductivist* (!) concept of corroboration – an explication, which, as we shall see, has *not yet* succeeded; as a quantitative concept it is to be explicated by the non-probabilistic concept of *degree of corroboration* (an explication which likewise has not yet been successfully resolved).

This observation casts some new light on what Carnap calls concept explication: as long as only the explicandum is available it must not be supposed as a matter of course that its clarification and precisioning must lead to a concept which satisfies certain formal rules. In particular, it must not be presupposed that probability as an explicandum will lead to *probability*. Popper's observation with regard to this would still be right even if the contrary Carnapian view holds true, viz. that all probabilities are also *probabilities*; for this could only be ascertained following a *complete* explication. Yet, in my opinion, everything seems to indicate that even with regard to the 'final phase of explication' it is Popper and not Carnap who is right.

(II) *One-dimensional or multi-dimensional perspective*? By a one-dimensional perspective we mean any line of thinking according to which only *one* point of view is decisive for the theoretical appraisal of hypotheses.[13] Various thinkers, especially Bar-Hillel, have pointed out that the one-dimensional perspective leads not only to a faulty one-sidedness, but this one-sidedness is *the common error of 'inductivists' as well as 'deductivists'*. The one-dimensional line of thinking holds for the early Carnap as well as for the earlier views expressed by Popper. According to Carnap what is decisive for the theoretical appraisal of an hypothesis is *only its degree of inductive confirmation* relative to the available empirical data. For Popper, on the other hand, what alone counts is *the degree of corroboration* of a strictly tested hypothesis competing with rival hypotheses and, consequently, the ability of the hypothesis to contribute to the growth of our knowledge.

Bar-Hillel objects to such a line of argument. On his view, many other dimensions have to be taken into account, in particular arguments of a pragmatic nature: the teachability of a theory, its technological applicability, indeed, even questions such as the cost of carrying out the strict test.

Although I consider Bar-Hillel's observations to be basically sound, it seems to me that his emphasis on the pragmatic approach has gone a bit too far. I want to make some positive as well as some negative comments about his position.

First the *positive* points: even if we suppose that the dispute between the 'deductivists' and the 'inductivists' has been satisfactorily settled, there still remain further dimensions in the theoretical appraisal of hypotheses. It does not quite suffice here to arrive at *isolated* clarifications of these other aspects. *The question of priority among these different theoretical aspects* must also be discussed. This can be illustrated rather easily by the example of two further 'dimensions': the Goodman-problem and the problem of simplicity. The former is surely the more fundamental. For before one discusses the question as to which element from the class of rival hypotheses should be chosen as *the most suitable* candidate for rigorous testing, one must first answer the more fundamental question as to which hypotheses may even *reasonably* be included in the list of potential candidates.

The following are my *critical* comments: as against Bar-Hillel, it seems to me that two quite different kinds of consideration have to be sharply distinguished from each other with regard to an hypothesis: the *theoretical* attitude and the *practical* attitude. The latter can also be systematically investigated. (This is done in rational decision theory.) It should not, however, be confused with the former.[14] Let me offer an analogy: a proof-theoretician conceives of a way of providing a constructive foundation for Zermelo's axiomatics. He is convinced that he would be able to solve the problem in seven years if he had eight qualified assistants. He finds them, but is, however, not in a financial position to pay them. He now faces the alternative of searching for the proof all by himself or turning his attention to much less ambitious projects. In view of the high subjective probability of never reaching his goal and of ending up in a mental hospital should he decide in favour of the first alternative, he opts for the second alternative. This will not in any way change the fact that he still considers his original goal *to be an important desideratum*. Yet, proof-theoretician though he be, he is no winged disembodied angel but a man of flesh and blood, and so he must take other things into account such as what Carnap would have called the relation between the micro-structure of his brain-stem and the micro-structure of his central nervous system. Considerations of such a nature are what motivates his decisions.

Every scientist finds himself caught in this double role of a knowing creature and a creature subject to the realities of life. It is nevertheless meaningful and legitimate to treat the problems of knowledge by themselves (even if, as we said, in more than one dimension). One cannot, it seems to me, criticize Popper for discussing these problems for their own sake, at least one cannot do this unless one wants to dispute the fact that *striving toward the growth of knowledge* represents a cultural achievement *sui generis*. As a fellow human being, in particular as a person responsible to his students and to society, the scientist is of course also obliged to answer other important questions regarding his research and teaching; nevertheless, despite their importance, they are still questions *foreign to epistemology*.

Formulated succinctly my position would amount to the following: *theoretical multi-dimensionality: yes! mixing up problems of theoretical appraisal with problems of practical decision: no!*

(III) *Distinctive approaches*: The demand to abandon the one-dimensional perspective should be *distinguished from the demand for drawing conceptual distinctions*. Let us, for example, examine the expression 'accept' as it is used in the phrase 'to accept an hypothesis'. Both Lakatos and Bar-Hillel urge us to make a distinction in the concept of *acceptability*. The latter distinguishes two concepts of acceptability whereas the former mentions no less than three! Such differentiations should contribute to our understanding of the deductivist concept of corroboration. And indeed they do, but it should be borne in mind at the same time that the discussion of this concept to date has not yet attained the status of an explication.

With *acceptance*$_1$ it is a matter of an hypothesis being *selected* for strict testing. We speak of *acceptance*$_2$, on the other hand, only if the hypothesis *has withstood the strict test*, that is, if it has been *corroborated*. The two authors differ essentially in that Bar-Hillel tries to render precise Popper's ideas whereas Lakatos, on the other hand, tries to improve them. (Acceptance$_1$ is taken by both to refer to the *prior* to the test.) From among all the available theories, says Bar-Hillel, it is the one with the greatest content that is *accepted*$_1$. As soon as the theory has passed the test it is *accepted*$_2$. According to Lakatos, it is the boldest theory which is *accepted*$_1$ prior to the test. The boldness of a theory is here judged not on the basis of its (absolute) content, but rather on the basis of its *excess content* relative to rival hypotheses. And this theory is *accepted*$_2$ if it possesses 'excess corroboration' relative to its competitors.

Conceptual distinctions such as the ones we have just mentioned are certainly valuable. Yet they are nothing more than intuitive hunches! We are still operating with the vague expression 'corroboration'. As long as this concept is not sufficiently clarified, it is futile to discuss the question as to whether or not Lakatos' proposal or Bar-Hillel's reconstruction represent an improvement. This discussion is bound to flounder in vague metaphors.

In my opinion the above discussion, together with Salmon's argument, demonstrate again that it is an urgent desideratum to explicate precisely the key concepts of Popper's theory: *it is only on such a basis that they will acquire the status of metascientific concepts*.

(IV) *Static and dynamic perspectives: is there a logic of scientific discovery*? It has been claimed by various authors that the essential difference between Carnap as well as most other philosophers of science on the one hand and Popper on the other does not lie so much in their position with respect to *specific* problems (e.g., the problem of induction) as in their perspective. Carnap's approach is *static* while Popper's is *dynamic*. In the former case we are dealing with the structure of a scientific language, with the axiomatic construction of science (which by virtue of an idealization is taken to be 'complete') and with the problem of the justification of theories already available, etc. The dynamic character of Popper's investigations, on the other hand, is immediately evident from the very title of his main work: it is the *process* of scientific discovery, the *progress* of scientific knowledge that captures his interest.

In this approach of his there is something fascinating; yet Popper's line of thought is at the same time also exposed to a potential danger; for it is not at all certain whether a *metatheoretical analysis of this dynamic aspect is at all possible*. If the answer is affirmative, then it is a project for the future and it will only be realized after the principle metatheoretical questions discussed in the 'static' view are answered. What would have to be considered then are not 'theories', 'basic sentences', etc., but such things as sequences of ordered quadruples of idealized models of these and similar components. If, on the contrary, the answer turns out to be negative, *then there is no such thing as a logic of scientific discovery*. Its place is taken by *empirical* disciplines like psychology, sociology, and the history of scientific discovery. This substitution will become dangerous only if the research devoted to the dynamic aspects of the growth of knowledge *is mistakenly regarded as metascientific analyses*. That this danger is not just a platonic possibility but something quite real is shown by the Kuhn-Popper discussion. I will not here address myself to that discussion; as a matter of fact I am not able to for I really don't know what exactly is at issue.

I *think* the question at issue here is simply 'how should the history of science be written?' With regard to this I couldn't really say anything for I lack the proper professional competence. The participants in the discussion will perhaps protest and stress that what is here at issue is the problem of the growth of knowledge as the title of the book clearly indicates. But as long as one is not told exactly what the problem is and shown that it involves an entirely different question, I will continue to stick to the above supposition.

I am quite content with the negative observation that *it certainly cannot be a metatheoretical discussion*. My reason for saying this is that one cannot find any metascientific theses and analyses in the writings of T.S. Kuhn.[15] How could Kuhn and the other participants in the discussion think otherwise? The answer might be traced to a certain ambiguity which plagues much of Popper's language: what Popper says about strategy in setting up theories, tests, hypotheses, what he says about the role of basic sentences, the background knowledge, and the competing hypotheses, etc. *should* be understood as the beginning of a rational reconstruction. But since it is often expounded in a 'narrative vein' it might also be construed *as an empirical report*. It is this empirical interpretation that Kuhn adopts, as witnessed by his quotation from [*L.F.*] which forms the starting point of all his polemical remarks against Popper ([*Growth*] p. 4).

But if one opts for such an interpretation, then the metatheory of science does not just simply end up on the wrong track; *it ceases to exist altogether*! The *metascience of science* has for its task the *critical* reconstruction of the sciences. If the word 'critical' is written smaller and smaller until it finally disappears altogether, then the metascience of science becomes a *science of science*, i.e., an investigation into the actual behaviour patterns of those doing science which then reduces to the three aforementioned disciplines.

There is a *parallel* danger to this degeneration of the metatheory of science. I mention it because in the current German literature one can find clear signs of it; namely, the *purely normative aspect* of the metatheory of science is being overemphasized. The word 'rational' is written larger and larger until it finally smothers that which was supposed to be reconstructed.

Since my colleagues in the English speaking countries have, presumably, no clear idea of what I am talking about here, I must pause for a moment to explain the situation. Kuhn says (*loc. cit.*, p. 3) that he and Popper appeal to the *same data*. To what data does the normativist appeal? None whatsoever.

This is exactly what can be designated as *the* characteristic of such a position: *no data is aknowledged*. This does not first begin with the empirical sciences but much before that; i.e., in logic, in semantics, in the whole of modern mathematics. A fictitious analogy may clarify this: if in the 12th century someone would have been critical of the investigations concerning God's essence and existence, one would have tried to justify these investigations by citing their 'progress' and 'success'. The critic would have remained unmoved by all this, and quite rightfully so, we should say today. But, asks the normativist, should we not then be just as critically minded when, for example, there is talk of the 'success' of logic and set-theory and of the sciences which rely on these disciplines? Is it perhaps only a traditional bias that regards such activities 'as great achievements'? We must, according to the normativist, get rid of such potential prejudices. This can only be accomplished by approaching textbooks of logic and mathematics as well as research reports with the critical attitude that we may perhaps be dealing here, for the most part, simply with ink marks and nothing more.

This is not the place to criticize this fundamental attitude. I simply want to point out the danger to which it gives rise; namely, the transformation of the metascience of science into a *metascience of science fiction*, the formulation of norms and rules which science is supposed to follow without ever taking into account the actual human practice of science. Though I am not at all a competent futurologist, I think I can quite certainly predict the end result of all this: the already numerous social utopias at our disposal will be augmented by a class of scientific utopias.

In my opinion, the metatheoretical attempts towards a metascience of science will continue for a long time to oscillate between these two menacing abysses: the *science of science* and the *metascience of science fiction*.[16]

The expression 'metascience of science' is, however, misleading in at least two ways: first of all the term 'science' embedded in the context 'metascience' tends to suggest that the theory of science itself employs *empirical scientific* methods (as opposed to logico-analytic) and this, in turn, leads to the unwarranted (or better yet, absurd) charge of *scientism*. Secondly, as will be shown by our new interpretation of Carnap's program, the metatheory of science should also include such extra-scientific activities as all the *rational actions involving risk*. It would be more appropriate to characterize the metatheory of science as the 'metatheory of science and rational action' (whereby 'science' is to be construed in a sufficiently wide sense so as to include also the 'humanities').

(V) *The question of formal precision*: Lakatos notes in [*Changes*], p. 328, footnote 1, that it is quite 'typical' of the Carnap school to avoid a critical discussion of Popper's ideas although Popper and his followers have published several critical papers on Carnap's views. Taking aim at Carnap (as can easily be gathered from the context) Popper poignantly says (*L.F.*, p. 346): "In this postrationalist age of ours more and more books are written in symbolic languages and it becomes more and more difficult to see why: what is it all about and why should it be necessary or advantageous to allow oneself to be bored by volumes of symbolic trivialities."

I feel called upon here to respond to both of these allegations even though, presumably, they have nothing to do with each other. I do this not because I am a 'Carnapian' – for I am not – but rather because I am definitely a 'formalist.' Since in terms of the above quotation I presumably represent the *very opposite standpoint* of Popper as regards the question of formalization, I will first make a few comments about this. The answer to Lakatos will then simply turn out to be a special application of my general remark. Again I begin with an analogy and will then take up the key concept of Popper's philosophy so frequently mentioned.

Suppose that a few mathematicians are sitting around during the afternoon coffee break. They chat about their research, the problems they have come up against and try to give some mutual stimulation. This can certainly prove quite fruitful. But still, such an activity would not be called logic. All of today's logicians will regard working with formal languages as an obvious part of their activity, for only in this way are they in a position to formulate in a concise and precise way their ideas and the result of their research.

Suppose now that the persons at this coffee break are not mathematicians but physicists who talk about their theoretical conjectures, testing them, etc., and by so doing also provide mutual stimulation. Once again this could be regarded as something quite reasonable. *Nevertheless, this should not, of course, be called metatheory of science even though 'common sense' prevails in these discussions*. As long as the ideas are not precisely formalized, everything remains more or less non-committal and vague.

This could be demonstrated in the case of all relevant metascientific concepts such as *definition, theory, axiomatization, explanation, functional analysis*, etc. This will be shown here in connection with a concept which is relevant to our present context.[17]

(VI) *Corroboration – what does deductivism (1) mean*? Popper's theory stands or falls with the concept of corroboration; but we can even go a step further: what is meant by calling Popper's theory a *deductivist theory* instead of an *inductivist theory* depends on the clarification of this concept.

We are initially dealing simply with an intuitive metascientific idea described in a more or less metaphorical way which, however, has not yet been explicated. One would have expected that the Popperian camp would have made an attempt at such an explication. Unfortunately this has not been the case. *Neither Popper nor his followers have so far clearly stated what they mean by 'corroboration' unless something is meant for which elementary counterexamples exist*. This also provides an answer – presumably in the spirit of Carnap – to Lakatos' challenge. Carnap would perhaps have said: "either 'corroboration' is understood as the concept defined by Popper (and discussed below), in which case one can categorically say that *this concept is inadequate*. Or something else is meant by it, in which case one must first spell out its meaning. *It does not make sense to ask me to discuss the ideas of the Popperians as long as they refuse to say (or are incapable of saying) what these ideas consist of*. This will hold as long as the concept of corroboration has not been explicated. To that extent it is also unclear what is meant by a deductivist theory for testing theories. *Popperian deductivism is provisionally a project and nothing more*. Whether or not this project is realizable can only be determined after concrete proposals are made available for discussion. If, on the other hand – as a result of the strange and in my view irrational reluctance to make things precise – no attempt whatsoever is made at presenting an explication, then what Popper and his school are doing remains at the level of 'common sense philosophy' *which, of course, does not constitute a metatheory of science*, but, at best, an intuitive precursor of it."

The only place, presumably, where Popper explicitly discusses his concept of corroboration is in Section 82 of his [*L.F.*] p. 211f, especially in the new footnote *1, Paragraph 2, p. 212. So as to make the definition more readily comparable to other definitions that have been proposed, I will use the expression 'observation sentence' instead of Popper's 'basic sentence'. Furthermore, I will speak of deductive confirmation instead of corroboration. Popper's definition is rendered formally by introducing the following binary relation of deductive confirmation: [18] *K is a deductive confirmation of T* (briefly, $DC(K; T)$) if and only if the following conditions are satisfied:

(1) ------ T is a theory;
(2) ------ K is the class of accepted observation sentences;
(3) ------ the class $T \cup K$ is logically consistent;
(4) ------ there exist two disjoint classes R and E such that
  (a) $R \cup E = K$;
  (b) $T \cup R \vdash E$;
  (c) E is not empty and contains as elements only observation sentences which are acknowledged as being the results of serious attempts to refute T.

This definition has the following consequences: (1) If $DC(K; T)$, then also $DC(K; T^*)$ as long as T^* represents *any* strengthening of T which satisfies the additional condition that $K \cup T^*$ is logically consistent. (2) Let T be: $\{\Lambda x(Fx \rightarrow Gx)\}$; let E be: $\{Hk\}$ where E also satisfies the second condition of (4) (c); and let R be: $\{(Fk \rightarrow Gk) \rightarrow Hk\}$. $DC(K; T)$ then holds although from a material point of view the sentence confirming the theory 'has nothing whatever to do with the theory.' (3) Let E be: $\{Gk\}$ where again Gk is acknowledged to be the result of a serious attempt at refutation; let R be: $\{Fk \wedge Gk\}$; and let T be any theory logically compatible with K. Again, $DC(K; T)$ holds true. Thus, disregarding trivial borderline cases, any theory whatever is corroborated by the given results of serious attempts at refutation.

These three absurd consequences show that the concept of the corroboration of a theory introduced by Popper in terms of deductive testing is inadequate in several ways. It must, therefore, be substantially improved. What will this improvement be like? No publication so far seems to have provided an answer.

There are, of course, several methods that one can resort to in coming to terms with the counterexamples; the third objection is the easiest to eliminate: one simply needs to add the further requirement that T occur *essentially* in (4) (b). The first objection could be neutralized if we could succeed in distinguishing precisely between *genuine* and *pseudo* strengthenings. The only response that could be made to the second objection would be to say that an atomic sentence formed solely by means of a predicate which does not occur at all in the theory does not describe the result of a *serious* (but unsuccessful) attempt at refutation. As long as one says *nothing more* than this, the response is surely unsatisfactory. It would amount to setting up a metatheoretical immunization strategy which, according to Popper, is strictly prohibited on the empirical level, and, hence, should be prohibited on the meta-level too. Otherwise one might reject *every* given counterinstance by claiming that the attempt at falsification does not constitute *a serious* attempt at refutation. One would thus expose oneself to the charge of having introduced by the expression 'serious attempt at refutation' an evasive concept to which the ensuing conceptual difficulties are then shifted. It is, of course, quite possible that even this difficulty may be removed.[19] I am the last to want to dispute this, all the more so in view of the fact that I think that the first successor problem to the riddle of induction consists in the explication of a *deductive* concept of confirmation. Developing Popper's ideas and making them more precise might well prove successful. (We may, however, presume that the concept of corroboration will then be over-determined since the above rule of inference (4) (b) would already be incorporated in the concept of refutation attempt.) But still other questions would have to be taken into account, such as whether we should not also consider consequences of confirmed theories as confirmed? For the sake of an exact *comparison* with other theories of confirmation which provide different answers to this and similar questions, a formally precise version of Popper's concept of confirmation would be highly desirable.

The brief sketch of a definition presented above should, however, enable us to answer clearly the question of when a theory of confirmation is to be designated as deductivist, namely: *a confirmation theory is deductivist if and only if concepts of deductive logic alone are used in the definiens of the confirmation relation* (including certain elementary set-theoretic concepts). Under this definition one must also consider in particular Hempel's definition of confirmation as a possible explication of the Popperian intuition even if it was rejected by Popper as well as by Carnap. There is, in other words, absolutely no way of knowing *how, from among the class of qualitative theories of confirmation, one might otherwise distinguish between those that are to be designated as inductivist and those that are to be designated as deductivist.* One should not make the mistake here of clinging to linguistic expressions.

(VII) *The quantitative theory of degree of corroboration. What is meant by deductivism (2)?* That the definition of 'deductivist confirmation theory' suggested above does not exhaust Popper's intention can be seen from the fact that in [*L.F.*], new appendix *IX, p. 339ff (cf. especially p. 352) he introduces a *quantitative* concept of *degree* of corroboration in whose definiens he draws on the concept of probability. Has he thereby abandoned the project of a deductivist theory of corroboration, or at least *expanded it by resorting to a probabilistic theory of confirmation that competes with Carnap's theory*? Without here going into the question of the adequacy of Popper's explication, I would respond to this question in the affirmative.[20] Popper would presumably protest, for in [*L.F.*] p. 352, he claims that his first discussion of the concept of degree of confirmation contains "a mathematical refutation of all those theories of induction which equate the degree to which a sentence is corroborated by empirical tests with the degree of probability (in the sense of the probability calculus)."

What have we then here? We must first hark back again to the two historical trends in the usage of the word 'probability'. Since many more people are familiar with the intuitive than with the technical use of the term, let us then resort to this common usage. The above expression 'probabilistic theory of confirmation' is consequently to be understood in this sense. But, as becomes apparent from the above quotation, Popper is instead thinking of *probabilities* in the sense of the mathematical calculus of probability.

Suppose Carnap's theory *were* a theory of the confirmation of scientific hypotheses – which it is not but which was mistakenly thought so at first – then something quite remarkable would now follow. The Carnapian quantitative concept of degree of confirmation is a probability which furthermore is a *probability*; Popper's quantitative concept, on the other hand, is a probability which is *not a probability*. If, now, Popper insists that his theory is deductivist, then what is the distinguishing feature that demarcates deductivism from inductivism?

It obviously cannot depend on the normalization axioms. The normalization to the interval from 0 to 1 is inessential (and can be carried through for *any* scale of intervals). There remains only additivity: Carnap's concept of the degree of confirmation is an *additive* concept, whereas Popper's concept of the degree of corroboration is, on the other hand, *non-additive*. We would thus have to accept the following definition:

A theory which operates with a quantitative concept of confirmation φ *is deductivist if and only if* φ *is a non-additive function; it is, on the other hand inductivist if and only if* φ *is additive*. I think that *every* empirical scientist to whom one tries to clarify the distinction between deductivism and inductivism in this fashion will shake his head in utter disbelief. His rejoinder might run like this: 'the difference between deductivism and inductivism upon which so much emphasis has been laid cannot surely boil down, after all, to simply a difference of opinion about a mere technical detail!' And yet, if we take the above definition as our basis, it indeed boils down to just that.

One can hardly escape the conclusion that Popper has over *dramatized* his opposition to Carnap and that his disagreement with Carnap has nothing to do with the antitheses 'deductivism – inductivism'. What we actually have here is at most a difference of interpretation as regards technical problems of a particular kind. This conclusion is furthermore driven home to us by the simple observation that *on the basis of the above definition we can transform Carnap's theory into a deductivist theory of confirmation by a simple change in a nominal definition*. We will come back to this later on.

It would be best to discard altogether concepts, or better: *words*, like 'deductivism' and 'inductivism' when thinking of the – merely apparent – antithesis between Popper and Carnap. Confirmation theories of the kind mentioned in (IV) can be developed; these can then be called either *qualitative* or *deductivist confirmation theories*. And likewise it is conceivable that a quantitative or probabilistic theory of confirmation be constructed (it need not be *probabilistic* in the technical sense of the word). The theories of Carnap and Popper represent competitive examples of such probabilistic theories of confirmation, at least according to Carnap's original intention.

(VIII) It might be asked whether the logical reconstruction of the qualitative (non-quantitative) corroboration concept in (VI) could not be simplified by using Nicod's criterion. One should not let himself be confused by Nicod's terminology. Indeed, he uses the *phrase* 'inductive confirmation'; but he makes no appeal to principles which could be called 'induction rules.' And a man who died long before [*L.F.*] was even published can hardly be blamed for using inductivistic *terminology* instead of the Popperian. The fact that Nicod, like Popper, did not resort to any 'rules of inductive inference' could be seen as a justification for such an attempt.

According to Nicod an object *confirms* an hypothetical universal conditional exactly when it satisfies the antecedence as well as the consequence. The object *violates* such an hypothesis when it satisfies the antecedence but not the consequence. In all other cases the object is *neutral* in respect to the hypothesis.

That such a reconstruction attempt would be inadequate can, apart from other possible objections, be recognized by the fact that Hempel's decisive argument against Nicod's criterion could then be brought against the corroboration concept. Hempel has shown, namely, that when the confirmation concept is made invariant in respect of logical transformations and satisfies the condition that the same observational data cannot confirm and falsify the same hypothesis, then the scientific language in relation to which the Nicod criterion is formulated dare not contain even a binary predicate (relation). For otherwise an hypothesis can immediately be formulated which will be both confirmed and violated by the same data.

Thus, such a reconstruction is not feasible – which is not surprising. This result is well in line with Popper's intuition according to which 'positive instances' do not warrent talking of 'corroborating instances' for an hypothesis.

(IX) *The paradoxes of confirmation and Goodman's paradox*. All theories of confirmation, whether they be characterized as deductivist or inductivist, are threatened by two types of paradoxes. By the 'paradox of confirmation' is generally meant simply a peripheral difficulty; it is also occasionally given the name of its author and called Hempel's paradox. A deeper lying difficulty relating to the concept of law was brought to light by N. Goodman.

My motive for mentioning both of these theories is the following: most of the authors who have taken a stand with respect to these paradoxes have formulated them as paradoxes of *inductive* confirmation. Goodman even went so far as to give the title 'The New Riddle of Induction' to Section III of his [*FFF*] pp. 59 – 83, where he formulated the problem. The impression might thus arise that the difficulties at issue here only threaten *inductivist theories of confirmation* whereas deductivist theories remain unaffected.

Such an impression, however, would rest on a mistake. It is certainly (trivially) correct that an *adequate* deductivist theory of confirmation might no longer be threatened by these two paradoxes. But that is only because *being an adequate theory* it must have developed methods to overcome these difficulties. *All* attempts to define the concept of confirmation are, however, (potentially) *threatened* by these difficulties. Thus, for example, Hempel's paradox can be translated into Popperian language. Consider, for example, the celebrated hypothesis 'all ravens are black' (briefly, the raven hypothesis). I take a white thing such as a piece of white chalk and after a brief examination I quite effortlessly ascertain that it is not a raven. *Is this an unsuccessful attempt at falsifying the raven hypothesis*? If no further qualifications are added, one would have to reply *'yes'*. For the raven hypothesis is logically equivalent to the statement; 'no non-black thing is a raven', and I have searched a non-black thing in vain for the property of being a raven.

Popper would object to this importation of the raven paradox into his theory: it surely cannot be treated as a *serious* attempt at refutation. Supposing that the explication of this latter concept is adequate, then, of course, such an objection is quite correct.[21] But whether it is adequate or not, it nevertheless goes to show that even his theory is potentially *threatened* by the paradox and nothing more than this is being claimed.

Feyerabend's response to Goodman's paradox shows how the paradoxes of confirmation may be mistakenly underestimated.[22] He claims that the difficulty arose only as a result of the fact that Goodman was operating with a concept of confirmation that rests on the concept of the positive single case. L. Foster has conclusively shown that such a claim is wrong and that the Goodman paradox crops up even if one is operating only with the concept of a negative single instance.[23] For anyone somewhat familiar with Goodman's ideas this would really be taken for granted. It is indeed quite true that Goodman speaks of positive single instances in his description of the problem as well as in his introduction of the conceptual framework for his theory ([*FFF*] p. 89). This, however, simply involves a perfectly harmless nominal definition. Had Goodman anticipated this objection on the part of a Popperian he would have chosen for his problem a more neutral title such as 'The New Riddle of Induction and *Corroboration*' and would have likewise described his own project in a terminology that would have dispelled the suspicion of a one-sided approach directed at an 'inductivist theory of confirmation'.

The extraordinary force of Goodman's argument lies exactly in the fact that it is free of any reference to a *particular* theory of confirmation. Let us (for the time being) speak of *confirmation* in the case of an inductivist theory and of *corroboration* in the case of a deductivist theory leaving the exact characterization of 'inductivist' or 'deductivist' open. One can then succinctly formulate the problem raised by Goodman in the following way: 'Given an hypothesis *h* which is confirmed (qualitatively) by the accepted body of knowledge or which enjoys a high degree of confirmation (quantitative) (which has been well corroborated (qualitatively) or whose degree of corroboration is high (quantitatively)), one can then present another hypothesis h^* which is just as well confirmed as *h* or whose degree of confirmation relative to the data is just as high as that of *h* (which is just as well corroborated or whose degree of corroboration is just as high as that of *h*) but which nevertheless is *incompatible* with *h* since it can be used to derive prognoses which contradict the predictions obtained with the help of *h*.' The qualitative *or* quantitative 'inductivist' *or* 'deductivist' theory of confirmation or corroboration *can be selected at will*.

The fact that this is all too easily overlooked stems again from the failure to explicate the expression 'corroboration'. It can easily be seen that the Goodman paradox arises in Hempel's theory (and was thus formulated by Goodman with occasional reference to this theory) for this theory is formally precise. One can likewise easily show that the problem also crops up in Popper's theory if the definition proposed above (or some other) is adopted. I repeat once again that the expression 'to render formally precise' means nothing else here but 'to state exactly what one really means'.

Since Goodman's paradox affects Popper's theory of corroboration (when stated precisely) exactly as it does every other theory of confirmation, there is no justification, unless one has a solution superior to Goodman's, for simply dismissing it as a theory which allegedly puts a premium on prejudices, as is claimed by H. Albert.

In any case, despite the extraordinary number of publications bearing on this topic, there does not seem to be any proposal so far that might compete with Goodman's.[25]

I hope it has by now become sufficiently clear why I have mentioned – though for lack of space not discussed – both kinds of paradoxes: the habitual use of certain modes of speaking, if not followed up by an attempt at formal precisioning, contains the danger of not taking problems seriously simply because they are formulated in a different terminology. This is especially true in the case of Goodman's paradox. There exists not the slightest difficulty in translating Goodman's [*FFF*] into a terminology favored by the 'deductivists'; for this simply amounts to 'transforming it into a jargon which sounds better to the deductivists than Goodman's own formulations'. (To give but one example: when Goodman uses a phrase like 'x is a positive single instance of h' one would simply substitute 'x is recognized as a serious attempt at refuting h which failed'.)

(X) *Complex logical statements, statistical hypotheses, and the borderline problem.* According to Popper, theoretical claims containing both unlimited universal as well as existential quantifications should, strictly speaking, be relegated to metaphysics. This seems a little strange if one bears in mind that the distinction between classical physics and quantum physics is characterized, for example, by the fact that a statement of the form $\Lambda x \, \Lambda t \, \mathrm{V} u \, \mathrm{V} v Sxtuv$ holds for the former whereas it fails to hold for the latter.

I will not, however, pursue this point for it has been often criticized along similar lines; I will instead turn to *statistical hypotheses* where again neither verifiable nor falsifiable statements are involved. With these hypotheses we enjoy the advantage of having at our disposal many detailed investigations.

Two questions must be distinguished here: the question of the *correct introduction of the concept of statistical probability* and the question of the *testing and confirmation of statistical hypotheses*. First a few words about the conceptual question.

In [*L.F.*] we are given an *objectivist version of probability*. Until now there has been an unbridgable gap between the representatives of the objectivist and of the subjectivist (or better, personalist) interpretation of probability. Prima facie the pro and con arguments seem to roughly balance each other out. Yet there is a decisive asymmetry: the objectivist conception is not just open to criticism because it is problematic and contestable: it is *simply false*. This is why the personalist can quite calmly listen to the counter-arguments of the objectivist all the while thinking to himself: 'the objectivist is fighting like a cornered rat.'

Unfortunately the views characterized here as objectivist are not distinguished by any one pervasive feature. Since there is not enough space here to discuss them all, I will limit myself to a nasty challenge:

> *'Tell me which variant of objectivism you favor and I will tell you how you will end up in DeFinetti's mousetrap!'*

Let me briefly sketch this trap: every exponent of the objectivist version of probability theory will have to admit at some point that *he too presupposes the subjectivist or personalistic concept of probability* unless he falls into one of two possible irrationalisms: either he lands in an infinite regress or he gets stuck with notoriously false statements.[26] Thus the 'objectivist' is operating with *two* irreducible concepts of probability, whereas the 'subjectivist' gets along with *just one*.[27] This can be seen most clearly in the case where statistical probability is defined, as for example by von Mises and Reichenbach, in terms of the concept of the convergence of a series of relative frequencies. The mistake here lies in the use of the concept of limit. Ordinary convergence must be replaced by measure-theoretical convergence: 'converges' is to be replaced by 'converges μ-almost everywhere'. The probability measure μ must, of course, on pain of an infinite regress, be construed as a subjective measure of probability.

One of the strangest and to me most incomprehensible psychological events in the history of science is that Reichenbach remained one of the staunchest exponents of the objectivist view of probability even though he was well aware of all of the difficulties mentioned. In one of his less well known German language reviews of Reichenbach's book (*Theory of Probability*) DeFinetti, quite puzzled, asked what Reichenbach expected to gain by admitting an infinite regress.

This question, which was addressed to Reichenbach, can likewise be directed to *all* objectivists: what do they expect to get out of the infinite regress into which they force themselves. *How can a rational scientist seriously and consciously put up with an infinite regress*? This 'putting up' is the only alternative which is left to the objectivist once he rejects the subjectivist version of probability.

The argument cannot be directly applied to Popper for he espouses a different variant of objectivism: the concept of probability is not introduced by the concept of limit but is identified instead with a more general concept whose existence is guaranteed by the Bolzano-Weierstrass theorem.[28] There is no need here to enter into technical details, for in a later section of [*L.F.*], particularly in p. 145 and p. 147, it becomes clear that the dilemma of objectivism simply crops up again at a different place. On p. 145 it is claimed that a probability estimate can only be contradicted by an infinite series of events. On p. 147 Popper attempts to delimit probability from metaphysical statements by asserting that existential statements can be inferred from assumptions of probability. One may infer even *more*: if the probability assumption for an alternative with the characteristic a and b represents a value p different from 0 and 1, then after *every* term-number *there is* a term with the characteristic a and one with the characteristic b.

Unfortunately all of these assertions are incorrect. Suppose we have at our disposal a homogeneous die all of whose sides conform to the equal distribution hypothesis. *An infinite sequence of tosses of threes is logically compatible* with the correctness of this statistical hypothesis of equal distribution. The probability principle cannot even stand in contradiction to an infinite sequence of events! *Whoever denies this is confusing practical certainty with logical necessity*. The same holds for Popper's other two claims: not only does it not follow from the statistical hypothesis that a 6 will be thrown again and again, but it does not even follow that a 6 will ever be thrown at all. *There is no logical law which obliges the homogeneous die to fall even once in such a way that 6 will turn up*.

In his new footnote *1, p. 147, Popper notes that in this problematic context the probabilistic concepts 'almost derivable' and 'almost contradictory' become useful. But in the first place these concepts are not just useful, they are *absolutely necessary*; and in the second place, the 'almost' must be linked to a *subjective* measure of probability (on pain of ending up in an infinite regress).

Popper's attempt to demarcate statistical hypotheses from metaphysical statements remained consequently unsuccessful. (For me this result is not at all shocking; it only goes to confirm my conviction that there exists no demarcation criterion between empirical science and metaphysics.)

Incidentally, the conceptual aspect does not seem very important since the antithesis described holds presumably only under the *overall reductionist hypothesis* and this has since been given up by Popper.[29] The failure to delimit empirical science from metaphysics holds true, then, even a fortiori.

I will now make a few comments about the second more important problem:

(1) The theoretical analogue to the concept of falsification is here the concept of *rational rejection*. *The extension of the concept of empirical refutation or falsification to that of rational rejection is no trivial task*.

The decisive difference consists in the fact that refutation represents something final, whereas rational rejection, on the other hand, does not. Falsification can *only* be challenged by contesting the basis. (Hence a falsified theory would be proved false in case one can assert the correctness of the falsifying basic statement.)

But that is not the case with a statistical hypothesis. Here it may well happen that an original rejection is rescinded *without having to challenge the data effecting the rejection*. It is not just the *revision* of the data but even its mere *extension* that may prompt the reversal. Any number of intuitive examples of this can be cited.

So far we have claimed that relative to acknowledged data (given an acknowledged basis) falsification of a strict universal hypothesis is something final, *whereas any rational rejection of a statistical hypothesis is in principle provisional and revisable* however one may want to define the concept of rational rejection. The '*modus tollens*' is not applicable here.

(2) Closely related to this first point is another. Although effective falsification does not entail falsity, one may well claim that Popper has developed his conception for the testing of scientific theories on the model of a danger which, in statistical test theory, is called the type-II-error. It is *the danger of mistakenly holding a false hypothesis to be correct*. In the statistical case, one must likewise take seriously a second source of danger, namely, *the danger of mistakenly rejecting a true hypothesis*. In statistical test theory this counts as a type-I-error. This is also the reason why in test theory one operates with *two* probabilities of error. (The power of a test R, for example, is the probability of not committing any type-II-error; the domain of R is the probability of falling victim to a type-I-error.)

The type-I-error is not adequately taken into account by Popper. It is not obvious how one is to act in the face of these two pitfalls. The prima facie requirement that comes to mind is to keep the two probabilities of error as low as possible; but upon closer examination this proves empty: 'choose a test with the smallest possible domain and the greatest possible power' amount to the rather well known demand: 'save your cake and eat it too.'

(3) With deterministic hypotheses a test can only lead to a result which is *in accord* with the hypothesis or to a result that *contradicts it*. In the case of a statistical hypothesis this metatheoretical TND no longer holds. The most rational response, under the appropriate circumstances, would be here to *temporarily suspend one's judgement and wait for further results*. This third possibility leads us out of the alternative 'either falsified or not falsified' (so-called 'sequential tests').

(4) Suppose we are confronted with the task of explicating a concept of corroboration for a statistical hypothesis. How would we go about it? It seems to me that this concept must be construed as a *five place relation*. This relation to be explicated would have the form: 'given background B the statistical null-hypothesis h is, on the basis of the empirical data E, the most corroborated hypothesis in terms of the test theory T relative to class K of rival hypotheses'. B consists of at most a finite number of general hypotheses; the class K can contain a finite or infinite number of competing alternate hypotheses.

The explicit reference to a test theory here will presumably meet with opposition from most quarters. Is it not the task of the philosophy of science to single out the adequate test theory? My doubts about such a claim are not due to the fact that I have been infected by Carnap's continuum; it is not the alleged fact that there is 'a continuum of inductive methods' that demands such relativization, but rather the fact that the concept of corroboration for statistical hypotheses has to be construed *as a pragmatic concept* and that the adequacy of a test theory may depend upon the circumstances. The dispute among the statistical schools is to a great extent a dispute about *the* adequate test theory. The uniqueness postulate hiding behind the definite article is presumably a silent dogma. Hacking (in Statistical Inference) has shown that certain test theories lead to satisfactory results only in particular situations. He too thought he would be able to construct an optimal likelihood test theory. The discussions which subsequently ensued have shown that the philosopher's stone has not yet been found even with this theory. All this tends to strengthen my belief that the search for *the* adequate test theory rests on an illusory hope. Test theories which are superior *in certain types of situations* must presumably give way to test theories of a different type in *situations of a different kind*; eventually to those which operate with concepts of an entirely different kind (the one, for example, with the concepts domain and power, the other with likelihood, etc.). Nevertheless we may well succeed in stating exactly which test theories are optimal in which types of situation.

And with these observations, which for a lack of space were formulated in a rather rudimentary and summary way, our discussion of the second question also comes to an end.

I am, of course, quite aware of the fact that Popper, [*L.F.*] p. 352, (9.1) and (9.2), introduces the two binary relational concepts E (for *explanatory power*) and C (for *degree of corroboration*); this latter concept should permit us, *inter alia* to determine the degree of corroboration of *statistical* hypotheses relative to the relevant statistical data. My problem is that *I am simply unable to read these definitions* (and thus am also not in a position to pass judgement on Lakatos' critique of them in [*Changes*] p. 408). In the definiens, the symbol 'P' stands for 'probability'. Since it cannot be taken to mean statistical ('objective') probability, P must be interpreted to mean logical probability.[30] *But since a constant cannot be defined by means of a variable*, both definitions have to be given a new interpretation. Presumably both relational concepts are to be construed as *four-place* relations $E(x, y, S, P)$ whereby S ranges over language systems while P ranges over the logical probability values of sentences out of S. Two-place relations would be obtained only if one had chosen *a particular language system* S_1 as well as *a particular probability measure* P_1 *holding for* S_1. Thus for both definitions we must first apply a method which fully corresponds to Carnap's method: choose a language plus an m- or c-function for this language. The question of the adequacy of E and C could only be raised after these two decisions have been made. Another possible interpretation would be to suppose S and P are universally quantified: 'for *any* (consistent) language system S and for *any* probability valuation P of S it should hold that ...' Still, I don't think this last mentioned interpretation is what was intended.

(XI) *Background knowledge*. Popper's concept of background knowledge seems to me extremely important and I think it is unfortunate that it has drawn so little attention in the philosophic literature. It may, after all, provide the key to eliminating a fundamental conceptual confusion that prevails especially in all of the German metascientific literature dealing with the nature of knowledge in the humanities. I mean the 'theory of the hermeneutic circle' which forms the basis of all of the hermeneutic theories of understanding.[31] I have had occasion to learn not only from extensive readings but also from numerous conversations with hermeneuticists that *a totally erroneous interpretation* – not of their *own* but – *of the method of the natural sciences* forms the basis of their thinking: the philosophizing humanist mistakenly *thinks* that, for example, a theoretical physicist who is in the habit of making complicated calculations is somewhat like a mathematician who *proves* his assertions in a mathematical way. But by comparing this to his own method, he then realizes this is not the way he himself actually proceeds; he instead approaches his subject with a 'preconception', i.e., with a theoretical hypothesis. He regards such a procedure to be circular (this constitutes the second mistake which now, however, refers to his *own* method) *for he in turn uses the data interpreted in the light of his 'preconception' to test his hypothetical assumptions*. And thus he finally arrives at the thesis that humanistic knowledge is fundamentally different from scientific knowledge for it is *essentially circular*. This hermeneutic circle is not perceived here as a drawback but rather as an *advantage* of the humanistic method.

But that is not all there is to it. The next step is to *extend this view to the natural sciences themselves*. As proof thereof let me cite the essay of the physicist Wolfgang Weidlich entitled 'How Certain Are Natural Laws?' (*Bild der Wissenschaft* (1970), No. 1, pp. 55 – 62) in which he contends that even the natural scientist has to start from a 'naive preconception' (p. 57) and that, therefore, *scientific understanding, like any other understanding, possesses a 'circular character'* (p. 56).

It is easy to see what has happened here: first, a misconstrual of the scientist's method led to a confused theory of the hermeneutic circle. The scientist then came across this interpretation, but instead of noticing the mistake that gave rise to this circle theory and realizing that this 'circle' is not a circle at all, he arrives, after comparing it to his own method, at the triumphant insight: 'my method, too, is essentially circular.' It is then but a small step to the theses that the hermeneutic method is a method that is universally valid for all of the sciences. All this could have been avoided had he understood the Popperian thesis which is *directly concerned with the natural sciences*: 'we approach everything in the light of a preconceived theory.'

The sociological-scientific process just cited does have a certain circular character. *This* circle is, however, definitely not a specifically hermeneutic one; it bears a rather amusing resemblance to a vicious circle.

I can think of yet another use that can be made of the concept of background knowledge, namely, in connection with a *critical analysis of Quine's thesis of the indeterminacy of translation*.[32] Such an analysis would also be indirectly relevant for the hermeneuticist, since the issue here is exactly the question of the correct interpretation of linguistic expressions.

Quine's thesis is of the utmost relevance in conjunction with the problem of clarifying intensions. However many other arguments Quine cites in favour of his *anti-intensionalism*, it is that thesis which plays a decisive role in establishing this more far-reaching view. Quine's thesis can be made more perspicuous by adopting a suggestion made by v. Kutschera: instead of using Quine's mapping of a language onto itself, one should consider directly the translation of a language into another. Quine's line of thought (put in a somewhat rough, schematic way) would amount to the following: *even if the syntax (grammar) and the semantics of the logical expressions were correctly inferred from a study of the language Y that is to be learned, the interpretation of this foreign language cannot be gathered from the observation of usage*.

The reason for this is that the observer must ultimately rely on descriptions of perceptual fields by the user of the language *Y* which also constitute perceptual fields for himself. It is easy to show, however, that a perceptual field *is describable in infinitely many different ways*. Nevertheless the observer must give an interpretation of the usage (of the speaker of *Y*) *on the basis of finite many observations.* That this interpretation involves a hypothetical component which can never permit absolute certainty about the meanings of *Y*'s expressions, Quine would presumably agree with most linguists, even with Popper. But in point of fact Quine draws a much more radical conclusion which, in turn, leads to the above mentioned thesis, namely: out of the infinitely many possible interpretation hypotheses only a finite number of them are ruled out; *the infinitely many hypotheses that remain are all equally justified* ('are all equally probable' or better still, 'are all equally improbable'). If in the place of *translation* we consider *the original acquisition* of language by a child, the Quinean consequence with regard to the question of intensions becomes apparant: since language can only be learnt by practice, it can be construed in countless different ways all of which are in accord with usage. Since, however, the meaning of a linguistic expression cannot consist in subjective imagery but must be an intersubjective consensual meaning, *one cannot speak about the meaning of an expression at all*.

But as v. Kutschera points out, such a result clearly stands in contradiction to the fact that we can often make quite precise statements about differences and similarities in meaning between the words and sentences of our language; we are likewise quite capable of weighing very exactly various shades of meaning of foreign language sentences given a bit of practice.

In order to shed some light on this issue, let us draw a few distinctions: suppose that one day we meet with an inhabitant X of a strange planet who bears no resemblance whatsoever to Man but who is obviously endowed with reason and with a capacity for language.[33] In such a case we would, presumably, find ourselves in the situation that Quine describes; this is because we have no *background knowledge* at our disposal about this creature, i.e., no reliable overall hypotheses about the biological and psychological characteristics of X nor about his socio-cultural environment;[34] we do not even know whether X was subject to an evolution which somehow parallels our own on this planet. It is quite possible we would not even be able to learn the language of X.

If, on the other hand, the speaker of the foreign language is human, then we have at our disposal a vast array of hypotheses which we quite intuitively apply in order to rule out immediately countless possible interpretations which per se are compatible with the observations of his usage. These hypotheses begin with our very familiar sensory faculties (same sensory organization), then go on to further physiological and psychological assumptions, and often to hypotheses of a sociological and cultural nature.

Here, of course, we have gradations. If a researcher discovers a new Indian language of an unknown tribe in the primeval forests of Brazil, it may well be that provisionally we are at a loss for socio-cultural hypotheses and that we can only rely on biological and psychological background knowledge. Learning such a language in such circumstances would thus be relatively difficult.

It seems to me that generally Quine arrives at the various consequences of his radical linguistic philosophy as a result of failing to pay sufficient attention to the various kinds of background knowledge. This neglect comes quite clearly to light in his attempt to prove his thesis of the indeterminacy of translation.

Empirical hypotheses do not constitute the only kind of background knowledge. It also encompasses tacit or explicit *assumptions of a logical, semantical, and mathematical nature*. If differences of opinion arise with respect to such assumptions, metascientific discussion becomes extremely complicated. Even in the discussion between Popper and Kuhn one can, I believe, observe such a divergence of views. There is a place where Kuhn attacks Popper's reference to *Tarski's concept of truth.* [35] He finally claims that what is at issue is the problem of the neutrality of the observation language. [36] But it becomes quite clear from the context that he rejects any talk of true and false theories. This attitude is very widespread among scientists, but it is also gaining currency among philosophers of science. Thus, for example, it is quite common to hear that theories can only be judged with respect to their usefulness, fruitfulness, etc. but not, however, with respect to truth. What is one to do in a situation where A considers the use of the truth concept to be meaningful and important whereas B rejects it (for whatever reason; e.g., because he thinks Tarski's idea rests on a faulty intuition; or because, being a constructivist puritan, he rejects the set-theoretic apparatus used by Tarski; or because he considers this concept inapplicable to physical theories, etc.)? There is but one answer: one must temporarily give up any further discussion from which this concept cannot be 'excluded' and first try to reach an agreement on the basic issue – in the present case about the usefulness of the truth concept with respect to scientific theories – before continuing the dialogue.

(XII) *Does Hume's problem of induction also come up in deductivism*? The most frequent attacks against Popper's theory of falsification and corroboration are based on *inductivist* arguments. As far as I can see, there is just one half decent argument of this kind that deserves to be examined more closely. It stems from W. Salmon. [37] In his critique Salmon makes exclusive use of Hume's problem; he construes it in a most general way, i.e., as the problem of the existence of truth preserving ampliative inferences.

Salmon begins by distinguishing two different aspects of Popper's theory. The *first aspect* concerns the strict testing and the retention of the non-falsified hypothesis. According to Salmon, this feature can in fact be characterized in a *purely deductive* way. The principle concept used here is the concept of falsification which uses exclusively the deductive rule of *modus tollens*. If the Popperian test theory were to possess just this feature, it would be unsatisfactory. The grounds for this are not simply that one cannot unambiguously single out an hypothesis which has successfully withstood a strict test (since the same facts which are supposed to be explained by the given hypothesis can also be accounted for by numerous other hypotheses) but above all because the non-falsification of an hypothesis represents a weaker statement than the conjunction of observation sentences reporting the results of the tests.

In order for science to be more than just a collection of observation sentences, *a second feature* is very essential. The concept of *corroboration* needs to be introduced. By means of this concept we should be able to *single out* and *accept* an hypothesis (in the earlier sense of acceptability$_2$) from the class of non-falsified hypotheses.

Salmon's thesis now reads: *with the introduction of the concept of corroboration, inductivism enters into Popper's test theory*. For the method bearing the name 'corroboration' effects *the choice (selection) of an hypothesis* from the class of non-falsified hypotheses whereby *the hypothesis chosen is richer in content than the relevant observation sentences which are available*. No deductive method can enable us to make such a selection. Basic sentences plus deduction do not provide us with a useful test. The concept of corroboration must also be brought in. But with such a concept one is introducing *a non-deductive rule of inference*.

By resorting to a perhaps somewhat far-fetched paraphrase of a celebrated saying of Kant, Salmon expresses his view succinctly as follows: "*modus tollens* without corroboration is empty; *modus tollens* with corroboration is induction."[38] It is consequently an illusion to believe that the problem of induction and with it the task of its positive solution are avoided by Popper's test theory. *According to Salmon the problem of induction as well as its attempted solution simply reappear under a different name in the guise of a non-demonstrative rule of inference*.

Lakatos also thinks that this argument must be taken seriously.[39] Suppose the theoretical appraisal of a scientific hypothesis, including the appraisal of the hypothesis as one that is well corroborated, is analytic or tautological (as Popper, for example, claims in [*L.F.*] p. 211). Then it remains incomprehensible how natural science can ever be for Popper 'a guide of life'. And yet that is what it can be on his view, at least within certain limits, since, after all, we do use the theories that are corroborated to make predictions and consider it rational to believe that these predictions will materialize.

To meet this problem, Lakatos introduces a third concept of acceptability: *acceptability*$_3$. It deals with the theoretical appraisal of a scientific hypothesis in terms of its future performance.[40] In order to characterize this concept Lakatos resorts to Popper's concept of *verisimilitude* which he calls "the Popperian reconstruction of non-probabilistic 'probability'."[41] This concept is defined as the set-theoretic difference between the truth content and the falsity content of a theory. (The technical variants of this theory are not taken into account here.) This concept is taken as *a measure of the approximation to truth*. (In the limiting case where the theory is true, the falsity content is, of course, empty.) For reasons which will readily become clear, we will not delve any further into this third concept of acceptability. I will proceed by first taking up Lakatos' proposal and then turning to Salmon's objection.

Apropos of Lakatos' standpoint I can only say that *it is totally incomprehensible to me how one can here operate with the concept of verisimilitude*. I can do nothing but present two reasons for my failure to understand. The first reason relates to the two shortcomings, mentioned by Lakatos himself, of the concept of acceptability$_3$ which is supposed to enable one to appraise the reliability of an hypothesis.

The *first shortcoming* consists, according to Lakatos, in the fact that via this concept we can only appraise the reliability of theories which, from the standpoint of the best available theories, *have already been eliminated.*[42] But then the concept of acceptability$_3$ is rendered completely worthless given the context of the present problem. The concept of verisimilitude is surely designed to explain why theories which slip through the acceptability$_1$-acceptability$_2$-filter, that is, theories which are not yet eliminated, should be used 'as guides of life' for rational programs. It is not supposed to provide us with an additional appraisal for theories already falsified. The *second shortcoming*, according to Lakatos, is that the reliability criterion based on verisimilitude is itself unreliable.[43] But in this critical assessment I see not so much evidence of a drawback as simply a decisive objection against such a concept: *if we mortals* – in contrast to the dear Lord – *are not in a position to appraise the distance of an hypothesis from the truth*, that is to measure the degree of verisimilitude, *then we cannot after all use the approximation or distance from the truth as a reliable criterion of the hypothesis*. At a later point Lakatos seems to want to use as a criterion not the actual verisimilitude, but rather its *estimate.*[44] Nevertheless a deductivist can quite easily see that he has then taken on a concept which is of the devil's own making.

It is therefore no wonder that Popper, who himself introduced the concept of verisimilitude, greets with skepticism the attempt to use this concept for the solution of the problem of acceptability$_3$ (in the sense of an appraisal of reliability). One can also easily gather from Popper's comments that such a use is bound to lead to an infinite regress. In [*Conjectures*] p. 234, he emphasizes the fact that one can never know whether the degree of verisimilitude of a theory T_1 is greater than the degree of verisimilitude of a theory T_2; here one can only guess and examine the conjecture critically; the infinite regress is just around the corner *if* one accepts the use Lakatos makes of this concept. For in so doing we are surely back again at our original starting point: an initial hypothesis H_0 was proposed, critically tested, and corroborated. Its reliability ought to be evaluated in terms of its degree of acceptability$_3$. It was for this purpose that the concept of verisimilitude was used. But this again can only be ascertained hypothetically. We thus have an hypothesis of a higher level H_1 and for it we must use an acceptability$_3$ of higher order, etc.

Concerning the second point I can be quite brief. Instead of speaking of the confirmation, support, corroboration, of reliability of a theory one can always speak of the confirmation, support, corroboration, of reliability of the claim *that the theory is true*. The truth is *the object and not the means* of appraisal. And it cannot in principle serve as the means if the metatheoretical conception precludes reaching a definitive conclusion either about the truth of the basis or about the truth of an hypothesis.

The explanation given by Lakatos in the first paragraph, p. 397, of [*Changes*] shows quite clearly that the idea of the whole history of science from some point onwards becoming *the history of a tragedy* is entirely compatible with Popper's conception of science; for it is quite conceivable that from a certain point on a series of theories could be produced, each one of which is better corroborated than the preceding ones and yet enjoys a smaller degree of verisimilitude than they do.

The foregoing comments are not directed at Popper but rather at Lakatos' attempt at coming to terms with Salmon's 'deductivist variant of the problem of induction' by means of the concept of verisimilitude. Does this problem then still remain unsolved? To answer this we must turn directly to Salmon's argument. *I consider Salmon's argument to be incorrect*. This argument is plagued by prematurity, an error, and a misconstrual.

Premature because he concedes too much to the 'Popperians'. He assumes we already know what 'corroboration' means. But as we had occasion to observe earlier, this is a mistaken assumption. Yet – and this is really what matters about the whole thing – our earlier attempt at an explication ought to have shown what formal structure an explicated concept of corroboration must have: only the concepts of formal *deductive* logic are used in the definiens. If one keeps this in mind, one can immediately recognize *Salmon's mistake*: he believes, namely, that it is *only* in the first stage, i.e., where we are dealing with falsification and non-falsification, that deductive concepts are used. According to him, however, it is in the second phase, viz. where the concept of corroboration is used, that inductivism enters into Popper's theory. *This claim is wrong.*[45] The concept of corroboration must be defined exclusively by using concepts of deductive logic. In other words, in Popper's theory one uses exclusively deductive logic not just at *one* place but at two quite different places: in the one place by virtue of *modus tollens*, and in the other place *via the definiens* of the concept of corroboration which is outwardly recognizable by the occurrence of the symbol '$\vdash$'.

This fact may be viewed as indirect support of my plea for a formally precise concept of corroboration: *this error could not have been committed by W. Salmon had he had at his disposal a formal definition of the concept of corroboration.*

This error then gives rise to the following misconstrual: since Salmon overlooks the fact that the concept of corroboration is to be characterized in a purely deductive way, he mistakenly thinks that corroboration is something like a 'non-demonstrative rule of inference' with the consequence that even Popper's theory is now confronted with the Humean problem of justifying induction. In this last claim there indeed lies a kernel of truth; it must, however, be formulated rather differently: *it is not Hume's* problem of justification that *reappears* – for since there is no non-demonstrative inference it cannot possibly reappear – but rather this problem is *replaced by another*, namely, by *the problem of proving the adequacy of the deductive concept of corroboration*. It is this problem alone which must be faced by any deductivistic theory of confirmation. Let's call it *the problem of the theoretical analogue to induction* (IA_t):[46] *how does one prove the adequacy of the deductive concept of confirmation?* (Or, should criteria of adequacy be used: *how are these criteria established?*)

We can discuss problem IA_t, which for the deductivist appears in the place of Hume's problem, *only if we have at our disposal a deductive concept of confirmation which we may presume or hope to be adequate*. We have seen that the Popperian concept fails to meet this requirement: it is either unclear or inadequate in more ways than one.

It should be noted that the problem IA_t crops up in lieu of Hume's problem in *every* deductivist theory of confirmation, whether or not this confirmation theory makes use of Popper's intuitions or is based on entirely different considerations.

Since I hold deductivism to be presumably correct, I don't want to fail to point out that my colleague Prof. Dr. M. Käsbauer has defined a deductive concept of confirmation which is neither plagued with the drawbacks of the Hempelian concept of confirmation nor with the drawbacks of the Popperian concept of corroboration. Whether it is adequate or not, I cannot yet say. In any event one can meaningfully raise the question and discuss (IA_t) in connection with this concept. Should it turn out to be adequate, one could then say that *for the first time it has been clearly stated what Popper actually meant.*

So far we have had only deterministic hypotheses in mind. *But the analogy to Hume's problem of induction* would, of course, also appear in connection with the concept of support or corroboration of *statistical hypotheses*, once such a concept is defined. If the conjecture advanced in (X) (4) is correct, we are here dealing with the appraisal of adequacy of a five-place relation.

The subscript '*t*' should remind us that we are dealing with the domain of *theoretical* reasoning. There is yet *a second analogy to Hume's problem of induction*. It belongs not to the theoretical domain but to that of *practical* reason. We will come across this second analogy in the course of our discussion of Carnap's theory. For now it suffices to say that the problem has a completely different formal structure: what is at issue there is not the proof of adequacy of a definition of confirmation but *the establishment of norms of human conduct* (and indeed *not* positive norms which dictate what one is to do but rather *negative* norms which state how one should not act).[47]

Since the discussion of the last point was based on Salmon's critique, we should, by way of conclusion, make some critical comments about Salmon's proposed solution of the induction problem which he has presented and expanded in his various works. (The most important of these works are cited in the bibliography.) Salmon seizes upon an idea of Reichenbach.[48] According to it one cannot indeed prove that any rule of induction is successful. One can, however, give a precise rule of enumerative induction *EI* and prove for it the conditional: '*if any method at all is successful, then the rule EI will lead to success.*' The difficulty here, says Salmon, consists solely in arriving at a clear, unambiguous demarcation. While Reichenbach was able to provide only an infinite class of equally qualified candidates – for his argument for the choice of a particular element out of the class was not convincing – Salmon believes that by adding further adequacy conditions (such as for example the normalization condition, or the requirement of linguistic invariance) we can arrive at an unambiguous and clear demarcation.

If one looks at the concept of statistical regularity that is used one can see that it is exactly the same as that of Reichenbach: *the assumption of the existence of a limes value for the relative frequency of an attribute in a series.* We here stumble, in my opinion, upon an insuperable difficulty: there exists no such limes value! To repeat once again: the correctness of the hypothesis that the probability of throwing a 6 with this die is 1/6 is perfectly compatible with the fact that 5 keeps turning up in an infinite number of tosses. Were this probability hypothesis correct then we could only say: *for μ-almost all sequences of tosses* the relative frequency of tosses of 6 converges on 1/6. (If, on the other hand, we have bad luck, then, as in the example we have just given, we get a series which lies in the μ-null set.) But in connection with this there again arises Hume's problem: out of the infinite totality of potential measures one has to select the 'subjective probability' in terms of which the measure-theoretical convergence is to be defined. *What are the criteria in terms of which this choice should be made and how can they be justified*?

My reason for raising this objection against Salmon's attempt is that it involves an argument which might not be acknowledged by Popper. It is easy to see that we are simply dealing with a variant of the first half of (X).

Though it is quite useful to bear Hume's critique in mind when posing our problem, it is nevertheless dangerous not to waive the search for rules of correct inductive inference. *Such rule-bound thinking can become a straitjacket.* It behooves us, therefore, to get rid of this straitjacket. That requires clear recognition of the question which nowadays appears *in lieu of* Hume's problem. With respect to the domain of '*theoretical* reason' we have already given a partial answer to this meta-question by means of (IA_t).

(XIII) *Concluding comments*: The radical nature of the various formulations proposed here has been dictated by the lack of sufficient space for more extensive explanations. Thus, it is perhaps not superfluous to emphasize by way of conclusion that *nowhere did I make a destructive critique of Popper.* Rather I have limited myself to carrying out *meta-scientific research programs* in a critical vein; my attempt has not been to overthrow, but to further clarify Popper's intuitions, all of which I consider to be in principle correct. A material point of disagreement exists, if at all, only with respect to the concept of verisimilitude.[49] A really substantial difference may, on the other hand, exist not so much with regard to content as with regard to the question of *formal precisioning.*

I should perhaps add a word about the kind of critique against Popper that I think really misses the mark: it has been claimed time and again in a variety of ways that Popper has not succeeded 'in overcoming inductivism' or that he himself presupposes something like a 'principle of induction' or 'inductive rule'. All of these objections seem *totally untenable* to me. To illustrate this let me cite the presumably most recent discussion (in the German literature) of the concept of falsifiability by E. Stöker.[50] On p. 500, line 4, Popper's conception is contrasted with 'the scientific meaning of the inductive methods'. But before one can speak of the meaning of such methods, one must first state what those methods are. Nowhere in the article, however, do we find any clues about this.

Three logically possible interpretations come to mind here: first, either no restrictions are imposed, in such a case, however, the expressions are not just simply ambiguous but *infinitely ambiguous*, for infinitely many rules qualify as possible candidates. To see this it is not even necessary to allude to Carnap's continuum. Even Reichenbach's asymptotic rules form an *infinite* class. But why only *asymptotic* rules? If no restrictions are given then one might just as well seriously consider the *apriori rules, the compromise rules, the vanishing compromise rules*, indeed even the *anti-induction rule* whether normalized or non-normalized.[51]

Or *secondly*, one limits oneself to *one particular method*. But then this method must be exactly described and Hume's problem must first be solved before one can go on to argue against Popper. But, as a matter of fact, the whole argument is bound to fail from the very start, for Hume's problem is unsolvable.

Or again, as a *third* move, neither the first nor the second tack should be pursued; instead, it must be emphasized that the conjectured 'regularities of natural events' must be tested empirically. But this no longer constitutes an *objection against* Popper but is simply a *repetition* of what Popper himself has said disguised in the misleading form of an objection.

This 'trilemma' is typical of all the arguments leveled against Popper: infinite ambiguity *or* dogmatic though unfounded assertion of the solubility of Hume's problem *or* repetition of the Popperian conception via other expressions (where possible in the form of an objection).

4. INDUCTIVISM I

4.1. *Carnap 1: Inductive Logic, Intuitive Sketch*

Carnap, in contrast to Popper, was[52] of the opinion that there is an interpretation of the probability calculus which renders precise the concept of the probability of an hypothesis. Thus the probabilities of hypotheses were for Carnap *probabilities*. He chose a starting point quite similar to that of the personalist: the probability of an hypothesis h is accordingly a measure of the belief in h relative to the empirical data e. One may not take the belief of just any person but must take as a model the belief of a *rational* person and this, in turn, leads to the problem of the criteria of rationality. To solve this problem, says Carnap, one must first *depsychologize* the concept of belief. Just as in *deductive logic* the psychological concept of necessary connection between thoughts (ideas) *was replaced* by the objective concept of logical entailment, so here the concept of degree of belief must be replaced by that of partial logical consequence. The theory of such a concept was called *inductive logic*. That the credibility of hypothesis h on the basis of the available data e is 1/3 – symbolically: $c(h, e) = 1/3$ – can be explicated as follows: 1/3 of the logical range of e is contained in that of h. This may also be expressed as follows: *the probability of the hypothesis* or the *degree of confirmation* of h relative to e is 1/3. The probability of an hypothesis is partial logical entailment and not weakened truth.

The concept of *statistical probability* is not rejected by Carnap but is sharply demarcated from the concept of *inductive probability*. Elementary statistical statements of probability are always hypotheses (neither verifiable nor falsifiable) whereas inductive probability statements are never hypothetical but, if true, they are provable and, if false, they are logically contradictory. Furthermore, inductive probability, in contrast to statistical probability which lies in the object language, is a metalinguistic concept: we are here talking *about* sentences of a formal scientific language.

The task of inductive logic is to provide a precise definition of the function c. This task is reduced to the problem of assigning a priori probabilities to state descriptions. A state description is a maximally strong consistent description of the given universe; in it one lays down for every individual and every predicate whether or not the predicate belongs to the individual. And since every molecular sentence can be represented as a disjunction of state descriptions we can also determine the a priori probabilities of any molecular sentence by means of the a priori probabilities of the state descriptions. The application to genuine general sentences is effected by a simple limit convention.

Carnap accepted *the usual probability axioms* for his c-functions. In his first theory he was able to justify this only with the help of intuitive plausibility considerations. These axioms are nevertheless much too weak for the foundation of an inductive logic; for their validity is compatible with infinitely many different a priori evaluations of state descriptions. An individual c-function is laid down only after a particular valuation has been decided upon.

Wittgenstein, and likewise Peirce, had chosen confirmation functions which assign to all of the state descriptions *the same* a priori probability. The function c^+ that thus results will be called the Wittgenstein function of confirmation. Carnap pointed out a fundamental drawback of such a function: it rules out learning from experience. The probability that the next ball drawn from an urn will be white is the same regardless of the number of white or black balls that have been drawn from the urn so far.

Carnap therefore suggested originally the following improvement: instead of treating every possible world alike, we must ascribe the same a priori probability to *types of possible worlds*. To this end state descriptions which are isomorphic are disjunctively connected to form a so-called *structural description*. Every such disjunction can be construed as the formal representative of a type of possible world. By assigning *equal* a priori probabilities to structural descriptions Carnap obtained the function c^*.

But even this method turned out to be plagued with numerous drawbacks. Carnap therefore finally lost hope for a single adequate inductive method and developed his one-dimensional continuum of inductive methods, also called λ-continuum since every method that belongs to the continuum (represented by a c-function) is unambiguously determined by the value of a parameter λ ranging from 0 to ∞. To be more exact, every inductive method is describable via appropriate arithmetical means consisting of an empirical factor (observed relative frequency) and a logical factor (predicate-width); thus the weights are built up from the number of objects observed plus the parameter λ. The reasons for the selection of a particular element out of this infinite class of possible inductive methods may be quite different: besides objective theoretical and pragmatic, there are also purely subjective grounds.

4.2. *Discussion and Critique*

(1) *Technical deficiency*. Carnap's first sketch of an inductive logic was plagued with numerous technical drawbacks. Among them are notably vari-

ous limiting conditions such as the requirement of the independence of all the descriptive constants as well as the requirement of completeness involved in the adoption of a synthetic principle of J.M. Keynes. A good part of Carnap's later works were designed to develop methods for eliminating these and similar flaws.

(II) *The Popper-Carnap discussion*. Popper had claimed, first in his essay on the degree of corroboration and then again in [*L.F.*] p. 345, that he had proved the logical inconsistency of Carnap's theory. This claim is incorrect (and should not therefore be endlessly repeated as is done for example by Lakatos [*Changes*] p. 355).[53] Nevertheless in the course of the discussion it became clear that Carnap had mistakenly conflated concepts of two different kinds. This can be explained psychologically by the fact that confirmation can be taken to mean either *posterior* confirmation or *increment* of confirmation. He had construed his quantitative concept in the former sense and the qualitative and comparative concept in the latter sense.

The difficulty could have been most simply resolved by dropping the whole seventh Chapter of [*Probability*] (pp. 428 – 482). Aside from Carnap's critique of Hempel, this Chapter contains no non-trivial result.[54] (Nevertheless it is a pity that Carnap was not aware of the above mentioned possibility for rendering Popper's theory precise. He would then have realized that Hempel's theory does *not* represent the qualitative analogue *to his own theory*, but must be construed *as a deductive theory of confirmation competing with that of Popper.* I think, however, that Carnap would have adopted the above critique and in his final negative comment on p. 482 relegated Popper's theory to the class of so far unsuccessful attempts at a qualitative (deductive) theory of confirmation.)

In the preface to the second edition of [*Probability*] Carnap considered the critiques of Popper and Bar-Hillel and distinguished sharply between two families of concepts: the concepts of *firmness* and the concepts of *increment of firmness*.[55] His concept of inductive probability corresponds to the quantitative concept of the former family. The quantitative concepts of the latter family are called *relevance concepts*.

As can be shown by a closer linguistic analysis, Carnap's use of the expression 'degree of confirmation' was bound to be misleading. *It would have been better, therefore, if Carnap had decided to take 'degree of confirmation' to mean increment of firmness, that is to identify it with his measure of relevance*. In such a case Carnap would have had to concede *to Popper that the content of confirmation does not have the structure of probability*. According to the definition given in 3.2. (VII), Carnap's theory would thus have become a *deductivist theory*.[56]

(III) *The null-probability of laws*. For all the *c*-functions out of λ-continuum, the inductive probability of laws relative to any finite datum is equal to 0. Carnap conceded that this result is not in accord with our intuitive expectations. He believed, however, this result was *only apparently* inadequate. In order to show this, he introduced (in the appendix of *Probability*, p. 572) the concept of the *qualified single instance confirmation* of laws. But against this proposed solution Popper[57] raised a decisive objection: according to Carnap's proposal it may turn out (and indeed quite often) that a long controverted law possesses a high single instance confirmation.

Carnap never came back again to this suggestion. I believe it may be viewed at best as a mistaken tack. Every subsequent attempt to salvage the positive probability of laws by proposing new interpretations of Carnap's project has likewise been futile. If the epistemological claim of Carnap's theory is taken for what it really was intended for, *then the null-confirmation of laws is a perfectly adequate and desirable result*.

(IV) *Partial implication. Hume's intuition versus Carnap's intuition*. The expression '*inductive logic*' stems from the fact that Carnap construed the concept of inductive probability as a metricized concept of partial logical implication. If the logical range of a sentence is completely contained in the logical range of another, then the latter is entailed by the former. If there exists only a patrial overlap, then we have a partial logical implication. If the logical ranges are distinct, then the two sentences are incompatible with each other.

The relationship of Kant and Carnap to Hume could be characterized in the following way: *Both of them* thought they had found a loophole in Hume's argument. *Both* were of the opinion they could exploit this loophole to overcome Hume's problem. Kant did this by *assuming synthetic a priori principles* while Carnap did it by *liberalizing the concept of inference* to that of partial inference.

Carnap's line of thought is extremely peculiar. This comes clearly to light if contrasted to Hume's ideas. According to Hume the relation of logical consequence is the most important case of logical dependency. Its counterpart is the concept of *logical independence*. This obtains especially between elementary statements about the past and those about the future (between, for example, a statement about the weight of a log of wood burned in the last century and a statement about the eye color of a child yet to be born). *In all the cases where Hume speaks of logical independence Carnap must speak of partial logical consequence*, since for him the concept opposed to logical consequence is not logical independence but rather *logical incompatibility*, which, in turn, represents a special form of logical dependency. (This becomes quite clear when one bears in mind that the logical incompatibility between two sentences is by definition reducible to the relation of logical consequence: logical incompatibility obtains, namely, only if the negation of the one sentence *logically follows* from the other.) What is happening here? It seems to me that Hume's intuition is correct, while Carnap's, on the other hand, is incorrect. If an adequate concept of partial logical consequence is introduced at all it must be placed between the genuine relation of logical consequence and that of *logical independence*, not between the genuine relation of logical consequence and *logical incompatibility* which is simply a particular case of logical consequence!

Against Carnap's construal Hume would presumably have raised an objection to the effect that *Carnap proposes a quasi Spinozian world in which there exist only logical dependencies between any states of affairs whatsoever*. He starts out, namely, from the strictest form of logical dependency: logical consequence; in a second step he arrives via liberalization at the concept of partial logical consequence; but in his third step, instead of moving even further away from the relation of logical consequence and introducing the concept of complete logical independence, *he again returns to a form of complete logical dependence: logical incompatibility* (which is construable as a special logical consequence). Hence Carnap lumps together two quite different cases: the case where a sentence (or its negation) is a partial logical consequence of another [58] and the case where it is logically independent from it. To both of them Carnap gives the misleading name 'partial implication'.

(V) *Material inconsistency in the concept of partial implication*. An explication should be called materially inconsistent if it can be shown that certain requirements placed on the explicandum cannot simultaneously be satisfied by the explicated concept. Such a case obtains in Carnap's inductive logic provided one is taking Hume's intuition as one's basis. Under such a presupposition inductive irrelevance must obtain exactly when there is complete logical independence. But this condition, to which Salmon has referred in [*Partial Entailment*], is satisfied only by the Wittgensteinian function. And so only such a function would represent an adequate inductive method. But upon second thought one can see that it too fails, for it rules out any learning from experience. *The interpretation of the basic inductive relation as a relation of partial logical implication is consequently logically incompatible with the requirement of rational learning from experience.*

(VI) *Inductivist falsification of the concept of partial L-implication.* The concept of partial logical consequence would be instrumental in the understanding of the basic inductive relation only if it could be introduced independently of the concept of inductive probability. This, however, is not the case. To realize this one need merely consider the following: it is ambiguous to speak of the intersections of the logical ranges of sentences. It might be taken to mean either the *absolute intersection* or the *intersection measured* by means of an already available measure. (An analogous distinction cannot and need not be made in the case of the consequence relation: here the one range is indeed completely contained in the other.) Carnap uses the *measured* intersection. But by so doing his procedure becomes circular: the partial logical implication which in its metricized form is supposed to enable us to understand the concept of inductive probability already presupposes the concept of the inductive measure of probability for its characterization. The concept of partial implication is *inductively falsified*, as one might say.

Only in a single case can this circularity be avoided; namely, if Wittgenstein's function is accepted. Only in this case are we using absolute intersections of logical ranges and not measured intersections. Should someone – contrary to all plausibility – prefer Carnap's intuition to Hume's and thus reject argument (V), then a new difficulty would crop up: in order to escape the circular reasoning he would now have to resort to the function which Carnap himself held to be completely inadequate since it rules out any rational learning from experience.

The foundations which have been sketched in our last three points are arguments against the concept of inductive logic. This is more than just a matter of terminology. Had Carnap taken the expression 'inductive logic' to mean 'logic of inductive reasoning', that is, as something analogous to expressions such as 'logic of explanation', 'logic of functional analysis', 'logic of statistical inference', etc. it would have been a trivial matter of terminology. But he took it to mean a theory having *a logical concept for its object*, namely, the concept of partial L-implication. If the critique in (IV), (V) and (VI) is right, then this concept, and consequently the idea of an inductive logic, must be completely abandoned.

(VII) *Three possible sources of Carnap's error.* Just like the subjectivists, Carnap also started out with the concept of degree of belief. Subjective probability is partial belief and metricized subjective probability is a yardstick for partial belief. Carnap thought this concept had to be depsychologized, and that the objectivation would lead to the concept of *partial L-implication*. This idea is indeed *prima facie* plausible; further analysis, however, will show that it is unrealizable. What we have here is not an objectivation but rather a normalization; that is, *norms* are set up to which a rational person is supposed to conform in his subjective probabilistic considerations. Carnap presumably overlooked the *circularity* just mentioned because he originally discussed L. Wittgenstein's and C.S. Peirce's theories and according to them all state descriptions possess the same a priori probability. In these theories (and only in them) can one speak of *absolute* intersections of two logical ranges: it suffices to enumerate the state descriptions to which both ranges belong. Carnap overlooked the fact that by relinquishing these theories (and proceeding first to c^* and then to the continuum) the concept of the intersection of logical ranges becomes infinitely ambiguous; for to one and the same absolute range there belong *infinitely many different measured ranges* depending on which measure function one opts for. And it is from this that there arose what we have called the inductivist falsification of the concept of partial logical consequence.

A third error of Carnap stems, in my opinion, from the statistical literature, in particular from statistical estimation theory with which he occupied himself very intensely for a long time. This is the view that *problems of evaluation are decision problems* which represent, in particular, evaluations of *actions* having advantageous or disadvantageous consequences. But by doing so he was bound to confuse the theoretical with the practical problems. If I comply with the request to estimate the distance between two houses I then venture a theoretical guess which may either be right or wrong. But I don't perform any action and it is meaningless here to speak of the practical consequences of my estimate, for only actions have such consequences. If, on the other hand, someone (e.g., a businessman, a general, the coach of a basketball team) makes an arrangement he performs an action whose possible advantages and disadvantages he must weigh. An *evaluation* can certainly be relevant for such an action. *But the best estimate in the theoretical sense does not necessarily lead to the best arrangement.* In preparing for an international match, the coach would do well, *inter alia*, to more or less overrate the opposing team.

If one tries to eliminate the first error mentioned, then the scope of

Carnap's theory must be sharply restricted. One can only speak of the degree of partial belief when one is in a position to supply a method of measuring this degree. As has long since been realized by F.P. Ramsey and B. DeFinetti, such a method is well illustrated by betting behaviour. It only makes sense to bet on events whose outcome can be determined; betting on natural laws, on the other hand, leads to a *subjectivist metaphysics of probability*. Hence the null-probability of laws is a perfectly acceptable consequence.

(VIII) *Analyticity and experience. An imaginary dialogue between D. Hume and R. Carnap.* [59] According to Carnap, who here seizes upon an idea of Bishop Berkeley, inductive logic ought to serve as 'a guide of life'. This should transpire by substituting in a provable equation $c(h, e) = r$ of inductive logic the respective hypothesis for h and for e all of the empirical knowledge which is relevant to this hypothesis. So as not to aggravate the problem at hand with the question of law hypotheses, let us here assume that h represents a singular statement about a future event.

How would D. Hume have responded to Carnap's claim? The least he would have said would have been that it is inconceivable how he could make such a claim. For e is a report about *past* observations, '$c(h, e) = r$' is a statement which is *analytically* provable in his (Carnap's) inductive logic, but h is an assertion about the *future*. Regardless of the technical apparatus of this inductive logic, one can set up the following alternative: either this c-equation is actually analytic, but this rules out the possibility that together with e it can provide information about h which justifies calling it a guide of life, for a statement about the past (namely, e) together with an analytic statement (namely, $c(h, e) = r$) can definitely not furnish us with any kind of knowledge or information whatsoever about the future; or again such information really does exist, but then – since e doubtlessly talks about the past and h about the future – $c(h, e) = r$ cannot, Carnap's reassurance notwithstanding, represent an analytic statement.

Lest things get too abstract, suppose that Carnap and Hume engage in a dialogue to determine whether, and how, a common acquaintance of theirs can use Carnap's inductive logic in a betting situation.

Hume: 'Our friend John came to see me yesterday and asked me whether the horse Mephisto will win the big race the day after tomorrow. I told him I had not the slightest idea: so long as the race is not run I don't know and neither does anyone else!'

Carnap: 'If, indeed, John is insisting on a categorical answer, then, of course, we are in no position to help him; for surely there is no certain knowledge about the future. Yet I suspect that he would be quite satisfied with simply a tip that will enable him to make a rational decision on how he should bet.'

Hume: 'The only advice that I can give him is to tell him to obtain a little information about the past performances of Mephisto as well as the other horses taking part in the race and then compare. John may well find such an investigation quite interesting; I don't think, however, it will serve his purpose very well; for he is not at all interested in the past, but in the outcome of the race that has yet to be run.'

Carnap: 'The next step that John must take after getting this information is to figure out the probability that Mephisto will win. Let's suppose, for the sake of simplicity, that the probability of victory given all the relevant data is 1/2. I would then tell John that a bet with these odds is rational.'

Hume: 'If John were to come back again to me for advice, I would put him on his guard. I would first point out to him that the probability statement containing the result of your calculation is a purely analytic statement without factual content, for your calculation follows from your definition of the *c*-function. I would futhermore remind him that the empirical data which you used to compute the probability of Mephisto's victory is based exclusively on past races and says nothing whatsoever about future races. I am afraid that once John takes all this into account he will start thinking and this will soon leave him restless so that he will quickly rush back to you with a reproach. For he had hoped, after all, to learn from you *something* about the coming race while your only source of non-analytic information was your knowledge of the past. But he had already obtained such information through my advice.'

Carnap: 'I will then try to show John that I have given him exactly the kind of information that he can rationally expect. I had alerted him from the very beginning to the fact that he cannot secure absolutely certain information. I will therefore try again to clearly explain to him that he cannot expect to learn more than which bet has reasonable odds in this case or, what comes to the same thing, what constitutes a degree of rational belief in Mephisto's victory. I will then point out to him that this is exactly the kind of information he has obtained from me.'

Hume: 'But if John is sufficiently critical, he will surely not be satisfied with this. He will, instead, try to probe the meaning of your expressions 'reasonable' and 'rational' in this context. Presumably, he will always somehow come back to the question as to how a belief that refers to the future can be regarded as rational if the only factual information upon which it is based is something in the past.'

Carnap: 'If *that* is the issue, then I must really get down to details. I would then have to explain to him the whole construction of my inductive logic or at least its main features. I will explain to him how values can be assigned to state descriptions, how this correlation carries over to sentences of any structure, and how, on this basis, the concept of degree of confirmation is introduced. The last part of my explanation will focus on the concept of rational belief; this concept can be reduced purely by definition to the concept of degree of confirmation. If he has understood my explanation, he will see that *this* is what is meant by rational belief. This should suffice, for this is exactly what he wanted to know.'

Hume: 'I don't think this will do, for he will soon realize that the probability statements obtained in your system are, in view of their analytic character, simply disguised statements about past observations. Things would be quite different, however, were you able to prove that one can expect *with certainty* that what, according to you, is more probable leads in the long run more often to success than what is improbable. But as you yourself have at one time emphasized, not even this can be proved.'

Carnap: 'It quite suffices for a rational procedure that there is in the long run a higher *probability* of success.'

Hume: 'Again I must contradict you: this will not do at all. For as long as there exists no logically provable connection whatsoever between that which is *probable* and that which will *actually* take place in the future, it is quite legitimate for John to raise the question: 'Why should one be rational in your sense of the word "rational"?' The possible answer: 'Because it is just rational to be rational', would, of course, amount to a mere sophism; for in the latter part of the sentence you would be referring to *your* concept of rationality. The whole sentence then would be taken to mean that it is rational to accept your concept of rationality. But that is exactly the very thing that is in question. Finally, our common acquaintance will not be unaware of the fact that *there are infinitely many different possibilities* for defining the concept of confirmation and, hence, the concept of rationality. (I have heard you have even constructed a whole continuum of such possibilities.) What seems rational depends upon the choice you make. *What is rational according to a particular choice is highly irrational according to a different choice and vice versa*.'

At this point, at the very latest, the dialogue would have to be broken off.

To meet Hume's objection they both would have to begin anew, and Carnap would have to present convincing grounds either for the choice of a particular *c*-function or, at least, the choice of such functions from a certain narrow class. Such a discussion would involve nothing less than *the problem of the justification of induction translated into the Carnapian idiom*.

As long as Carnap's theory is construed as a theory of the confirmation of hypotheses, as was originally intended, then I believe this problem is insoluble – *just as all the theoretical variants of Hume's problem are insoluble*. Only *the successor problems* to Hume's problem can be discussed with some prospect of success. And the problem here – in contradistinction to the successor problem mentioned in 3,2 (XIII) – does not involve a *theoretical* question at all, but is rather *a problem of the justification of norms of action*. With regard to this we have to mention briefly Carnap's later theory.

5. INDUCTIVISM 2

5.1. *Carnap II: Normative Theory of Inductive Reasoning: Intuitive Sketch*

In contrast to the critique leveled against Popper's theory, the critique in 4.1 was in its most important aspects – that is, all those aspects which dealt not simply with technical shortcomings – purely destructive. The impression might thus arise that with its acceptance Carnap's theory is totally destroyed. Yet, as far as I can see, that is not the case. I believe that only when we have abandoned the idea of an inductive logic are we really in a position to see what Carnap has actually accomplished.

The second version of his theory is substantially different from the first both as regards intuitive approach as well as technical construction.

I here reverse the order of presentation and begin by saying a few words about its *technical construction*. The expected did not come about. It was expected that Carnap would expand his system to include richer and richer languages and simultaneously remove the original technical shortcomings. But what actually happened was that his thinking, as was often the case, took an unexpected turn: *he abandoned the linguistic approach altogether*. To be sure, there is still talk of languages in [*Basic System*]; this, however, is completely inessential. The real object of his investigations are purely *conceptual systems* consisting of individuals, attributes, and functions. Since some of these contain much more than can be expressed by any language created by man (including languages with expressions of infinite length) he has consequently greatly extended the domain of application of this theory.

The second essential innovation regards the inclusion of the modern theory of measurement into his conceptual apparatus, He has here succeeded in establishing a quite natural connection between Tarski's semantics or model theory and the theory of mathematical measurement and probability. *I think that Carnap's most significant technical contribution lies exactly in this connection between model theory and measurement theory*: this will presumably survive even if his ideas about 'induction' should not prevail. Thus, I would like to make a few comments about this. Carnap's procedure relies essentially on two conceptual devices. The *first* consists in *construing models by means of* one or many-place *numerical functions*. To do this three types of indices are necessary: first the (denumerable or non-denumerable) individuals are numbered. The attributes are divided into (at most denumerably many) families every one of which is numbered. Within every family the attributes are then numbered; here a non-denumerable set is in principle permissible. (For example: the family of colors construed as a color spectrum with the single colors being identified with the points of the color spectrum.) A model Z (a 'possible world') is rendered by a two-place function. The statement $Z(m, i) = j$ is to be read as follows: 'the individual with the number i has the attribute with the number j of the family with the number m.'

If the family contains n-ary attributes, then the corresponding statements assume the form: $Z(m, <i_1, ..., i_n>) = j$. (The functions Z cannot be described in the intuitive sense here portrayed. A technical complication arises from the fact that the respective domain of values depends on the domain of the first argument. Carnap is therefore forced 'to piece together' the model functions out of sequences of model components every one of which refers to exactly one family.)

Carnap's *second conceptual device* consists *in choosing these model functions as points of the probability space* γ. An appropriate σ-body of subsets of the set γ must be selected for the application of the theory of probability. This σ-body is identified with the class of propositions. The atomic propositions form the starting point: $P^m_j a_i$ (j being an element of the index of the m-th family). Such an atomic proposition consists of the class of models Z such that $Z(m, i) = j$. (*First example*: let $m = 1$ and let's suppose we are dealing with the family of color attributes. If the domain of individuals as well as the class of colors is taken to be non-denumerable, then the class of atomic propositions is of a higher power than the power of the continuum, that is, it has the same power as the class of real functions. Only a very small part of the atomic propositions could be exhibited by means of a language.

Second example: Let $m = 1$ and let the family contain only two attributes A and B. Let the domain of individuals be denumerably infinite. An atomic proposition might state that every individual with a prime number index has the attribute A while, on the other hand, every other individual has the attribute B. Although there are only denumerably many individuals and merely two attributes, such an atomic proposition could be described only by means of a sentence of infinite length.) Since the class of atomic propositions can easily be constructed, *the class of propositions* ξ can be identified with the σ-body generated by means of this class. It should be noted that by so doing we can gain a substantially greater number of propositions than could be introduced by means of the usual recursive definitions of a sentence.[60]

We can now introduce a probability measure defined for all propositions. In contrast to the procedure in the abstract calculus of probability, we must justify the basic axioms of probability. For this Carnap appeals to the factors considered by a person who *makes decisions involving risk*. In such situations the agent must choose between different possible courses of action: all of the possible natural states of affairs that might ensue lie before him, but still he does not know which particular state of affairs will actually materialize. He has *only the subjective probabilities of their occurring*. What is meant by the subjective probability of a natural state of affairs is the degree to which the subject believes in the occurrence of this state of affairs. In the case of a *rational* person one then *speaks* of the *degree of rational belief*. This concept is no longer a descriptive psychological concept but rather a *normative* concept whose exact determination depends upon the definition of the criteria of rationality. So as to distinguish this normative concept from the empirical concept of subjective probability let us call it *personal probability*.[61]

Carnap, just like the personalist, is concerned with the formulation and justification of certain norms which every reasonable person ought to follow when making decisions involving risk. Since the considerations involved here are of a *subjective probabilistic* nature, it makes sense to regard them as inductive reasoning. Carnap is here striving for a *normative theory of this inductive reasoning*.

The degree of belief of a person X at a particular time T is given by a belief function *Cr*. Carnap takes over from the personalist probability theoreticians (F.P. Ramsey, B. DeFinetti) the method for justifying the requirement that the basic axioms of probability should hold for *Cr* : *Cr* is construed as a betting quotient and it is shown that these axioms are *a consequence of the coherence requirement*. This means that if someone considers it unreasonable to accept a system of bets in which *loss* is *necessary* (that is in which one loses regardless of what actually happens), then the validity of the axioms of probability must be assumed for *Cr*. If it is admitted that it is likewise unreasonable to include betting systems in which it is impossible to win, yet quite possible to lose, then a further axiom can be established: *the axiom of regularity*.

So far Carnap and the personalists are in agreement. But at this point an essential difference crops up in their interpretations; a difference of opinion which, *inter alia*, shows that despite this common point of departure *the real metascientific opponents of Carnap are not the 'Popperians' but the personalist theoreticians of probability*. Carnap is of the opinion, namely, that (1) the search for additional norms of behavior is urgently called for, and (2) it is also possible to develop a method for justifying such additional norms.

The urgency is quite simple: it can easily be shown that in every situation countless functions *Cr* would be considered unreasonable even though they satisfy the theoretical axioms of probability.[62] So as to reduce this vast amount of arbitrariness and to justify further norms, one must pass from the analysis of the manifest belief function *Cr* at a particular point in time to the analysis of the deeper-lying non-manifest function *Cred* (for 'credibility') which describes a *permanent dispositional structure* of the person. The function *Cr* is its mere manifest expression. This can be illustrated by means of analogies from the domain of moral philosophy and of natural science.

Suppose we have to pass judgment on the morality of two persons *X* and *Y*. An appraisal that relies on the descriptions of their actions in different situations would be superficial: for it may well be that *Y* receives a better mark than *X* because he has never been in as difficult conflict situations as *X*. If a comparison of both characters brings to light the fact that in similarly difficult situations *Y* had conducted himself worse than *X*, then we would judge *Y* less favorably than *X even though their actual conduct would seem to indicate the opposite. But in this comparison we are basing our judgment* on their moral characters and we do not count it as a merit of *Y* that he was spared the conflict situations of *X*.

The analogy to our case lies in the following: if in a certain situation two persons *X* and *Y* believe the same thing, they need not on that account be equally rational. For the 'data' at their disposal (past experiences, basic convictions acquired in growing up, etc.) may be completely different. If we draw the conclusion that the conviction of *X* is (relatively) rational while that of *Y* is irrational, then this judgment cannot be based on a comparison of the functions Cr_X and Cr_Y, for these are by hypothesis supposed to be the same. Our appraisal of the two persons is based not on their factual beliefs but rather on a comparison of the *Cred* functions, that is, on their *dispositions* to arrive at such and such convictions in certain situations.

Such a method is also urged in view of its success in the natural sciences: in the search for general law-like regularities it has always proved useful, indeed often indispensible, to proceed from manifest characteristics, which are at first used in descriptions, to permanent theoretical dispositions.

To arrive at an adequate characterization of the function *Cred* of a particular person can be, depending on circumstances, extremely difficult. But this problem would, after all, appear only in connection with the *descriptive* theory of decision. It does not crop up within the *rational* or *normative* theory of decision which Carnap was trying to establish. Since we have to obtain additional criteria of rationality, it is permissible to make idealizations about the rational person and his *Cred* function. The idealizations gain in clarity if we imagine the rational person replaced by a robot who has the structure of a discrete state system.[63] Furthermore, Carnap here also replaces the static point of view with a dynamic one: in lieu of the momentary state *Cr*, which can be construed as the instant recording of the brain state of the person (of the robot), there is a temporal sequence of belief functions Cr_0, Cr_1, ..., Cr_n, ... It begins with the initial belief function Cr_0; and the transition from every function Cr_i to the next Cr_{i+1} is nothing but the transition from the function connected with time T_i to the one connected to the next point in time T_{i+1}. (Time is conceived as consisting of discrete units.) The experiences acquired between periods are stored up; the robot is supposed to be equipped with a prefect memory and every transition from a Cr_i to a Cr_{i+1} should entirely depend on the experience accumulated in the intervening period. It can be shown that for every proposition H and every n we can calculate the value $Cr_n(H)$ by means of the conditional initial credence function which is to be identified with the function *Cred*. The knowledge upon which this calculation draws need not be factual but may simply be *possible* knowledge. And it is precisely this that constitutes the advance from a series of manifest characteristics to a theoretical disposition.

The transition from decision theory to abstract probability theory consists in the replacement of the function *Cred* by the two-place function $C(H, E)$. But for the justification of further principles one always resorts to the credibility interpretation. Additional axioms which are justified by *Cred* are: the *symmetry axiom* which demands that logically isomorphic propositions be given the same treatment; furthermore various *invariance axioms* according to which the value $C(H, E)$ is required to be independent of the existence, number, and properties of the individuals and families not mentioned in E and H. The net result of this is that Keynes' postulate of limited variety in the world becomes superfluous. The concept of rational learning from experience is rendered precise via the *principle of the relevance of single instances*.

Carnap, on the other hand, does not assume any further axioms that restrict the C-functions to the class of the λ-family. The λ-family is only *one* class of possible rational C-functions. The so-called *analogy influence* in attribute spaces can dictate the choice of C-functions which do not belong to the λ-family.

In his (fragmentary and incomplete) examination of the structure of attribute spaces, Carnap develops by means of sophisticated methods ideas that had already occupied him in his [*Logical Structure*]. *In order to arrive at a* rational metricization of attribute gaps he resorts to topological and measure theoretical aids. A priori connections beside being determined by *postulates of analyticity* are also determined by *basic phenomenological postulates* (synthetic a priori propositions). By so doing we succeed in *freeing non-logical constants from the requirement of independence*. Salmon's so-called problem of *linguistic invariance* is thus solved.

Two limit axioms form the conclusion of the axiom system: Reichenbach's axiom and the principle of σ-additivity for the absolute probability function.

Carnap *does not*, of course, succeed in singling out a *particular* C-function. He does, however, provide an exact analysis of the possible strategic considerations which may motivate a rational person in his choice of a particular *Cred* function.

The subdivision of axioms into different subclasses has the practical advantage that the grounds offered for their acceptance can be discussed independently of each other. The further discussion can thus lead either to additional restrictions or to the abandonment of certain postulates.[64]

5.2. *Discussion of Carnap II*

From what epistemological sources does Carnap derive support for his axioms? A very tempting interpretation comes to mind. Since I am quite sure it will some day emerge, I want to anticipate it here. It would seek to bring Carnap very close to Kant. This might be justified by appealing to the fact that Carnap by assuming synthetic a priori propositions – even *quantitative* synthetic a priori principles – into his domain of objects has long since become a Kantian. We might, therefore, be tempted to look for a Kantian interpretation of his inductive metatheory too: Carnap's grounds of justification are intended by him as synthetic a priori metatheoretical propositions. He has abandoned empiricism not just in the object theory but in his metatheory as well. A direct proof of this can be found in Carnap's Schilpp Volume, p. 978, Sentence (II) (b), as well as in the first sentence of p. 979. According to them there are neither logically provable nor inductively derived *a priori grounds* for accepting his axioms.

To be more precise this interpretation would run something like this: for Kant theoretical reason is not identical with logical reason since the theoretically possible represents a substantially narrower class than the logically possible, whereas for Carnap, on the other hand, theoretical reason is divided into two subclasses: the domain of *deductive reason* and the domain of *inductive reason. Deductive reason is reflected in the avoidance of logical contradictions, deductive irrationality in their acceptance. Inductive reason is reflected in coherent behavior while inductive irrationality is manifested by incoherence.* (This analogy would then have to be expanded, of course, beyond the personalistic basis.)

In my opinion, however, all such speculations are mistaken. If one looks at the context of the sentences cited above, one is struck by something even more remarkable: Carnap denies not only that his axiomatic statements have been gained deductively or inductively, but he even denies that they are synthetic principles whether a priori or empirical.

Such a characterization reminds one of the descriptions of God in negative theology. The contradiction can only be resolved by discarding the supposition that Carnap was attempting to justify *theoretical* sentences.

His real objective was, as we have already said, tó *establish norms for rational action in cases that involve decisions under risk.* One may perhaps not consider all of these justifications convincing: one may also quite rightly demand that the method of justification be given a more precise explanation. But alone the very fact that a logician has here for the first time illustrated *the justification of norms* by means of concrete examples is enough to lend a significance to Carnap's thinking far exceeding the topic of 'induction'.

In 3.2 (XII) the successor problem to the problem of induction which belongs to the domain of 'theoretical reason' was called *the problem of the theoretical analogy of induction* IA_t. Correspondingly, the successor problem to the problem of induction belonging to the domain of 'practical reason' and appearing in connection with Carnap's investigations might be called *the problem of the practical analogy of induction* IA_p. It reads as follows:

(IA_p) *What norms hold for the subjective probabilistic considerations used in decisions involving risk and how are these norms to be justified?*

Surely we are still left with many difficult questions by Carnap's theory. I, too, am convinced that some essential additions and revisions of Carnap's principles are in order.

I will nevertheless content myself with providing a justification for the claim made in (17) of the introduction; for it is in the three points raised there that we encounter what are generally regarded as the worst shortcomings of the Carnapian system. The apparent shortcomings turn into desiderata with a decision theoretical reinterpretation.

(1) *The lack of rules of acceptance and rejection.* In the case of decisions involving risk such rules are *not only superfluous*, they are simply *obstructive*. Someone having to decide whether he should leave for Boston by train or by plane tomorrow will, on the basis of the available information, make probabilistic considerations such as whether or not the destination will be fogged in or not (and if so the plane, not the train, must be diverted with a consequent loss of time). His final decision will probably conform to Bayes' principle. It would be quite irrational on his part were he to act *as if he knew* that the Boston airport will be free of fog or *as if he knew* that it would be covered with fog.

(2) *Declining to single out one particular C-function.* The decision theoretician must content himself with setting up *negative normativity barriers*, that is, with stating which principles ought not to be violated when acting rationally. It is not his task, however, to tell a person what he ought to do. This would amount to *making robots of men*, who in every possible situation would pull the 'true' *C*-function out of their pockets in much the same way as a compass and thus learn the only right way. It is not the task of the rationality criteria to reduce to zero the free play of rational persons (agents).

(3) *The null probability of laws.* Personal probability is normalized partial belief. This can be measured by studying rational betting behaviour. A partial belief exists only relative to things upon which it makes sense to bet. One can only bet on events whose outcome can be ascertained. 'Betting on laws' has no clear meaning whatsoever. In order to interpret such an expression one would have to resort, presumably, to mythological ideas such as betting with an omniscient mind, that is, to what I would call the 'metaphysics of subjectivist probability.' That laws are dropped from Carnap's theory is simply a consequence of the decision theoretical interpretation of this theory.

By way of conclusion I will try to make clear by an illustration what I mean by a mythological idea. Suppose that on my way to Munich I have to drive over the Friedenheim bridge tonight. I am quite aware of the fact that this bridge was constructed on the basis of computations which in the final analysis rest on the Newtonian theory. I am prepared to bet $ 100,000 against $ 100 that the bridge won't collapse under the weight of my car. I would consider such a bet as a practically risk-free way of getting $ 100. *Does this mean that I am likewise prepared to make a similar bet about the validity of Newton's theory*? I must first ask what this is supposed to mean. It surely cannot mean anything else but that I ought to make a bet with an omniscient creature about the truth of the Newtonian theory. I would be on my guard against any such thing! The imperative: 'Thou shalt not make any bets with the good Lord on natural laws regardless of the odds' seems to me so self-evident that it needs no additional justification. The null probability of laws is nothing else but the content of this rational imperative as reflected in Carnap's formalism.

6. CONCLUDING REMARKS

Since many of the theses portrayed here will not be found acceptable, I would like to say a final word on what seems to me to be the crux of the matter: clarity about the problems which must replace the so-called problem of induction as well as clarity about what lies behind the antithesis between deductivism and inductivism.

The 'problem of induction' really consists of two questions: one concerns *conceptual clarification* while the other concerns *justification*. These two questions can be distinguished as J_1 and J_2:

J_1: *What is the principle of induction*? (or if one believes in pluralism: *What are the rules of inductive inference*?)

J_2: *How can the principle of induction (the rules of induction) be justified*?

These two questions have to be replaced by classes of other problems: I call them the successor problems to the problem of induction. The basic distinction that one must start out from is the division into *a theoretical and a practical family of problems*.

5.1. *Family of Theoretical Problems*

As long as we are dealing with the theoretical appraisal of *deterministic* law hypotheses, the two successor problems are the following:

(1) *What is the precise definition of a deductive concept of confirmation (corroboration concept)?*

(2) *How does one establish the adequacy of this deductive concept of confirmation?*

In my view, the significant insight of Popper lies in his recognition that problem J_1 does not exist, and that consequently, of course, problem J_2 is likewise void, since one cannot demand a justification for something that does not exist. If, furthermore, my critique of Salmon's critique of the concept of corroboration proves correct, then it is exactly the two successor problem (1) and (2) which appear in Popper's deductivism.

Without wishing to underestimate these problems, I nevertheless want to point out that their solution should not be presumed too difficult. Even though the explication of a pragmatic concept may require greater efforts than that of a semantic concept, both of these successor problems are, in principle, questions of exactly the same kind as were faced, for example, by Tarski in his work on the concept of truth; namely, first *to describe precisely the method of definition* of the concept of truth (for languages of a different structure and different content) and secondly, *to establish the adequacy of this method.*

But in any event one should not run the risk here of falling into the plethora of snares and conceptual confusions in which the philosophic attempts at a solution to the problem of induction have regularly ended up for so many centuries – not to say millenia (going all the way back to the attempts of the Aristotelian epagoge). Such questions as: 'How can a well confirmed theory be a "guide of life" for the future?' would be viewed as serious problems only after they have been converted into objections against the adequacy of the proposed concept of confirmation and brought up to the standard of *exactness* of the proposed explications.

Two analogous successor problems also come up as regards the question of the theoretical appraisal of *statistical hypotheses*. A conjecture was ventured in 3.2 (X). If this conjecture proves to be correct then we are here dealing with the problem of rendering precise a five-place relational concept and of justifying its adequacy. (If, on the other hand, we should succeed in showing that a particular theory of statistical support and of statistical test is superior to any other *in every situation*, then our job would be to render precise and to justify the definition of a four-place relation.)[65]

If the thesis of theoretical multi-dimensionality presented in 3.2 (II) is accepted, *then the two pairs of questions mentioned are not the only theoretical successor problems to the problem of induction*. If one considers the concept of *simplicity* to be amenable to formal precisioning, then the problem of a correct definition and proof of adequacy will likewise arise in connection with this concept. This is likewise the case with regard to Goodman's problem of *law-likeness*.

Yet a further problem would arise in this case – a successor problem of second order vis-à-vis the problem of induction. It would concern the priorities of these characteristics; e.g., establishing the thesis that only law-like hypotheses are to be admitted as potential candidates for confirmation (degree of corroboration, etc.) appraisals.

6.2. *Family of Practical Problems*

Here we are not dealing with a theoretical appraisal of hypotheses but rather with *norms of human action*. Presumably the most important class can be described by the slogan: '*decisions involving risk*.' Here the two successor problems to the problem of induction are the following:

(3) *What are the norms for rational decisions involving risk*?

(4) *How does one justify such norms*?

The difference between Popper and Carnap amounts to a distinction in the kinds of problems; it can be concisely characterized by the fact that Popper's theory of science is confronted with questions (1) and (2) whereas Carnap's theory must answer questions (3) and (4).

The difference between Carnap and the personalist probability theoreticians can be succinctly characterized as follows: according to the personalists *only the basic axioms of probability theory* can be justified as norms for one's subjective probabilistic considerations (inductive reasoning); it is upon them that decisions are based. According to Carnap, however, this is far too little: *additional norms* can be established (by passing from the 'manifest' function *credence* to the dispositional function *credibility*).

The methods of Ramsey and DeFinetti as well as Carnap's more extensive attempts provide an interesting example of how we can arrive at a justification of norms. Again, questions (3) and (4) do not constitute *the only* successor problems to the problem of induction. Analogous questions arise, for example, with regard to decisions involving uncertainty.

The problems of *family A* could be construed as the modern version of the Kantian question '*What can we know?*' while the problems of *Family B* involve the question '*How are we to act?*'

NOTES

[1] This error can also be found, for example, in J. Katz [*Induction*] p. 115.

[2] [*Justification*] p. 30.

[3] As far as I know, this idea was first used by M. Black in [*Analysis*] p. 171. W. Salmon has resorted to this example in various works partly for the same reasons we have already cited, partly to show how the rejection of the rule can be justified on the basis of Reichenbach's theory of probability.

[4] This rule can be rendered precise in two ways: as a rule for 'guessing in the long run' as well as a rule for 'guessing the next particular case.'

[5] The most important objections can be found in the works of W. Salmon with a rather condensed summary in [*Regular Rules*].

[6] We are here dealing with a very schematic characterization. The word 'party' is somewhat misleading since the 'inductivists' do not form a homogeneous group. It includes thinkers who in many ways have quite different views. This holds in particular for Reichenbach and Carnap.

[7] Cf., for example, Carnap [*I.L.*] p. 69.

[8] By Carnap's theory I mean *the usual version* of his theory which is based on his published writings. Carnap II should be taken to mean my normative decision theoretical reinterpretation of his theory which is based mainly on the two so far unpublished manuscripts [*Axiom System*] and [*Basic System*] which he worked on in the 15 years from 1955 to his death.

[9] [*L.F.*] p. 223.

[10] [*L.F.*] p. 15.

[11] In any case it was nearly always in *negative* contexts that I have had occasion to observe this manner of speaking, that is, in expressions such as: 'This hypothesis is surely too *improbable* to be taken seriously' and the like.

[12] Roughly speaking only what fulfills the Komogoroff axioms is called a probability.

[13] As far as I know this somewhat metaphorical yet quite illuminating use of the expression 'one-dimensional' stems from Bar-Hillel. It might, in principle, correspond to what Lakatos has called the 'monolithic appraisal of hypotheses' in [*Changes*] p. 375.

[14] Unfortunately this mixup is very much in fashion nowadays. It is not just found in Carnap. It can be found practically everywhere in mathematical statistics, particularly in statistical test and estimation theory – this odd combination of mathematical virtuoso performances and partly premature, partly confused metascientific ideas.

[15] I do not thereby mean to deny, of course, that Kuhn's statements are of metascientific *relevance*. Of course they are! But what interesting *inner-scientific* processes are not of relevance to metascience! A dispute between two astronomers about the enigma of the quasars or an argument between two German philologists regarding the correct interpretation of a poem by Walther von der Vogelweide can also be of the greatest metascientific relevance.

[16] Still, I don't want to conceal the fact that I consider the second danger to be substantially greater. Well founded empirical investigations on the actual behavior of scientists are not only valuable in themselves but are also indispensible for metascientific investigations. Purely normative considerations, on the other hand, threaten to degenerate into inane speculations.

[17] In my positive stand with regard to formalization I wish neither to deny that there is such a thing as *trivial precision*, which may become a vice, nor that formal precision almost always poses the potential danger of letting *technical questions* smother important philosophical problems.

[18] This proposal as well as the objections that will be raised originate with my colleague Prof. M. Käsbauer.

[19] I am unable to interpret Popper's attempt at defining the concept of a 'severe test' in [*Conjectures*] p. 388. The reasons are analogous to the ones concerning his concepts *E* and *C*, [*L.F.*] p. 352 (cf. the concluding comment to (X)).

[20] For a material critique cf. I. Lakatos [*Changes*] p. 403.

[21] In [*L.F.*] p. 354 Popper remarks that one cannot fully formalize the idea of a serious and well thought out test. In [*Conjectures*] p. 390ff. he does nevertheless propose two formalizations. It would be beyond the scope of this paper, however, to discuss the question of the adequacy of this precisioning and the solution of the paradoxes of confirmation connected with it. As to the difficulties in interpretation I have already mentioned, cf. the last paragraph of (X) below.

[22] Cf. his [*Induction*] p. 253.

[23] Cf. L.Foster [*Feyerabend's Solution*] p. 260, last paragraph.

[24] H. Albert [*Traktat*] p. 25; cf. also footnote 31 there. Albert's observations rest on two errors: first of all, Goodman does not single out any *propositions* (and 'prejudices' *are* propositions) but refers instead to *predicates*. Secondly, nowhere does Goodman demand that predicates well entrenched in the language be *favored*. To remove the above contradictions he instead formulates rules of elimination that exclude non-law-like statements. It is only in the definition of these rules of elimination that the concept of the linguistic embedding of predicates is used *in the definiens*.

Quite apart from this, however, I would suggest that in the theory of science one should follow the imperative 'Don't reject anything as long as you have nothing better to offer!' (Advice of this kind has, incidentally, first been given in statistics by J. Neyman; and this advice is today generally followed in statistical test theory.)

[25] With the exception perhaps of a new *approach* to a solution by Carnap in his [*Basic System*] as well as Richard C. Jeffrey's essay [*Goodman's Query*]. Jeffrey's observations, however, rest on an explicit confession of *intensionalism* which is rejected by Goodman. The above remark would have to be amended by saying that there exists so far no *extensionalistic* theory which might compete with that of Goodman.

[26] For a clear philosophical discussion of the relation between objective and subjective probability cf. F. v. Kutschera's essay [*Subjektiver Wahrscheinlichkeitsbegriff*].

[27] For in DeFinetti's theory there is an *analogue* to the objective concept of probability which contains all that you like but is, of course, still only a façon de parler. On this account one could, if one wishes, call even DeFinetti a *frequency theoretician* of probability, though 'true' probability consists for him only in the degree of belief (or 1 minus the degree of doubt).

[28] Cf. [*L.F.*] p. 141.

[29] Cf., for example, [*Propensity*].

[30] This follows from the observations in footnote 1 of [*L.F.*] p. 348.

[31] One can distinguish at least five variants of this theory of the hermeneutic circle: a *psychologistic* (Schleiermacher, Dilthey), an *existentialist* (Heidegger, Staiger), a *cultural philosophical* (Gadamer), a *sociological* (Habermas), and a *linguistic* (Apel); and, of course, various complicated combinations of these. The above mentioned characteristic, however, can be found in all the forms under which the theory has appeared.

[32] The thesis is formulated briefly in Quine's work [*Word and Object*] p. 27. For a more detailed description and critique of this thesis cf. F. v. Kutschera, *Sprachphilosophie* 3.3.3.

[33] This language, in contrast to ours, might be 'multi-dimensional, that is, it might consist in the simultaneous production of sounds plus visual signals plus odors etc.'

34 So as to make this concrete let's suppose that 'thinking in terms of things' is completely foreign to creature *X*. While I, for example, see a crowing rooster on a dunghill, *X* sees only structures of the kind: rooster-phase-at-time-*t* on a dunghill-phase-at-time-*t* with $t = 10^{-3}$ sec. Thus, if, for example, I see the rooster for six seconds, *X* has seen 6000 perceptual fields and provides what for me are complicated structural descriptions; the relations between these various fields are likewise described in a very complicated way. In order to express in our language the descriptions which are *short in his language*, one would have to write a bulky volume.

The real difficulty would not be, of course, in producing this volume but rather in picking out the right volume from the potentially infinite list of such volumes *without knowledge of X's way of describing things.*

35 [*Growth*] p. 265.

36 *Loc. cit.*, p. 266.

37 W. Salmon [*Inference*] p. 24ff, especially p. 26; cf. also [*Justification*] p. 28 and p. 95.

38 [*Inference*] p. 26; [*Justification*] p. 28.

39 [*Changes*] p. 401.

40 [*Changes*] p. 391.

41 [*Changes*] p. 393; the first definition of 'verisimilitude' can be found in [*Conjectures*] p. 234. Alternative definitions are given on p. 391.

42 Lakatos, *loc. cit.* p. 395.

43 "The second *serious shortcoming* of our criterion of reliability is that it is unreliable," *loc. cit.*, p. 397.

44 At any rate in the place cited from p. 398 on there is more talk of 'estimates' with relation to verisimilitude or with relation to reliability.

45 In [*Justification*] this error occurs to him first on p. 27, lines 3 and 4; in [*Inference*] the error can be found on p. 26 where he says: "Corroboration is a nondemonstrative form of inference."

46 If someone does not like the word 'analogue' because he associates with it the idea of an 'inductive analogical inference', he can speak instead of the successor to the problem of induction. One would then have to distinguish between (IN_t) and (IN_p).

47 On the other hand, the problem *does not* consist, as may be suggested by Carnap's formulations, in the question as to which confirmation function should be picked from a 'continuum of inductive methods'. If the problem is posed *this way* then the 'solution' inevitably degenerates into a game of subjective preference.

48 Namely the class of asymptotic rules.

49 I insert the clause 'if at all' here because I was only referring to the use of this concept for Lakatos' acceptability$_3$; on p. 401 of [*Changes*] Lakatos himself says that Popper does not place much value on this use.

50 [*Falsifiability*].

51 Cf. W. Salmon [*Inference*] p. 50ff, and '*Inductive Inference*' p. 359.

52 With regard to Carnap's first theory, called Carnap I for short, I use the past tense. The present tense always refers to the later theory, Carnap II.

53 A very objective and detailed discussion was offered by Harry V. Stopes-Roe in *JSL* 33, # 1 (March 1968), 142 – 146. On p. 144 he arrives at the conclusion that "the contradiction, therefore, is of Popper's making and Carnap is free of it."

54 An analysis of concepts is to be viewed as trivial if a lower concept can be characterized by means of an already available higher concept. Thus, for example, it is a *trivial* task to define 'warmer than' if the quantitative concept of temperature is already at our disposal. But this is exactly what Carnap is doing in the chapter in question.

55 It seems to me that the term 'increment of' proposed by Bar-Hillel should be preferred to Carnap's own term 'increase of'.

[56] The fact that a nominal definition can transform an inductivist theory into a deductivist theory and vice versa goes to show, after all, how unimportant the stereotypes 'inductivism' and 'deductivism' become when one decides to develop a quantitative theory of confirmation.

[57] [*Reply to Bar-Hillel*] p. 161.

[58] What is meant here is partial logical consequence *on the basis of Hume's intuition*. This concept of partial logical consequence would have to lie between the relation of logical consequence and a relation of logical independence yet to be explicated. The form these explications might take has been shown by W. Salmon in [*Partial Entailment*].

[59] The following considerations have been prompted by W. Salmon's works, especially his essay 'Carnap's Inductive Logic'.

[60] It is not perhaps superfluous to stress that this model theoretic concept of the proposition belongs to *extensional semantics*. By such a construction Carnap is not, therefore, exposed to the objections that Quine brings against *intensional semantics*.

[61] Popper says in [*L.F.*] p. 359. last paragraph – as he himself remarks 'only in parenthesis' that the expression 'degree of rational belief' should perhaps be viewed as a sign of conceptual confusion; what is really meant is 'degree of rationality of belief'. This interpretation surely does *not* correspond to the intention of the personalists. Popper himself subsequently notes "that the intensity of our belief often depends, in fact, more upon our wishes or fears rather than upon rational arguments" (*loc. cit.*, p. 360). But this constitutes no objection to the subjectivist, or better, the personalist interpretation. For the degree of irrational belief can by means of an analysis of betting behavior be measured *just as well as* the degree of rational belief. The difference between subjectivism and personalism consists in the fact that the former uses this method as an empirical measure of the actual rational *or irrational* (!) degree of belief, while the latter uses the method to formalize the minimal conditions of rationality, that is, to set up *norms for behavior*. The expression 'degree of rational belief' (in German as well as English) is a rough abbreviation for the longer expression 'degree of actual belief that a rational person would have (in this situation)'. This expression is meaningful only after the criteria of rationality are formulated.

[62] Technically speaking, for *any* real number r between 0 and 1 and *any* pair of molecular propositions E and H – except the borderline cases of logical incompatibility between E and H as well as the L-implication of H by E – there exists a belief function Cr satisfying all the basic axioms of probability theory as well as the axiom of regularity, such that $Cr(H, E) = r$.

[63] For a general description of systems such as those given by N. Rescher, cf. Vol. I, Chapt. III of my *Wissenschaftstheorie*: *wissenschaftliche Erklärung und Begründung*.

[64] An example of a problematic postulate is furnished by Reichenbach's axiom. As far as I can see, this axiom has so far served only two purposes: first as a foundation for a partial claim of the principle of the relevance of single instances, and secondly to formally exclude Wittgenstein's function from the λ-continuum. The question as to whether one should be burdened with a separate limit-axiom in order to attain two such relatively modest scientific goals is a matter of opinion.

[65] I believe I can prove that the place number of the relation cannot be further reduced: the reference to statistical hypotheses (representing 'background knowledge' here) *as well as* the reference to classes of rival hypotheses is unavoidable.

BIBLIOGRAPHY

In view of the vast amount of literature I must limit myself to a very small selection. The works cited are either those which I have expressly cited or used in my article. This also holds for the authors whose ideas are discussed in some detail. I shall cite the page only when it will expedite the search for the article in a journal. For quotations I will use the short title enclosed in brackets.

Albert, H. [Traktat], *Traktat über Kritische Vernunft*, Tübingen 1968.

Bar-Hillel, Y., 'Comments on "Degree of Confirmation" by Professor K.R. Popper', *The British Journal for the Philosophy of Science* 6, 1955-6.

'Further Comments on Probability and Confirmation. A Rejoinder to Professor Popper', *ibid.*

[Corroboration], 'Popper's Theory of Corroboration' (Manuscript, 27 pp.), 1970.

Black, M. [Analysis], *Problems of Analysis*, Ithaca, N.Y., 1954.

Carnap, R. [Logischer Aufbau], *Der Logische Aufbau der Welt*, 2nd ed., Hamburg 1961.

[Probability], *Logical Foundations of Probability*, 1st ed., Chicago 1950, 2nd ed., 1962.

The Continuum of Inductive Methods, Chicago 1952.

'Remarks on Popper's Note on Content and Degree of Confirmation', *The British Journal for the Philosophy of Science* 7, 1956-7.

[I.L.], *Induktive Logik und Wahrscheinlichkeit*, Wien 1959.

'The Aim of Inductive Logic', in: Nagel, E., P. Suppes und A. Tarski (eds.), *Logic, Methodology and Philosophy of Science*, Stanford 1962.

[Axiom System], *An Axiom System for Inductive Logic* (Manuscript, 503 pp.), 1959-1964. 'Inductive Logic and Rational Decisions' (Manuscript, 38 pp.), 1969.

[Basic System], *A Basic System for Inductive Logic* (incomplete Manuscript, 371 pp.), 1968-1970.

Feyerabend, P. [Induction], 'A Note on two "Problems" of Induction', *The British Journal for the Philosophy of Science* 19 (3), 1968.

Finetti, B. de. 'Rezension der Wahrscheinlichkeitslehre von H. Reichenbach', *Zentralblatt für Mathematik* 10 (1935), pp. 364f.

'Foresight: Its Logical Laws, its Subjective Sources', 1937; English translation in: Kyburg, H.E. und H.E. Smokler, *Studies in Subjective Probability*, New York 1964.

'Initial Probabilities', *Synthese* 20, 1969.

Foster, L. [Feyerabend's Solution], 'Feyerabend's Solution of the Goodman Paradox'. *The British Journal for the Philosophy of Science* 20 (3), 1969.

Goodman, N. [FFF], *Fact, Fiction and Forecast*, 2nd ed., New York 1965.

Hacking, I. [Statistical Inference], *Logic of Statistical Inference*, Cambridge 1965.

Hempel, C.G. [Confirmation I], 'Studies in the Logic of Confirmation (I)', *Mind* 54, 1945.

Hume, D. *An Inquiry concerning Human Understanding*, Sec. IV.

Jeffrey, R.C., 'Goodman's Query', *The Journal of Philosophy* 63 (II), 1966

Käsbauer, M., 'Deduktive Bestätigung' (Manuscript, 32 pp.)

Katz, J.J. [Induction], *The Problem of Induction and its Solution*, Chicago 1962.

Kemeny, J.G., 'Review of K. Popper, "Degree of Confirmation" ', *The Journal of Symbolic Logic* 20 (1955), pp. 304f.

Kuhn, T.S., 'Logic of Discovery or Psychology of Research?', in: Lakatos, I. and A. Musgrave, (eds.) [Growth].

'Reflections on my Critics', *ibid.*

Kutschera, F.v. [Subjektiver Wahrscheinlichkeitsbegriff], 'Zur Problematik der naturwissenschaftlichen Verwendung des subjektiven Wahrscheinlichkeitsbegriffs', *Synthese* 20, 1969. *Sprachphilosophie* (in publication).

Lakatos, I. [Changes], 'Changes in the Problem of Inductive Logic', in: Lakatos, I., [Inductive Logic].
(ed.) [Inductive Logic], *The Problem of Inductive Logic*, Amsterdam 1968.
Lakatos, I. and A. Musgrave (eds.) [Growth], *Criticism and the Growth of Knowledge*, Cambridge 1970.
Popper, K.R. [Reply to Bar-Hillel], ' "Content" and "Degree of Confirmation: A Reply to Dr. Bar-Hillel" ', *The British Journal for the Philosophy of Science* 6, 1955-6.
'Reply to Professor Carnap', *ibid.*
'Adequacy and Consistency: A second Reply to Dr. Bar-Hillel', *ibid.*
[Propensity], 'The Propensity Interpretation of the Calculus of Probability, and the Quantum Theory', in: Körner, S. (ed.), *Observation and Interpretation*, London 1957.
[L.F.], *Logik der Forschung*, 3nd ed., London 1969.
Quine, W.V. [Word], *Word and Object*, Cambridge, Mass. 1960.
Reichenbach, H. [Theory of Probability], *The Theory of Probability. An Inquiry into the Logical and Mathematical Foundations of the Calculus of Probability*, Berkeley 1949.
Salmon, W. [Regular Rules], 'Regular Rules of Induction', *The Philosophical Review* 65, 1956.
Inductive Inference', in: *Philosophy of Science. The Delaware Seminar*, vol. 11, New York 1963.
'On Vindicating Induction', *Philosophy of Science* 30 (3), 1963.
[Inference], *The Foundation of Scientific Inference*, Pittsburgh 1967.
'Carnap's Inductive Logic', *The Journal of Philosophy* 64, 1967.
[Justification], 'The Justification of Inductive Rules of Inference', in: Lakatos, I. (ed.) *Inductive Logic.*
[Partial Entailment] 'Partial Entailment as a Basis for Inductive Logic', in: Rescher, N. (ed.) *Essays in Honor of Carl G. Hempel*, Dordrecht 1969.
Schilpp, P.A. (ed.), *The Philosophy of Rudolf Carnap*, La Salle, Ill. 1963.
Stegmüller, W., *Wissenschaftliche Erklärung und Begründung*, Berlin-Heidelberg-New York ^{2}1974.
Stopes-Roe, H.V., Review of Discussions between Y. Bar-Hillel, K.R. Popper, R. Carnap and R. Achinstein, in: *The Journal of Symbolic Logic* 33, (1968), p. 142ff.
Ströker, E. [Falsifizierbarkeit], 'Falsifizierbarkeit als Kennzeichen naturwissenschaftlicher Theorien. Zu K.R. Poppers *Logic der Forschung*', *Kant-Studien* 59, 1968.

CHAPTER 5

CARNAP'S NORMATIVE THEORY OF INDUCTIVE PROBABILITY

When I was asked to give a talk on Carnap's late and still unpublished philosophy of induction I immediately realized that I would be unable to do this without suggesting a drastic reinterpretation of Carnap's program. I can only hope to make this reinterpretation comprehensible by trying to give a systematic sketch of my own position on the so-called problem of induction and to describe the role of Carnap's theory within the conceptual framework.

In principle I can make my point in a few words though it will take some time to explicate it. The point is simply this:

I do not believe in the problem of induction.

The title 'the problem of induction' is to include all kinds of endeavor to formulate rules either for finding yet-undiscovered laws or for justifying proposed hypothetical laws.

The list of possible candidates for such rules is nondenumerably infinite. As we cannot ask an infinite number of questions we are forced to formulate the problem in an abstract way which points to a common feature of all possible candidates. The rules we are looking for must be correct. This means that they have to be *truth-preserving*. But as distinguished from rules of deduction the content of the conclusion must not be part of the content of the premises, in other words: the rules have to be *amplifying*. So we get the following version of the problem of induction which is already implicit in the work of Hume:

(J) Are there inferences which are truth-preserving as well as amplifying?

The answer to this question is: 'No, of course not.' Therefore if by the problem of induction we understand the question (J) then it has a trivial negative solution. As this answer is ridiculously obvious, it seems to me preferable to say that in the field of theorizing such a thing as the problem of induction does not exist at all.

This sounds as if I were a Humean. But in that case I would presumably stress that I do not believe in a *positive solution* of the problem of induction. This formulation would seem to me completely misleading for it would give the impression of a skeptical position which urges us to resign. But far from recommending resignation I think there are very important problems which must take the place of the problem of induction and which therefore I suggest to call *successor problems of the problem of induction*.

I will try to relate these successor problems to Carnap's theory of inductive reasoning. This theory was under heavy attack from various sides. The strongest arguments have been brought forward by W. Salmon. Salmon also gave an interesting criticism of Popper whom many people still regard as Carnap's intellectual antipode. A brief examination of one of Salmon's arguments will help to clarify the problems which are at stake. While in my opinion Salmon's criticism of Carnap's *original* theory is basically correct it seems to me that his critical remarks on Popper are based on a misunderstanding.

Therefore I will begin my talk about Carnap with a defense of Popper. Salmon points out that within Popper's theory of testing the key concept is the concept of *corroboration*. In view of the fact that this concept provides 'a method for selecting among unfalsified hypotheses', Salmon (1967a, p. 26) comes to the conclusion that Popper's theory is not properly characterized as 'deductivism'. For 'Popper's theory furnishes a method for selecting hypotheses whose content exceeds that of relevant available basic statements'. 'Corroboration', Salmon says, 'is a nondemonstrative form of inference'. This is a misinterpretation of Popper which paradoxically is partly due to his granting the Popperians too much. Actually, with one single exception, neither Popper nor his students ever told us what they mean by 'corroboration'. The exception mentioned is the second paragraph of Popper (1959, p. 267). The following definition gives a detailed account of Popper's remark (with some slight changes in terminology): 'Corr(B; T)' ('B corroborates T') if

(1) T is a theory
(2) B is the class of accepted observational sentences
(3) the class $T \cup B$ is logically consistent
(4) there exist two disjoint classes R and E such that
  (a) $R \cup E = B$
  (b) $T \cup R \vdash E$
  (c) E is not empty and contains only such elements which are sincere attempts to refute T.[1]

Within the present context we may refrain from entering into a discussion of the vague phrase 'sincere attempt to refute' ('*ernstzunehmender Widerlegungsversuch*').[2] Then we can easily discover the root of Salmon's error. He erroneously believes that exclusively deductive logic is used only insofar as

Popper speaks of falsifiability and falsification. But as a matter of fact it was Popper's intention to define the concept of corroboration exclusively in deductive terms (plus certain terms of elementary set theory). So within Popper's theory '$\vdash$' occurs in two quite different places: first within the definition of falsification and second within the definition of corroboration.

Philosophers of very different persuasions, like Reichenbach, Carnap and Salmon, tried to give an adequate account of induction either on the basis of a frequentist or a logical conception of probability or on pragmatic grounds. Popper was presumably the first one who recognized that we must simply stop seeking for a solution to 'the problem of induction'. Thinking in terms of 'rules of nondemonstrative inference' has become a straitjacket we are called upon to strip off. Popper's concept of corroboration, far from being 'quite distinct from confirmation', as Salmon maintains, is the very first step toward defining a concept of *deductive confirmation*. For this reason Popper's concept ought to be considered as a competitor of Hempel's definition of confirmation (and of various other suggestions, e.g., those discussed by Hempel). Though very different in content, Hempel's and Popper's definitions have the same formal structure insofar as Hempel's concept of confirming evidence also makes use only of the tools of deductive logic. (That this fact has not been realized is presumably due to at least two different factors: first to the prevailing vagueness in the characterization of corroboration and second to Carnap's mistaken assumption that Hempel's concept was intended as a qualitative analogon to his quantitative concept of degree of confirmation. Since that time Hempel's definition has been running under the wrong title 'theories of *inductive* confirmation'.)

I will now try to confront schematically the problem of induction with what I call the *theoretical* successor problem of induction.

The problem of induction might be thought to consist of two questions:

(I_1) What is the precise formulation of the principle of induction?

(I_2) How can we justify this principle?

These two questions are to be replaced by the following ones:

(SI_1^T) What is the precise definition of the concept of confirmation?

(SI_2^T) How can we prove the adequacy of this definition?[3]

Popper's expression 'corroboration' neither designates a successful alternative to a rule of induction nor a new kind of a nondemonstrative rule of inference. Rather it ought to be considered as the name of a metascientific research program consisting of the two questions (SI_1^T) and (SI_2^T). These two questions are the analogies to the problems Tarski was confronted with when defining his concept of truth. But of course there are various differences.

Therefore qualifications have to be made of which I will mention the four most important ones:

(1) Popper's *definition* of corroboration is inadequate though for very different reasons than other attempts to define 'deductive confirmation' are inadequate. As the second question (SI_2^T) can only be raised after an answer – and indeed a correct answer – to the first one has been found, it is still too early to ask the second question. In my opinion deductivism is right but I cannot prove it. If I am not mistaken in my conviction then the first question can be specified to the following one:

(SI'^T_1) What is the precise definition of the concept of *deductive* confirmation?

(2) Truth is a semantic notion, confirmation is a pragmatic one. This makes an essential difference. Up to now we do not even know exactly what adequacy criteria hold for the concept of deductive confirmation. Popper, in this respect following Carnap, rejected some of the adequacy criteria of Hempel, e.g., the criterion of consistency. On the other hand Hempel would certainly criticize the attempted reconstruction of Popper's definition, partly because it satisfies conditions which he like Carnap rejects, e.g., the converse consequence condition, partly, because it violates conditions which he, in this respect diverging in opinion from Carnap, would require as necessary, e.g., the consequence condition.

On the other hand a general agreement on adequacy conditions is urgently needed. If, for instance, somebody objects: 'A concept of deductive confirmation (corroboration) cannot be a guide for life' I would counter: 'Either you mean that the concept is *inadequate*. In this case I can answer you only after your objection is made precise in such a way as to show *why* the concept is inadequate. Or I must refuse your objection because it is too vague to be understood'.

(3) Suppose there is such an entity as the theoretical disposition called 'statistical probability'. In this case the two successor problems to the problem of induction would arise with respect to statistical hypotheses as well. Hacking (1965) has tried to give a definition of comparative confirmation for such hypotheses in terms of likelihood comparison. The definition whose adequacy of course I cannot discuss here convinced me that the alternative 'deductivism-inductivism' is not an exhaustive one. Hacking's definition is not a deductive one because 'likelihood' is not a concept of deductive logic; nor is it an inductive one because likelihoods are not probabilities. And a non-probabilistic concept of confirmation or of support should not be called

'inductive'. It may possibly turn out that the most interesting cases of confirmation are neither deductive ones nor inductive ones, i.e. they are *neither* of the 'Popperian kind' *nor* of the 'Carnapian kind'.

(4) Theoretical evaluations of theories ought to be distinguished from nontheoretical ones. This does not mean that I favor a 'monolithical appraisal of theories', as Lakatos called it. If one believes as I do in the necessity of a many-dimensional appraisal of theories then there are as many successor problems to the so-called problem of induction as there are dimensions of evaluations. To mention only two: the problem of *simplicity* and the problem of *lawlikeness*. If one believes in such a multi-dimensionality then one even encounters a successor problem of higher order. This problem is concerned with the *ranking* of the concepts representing the various dimensions of theoretical appraisals. For instance, it may well be the case that Goodman's problem is a deeper one than the problems of defining 'confirmation' and of giving an adequate account of simplicity. (On the other hand it may turn out that there are rather complicated connections between these aspects so that these problems can be attacked only 'in one single stroke' by what could be called a 'simultaneous recursive procedure of problem solving'.)

Now what about Carnap? Undoubtedly according to Carnap's *original* conviction his theory was intended as a quantitative theory of confirmation based on a concept of inductive probability. The name of this theory 'inductive logic' was chosen because Carnap identified inductive probability with partial implication. It seems to me that Salmon has shown conclusively that the difficulties arising for such a theory are insurmountable. On the whole there are four fatal arguments:

(1) Whenever Hume speaks of logical independence Carnap must speak of partial entailment. Hume would have objected, correctly in my opinion, that Carnap is building up a quasi-Spinozistic world in which there are only implications between two arbitrary states of affairs (propositions) or their negations.

(2) If we substitute a concept of partial entailment based on the Hume-intuition for the Carnapian concept of partial implication then we become involved in a logical conflict with the principle of learning from experience. Although there is, we could say, no formal inconsistency in Carnap's system, as Popper wrongly maintained, this system contains an *intuitive inconsistency*.

(3) Carnap's characterization of the concept of partial implication is circular because, except for the Wittgenstein function C^{+}, Carnap always uses

measured intersections of ranges. Therefore the concept of probability measure is required to explicate partial implication. Carnap tried in an explication in the opposite direction.

(4) As the analysis of the predictive inference shows, Carnap's theory would also become a victim of the insolvability of the Hume problem. Since in $C(H, E) = r$ the proposition E is about the past, H is about the future and the C-statement itself is an analytic proposition of inductive logic, Carnap's claim that inductive logic is a guide of life would be unrealizable.

But these arguments do not show that Carnap's project is doomed to failure. They only prove that this project is in need of a more or less radical reinterpretation.

To this end let us go back to Immanuel Kant's division of the domain of philosophical endeavor into two different fields: *the domain of theoretical reason* and *the domain of practical reason*. All the theories mentioned so far belong to the first domain. Carnap's late theory does not. Applying a terminology used by Kant we could say that the usual theories of confirmation ('deductive' ones as well as 'inductive' ones) tackle problems which are to be subsumed under the heading: *What can we know*? By contrast, Carnap's investigations belong to the family of questions entitled: *How am I to act*? (but not, as Kant had put it: What am I to do?). Many disputes, in particular the so-called Popper-Carnap discussion, were based on a complete misunderstanding, partly produced by Carnap's own description of the aims of his so-called inductive logic. As a matter of fact there is not even a partial overlapping of Carnap's and Popper's domains of research. To be more concrete: While Popper, like most of the other philosophers of science, was only interested in the theoretical appraisals of unverifiable scientific theories Carnap's concern was the fundament of *rational decision making under risk*. This by the way is the deeper reason for the strong parallelism between the theories of Carnap and of the personalists. In particular *both* are *normative* theories. By using Popper's criterion not as a criterion of demarcation between science and metaphysics, but as a criterion of demarcation between descriptive and normative theories, Carnap once came to this conclusion by pointing out that a personalist would not consider an incoherent behavior of people as a falsification of his theory. He would rather declare those people to be irrational. Though I very much dislike using the term 'inductive' for all kinds of theoretical evaluations of hypotheses I not only have no objection against using the name '*inductive reasoning*' to designate the common field of research of the personalists and of Carnap, but it even seems to me that this is indeed the field of induction proper. The phrase 'inductive reasoning' can be taken as a synonym for 'subjective-probabilistic reasoning'. The justification for using the predicate 'inductive' lies in the fact that this kind of reasoning has the structural characteristics of a probability in the technical sense of the word.

What distinguishes Carnap's work from the procedure of the other personalists is the degree of precision arrived at in the first steps of a personalistic probability theory. In Carnap's late theory we find, presumably for the first time, definitions of concepts like 'bet', 'betting system', 'coherence' which meet present standards of mathematical logic. But of course this is an incidental difference. A closer inspection will show something which is much more important, namely, that in spite of all the analogies between their conceptions *the personalist and not the Popperians are the very opponents of Carnap.*

Before coming back to this point let me make a brief remark on *one* of the many technical aspects of Carnap's late work: He abandoned his earlier linguistic approach in favor of a *model theoretical* one. The objects he investigates are not any more formal object languages but *conceptual systems* consisting of individuals, families of attributes and functions. Systems of this kind usually contain much more than could be expressed within a language. With the help of two devices Carnap succeeds in *connecting Tarski semantics with mathematical measure theory*. His first device consists in representing whole models by n-place functions Z based on an indexing of the various entities of his domain. In the simplest case we get an elementary statement of the following type: $Z(m, i) = j$. This means: 'the individual with the index number i has the attribute No. j from the mth family'. The class of all models such that $Z(m, i) = j$ for particular values i, m and j gives the atomic proposition $P_j^m a_i$. (Suppose, e.g., we have only one family, namely, the family of colors, each color represented by a point on the circumference of the unit circle. Furthermore let us assume that the domain of individuals is nondenumerable. Then the class of atomic propositions is of higher power than the power of the continuum.) Carnap's second device consists in *identifying the model functions with the points of the possibility space and taking as the class of propositions the σ-field generated by the class of atomic propositions.* The class of propositions so defined is of course closed with respect to logical connections and quantifications. (But for obvious reasons this definition of 'proposition' gives much more than could be obtained by a recursive definition of 'sentence' with respect to a particular language.) In this way the apparatus of measure theory becomes applicable. In particular, probability measures with this σ-field of propositons as domain can be introduced.

Let us now concentrate on the philosophical aspect. It is important to see clearly the problems Carnap was confronted with. To this end I will try to formulate what I call the *practical* successor problem of induction. The adjective 'practical' is used to remind us that we have moved from the field of theoretical reason into the field of practical reason. We get the following two questions which show that there is a structural analogy between the two families of successor problems:

(SI_1^P) What are the norms holding for rational decisions under risk?

(SI_2^P) How can we justify these norms?

Let us consider for a moment the partial answer to this problem: According to this answer the reasoning on which such rational decisions are based is *probabilistic* by nature. Let us furthermore decide to reserve the term 'inductive' for probabilistic thinking. Then the two questions (SI_i^P) ($i = 1, 2$) are not *successor* problems of induction but *comprise exactly the rational kernel of the traditional problem of induction*. If we put it this way then we must immediately add that the so-called laws of nature are not possible objects of inductive reasoning. Therefore this resurrection of the problem of induction as a normative problem is not at variance with Popper's claim that there exists no theory of inductive confirmation of unverifiable hypotheses.

But there is a real conflict between Carnap and the personalists. They agree only in the first steps. The personalists stop as soon as they have succeeded in justifying the basic axioms of probability theory by deriving them from the requirement of coherence. According to Carnap much more has to be done. There are infinitely many belief functions of adult persons which we would consider as irrational although all of them are normalized measure functions. Thus additional principles of rationality are required.

Now of course Carnap's admonition to look for further principles would be empty if we did not have an idea of how to proceed. Carnap combined his request with the following suggestion: We must not rest content with analyzing belief functions or credence functions of adult rational persons. We should rather dare to make one deeper step from the time-depending manifest credence function to the permanent *dispositional* structure which manifests itself at any time in particular credence functions. Carnap justifies his suggestion with the successes of thinking in dispositions within science where the discovery of more and more general laws goes hand in hand with a replacement of manifest attributes by dispositions. But since in the present case we are confronted with the justification of norms an analogy taken from moral philosophy may be more convincing. Suppose we have to judge two persons A and B from a moral point of view. Let the moral codex be given. It would be very superficial to base our judgment only on the actual behavior of the two persons. *A* may be judged better than *B* but only because he never became involved in difficult conflict situations such as haunted *B*. Hence instead of the overt behavior the *moral character* ought to be made the object of moral judgment. The attribution of moral character amounts to the attribution of dispositions of a certain kind. If we know the moral character of a person we are in a position to derive contrary-to-fact conditionals of the following form: 'If the person *A* got into a situation of such and such a kind he *would* behave in such and such a way'.

Rationality is on a par with morality. That two persons believe the same in the same situation is no proof of the sameness of their degrees of rationality. The investigation of rationality requires the analysis of the *disposition* to form beliefs in various kinds of situations. Carnap gave the function which represents this disposition the name 'credibility'. One could call it a basic philosophical thesis of Carnap that *the transition has to be made from credence to credibility*. To be sure, this transition is a big step. Whether we are willing to perform it depends on our willingness to accept several idealizations from which some philosophers shrink. In order to stimulate our readiness Carnap suggested replacing the rational human being as the object of investigation by a robot. This robot has among other things an infallible memory and is determined in its beliefs by logical deductions and experience only but never by emotions like fear and hope.

Even if one accepts Carnap's concept of credibility one need not accept all of his additional axioms. Actually Carnap facilitated potential criticism of his system by subdividing the additional axioms in different groups according to the procedure of justification used. The five classes of axioms to be added to the basic axioms are the following ones:

(1) The *axiom of regularity*, justified by the requirement of strict coherence;

(2) The *axiom of isomorphism* or of symmetry which claims invariance of a priori probability with respect to finite permutation of individuals;

(3) Further *axioms of invariance* which in Carnap's view exhibit the rational core of the classical principle of indifference. Roughly speaking these axioms tell us that the value of Cred(*H,E*) is independent of the number and of the properties of individuals and attribute families which are not mentioned essentially in *H* or *E*.

(4) The *principle of relevance* which explicates the concept of rational learning from experience.

(5) Two *limit axioms*: the axiom of σ-additivity and the Reichenbach axiom.

In one important respect Carnap's system contains a *liberalization* of his earlier views: There is no axiom which restricts the class of admissible *C*-functions, i.e., the abstract counterparts of the credibility functions, to the class of λ-functions. The λ-family is only *one* possible class of *C*-functions. Whenever one kind of *analogy influence* emerges, a *C*-function has to be chosen which does not belong to the λ-family. On the other hand Carnap took into consideration additional restrictions depending on the domain of application of inductive reasoning. They mirror particular a priori connections which cannot be expressed with the help of analyticity postulates. In the traditional philosophical terminology they would be called synthetic propositions a priori. Carnap gave them the name *phenomenological postulates*.

There are lots of other new results he obtained in the course of his study of attribute spaces. I only mention in passing that he made a fresh start to solve the Goodman paradox. (Ironically Carnap's ideas contain rather a contribution to ordinary language philosophy than to probability theory for he approaches the problem by asking how to talk about individual objects. In his answer he makes a strong distinction between *identifying* and *describing* individuals, the latter based on relative space-time coordinates, the former on absolute ones.)

I will conclude my sketch about Carnap's philosophy of probability with some remarks on three features of this theory which for many people disclose serious defects of Carnap's whole approach: (1) the lack of rules of acceptance and of rejection; (2) the 0-confirmation of laws on any finite evidence; (3) Carnap's failure to single out one particular *C*-function as *the* function representing adequate inductive reasoning.

These three features cease to be disadvantages and even become desirable consequences of Carnap's system if one is prepared to accept the suggested reinterpretation of Carnap's theory. We must remember that in the light of this interpretation Carnap neither wrote an inductive logic nor a theory of partial entailment. He did not even write a quantitative theory of confirmation. He was only concerned with the probabilistic aspect of normative decision theory. Looked at from this point of view we get rather simple answers to the three problems:

(1) Rational action under risk requires the assignment of subjective probability values to the relevant states of nature. If you finally choose the act whose expectation value of desirability is the greatest, this by no means amounts to acting *as if you knew* that one of the states is the real one.

(By the way it seems to me that Carnap's strong dislike of rules of acceptance and of rejection gives an indirect support of my reinterpretation. Otherwise Carnap's position would be somehow incomprehensible. For even a very cautious scientist who shrinks from believing in the truth of any of his projected hypotheses must accept certain hypotheses and reject others for the sake of explanation and prediction.)

(2) Subjective probability is partial belief, and partial belief can be measured by betting behavior. Betting on a hypothesis has sense only *if you can wait for the outcome of the bet*. Betting on an unverifiable hypothesis, e.g., a lawlike statement, does not even make sense. (Presumably we must appeal to mythological conceptions like an omniscient arbitrator in order to explain what 'betting on a law' should mean.) The 0-confirmation of laws is just the way the imperative: 'Thou shalt not bet against the Lord with nonzero betting quotient' articulates itself within Carnap's system.

Lawlike hypotheses which attract the attention of most philosophers of science, certainly of all Popperians, are completely beyond the scope of Carnap's theory.

(3) I called Carnap's theory a *normative* theory. One must be careful in interpreting the adjective 'normative'. The principles of rational reasoning on which rational action is based are not principles which tell you what to do. Metaphorically speaking we could say that Carnap tried to erect *negative normativity walls*. His axioms are intended as principles that ought not to be violated in subjective-probabilistic reasoning. To be sure whatever the axioms may be the number of admissible C-functions will remain infinite. But this only shows that *it is not the task of a theory of inductive reasoning to transform human beings into automatons*. A man would become an automaton if he would have at his disposal one single C-function which he could use as the correct inductive compass in all situations of his life.

I am aware of the fact that the strong Kantian division of the domain of reason in a theoretical and a practical field is an oversimplification. Although theories never become objects of inductive reasoning the results of theoretical reasoning are *of relevance for* inductive reasoning. Accepted theories always become in some way relevant for practice. It seems to be an open problem how one can describe in precise terms the rules which connect the theoretical field with the field of decision theory. Carnap's concept of qualified instance confirmation of laws will best be considered as a first and unsuccessful attempt to formulate such rules. The simplest solution of this problem would perhaps be to relativize all concepts of subjective probability theory to a background knowledge and to incorporate theoretically accepted theories into this background knowledge. Such a procedure would have the advantage that the problem at hand could be shouldered by philosophers of science who toil with problems of confirmation and acceptance. Whether I am right in this assumption I do not know.

NOTES

[1] I am indebted to my colleague, Professor M. Käsbauer, Munich, for giving this reconstruction of the concept of corroboration.

[2] But compare the remarks on this point on p. 88 (plus note 19 on p. 132) and p. 98.

[3] The index 'T' is to remind us that we are dealing with the successor problem in the *theoretical* field.

BIBLIOGRAPHY

Carnap, R., 1950, *Logical Foundations of Probability*, University of Chicago Press, Chicago, second edition, 1962.

Carnap, R., 1952, *The Continuum of Inductive Methods*, University of Chicago Press, Chicago.

Carnap, R., 1959, *Induktive Logik und Wahrscheinlichkeit*, bearbeitet von W. Stegmüller, Springer, Wien.

Carnap, R., 1962, 'The Aim of Inductive Logic', in: *Logic, Methodology and Philosophy of Science, Proceedings of the International Congress* (ed. by E. Nagel, P. Suppes and A. Tarski), Stanford University Press, Stanford, pp. 303-318

Carnap, R., 1959-1964, *An Axiom System for Inductive Logic*, Manuscript, 503 pp.

Carnap, R., 1968-1970, *A Basic System for Inductive Logic*, Manuscript, 371 pp.

Hacking, I., 1965, *Logic of Statistical Inference*, Cambridge University Press, Cambridge, England.

Hempel, C.G., 1945, 'Studies in the Logic of Confirmation (I)', *Mind* **54**, 1-26.

Hempel, C.G., 1945, 'Studies in the Logic of Confirmation (II)', *Mind* **54**, 97-121.

Popper, K.R., 1934, *Logik der Forschung*, Springer, Wien, third edition, 1969.

Popper, K.R., 1959, *The Logic of Scientific Discovery*, Hutchinson, London.

Popper, K.R., 1963, 1969, *Conjectures and Refutations. The Growth of Scientific Knowledge*, Routledge and Kegan Paul, London.

Salmon, W.C., 1967a, *The Foundations of Scientific Inference*, University of Pittsburgh Press, Pittsburgh.

Salmon, W.C., 1967b, 'Carnap's Inductive Logic', *The Journal of Philosophy* **64**, 725-739.

Salmon, W.C., 1969, 'Partial Entailment as a Basis for Inductive Logic', in: *Essays in Honor of Carl G. Hempel*, (ed. by N. Rescher), Reidel, Dordrecht, pp. 47-82.

Stegmüller, W., 1969, *Probleme und Resultate der Wissenschaftstheorie und Analytischen Philosophie*. Vol I: *Wissenschaftliche Erklärung und Begründung*, Springer, Berlin.

Stegmüller, W., 1970, *Probleme und Resultate der Wissenschaftstheorie und Analytischen Philosophie*. Vol. II: *Theorie und Erfahrung*, Springer, Berlin.

Stegmüller, W., 1971, 'Das Problem der Induktion: Humes Herausforderung und moderne Antworten' in: *Neue Aspekte der Wissenschaftstheorie* ed. by H. Lenk, Vieweg, Braunschweig, pp. 13-74. Appears in translation as Chapter 4 of this book.
Stegmüller, W., 1973, *Personelle und statistische Wahrscheinlichkeit*, Springer, Berlin.
Stegmüller, W., 1973, *Statistisches Schließen, Statistische Begründung, Statistische Analyse*, Springer, Berlin.
Stegmüller, W., 1973, *Theorienstrukturen und Theoriendynamik*, Springer, Berlin.

CHAPTER 6

LOGICAL UNDERSTANDING AND THE DYNAMICS OF THEORIES

Kuhn's work on scientific revolutions represents the greatest existing challenge to today's theory of science. It has also been viewed as such by several philosophers. Yet, so far, no satisfactory response seems to have successfully answered it.

Kuhn's conception of science has deeply disturbed most of the philosophers who have come to grips with his ideas. His conception seems to question the very basic presupposition of *any* theory of science, namely, that the natural sciences represent a *rational* undertaking. This fact can clearly be seen by the way in which Watkins and Lakatos distinguish Kuhn's position from that of three others, viz. Hume, Carnap, and Popper respectively. According to Hume, the natural sciences employ inductive methods. Nevertheless, as Hume says, the progress of these sciences is irrational to the extent that these methods cannot be logically justified. Modern inductivists, among them especially Carnap, have tried to provide a rational interpretation for inductive inference. In such a view, the natural sciences develop in an inductive and rational way. For Popper, on the other hand, so-called inductive reasoning is a philosophical will-o'-the-wisp. Scientific methods of testing can be characterized by resorting exclusively to concepts of deductive logic: the natural sciences follow a rational, though non-inductive course; it is by the application of deductive methods of testing that rationality comes into play.

Kuhn's view represents quite a radical departure from any of these views. Together with Popper he shares the conviction that there are no inductive methods; likewise, he agrees with Hume's view that scientific progress is not at all rational. *Such, at least, is the picture which Kuhn's critics draw from his conception*, which, in effect, says that historical studies have allegedly shown that even the most exact natural sciences, e.g., physics, are such that neither inductive methods nor any criteria of rationality seem to play a part.

Some philosophers have sought solace in the thought that the history of science is a discipline quite different from that of the philosophy and logic of science, and that the only conclusion that needs to be drawn from Kuhn's descriptions and analyses is that there is little, if any, point of contact between these two disciplines even as regards their results.

But to play down the antithesis in such fashion is quite untenable. It cannot be claimed that no points of contact exist. In fact, what we really have here is a situation of complete, unmitigated opposition. Consider, for example, the form of scientific undertaking which Kuhn designates as *normal science*. This would have been quite compatible with Popper's position, had Kuhn arrived at a conclusion like the following: inventors of new theories take no great pleasure in testing their ideas critically. Such tests are undertaken instead by their competitors. If the test turns out negative, this is often simply disregarded by the former, etc.

What Kuhn actually says, however, is that *not one single case* so far uncovered by historical studies has even *the slightest resemblance* to the falsification model. Kuhn too concedes that a theory can be abandoned in the face of empirical counterinstances; but this is simply a consequence of the fact that the scientist is forced to change his career when he is no longer able to cope with the counterinstances; for, according to Kuhn, recalcitrant experience can never discredit the theory but only the person holding it.

Popper concedes that he has directed his attention exclusively to what Kuhn calls 'extraordinary research', and that in so doing he has completely overlooked the phenomenon of normal science. But Popper emphasizes at the same time, however, that the normal scientist, as Kuhn describes him, is a person one ought to be sorry for. He is a person who accepts uncritically everything that he has been taught and who demands the same uncritical attitude on the part of his students.

From this observation, the followers of Popper's school have concluded that normal science is something that must be overcome. It becomes thus necessary to design a *normative methodology* in such a way that by following its rules we can banish normal science and ensure a permanent scientific revolution.

It would be a mistake to think that the difference of opinion between Kuhn and his opponents is merely confined to the phenomenon of normal science. The revolutionary changes which follow periods of extraordinary research are described by Kuhn in such a way that here again we can hardly avoid the impression that they involve completely irrational processes. In Kuhn's view there never is a case where the old theory fails in the face of experience and *on account of such failure* leaves the way open for a new successful theory. Rather, the old theory is *directly dislodged*, regardless of experience, *by the new theory*. And it is Kuhn's view that neither in the beginning nor at the successful termination of such a process of dislodging do logic and experience play any role whatsoever. Rather, the originators of the new theory undergo experiences which resemble Gestalt-shifts and which lead them *to look at the world with new eyes*. And it is their conviction, strengthened by such experiences, that the new theory is correct; this spurs them to advocate its dissemination with quasi-religious fanaticism. This is not accomplished by resorting to arguments but is launched, instead, with the help of persuasion and propaganda. Opposition against what is new comes mainly from scholars of the older generation who realize much more clearly than the mostly young innovators that the new theory is, in its present form, plagued with even worse problems than the old theory which is under fire. This notwithstanding, even their opposition is broken; this is to be attributed to the fact that the scientific revolutionaries are assisted by nature itself, namely, by the biological process familiar to us all by the name of 'death': the older generation of scientists ultimately dies out and, as a result, the victory of the revolutionaries is thus rendered complete.

The call for a normative methodology we have just mentioned, was not the only response that was made to Kuhn's challenge. The critiques of Kuhn's arguments range from the accusation of a one-sided and mistaken description of historical processes over assertions to the effect that he is obviously blind to the rational aspect in the history of science, to the claim that he is completely incompetent in matters of history.

The person who maintains such an attitude or any variation thereof cannot be logically refuted. There are, however, two things indicating that such a response is taking an all too easy way out: first of all, the explicandum which the logician has at his disposal does not merely consist of his personal knowledge and intuitive ideas about the sciences but derives in no small measure from what he learns about them from historians of science. Secondly, one can hardly deny that Kuhn is much better versed in the history of science, in particular in patterns of thought unfamiliar to our present-day scientific thinking, than those who call themselves philosophers or theoreticians of science. The present discussion at any rate is motivated by the conviction that what the philosopher of science must do is not to contest, dispute, or dismiss Kuhn's principle theses but, instead, *take into account and logically process* the claims of a competent historian of science.

According to the interpretation advocated here, Kuhn, in contrast to his critics, is right on almost every essential point. With the help of the concepts of a theory, holding a theory, and the relationship between theories, which will be outlined here, we want to show that we can gain a logical understanding of the processes described by Kuhn; such an understanding will enable us to show that the claim that Kuhn ascribes an irrational character to the natural sciences is incorrect.

Of course countless interesting details about the dynamics of science can only come to light by a combination of historical, psychological, and sociological investigations. What is here claimed is simply that the rational character of *science* cannot be clarified via such studies *alone*. No matter how extensive our empirical analyses of what has taken place in a scientific revolution, we still cannot answer the question as to whether these revolutions constitute scientific progress or involve a setback which, for some time (perhaps always), has mistakenly been interpreted as progress.

I must first make a few comments about the two mistakes which, in my view, have blemished the analysis of theories given so far by logicians. Both mistakes are rather deeply rooted in basic assumptions which if abandoned might occasion serious (psychological) difficulties. The first mistake consists in *imitating the procedure of the metamathematician*. 'Metamathematics' is here understood not in the special sense of 'proof-theory', but rather in the much more general sense that includes all the metatheoretical investigations of mathematical disciplines. The second mistake consists in what might be called *the monistic conception of scientific rationality*. Both of these mistakes are closely connected.

In metamathematics *theories* are construed *as sentence classes* (finite or infinite, axiomatized or unaxiomatized, axiomatizable or unaxiomatizable). This identification has proven fruitful since the problems which arise there such as, for example, consistency, decidability, completeness, the independence of axioms, etc. are reducible to questions about the existence of inference or consequence relations between sentences (propositions). But, as we shall see, such an identification serves poorly when it comes to clarifying, for example, the nature of a physical theory. We will therefore abandon the *statement view of theories*, as this position might be called. Only by abandoning this conception and by introducing a concept of physical theories according to which a theory *does not* represent a sentence class or a class of propositions are we in a position to throw some light on the phenomenon which Kuhn calls normal science. Normal scientists, i.e., those scientists who feel themselves committed to a particular tradition, hold one and the same theory. It is nevertheless inappropriate to construe holding a theory as a belief in a class of sentences, the acceptance of these sentences, or again as the conviction that these sentences are correct; for the persons holding one and the same theory attach quite *different convictions* and quite *different hypothetical assumptions* to it.

The second mistake is connected with the first in the following way: in the mathematical domain, rationality is signaled by correctness of logical reasoning. If empirical theories are construed as sentence classes, the question immediately arises as to what kind of reasoning then corresponds to the logical reasoning in mathematics. According to some, it is *inductive inference*, whereas according to others it is the *deductive method of strict testing*. According to Kuhn's conception of science, however, there is here absolutely no counterpart; Kuhn's answer to such a question seems to be: *none*. And this again seems to lend support to the thesis that Kuhn is ascribing a totally irrational attitude to natural scientists. If, on the other hand, the statement view is abandoned, then one can no longer even formulate the problem of rationality in this way. We should not pretend we are metamathematicians who by chance, so to speak, happen to be concerned with empirical instead of mathematical sentence classes. Only if one sets out from this as-if-position, which, as will be shown, is inappropriate, is one forced to answer the question of what kind of logical relation between sentences establishes the rationality of the empirical sciences. If, on the other hand, this fiction is dropped, then not only is it no longer necessary to establish the rationality of the empirical sciences via some concept of specifically empirical argumentation, but one is no longer even forced to accept that there is only one *single* kind of scientific rationality.

As a matter of fact, we will try to replace the monistic conception of rationality by a dualistic one: the normal scientist in Kuhn's sense engages in quite different activities than the man engaged in extraordinary research; the criteria of rationality for the former are quite different from those involved in the latter.

The logical understanding that we are aiming at will render possible, in a certain sense, a more radical critique of the programs of normative methodology than, for example, Feyerabend's. Whereas Feyerabend warns against the consequences of such methodologies, we, instead, *contest the very presupposition upon which they are based*. Their advocates, for example, do *not* start out from the trivial fact that in the empirical sciences we meet with irrational modes of conduct. (We encounter narrow-mindedness, dogmatism, and intolerance in all human endeavors: so why not then also in science?) They are instead firmly convinced that certain forms of science are *as such* irrational and, hence, must be eliminated. According to Popper, for example, the normal scientist *is just like* a narrow minded dogmatist. The explication of the concept of normal science in terms of the concept of holding a theory will enable us to see where Popper has gone wrong. Such an explication will also show that a theory is, as a matter of fact, very *insensitive to possible falsifying experience* and that it is, therefore, a mistake to believe that such a feature is the result of an objectionable immunization strategy and, hence, a corruption of rational scientific thinking. Perhaps the reader will now begin to understand what was meant by saying that our task is to replace the *distorted picture* of Kuhn's conception of science by a more adequate one.

The conceptual apparatus for gaining such an understanding has been provided essentially by J.D. Sneed.[1] We will briefly describe it here. It must be emphasized, however, that a number of Sneed's special assumptions such as, for example, his criterion for the theoreticity of terms *does not* form an essential part of our subsequent attempt at a reconstruction.

So as to arrive at a uniform formulation, we will confine ourselves to theories which are, on the whole, formulated in quantitative language; that is, those which only permit descriptions by means of functions (numerical, real, etc.). All such theories can be thought of as formulated in axiomatic form. The simplest method of axiomatizing a theory consists in defining a set-theoretic predicate which describes the mathematical structure characteristic of this theory. Thus, for example, the axiomatization of group theory is achieved by introducing the set-theoretic predicate 'is a group'. In much the same way, the Newtonian version of particle mechanics can be axiomatized by defining the set-theoretic predicate 'is a classical particle mechanics'.

The content of the set-theoretical predicate in terms of which a physical theory is axiomatized is to be called the *mathematical structure of the theory*. One arrives at *empirical* claims by applying this structure to physical systems. Let a be such a system (e.g., the solar system). Let S be a mathematical structure (e.g., the structure expressed by the predicate 'is a classical particle mechanics'). If no further complications would arise, then the empirical statements formulated with the help of a physical theory would all have the form: 'a is an S'; for this statement expresses exactly the hypothetical assumption that the physical system a is an entity having the mathematical structure S. As long as applications are involved such a mathematical structure will occasionally be called *the fundamental law of the theory*; for this structure is basic in the sense that it recurs identically in all of its applications.

The reason why things are not that simple is due to the fact that physics uses *theoretical* quantities. There has been much speculation about the nature of theoretical functions. Most of the attempts at clarifying them have not succeeded due to the fact that one has tried to follow a logico-linguistic approach; but it is exactly this imitation of the logician's method of constructing formal languages that is at fault. Guided by intuitively plausible considerations the vocabulary of the scientific language was divided into observational terms and theoretical terms. All further constructions and analyses were designed to show that, and in which manner, the theoretical terms obtain an indirect and partial interpretation through the observational terms which alone are fully understandable.

In contrast to this method which marks off the theoretical quantities only negatively (i.e., as *not* observable, *not* fully understandable, etc.), Sneed introduces a criterion of theoreticity that demarcates the theoretical quantities positively, i.e., by citing the role these quantities play in the application of the theory: in every application *they are measured in a theory-dependent way*. We have a theory-dependent measurement of a quantity if the determination of the values of this quantity requires that there exists a successful application of *just that theory in which this quantity occurs*. In the Newtonian version of classical particle mechanics, for example, both of the functions *force* and *mass*, and only these two, are, according to this criterion, theoretical quantities. Sneed's criterion of theoreticity does not rest, consequently, on a linguistic convention, that is, on an arbitrary decision on the part of a philosophically minded logician of science. Moreover, it is not burdened by the epistemological problems of the observation language. (That does not mean that the concept of the observation language is thereby rendered worthless, but that *for the purpose of introducing the dichotomy: theoretical – non-theoretical* such a concept is not necessary.) Finally the theory with reference to which a quantity is theoretical must always be given since one and the same function may be theoretical relative to one theory and yet not theoretical relative to another theory.

Behind a theoretical function lies hidden the danger of a paradox. In calculating its values one is referred to other successful applications of the theory; but in order to test the claim that the other application of the theory has been successful, one must again calculate the values of this function and in so doing one is reverting back again to a successful application of the theory, etc. In order to escape this circle or an infinite regress, one has to resort to *Ramsey's solution* of the problem of theoretical functions.

Apropos to this, a few terminological points: everything which the mathematical structure S applies to will be called a model of S. Suppose that in the description of S there occur functions which turn out to be theoretical when applied. We leave aside such functions and call all the entities which can be described in terms of the non-theoretical functions remaining in S *partial possible models of* S. If, now, the discarded theoretical functions are again added to the partial model, the result is called a *theoretical enrichment* of the partial possible model. It can then be meaningfully asked of this *theoretical enrichment* whether or not it is a model of *S*. The physical system *a* is described solely by means of the non-theoretical functions. If the mathematical structure *S*, under which it is supposed to be subsumed, contains theoretical functions, then *a* is merely a partial possible model of *S*. The original attempt at using the theory to make an empirical claim about *a*, which took the form '*a* is an *S*', must, therefore, be replaced by the following statement:

(I) *There exists a theoretical enrichment x of a which is a model of S.*

By means of this statement the aforementioned danger is thus eliminated. To test the correctness of (I) there is no need to calculate any of the values of the theoretical functions; one must simply ascertain whether the *non-theoretical* functions used in the description of *a* satisfy the condition imposed by (I). With respect to empirical content, on the other hand, statement (I) is demonstrably no weaker than the original attempt which was plagued by a paradox. (The difference between Ramsey and Sneed as regards the interpretation of (I) is the following: according to Ramsey the empirical content of a theory *can* be rendered by a statement of the form (I), whereas according to Sneed the content *must* be rendered by (I). Thus, on Sneed's view, it is an abstract statement of this form that the physicists *really mean* when they employ theoretical quantities in their claims. Whether or not Sneed is right in this is of no consequence for what follows.)

Let's call (I) the *primitive form* of the Ramsey-formulation of the empirical content of a theory. This primitive form must be transformed into the *final versions* of the Ramsey-formulation by means of various modifications. One must first get rid of the fictitious supposition that a physical theory has just a single (so to speak 'cosmic') application. Almost every such theory has *various intended applications*. Classical particle mechanics, for example, has, inter alia, the following applications: the solar system, certain of its sub-systems (such as the earth-moon system), the tides, the pendulum, etc. These applications, however, do not stand completely isolated but are linked to each other by means of constraints which are placed on the theoretical functions. *One* such constraint states that one and the same object occurring in different applications is assigned the same function value each time. (Thus, for example, the planet Earth has the same mass regardless of whether it is considered as an element of the solar system or as an element of the moon-earth system.) For clarity's sake this condition will be called the identity condition. As a more exact analysis will show, even the following statement describes a constraint for the mass function, although, in ordinary language, it sounds more like a particular natural law: 'mass is an extensive quantity.' Both of these facts, i.e., the existence of several applications of a theory as well as the constraints connecting these applications to each other, raise considerably the theory's power of prediction and explanation. Via a miniature theory Sneed was able to show that the intrinsic property condition alone produces substantial results even in elementary cases.[2] A third modification of the Ramsey-formulation is required by virtue of the fact that, though the *fundamental law* of the theory represented by the aforementioned mathematical structure S holds *in all of its* applications, there are furthermore, as a rule, *special* laws which hold in *certain* applications. Each of these laws can be represented by a specific restriction on the structure S. (As examples of special laws in classical particle mechanics we may cite the Law of Gravitation or Hooke's Law.) Thus by a threefold modification of the method used to arrive at statement (I), one reaches the final version of the Ramsey-formulation. The object about which the empirical claim is made is now no longer a specific physical system (partial possible model) a, but a set $\mathfrak{a}$ of partial models of the structure S. The content of such an assertion may be rendered, for example, in the following words:

(II) *There exists a theoretical enrichment $\mathfrak{E}$ of the set $\mathfrak{a}$ of physical systems to models of the mathematical structure S such that the theoretical functions employed in this enrichment satisfy a class of given constraints, and certain proper subsets of $\mathfrak{a}$ can be enriched to models for a specific restriction of the structure S.*

This final version of the Ramsey-formulation has the following feature in common with its primitive form: within it the empirical content of a physical theory at a particular time is rendered by *a single non-fractionable statement*. It is therefore permissible to use the definite article and to speak of *the* empirical claim of the theory characterized by the mathematical structure S. As we shall see later on, this empirical assertion should be furnished with a time index t, since various empirical claims of form (II) can be formulated with one and the same theory at different times.

What we have just said already contains implicitly the claim that a physical theory is not to be identified with the empirical content it may have at a particular time. (Thus, the abandonment of the statement view of theories *does not* consist in the fact that a theory is construed as *one* statement of the form (II) instead of a *class* of statements.) Such an identification would be most inappropriate. For in that case, the slightest change in (II), e.g., in a special law pertaining to very specific applications of the theory, would have to be considered a change of theory. As against this, it would be much more consonant with linguistic usage and conducive to a more appropriate analysis both from a logical as well as from a historical point of view, if one simply says that *the theory remains constant while the empirical hypotheses of form (II) built with its help change*. It is thus a question of introducing a theory concept that will enable us to say that the followers of a particular scientific tradition (e.g., the Aristotelian physicists, the Newtonians, the Quantum-physicists) hold *one and the same theory*, even though quite different convictions and divergent hypothetical assumptions are associated with this theory from time to time and even from person to person. The concept of holding a theory employed here might then serve *as an explicans for Kuhn's concept of normal science*. The insensitivity of a theory vis-à-vis recalcitrant experience, which Kuhn so emphatically stressed, is thus not the result of immunization strategies on the part of theoreticians, but an innate property of theories themselves.

Can these vague intuitions be made precise? The answer is *yes*. The first step toward this objective consists *in describing in a purely set-theoretic way* the sub-structures which are used in claims of form (II). These will be briefly sketched.[3]

In a theory we can distinguish between a *logical component and an empirical component*. The structures we have just mentioned concern the former. Let us look a little more closely at the structures belonging to the logical component! The most important among them is the mathematical structure S which can be characterized set-theoretically as the *set M of models satisfying this structure*; we have likewise already cited the corresponding *set of partial possible models*. The members of this set are the physical systems which can be considered as potential candidates for the application of the theory in so far as they can be described exclusively by means of the non-theoretical functions. Hence, every partial possible model becomes a *possible model* by adding the theoretical functions occurring in the mathematical structure S regardless of whether the resulting structure is likewise a model of S.

To every possible model is assigned its corresponding partial possible model by means of a reduction function which serves no other purpose but to 'cancel out' the theoretical functions. Lastly we have still to name the *constraints* which have already been mentioned. All of these can also be defined in a set-theoretic way.

The *logical components* of a theory should have exactly these five constituents: the set of partial possible models, the set of possible models, the reduction function, the set of models (the mathematical structure of the theory), the set of constraints. The ordered quintuplet of these constituents is to be called the *core* of the theory.

Before we turn to the empirical components, let us cast a glance at the final version of the Ramsey-formulation of the empirical content of a theory so that it becomes clear that the structural core of a theory does not yet contain the whole conceptual apparatus employed in (II). In (II) *special laws* which hold only in certain applications also appear, and they are all obtained by appropriately restricting the mathematical structure S. Suppose now that at the very same time that the empirical claim (II) is made, we add these *special laws* to the core. It must then be specified more exactly *which* of these laws hold in *which* applications. This can be done with the help of a *correspondence relation*. (This relation is, obviously, not a function, because on the one hand *several* special laws hold, as a rule, in one and the same physical system, while, on the other hand, the same special law may be valid in *several* intended applications. The only requirement is that it does not hold in all applications, for otherwise it would become a part of the fundamental law.) The result of adding these two entities to the core of a theory is called an *expanded core*, or, respectively, an *expansion of the core* (briefly: *core expansion*) E of this theory.

The fact that we identify the logical component of a physical theory not with the expanded core but exclusively with the structural core itself, is dictated by the goal of our explication; for concerning the logical aspect, the course of normal science in Kuhn's sense is characterized by the fact that the core of the theory is indeed retained, but nevertheless expanded at various times by the addition of *different* laws. Empirical corroboration (progress in normal science) and empirical falsification (setback in normal science) involve then only these special laws, which at a later time may either be retained or be replaced by new ones. The score of the theory is not subject to such change dictated by experience. As may already have become evident by now, this fact is the source of the considerable stability of theories vis-à-vis the danger of potential falsification.

In order to arrive at the *empirical component* of the theory it's best we take as our point of departure an empirical claim of form (II). The name $\mathscr{A}$ occurring in it designates the set of intended applications which the researchers accept at the time this claim is made, i.e., the set of physical systems to which the conditions cited in (II) have been claimed to apply. We weaken the claim (II) by neglecting the special laws and replacing the name $\mathscr{A}$ with a variable. By so doing we obtain a sentential form. Let us call the sets of physical systems which satisfy this sentential form *the class A of possible intended sets of applications of the theory*. This class might be called the *empirical framework* which is laid down by theories with the core K. The reason for speaking here of the theory itself is that since we are neglecting the special laws, it is the core alone that is decisive in determining the class A. To put it more exactly: one can define a function which when applied to any core K yields the pertinent class A just described.[4] In a similar way we can specify a function which yields a class (substantially narrower, as a rule) when applied to an expanded structural core E.[5] Although, strictly speaking, we have here two different functions, let us for simplicity's sake give both of them the same label 'application of'. The class A is thus either the application of K or the application of E.

It would not be enough to identify the empirical component of a theory with its empirical framework. For we still need the fact that this framework can be 'filled in' empirically, and this is tantamount to saying that there is a set I of physical systems which is an element of A. One must furthermore require that the elements of the set I satisfy certain conditions; these details will, however, be omitted here.[6] Since our theory concept does not include special laws, we at first identify a *physical theory* with the ordered pair $\langle K;A \rangle$ consisting of the core of the theory as well as the application A of K and require the existence of a set I which is an element of A. We have indeed used the expression 'theory' often. Yet this method of introducing the concept of a theory is in no way circular, for previously the expression 'theory' was used *only in certain contexts* like 'empirical claim of a theory', 'core of a theory', 'expanded core of a theory'. What a theory itself is, was thus left open and has only now been stated explicitly.

The concepts introduced above permit us to express the *propositional content* of the empirical statement (II) by an atomic set-theoretic proposition. To see this one need only remember that (1) the set designated in (II) by $\mathfrak{a}$ is nothing else but the set I of the intended applications of the theory accepted at time t by the speaker; and (2) the mathematical structure S, modified and restricted as indicated, is nothing else but an expanded structural core E of the theory. The propositional content of (II) can therefore be rendered by the atomic proposition:

(III) *I is an element of the application of E.*

We can now proceed to realize the above program and explicate the concept of holding a theory. This will be accomplished in two steps. In a preliminary step we will introduce the concept of holding a theory in the semantical sense while in a second step we will introduce the concept of holding a theory in a pragmatic sense. This second step should enable us to explicate, at least roughly, Kuhn's concept of normal science.[7] We say that a person (or group of persons) *p holds (hold) a theory T in the semantical sense* at the historical time *t*, if *T* is a theory in the sense given and if, furthermore, there exists an expansion *E* of the core of this theory as well as a set *I* of physical systems such that *p* at time *t* knows the following three things: (1) *I* is an *element* of the application of *E*; (2) this *E* is the strongest known core expansion to whose application *I* belongs; (3) *I* is a *maximal* set in the application of *E*. The expression '*p* knows that *X*' should mean here the same as '*p* believes that *X*, and furthermore *p* has at his disposal empirical data which support this conviction'. (The concept of knowledge so introduced serves as a linguistic abbreviation and it also isolates the problem of confirmation that enters into the concept of support.)

So as to be in a position to carry out the second step of the explication, we must first turn briefly to the concept of a paradigm. Instead of speaking of theories Kuhn, almost without exception, speaks of *paradigms*. The fact that he shuns the concept of theory may rest on psychological grounds: he would like to prevent his readers from thinking of *formalized* theories. (When philosophers of science employ the word 'theory' they almost inevitably think of formalized theories.) The fact that Kuhn resorts to the concept of paradigm as introduced by Wittgenstein can be explained on grounds that both Wittgenstein and Kuhn share the opinion that in the non-mathematical domain concepts are often, if not exclusively, introduced by the *method of paradigmatic examples*. In response to the question as to what a game is, one cites paradigmatic examples. Analogously one cannot, according to Kuhn, answer the question as to what a Newtonian physicist (a relativity theoretician, a quantum physicist) is in any other way except by giving paradigmatic examples of the activities of Newtonian physicists (relativity theoreticians, quantum physicists). We will confine ourselves to applying the concept 'paradigm' only to a quite specific component of a theory, namely, the *set of intended applications of the theory*.

There are, in principle, three possibilities for determining the set *I* of intended applications of a theory at a given time.[8] The first consists in presenting this set in an explicitly extensional way, i.e., by enumerating all the applications of the theory by means of a list. The second possibility consists in defining a characteristic which is a necessary and sufficient condition for belonging to *I*. The third possibility consists in giving *typical, i.e., paradigmatic, examples belonging to I*. This third type of case may be realized most often in the natural sciences. Thus if someone were asked, for example, to what sorts of things classical particle mechanics may be applied, one would today give the same answer that Newton would have given, namely, enumerate the paradigmatic examples of this theory such as the solar system and some of its sub-systems (e.g., the Earth-Moon system, Jupiter and its moons), the pendulum, the tides, free falling bodies near the surface of the Earth.

The (weak) semantical concept of holding a theory can now be strengthened into a (strong) pragmatic concept of holding a theory by referring explicitly to the historical origin of the theory as well as to the manner of presenting I just described. Moreover, the 'belief in progress' can be embedded into this concept. To be more exact, one may say: a person (or group of persons) *p holds a theory T at time t in the pragmatic sense* if T is a theory held by p at t in the semantical sense (in accordance with the above definition); if, furthermore, there exists a person p_0 (the 'creator' of the theory, e.g., Newton) who has laid down the intended applications of T by means of a paradigmatic set of examples I_0; and if, furthermore, p accepts this paradigmatic set of examples so that I_0 is a subset of the applications I of T chosen by him at t; if, furthermore, p is convinced that there is a restriction of the core E of the theory chosen such that I is an element of the application of this restriction; and if p, moreover, is convinced that there is a genuine expansion of the set I which is an element of the application of E. The next to last stipulation might be thought of as the *theoretical belief in progress* on the part of p since it expresses the conviction that the behavior of the physical system I may some day be better explained, i.e., by more and more exact laws. The last stipulation might be called the *empirical belief in progress* of p; for it expresses p's conviction that further applications of the theory will be found.

We now direct our attention to two important consequences which follow from our decision to choose this pragmatic concept of holding a theory as an explicans of Kuhn's concept of normal science. The first consists in the fact that persons who hold one and the same theory may espouse *mutually incompatible hypotheses*. The differences of opinion may even proceed along two different dimensions; on the one hand, one and the same core can be employed for different expansions and, on the other hand, holding a theory is compatible with the fact that the views about the sets of physical systems to which the theory is applicable differ widely. So as to be able to say that in this second case too the same theory is employed, the advocates of the mutually divergent views must simply select the same paradigmatic initial sets.

A further consequence is logical support for the thesis so emphatically advocated by Kuhn with regard to the *immunity of theories against 'recalcitrant' experience*. Empiricists as well as Critical Rationalists are known to share the view that such stability of theories in the face of 'falsifying experience' can only be achieved at the price of a certain intellectual dishonesty, namely, by resorting to ad hoc immunization strategies. As opposed to this, it can now easily be shown that a physical theory *is immune* to potential falsification in no less than three respects and need not be 'immunized'.

In order to arrive at an empirical claim of a theory, i.e., at a statement of form (II), it is necessary that the scientist holding the theory use the core of this theory for an hypothetical core expansion E. Should the empirical statement (II) be empirically falsified, that only means that the scientist did not succeed in his attempt to expand K to E. No matter how many such attempts end up in failure, they cannot serve as proof for the uselessness of the core and, hence, of the theory. *It is, therefore, not Kuhn, but his rationalist and empiricist opponents who here commit a logical error when they speak of the falsification of theories*. It is the fallacy of concluding from a finite number of unsuccessful expansion attempts that a successful expansion of the core is impossible. This involves a logical error because the number of candidates which may qualify as expansions of a given core is potentially infinite. Many of Kuhn's claims which have provoked astonishment and utter dismay – since they seem to lay emphasis on the complete irrationality of the behavior of researchers within the context of normal science – can here be given an easy explanation as, for example, the following: the inability to find a solution with the help of his theory *discredits only the scientist* but never the theory; also that (in the context of normal science), the only way of giving up a theory because of counterinstances is to *give up science as a career*.

For an interpretation of the first claim let us start out from the additional premise (which in the context of the tradition of normal science is always satisfied) that the theory which the scientist holds has been successful in the past, i.e., that the core of this theory has been successfully expanded. Should, then, an expansion E of the core K not succeed, it is actually not at all unreasonable but the most natural thing in the world *to place the blame for the failure not on the theory, whose core is K, but on the scientist who has attempted this unsuccessful expansion of the core*. This is the most natural thing in the world because it is in fact well known that this theory has been successful in the past: the unsuccessful scientist who, in spite of this, insists that the failure must lie with the theory behaves, therefore, as Kuhn says 'like a poor carpenter who blames his tools.'

In order to interpret the second claim we assume that the statement refers to 'normal scientists' as men who have to earn their living by working ('physically' or 'mentally'). The scientists who in Kuhn's sense are engaged in *extraordinary research are those scholars who design new cores. Normal scientists*, on the other hand, are not in a position to carry out such a task; in our terminology *they must limit themselves to holding a given theory and to using the core of this theory for making hypothetical expansions*. When these individuals do not succeed in using their theory, *what else are they to do but change their profession*? The analogy with the working man is here even more appropriate: if a carpenter is confronted by a job which he can no longer master with the tools which up to now were adequate and if he furthermore does not have the talent to invent a better tool (and fails to find anybody else who is up to the task), then, unless he wants to starve, he must change his profession.[9]

The astonishing thing about Kuhn's metaphors, such as those we have just mentioned, is not that he describes the behavior of scientists in such a way as to rule out any interpretation of this behavior as rational, but that he is right on target each and every time even though he did not have at his disposal the conceptual apparatus which would have made possible a logical understanding of the processes he describes.[10]

The immunity of a theory we have just described holds with respect to *every* application. The one we are about to discuss next holds only for those applications which do not belong to the paradigmatic set of examples. On this account it is stronger than the former case: it (the theory) remains unaffected *even if whole generations of scientists fail to apply the theory successfully* and not just single researchers. In such a case, the decision will some day be made to remove the domain in question from the class of intended applications of the theory. Thus, once the conviction had spread among the experts that Newton's hope of being able to explain light phenomena in terms of classical particle mechanics could not be fulfilled, they did not declare Newton's theory to be falsified, but concluded, instead, that light does not consists of particles.

The philosophers who often like to call themselves Critical Rationalists presume that such behavior, should it turn out to be the rule, betrays a dubious pseudo-scientific attitude, a *tendency toward the autoverification of a theory*. What is actually the case is something quite different, viz. an adherence to *the rule of autodetermination for the domain of application of a theory*. This method lets the theory itself decide on its applications, i.e., on what is or what is not an application. Following such a rule is perfectly consonant with a rational attitude, since, in distinction to the cases studied in mathematical logic and metamathematics, membership in a domain of application involves an unavoidable vagueness because the paradigmatic examples do not unambiguously lay down, *independent of the theory*, what belongs and what does not belong to its applications.

A Rationalist might claim here that it is exactly this shortcoming that needs to be remedied. And this can only be done by demanding that every theoretician sharply define necessary and sufficient conditions for membership in the class of intended applications of this theory. Such a requirement would correspond to Popper's conception; for Popper does indeed demand that, in a doubtful case, it is the more risky and hence more easily falsifiable hypothesis which should be given preference. How is one to decide when confronted by such an alternative? Well, history *has* already decided and indeed in favor of Kuhn and against Popper. *For so far no physicist seems to have been disposed to incur the risk of falsification connected with a formulation of necessary and sufficient conditions for belonging to the set I.* And so it will probably remain in the future. A Rationalism that contests this and strives to impose the requirement just formulated expects something superhuman of man, and ought, therefore, not to be called *critical* but rather *exaggerated*.

Finally, a word about the *third form of immunity of theories*. Given the difficulty of this matter, we must here remain content with just a few hints. So far we have omitted from our considerations the fundamental law of the theory. May not this law be empirically refuted and thus the core and with it ultimately the theory itself collapse? If as an example of a theory we again choose classical particle mechanics, then the question would be: is Newton's second law empirically falsifiable? The unfalsifiability of the law has often been observed. The reasons given were the following: the law is an analytic truth; it amounts to nothing more than a definition of force; it involves a truth of reason (a synthetic proposition a priori), etc. All of these suppositions are mistaken even though the assertion which they attempt to establish is quite correct. The error of all such speculations is to be attributed to the false assumption that one can measure the values for the functions of location, force, and mass *independently of the theory* and, *after having undertaken the measurement*, find out whether Newton's second law is satisfied. Both of the quantities *mass* and *force*, being theoretical quantities, are, however, *measurable only in a theory dependent way*, and this is why *any* contradiction between the law and experience can be laid to the measurement instead of the law.

These remarks should suffice to make us realize why Popper is wrong when he identifies Kuhn's 'normal scientist' with an uncritical and narrow minded dogmatist. There *may* well be an uncritical attitude in science; and it unfortunately occurs perhaps all too often in the so-called applied sciences. But it is nevertheless quite absurd to make the normal scientist *as such* responsible for this attitude and to view him as the very prototype of an uncritical attitude.

We had said at the beginning that Popper has professed to concentrate exclusively on what Kuhn calls '*extraordinary research*'. Even here, however, the decisive difference between the two thinkers consists in the fact that they characterize these processes in mutually incompatible ways. Whereas, according to Popper, a new theory is accepted only after the old one has been falsified, according to Kuhn a new theory always replaces the old one directly. Let us call this *the phenomenon of the direct dislodging of a theory by another theory*. The term 'direct' should serve here to indicate that 'no experience enters into' this process. An additional thesis of Kuhn states that the dislodging and dislodged theories are *incommensurable with each other* (and, therefore, the widespread idea that the old theory is a special limiting case of the new is incorrect). The dislodging of a theory by a new theory incommensurable with it, is the essential mark of a *scientific revolution*.

But with respect to these processes, too, our view is that the task of the logician is not to contest Kuhn's conception but rather *to make logically understandable the phenomenon he describes*.

The preceding observations have, in a certain sense, already paved the way for this logical understanding. For since a theory is not, strictly speaking, falsifiable, no act of falsification can be involved in the revolutionary process of theory dislodgment. On Kuhn's view, such a process of theory dislodgment is preceded by a *crisis* characterized by the fact that the difficulties which face the old theory keep mounting and grow into anomalies. What has disturbed most of Kuhn's critics is the fact that the process beginning with such a state of affairs and ending with the victory of the new theory over the old one is described in purely psychological and sociological terms. Nothing whatever can be said against such a description per se; it may even be the only one possible for a philosopher of science *as* historian. The task of the philosopher of science consists in pointing out a gap in this description and in specifying how this gap is to be filled. The gap exists only for someone concerned with *understanding* the historio-scientific process of one theory dislodging another *as a rational process*, and this despite the fact that at the inception and during the propagation of the theory there prevailed irrational processes such as sudden flashes of new ideas in the mind of particular researchers, or the spread of the new ideas via persuasion and propaganda, etc. The rational construal of such an event requires two things: first, correctly *locate the rationality gap*, and second, *bridge it.*

It seems that a number of Kuhn's critics have failed even in the first of these two tasks, for they have incorrectly located the gap. It might also be added that they have seen a gap where none exists. What these critics are demanding is a *critical region* that *specifies exactly when a theory has to be abandoned*, whether or not we have another theory on hand which can take its place.

If such a critical region existed, then not only would there be a rationality gap in Kuhn's descriptions but even one of his basic theses would turn out false, namely, the thesis that a theory is abandoned only when there is another candidate on hand to replace it. But here again the mistake lies not with Kuhn but rather with his critics. The only thing that can be done is *to make one realize why the search for such a critical region amounts to an idle quest.* The factor responsible for the persistence of the demand for a critical region is the adherence to the *statement view*; it is this that leads us astray in our thinking about theories. The analogy from which one sets out is roughly the following: 'Even with hypotheses which are not strictly deterministic, as for example statistical claims, every rational test theory has to give a critical region such that the hypothesis is to be rejected if the observational data fall within this critical region; and so there must be such a critical region even for theories.' This analogy is, however, mistaken; a statistical hypothesis is a sentence but a theory, on the other hand, is not.

The insight mentioned can be gained by a combination of elementary psychological analogies and logical analysis. The fact that a theory is increasingly plagued with anomalies can be compared with other human situations such as for example: the roof of a house getting more and more leaks; a ship being damaged by a storm; a tool gradually failing to perform its job. The fact that the 'normal scientist' holding a traditional theory clings to it despite repeated failures can be explained, just like the other cases, by the *trivial psychological truth* that a tool that is urgently needed, however battered it may be, is always better than none. The wanderer threatened by the freezing snow storms will be more than happy to stumble upon even a dilapidated hut. To the shipwrecked, a boat with a shattered rudder and broken oars is always better than no boat at all. In none of these cases is it conceivable that the helpless victim will concede that having nothing at all would be better than making do with the little one has.

The logical grounds for not being able to meet the demand for a critical region has already been explained; namely, no finite number of unsuccessful core expansions constitutes a final proof that a successful core expansion is impossible. The appearance of anomalies can be equated, at least in the case of physics, with the frequant and repeated failures of the core expansions. It is only natural that in such a situation life for the adherents of the scientific tradition caught in a crisis will become more and more uncomfortable. But it is nonetheless quite *understandable psychologically* why they would still pin their hopes on the old theory which has proven so successful in the past, at least until such time as a new theory emerges which shatters altogether the belief in the efficacy of the tradition.

In our attempt to determine the locus of the rationality gap we may start out from Popper's simple observation that it is only in science that one can speak of *progress*. As a matter of fact, one cannot distinguish, on the basis of Kuhn's exposition, between *theory dislodgment that leads to progress in knowledge and theory dislodgment without such scientific progress*. It seems, at times, as if Kuhn wants to solve this problem by appealing to sociology and declaring the progressives to be those that manage to prevail (cf. especially p. 166 of his book *The Structure of Scientific Revolutions*).

In the last pages of his book (p. 191) it nevertheless becomes evident that he has something else in mind and hence considers the following as a desideratum: *the introduction of a non-teleological concept of progress* which, in a certain sense, is supposed to represent the metascientific parallel to Darwin's non-teleological concept of evolution (and might, therefore, be viewed by many as being just as exasperating as Darwin's claim of being able to explain the development of life without resorting to a plan). Kuhn's critical remarks are directed against *teleological concepts of progress* such as, for example, Popper's concept of increasing verisimilitude. This latter concept is both teleological and useless; it is teleological because it sets truth as the goal of all epistemological endeavors; and it is useless because only God or the Hegelian world spirit have at their disposal a yardstick by which to measure the distance of a theory from the 'true state of nature'.

Can Kuhn's demand for the introduction of a non-teleological concept of scientific progress be met? The answer is yes! The demand is satisfied by providing a sufficiently precise concept of theory reduction. *Revolutionary scientific progress takes place when the dislodged theory is reducible to the new theory*. At this point we can only assert quite dogmatically that an exact and materially adequate concept of reduction can be introduced set-theoretically and that its degree of precision (just like the rest of the concepts mentioned earlier and explained only intuitively in this essay) is no less than that of other set-theoretic concepts such as, for example, the concept of ordinal number. Only to the extent that these concepts contain pragmatic components such as the concept of holding a theory in a pragmatic sense, must one resort to concepts like 'man', 'time' (in the historical, non-physical sense) etc.; they can nevertheless be regarded here as being just as unproblematic as in the countless other contexts in which they are employed.

The claim we have just made, namely, that the concept of scientific progress can be clarified in a non-teleological way by means of a suitable concept of theory reduction, appears, quite obviously, to be logically incompatible with Kuhn's thesis of incommensurability. Such a contradiction is, however, merely apparent. Whenever Kuhn, and similarly Feyerabend, speak of the *incomparability* of theories that supercede each other, they do not use a two-place but a three-place relational concept. If a theory is designated as incomparable with another, then in order to understand such an assertion, one must answer the additional question: incomparable *in relation to what*? If one looks more closely at the arguments it is not hard to realize that what is meant is merely an incomparability *within the statement view of theories*: the basic concepts of the dislodged theory are not definable in terms of the concepts of the new theory, and hence the axioms and theorems of the former are likewise not derivable from the axioms and theorems of the latter. This point is doubtlessly right. Translated into our set-theoretic terminology, this amounts to saying nothing else but that *the core of the new theory is not identical with the core of the dislodged theory*. That in spite of this it is still possible to speak of reduction even in cases where we have different cores (and *in this sense* 'incomparable' theories) is due to the fact that a concept of reduction can be introduced which rests on a comparison of achievements: the reducing theory accomplishes in an explanatory and prognostic sense *at least as much as* the theory that is reduced. This idea can be found for the first time in an unpublished dissertation of E.W. Adams. Sneed has seized upon this idea and has refined it and modified it in such a way that it becomes applicable to the complicated conceptual apparatus that is employed in the present concept of theories. (To be more exact, we are here dealing not with *one* concept of reduction but with *three*: one of them involves the cores, the second one has to do with expanded cores, only the third deals with theories.[11])

By bridging the rationality gap in the way just described it becomes possible to reconcile two basic ideas which have so far seemed diametrically opposed: *Kuhn's thesis that the form of progress involved in the revolutionary dislodgment of theories is non-cumulative is perfectly compatible with the idea of a cumulative increase of knowledge in the course of such revolutionary phases*. The apparent contradiction disappears as soon as one recognizes the equivocation in the expression 'cumulative': the process is *non-cumulative* in Kuhn's sense in so far as the cores of the dislodging and dislodged theories are different (and hence within the statement view there exists an incomparability as regards the conceptual and sentential apparatus of both theories). The process is *cumulative* in so far as there occurs a reduction of the old theory to the new theory. The 'in so far' of this last statement is important: such reducibility need *not*, of course, obtain. If it does not, the concept of progress does not thereby become meaningless; it simply does not apply to such cases. This is a perfectly desirable result; for an important achievement of the concept of reduction is exactly the fact *that it enables us to differentiate between a revolutionary theory dynamics with progress and such a theory dynamics without progress*. (And corresponding to the setbacks of normal science, should we not also have *revolutionary* setbacks? They are at least conceivable. Whether such a thing has actually ever occurred, and how often, can only be determined by a combination of historio- and logico-scientific analyses.)

Lakatos' efforts to introduce a concept of *sophisticated falsification* can also be viewed as an attempt to bridge the rationality gap. Lakatos' method seems at first quite different from the one outlined above. But *the concept of sophisticated falsification*, apart from its misleading designation,[12] *amounts essentially to a concept of theory reduction*[13] or better, to the intuitive sketch of such a concept). The question of confirmation which we bracketed is, however, included here. It is expressed by Lakatos' demand that the extra power of the new theory vis-à-vis the old theory must be empirically corroborated. (For this kind of corroboration he employs the expression 'excess corroboration'). His concept of a *research program* turns out, on the other hand, to be less important since it involves just a variant or a special case of normal science in Kuhn's sense.[14]

One of the arguments usually brought up in various forms against this by the opponents of the traditional philosophy of science relies on *the thesis that all observations are theory-laden*. This thesis, according to which there exist no 'theory-neutral' observations, is directed especially against the conception of an observational language; but since we did not have to resort to any such conception at all, there is no compelling reason why we need to take a stand in this matter. This seems, nevertheless, quite appropriate; for behind the slogan that observations (or the observation language) are theory-laden there lies hidden a fundamental equivocation which has led to much confusion. The conceptual framework previously described enables us not only to detect this ambiguity but also to take a clear unambiguous stand.[15]

Suppose that a theory T and certain observational data relevant for this theory are under discussion. If, now, someone were to assert that theoretical assumptions enter into these very data of observation themselves, one should immediately retort: 'theoretical assumptions *of which theory*?' It makes quite a difference in the problem whether in alluding to the dependence on a theory one is referring to a *different* theory, i.e., to a theory *distinct from* T, or *to this very theory itself*. We will examine both possibilities briefly.

In most cases the proponents of the thesis would espouse the first version. In our idiom, the situation should then be presented in the following way: the physical systems which are potential canditates for membership in the domain of intended applications of a theory T must first be described *by means of a different theory*. Or, to put it even more briefly and concisely: the description of physical systems as partial possible models of T – more exactly, as partial possible models of the mathematical structure of T – must employ the concepts of a different theory.

If the concept of a theory is narrowed down to theories of the kind we have studied, then the thesis, construed in that sense, is *doubtlessly correct*. But it is then harmless and cannot be brought forward as an objection against the attempts at a rational reconstruction. The important thing about this thesis is that it contains an implicit clue about the hierarchical structure of a system of theories. Thus, particularly the so-called 'facts' for a physical theory are only 'there' if there already exists another theory which supplies the 'quantitative vocabulary' necessary for their description. One should remember, for example, that to describe the intended applications of the simplest physical theory, e.g., classical particle mechanics, one needs a concept of place in the form of a place function which can be doubly differentiated with respect to time; this is a concept which not only plays no part in our everyday thinking, but which was for many centuries not known even to the scientists who studied the phenomena of motion.

At this point, however, instead of pursuing further the phenomenon of the hierarchy of theories (or the hierarchies of theories) we will probe the second alternative: when there is talk of the dependency of observations or of the empirical data of a theory can it be *the theory T itself* that is meant? This is actually possible, provided one is generous enough to count among the data relevant for this theory not just the descriptions of partial possible models but the descriptions of *possible* models of the theory as well. As we may recall, these latter descriptions do indeed contain the names of T-theoretical functions and consequently rest, in a sense that can be made quite precise, on the very theory itself under discussion. This fact, however, raises at the same time a big problem, namely, *the problem of theoretical terms*, which, at least as far as we now know, can only be resolved by resorting to Ramsey's solution.

By way of summary we can thus say that talk about the theory dependence of observational descriptions is ambiguous and that, depending on the interpretation, it contains either a reference to the hierarchical structure of systems of theories or a metaphorical paraphrase of the problem of theoretical concepts. The problems of *both* versions prove solvable.

I should like to add a few remarks here about Feyerabend's call for *epistemological tolerance*; they may very well depart from all previous commentaries on Feyerabend's ideas. The present author shares to a large extent Feyerabend's suspicions about normative methodology in general as well as about the various forms of 'critical rationalism' in particular. A realization of the Rationalist's requirements would amount to a decisive contribution not toward optimizing but rather toward extinguishing the natural sciences on this planet.

Feyerabend derives his call for tolerance from such critical considerations. What should be said at this point is that Feyerabend himself does not practice the tolerance which he advocates. We find in him a *partial intolerance at the object-level* and, in a certain sense, *an altogether total intolerance at the metalevel*.

In support of the former allegation we need only be reminded that the imperative 'against normal science!' as well as the call for a permanent scientific revolution which have recently been seized upon by Watkins hark back originally to Feyerabend. Even in his latest writings he repeatedly demands that the scientist *ought* to think up new theories all the time. Since he is probably not thinking of calculi which without empirical applicability turn out at best to be amusing logico-mathematical games, but rather of *productive* theories, such demands amount to an imperative such as: 'be like Newton or Einstein!' To the extent that this imperative is directed at the 'normal scientist' who, in his field does perfectly good productive work and who, of course, makes up the overwhelming majority, it is cruel and inhumane. It implies that the judgment of scientific competence be made dependent on the extent to which this demand is met and consequently an annihilating value judgement is passed on practically every scientist.

The second aforementioned assertion (i.e., intolerance at the metalevel) concerns Feyerabend's radical rejection of any kind of logic of science. According to him, the dynamics of a science can only be grasped by means of psychological, historical, and sociological methods. All attempts toward a logical understanding, on the other hand, are for him nothing but a laughable and misguided intellectual investment of decrepit philosophers of science.

Let us here disregard the moral tone of this attitude and content ourselves with pointing out the logical consequence of such a stand. Feyerabend designated the sciences as a *rational* undertaking. There consequently arises for him the fundamental problem of supporting this thesis solely with the means he acknowledges for describing and understanding this phenomenon. This difficulty cannot be removed. For however exact the historio-psychological descriptions may be and with however much empathy they may be carried out, one will not discover any difference in rationality at all between scientific and political revolutions; both kinds will appear equally irrational.

Feyerabend has recently discovered his sympathy for the Hegelian dialectic. Perhaps he hopes this method will help him overcome his difficulty. But quite apart from the great implausibility of this idea, such an expedient is not at all necessary. It is indeed psychologically understandable that Feyerabend distrusts the logic of science since he has been disillusioned by what it has accomplished so far. But if, however, the ideas we have outlined here for a metatheoretic treatment of theory dynamics prove useful, we would then be justified in claiming that Feyerabend's skepticism rests on a premature inductive inference, namely, from present inadequacy to future uselessness. It is possible to have a rational reconstruction of theory dynamics which contributes to our logical understanding of this phenomenon and yet does no violence to history nor makes an inhuman methodological demand on the individual researcher. If one really understands the expression 'tolerance in matters of epistemological theory' in Feyerabend's sense, then one ought to plead for much more tolerance and openness if we are to reach the goal that Feyerabend too desires.

Finally, one more word about falsification: as we have already said, Popper admits, on the one hand, that he has neglected the phenomenon of normal science and that he has concentrated entirely on extraordinary research; but, on the other hand, it is well known that in his theory the concept of strict proof, falsification, and corroboration stand very much in the foreground. If the explications proposed in this essay are in principle accepted, in particular, the explication of normal science in terms of the concept of holding a theory and the explication of scientific revolutions in terms of the concept of theory dislodgment, then these two aspects of Popper's theory of science are mutually incompatible. For only in the context of normal science are we involved with setting up hypotheses, namely, the attempted core expansions; consequently, it is also only within normal science that we have strict tests and corroborations or falsifications. Neither extraordinary research not its successful (theory dislodgment with reduction) or unsuccessful (theory dislodgment without reduction) results are accompanied by processes which, according to Popper, ought to be characteristic of a critical science. What has presumably deeply disturbed Kuhn as well as those holding similiar views and led to Kuhn's arguments against Popper is Popper's unsuccessful attempt to establish a rationalistic monism by fusing these two aspects of the dynamics of science. One should not, however, overlook the fact that the problems of confirmation connected with empirical hypotheses will henceforth have to be recognized, and that Popper might, presumably, be right in thinking that a deductive concept of confirmation (concept of corroboration) will suffice in a deterministic case. [16]

NOTES

[1] J.D. Sneed, *The Logical Structure of Mathematical Physics.* A simplified and somewhat modified exposition of this conceptual scheme can be found in Stegmüller's *Theorienstrukturen und Theoriendynamik*. [*Theoriendynamik*]

[2] Sneed, *loc. cit.*, p. 74. The general as well as the special case of the miniature theory of Sneed is discussed in greater detail in Stegmüller's [*Theoriendynamik*], pp. 81 – 90.

[3] These set-theoretic concepts can be found in Chapter VII of Sneed's book. An explication that departs somewhat from his version and which, in certain respects, is more extensive can be found in Stegmüller's [*Theoriendynamik*] Chapter VIII, Sections 7, 8, and 9. To allay any suspicions on the reader's part, it should be added that we will not make use here of the 'higher' concepts of set-theory about which there is disagreement in the discussion of mathematical foundations. Most, though not all, of the nine concepts presented there are mentioned in the above text.

[4] For a more exact definition of this function cf. Stegmüller, [*Theoriendynamik*] p. 129.

[5] Cf. *loc. cit.*, p. 133.

[6] The minimal conditions cited by Sneed are contained in the specifications (4) – (6) of the definition on p. 189 of [*Theoriendynamik*].

[7] The following text does not merely contain an intuitive description of the formal explications given in [*Theoriendynamik*], pp. 221 – 223. Instead, I will try improve the line of thought presented there. The decisive difference consists in *getting completely rid of the platonism that can be found in Sneed*, which consists of postulating an 'absolute' set *I* of 'true' intended applications of a theory. The attempt I have made in [*Theoriendynamik*] p. 224 is not entirely satisfactory.

[8] A systematic, exhaustive classification along the lines of Sneed which also takes into account the matter of presenting individual domains and functions used in a physical theory may be found in [*Theoriendynamik*] pp. 207 – 215. The paradigm concepts of Kuhn and Wittgenstein are discussed on pp. 195 – 207.

[9] The danger lurking in metaphors and analogies like these is that the reader gets the

impression that a 'purely instrumentalist conception' is being advocated here. Apropos this question cf. [*Theoriendynamik*] p. 294 *et passim*.

[10] And it is exactly because such a conceptual apparatus is unavailable that it is quite absurd for someone to expect (as seems to have been done in some universities) that young students of the theory of science, natural philosophy, and the history of the natural sciences be in a position to read and discuss Kuhn's book; for it is very likely that these young students do not possess Kuhn's intuitive genius (let alone his profound mastery of history), nor are they in a position to equip themselves with the necessary logical wherewithal alone, and so such reading is inevitably bound to create in their mind a fantastically distorted picture of science and its development.

[11] Sneed has introduced and discussed this concept in Chapter VII of his book. The present author has attempted a simpler and clearer presentation of these reduction concepts in [*Theoriendynamik*] Chapter VIII, Section 9.

[12] The reasons why this terminology is misleading are given briefly in [*Theoriendynamik*], p. 264.

[13] For an attempt at reconstructing diverse variants of this concept of sophisticated falsification within the context of our conceptual scheme cf. [*Theoriendynamik*], p. 259.

[14] Attempts at explicating the concept of a research program by means of our set-theoretic concept can be found in [*Theoriendynamik*], p. 257. It should be added here that according to the view expounded there the expression 'theory' as used by Lakatos is ambiguous. At times it is taken to mean something which is also regarded as theory in our reconstruction; but at other times theories *as elements of research programs* are hypothetical assumptions which, in the present conceptual frame of reference, must be interpreted either as sentences of form (II) or their propositional counterparts (III).

[15] Cf. [*Theoriendynamik*], pp. 28, 33, 233, and 277.

[16] And if the view presented in Volume IV (second half) of the history of science of the present author proves correct, then even the concept of confirmation for statistical hypotheses, though quite different from the concept of corroboration, is not probabilistic but 'non-inductive'.

CHAPTER 7

STRUCTURES AND DYNAMICS OF THEORIES

Some Reflections on J. D. Sneed and T. S. Kuhn

I. THEORIES AND THEIR EMPIRICAL CLAIMS

The most natural way to formulate a scientific theory is to axiomatize it. Among the various possibilities of interpreting the phrase 'to axiomatize a theory', a particularly attractive one for logical studies consists in taking it as meaning 'to define a set theoretic predicate'. We shall therefore sometimes speak of the set theoretic predicate *corresponding to* the theory in question; e.g., the theory of groups is axiomatized by introducing the corresponding set theoretic predicate 'is a group'; quantum mechanics is axiomatized by introducing the set theoretic predicate 'is a quantum mechanics'. We shall not presuppose that the set theory itself is formalized. The set theoretic predicate used to axiomatize a theory will, therefore, always be an *informal* predicate.

If the non-logical vocabulary of the theory contains only quantitative concepts, i.e. functions of various kinds, the set theoretic predicate corresponding to the theory describes a mathematical structure S. For the time being we will use only an intuitive concept of a theory. What matters for the moment, given a theory T, is only its mathematical structure $S(T)$ and the extension of this predicate 'S' which we call the set $M_{S(T)}$ of *models* of our theory. The empirical statements made with the help of our theory are sentences of the form

(I) $\quad a \in M_{S(T)}$,

whereby a is the physical system to which we claim our theory applies.

According to Sneed this traditional view of the empirical sentences of a theory is confronted with insurmountable difficulties if the theory contains theoretical functions. What has to be counted as a theoretical function φ of T is, according to Sneed, not a question of linguistic convention, as it seems to be for the empiricist. It is rather a matter of whether *the values of* φ *are T-dependent*. Roughly speaking, his theory-relative concept of a theoretical function can be characterized as follows:

Reprinted from Erkenntnis 9 (1975), pp. 75-100.

The function φ is *theoretical with respect to T* iff for every $a_i \in M_{S(T)}$ any method of measuring the values of φ for some individuals of a_i presupposes that there is an a_j such that $a_j \in M_{S(T)}$. (It must be observed, however, that i need not be different from j!) Thus, the measurements are T-dependent and any attempt to test the truth of (I) presupposes that there already is a true empirical claim of this form. Consequently, where T-theoretical functions occur, the traditional view of empirical statements of a theory gets involved either in a vicious circle or in an infinite regress (depending on the number of applications of the theory). It is this difficulty which Sneed calls *the problem of theoretical terms.*

It should not be overlooked that the difficulty just mentioned does not concern the *semantic* status of T-theoretical concepts but only their *epistemic* status. Thus, the assumption that (I) *is true* is unproblematic in the sense that it is not based on the assumption that another sentence of this form be true. But all the attempts *to find out whether* (I) *is true* get involved either in a vicious circle or in an infinite regress.

One could express this fact by saying that the occurrence of T-theoretical functions in (I) prevents (I) from being an empirical sentence, i.e., a sentence which could be tested on empirical grounds.

The difference becomes obvious in cases where $i=j$ (which is always the case where there is only one application). Here, the measuring of the values of the T-theoretical function φ for certain individuals in order to find out whether $a_i \in M_{S(T)}$ is true presupposes that *this very sentence itself* be true. Take, for example, a balance B which is used to determine the weight of a physical body. What does it mean to say that this weight is measured in a T-dependent way, where T is a classical particle mechanics? It means that we presuppose B to be a model of T. If we agree that *mass* and *force* are T-theoretical functions, and for simplicity take B to be *the only application* of T (i.e. $i=j=1$), then the latter sentence cannot be an empirical one. This becomes immediately evident if we imagine a person questioning the correctness of our measurement because he thinks that the balance is defective. There is no possible empirical way to remove his doubts.

The only way out of this difficulty known to us at the present moment is what Sneed calls *the Ramsey-solution of the problem of theoretical terms.* In order to explain it we shall first introduce a bit of technical terminology.

Suppose a set theoretical predicate S of the kind mentioned at the beginning be given and further, that the theory T, axiomatized with the help of S, contains T-theoretical functions. An entity which is similar to a model of T, but which need not satisfy the axioms proper, is called a *possible* model of T. If we take a possible model and eliminate from it all T-theoretical functions we get a *partial possible model* of T. Sneed's suggestion of making empirical claims by using set theoretical predicates amount roughly to this: We are to take as intended applications of a theory not models but partial possible models. As they do not contain T-theoretical functions we can take them as the objects referred to by names or descriptions in an empirical sentence.

If x is a partial possible model of T, y is called *a theoretical supplement of* x: $y\Sigma x$ iff y is that possible model of T from which x is obtained by eliminating the theoretical functions. Alternatively, we shall say that x is the *non-theoretical reduct* of, or simply, the *reduct* of y. For a given particular possible model a, e.g., that mentioned in (I), we designate the corresponding reduct by a^r. Similarly, M^r is used to designate the set of reducts of the elements of $M_{p(T)}$ where $M_{p(T)}$ is the set of possible models of the theory T. Obviously M^r is the set of partial possible models corresponding to $M_{S(T)}$. By $M^r_{S(T)}$ we designate the set of reducts of elements of $M_{S(T)}$. Of course, every element of $M^r_{S(T)}$ must be an element of M^r but not vice versa. As a rule, M^r will be much larger than $M^r_{S(T)}$.

In a first step we replace claims of the form (I) by their Ramsey-substitutes:[1]

(II) $\qquad \bigvee y(y\Sigma b \wedge y \in M_{S(T)})$,

whereby b is a partial possible model of T. We can call (II) the *Ramsey-translation* of sentence (I) in case b is the same as a^r. Intuitively speaking, what (II) says about the partial possible model b of the theory with the mathematical structure S is this: 'There is a theoretical supplement of b which is an element of the set $M_{S(T)}$ of all models of the theory'.

Using the terminology of reducts, (I) could be replaced by:

(II*) $\qquad a^r \in M^r_{S(T)}$,

which says: 'The reduct of a is an element of the set of reducts of those possible models of the theory which turn out to be models of the theory'.

Sentences of the type (II) or (II*) can, in contrast to sentences of the type (I), be considered as *empirical in character*. For when testing (II) or (II*) we have to find out whether an entity b, *describable in purely non-theoretical terms,* satisfies certain conditions which are imposed on the *non-theoretical* functions occurring in it.[2] Difficulties may of course arise but they are of mathematical nature only. Thus, the problem of theoretical terms has disappeared.

But, the Ramsey-substitute of the original sentence (I) is still defective in at least three respects. First, *the number of intended applications* of the theory will usually be *greater than one.* (In the case of classical particle mechanics, e.g., possible applications are: the solar system and certain subsystems of it; the class of pendulums; the class of tides; the class of free falls near the surface of the earth etc.) These applications can have, and as a rule will have, non-empty intersections. Secondly, the various intended applications are 'cross-connected' by *constraints* imposed on the theoretical functions. This means that the theoretical functions employed in different applications are not independent of each other, but that certain relations hold between their values. A simple example of one such constraint says that an individual, if it occurs in different applications, gets the *same* value for one type of function, e.g., mass. Another one can be formulated with the help of the sentence: 'Mass is an extensive quantity'. Although this phrase makes it appear 'as if we were formulating a law' holding for the mass function, it actually expresses a constraint.

This becomes obvious as soon as we realize that the individuals whose combination is to be assigned a value of the mass function may be taken from *different* applications. Finally, *special laws* may hold in *particular* applications without holding in others.

Let us now see how sentence (II) (or (II*)) has to be modified in order to take account of these complications. The first and simplest modification consists of the use of bold-faced letters to designate sets of entities mentioned in sentence (II). '$\mathbf{y}\Sigma\mathbf{x}$' is now to be read as '$\mathbf{y}$ is a set of theoretical supplements of the set of partial possible models $\mathbf{x}$'. The second involves the requirement that a union of functions be restricted by $\langle R_i, \rho_i \rangle$. This will mean that if the relation R_i obtains between elements of the union of the domains of these functions, then the relation ρ_i obtains between the values which these functions take for the given elements. Let us take $\langle R, \rho \rangle$ as a formal representative of the class of all restrictions of this kind. The class of constraints C can then be defined as a 4-place relation such that '$C(\mathbf{y}, \mathbf{x}, R, \rho)$' is synonymous with '**y** is a set of theoretical supplements of **x** and the union of the theoretical functions constructing elements of **y** from elements of **x** is restricted by $\langle R, \rho \rangle$'.[3]

These first two kinds of modification are now taken into account if we replace (II) by:

$$\text{(III)} \qquad \bigvee \mathbf{y}(C(\mathbf{y}, \mathbf{b}, R, \rho) \wedge \mathbf{y} \subseteq M_{S(T)}).$$

(Observe that the member '$\mathbf{y}\Sigma\mathbf{x}$' need not be mentioned because it has become part of $C(\mathbf{y}, \mathbf{b}, R, \rho)$.)

The same modification can be made with respect to (II*) as well. Here we have to use a set theoretical characterization of the class C of constraints of which we think to single out certain elements of the power set of $M_{p(T)}$, i.e. of the set of all possible models of T. C is to be considered a *constraint for* $M_{p(T)}$ iff

(1) $\quad C \subseteq Po(M_{p(T)})$ (with 'Po' for 'power set of') and

(2) $\quad \bigwedge x(x \in M_{p(T)} \rightarrow \{x\} \in C)$.

Condition (2), specifying that the unit set of every possible model is an element of C, insures that constraints may exclude *combinations of* functions while they never can exclude *particular* functions.

(II*) would have to be replaced by:

$$\text{(III*)} \qquad \bigvee \mathbf{a}(\mathbf{a}^r = \mathbf{b} \wedge \mathbf{a} \in C \wedge \mathbf{a} \subseteq M_{S(T)}),$$

i.e.: 'there is a set **a** of models of T which satisfies all constraints and whose reduct $\mathbf{a}^r$ is identical with the given set **b** of intended applications'.

Now, what about the special laws? A theory T is formally represented by the mathematical structure S. We obtain a special law L by confining the functions of S to functions of special forms. (As a rule, this procedure will be applied to T-theoretical functions.) We can therefore represent each *special* law by a predicate S^i which is *stronger than* the original predicate S. Let us call S^i a *specialization* or a *limitation* of S. The set of models of S^i shall be designated by $M_{S^i(T)}$. Obviously, this representation can be iterated. In order to avoid the use of multiple indices let us allow that for two different limitations S^i and S^k of S it may be the case that one of them, e.g. S^i, is a limitation of the other, e.g. of S^k. Furthermore, we shall incorporate a generalization of the concept of constraint. Besides the *general* constraints, there may be *special* constraints holding only for those theoretical functions which occur within special laws. For obvious reasons these special constraints can be named *law-constraints.* Whenever it seems to be advisable to contrast the basic predicate S with predicates S^i obtained from it by specializations we shall say that S *represents the fundamental law of the theory.*

If $\mathbf{b}$ is the given set of intended applications of the theory and $\mathbf{b}_1$, $\mathbf{b}_2$, ..., $\mathbf{b}_n$ are those subsets of $\mathbf{b}$ in which the special laws represented by S^1, S^2, ..., S^n are supposed to hold respectively, then (III) has to be replaced by the following sentence:

$$\text{(IV)} \quad \bigvee \mathbf{y}[C(\mathbf{y}, \mathbf{b}, R, \rho) \wedge \mathbf{y} \subseteq M_{S(T)} \wedge$$
$$\wedge \bigvee \mathbf{y}_1(\mathbf{y}_1 \subseteq \mathbf{y} \wedge C(\mathbf{y}_1, \mathbf{b}_1, R_1, \rho_1) \wedge \mathbf{y}_1 \subseteq M_{S^1(T)})$$
$$\ldots\ldots$$
$$\ldots\ldots$$
$$\wedge \bigvee \mathbf{y}_n(\mathbf{y}_n \subseteq \mathbf{y} \wedge C(\mathbf{y}_n, \mathbf{b}_n, R_n, \rho_n) \wedge \mathbf{y}_n \subseteq M_{S^n(T)})].$$ [4]

(IV) is supposed to reproduce the whole empirical claim made with the help of the theory T. Roughly speaking it has the following content: 'There is a set of T-theoretical functions satisfying a given class of constraints such that all partial possible models, i.e., all intended applications, belonging to $\mathbf{b}$ can, by adding these T-theoretical functions, be supplemented to become models of S in such a way that the elements of certain subsets $\mathbf{b}_i$ of $\mathbf{b}$ can be theoretically supplemented to become models of the limitations S^i of S and that some of the T-theoretical functions used for these special limitations satisfy the law-constraints $C(\mathbf{y}_i, \mathbf{b}_i, R_i, \rho_i)$'.

We call (IV) the *Ramsey-Sneed-Sentence* expressing an empirical claim made with the help of the theory. As each empirical claim is made *at a particular time* we should, for the sake of explicitness, add a time-index to this sentence and speak therefore of $(\text{IV})_t$ instead of (IV). (Of course t, being a historical and not a physical time, can be taken to be discrete). Whoever prefers the language of (III) may 'translate' (IV) accordingly – a routine matter we leave to the reader. Later we shall give a simplified 'translation' of (IV) into the language of set theory anyway.

If we compare the Ramsey-view of physical theories with Sneed's we realize that there are three major differences:

(1) The first consists in replacing 'can' by 'must' when evaluating the service done by sentences which, starting with (II), suppress any mention

of theoretical terms via existential quantification. According to the current Ramsey-view the empirical content of a theory *can* be expressed with the help of a sentence having the structure (II). According to Sneed this empirical content *must be* expressed by a sentence in which theoretical terms are 'quantified away'. For him there seems to be no other way than doing so, at least as long as we try to formulate *empirical* claims. The reason for this is the simple fact that *a sentence of form* (I) *cannot be an empirical sentence as soon as T-theoretical terms are involved.* Therefore, in a certain sense, only sentences having the form of (II), (III) or (IV) tell us *what physicists really mean* when they try to make empirical claims.

This difference between the usual Ramsey-view and the Sneedian view of the Ramsey-sentence was mentioned only for the sake of completeness. It is not essential to what follows.

(2) The second difference is mirrored by the transition from the 'naive version' of the Ramsey-sentence (II) into the much more 'sophisticated version' (IV). We remember that for the latter, by contrast to (II), the intended application of the theory consists not of a single partial possible model but rather of a *set of* such models.[5]

(3) The third difference, which has so far not been discussed, is of at least equal importance. Roughly speaking, it can be summarized as follows: *An empirical claim made on the basis of a theory*, i.e. a claim of type (IV), *must not be identified with the theory itself.* We shall dwell on this point for a moment because its proper understanding will pave the way for a new conception of theories, the *non-statement view* or positively characterized, the *structuralistic view of theories.*

Before entering into this discussion it should be *stressed* once more that, although the following remarks will rely highly on the three modifications of the original Ramsey-view mentioned in (2), the point emphasized in (1) will not be incorporated into the considerations in the rest of this paper. This means that the reader will not be asked to accept Sneed's criterion of *T*-theoreticity. If he either believes that one of the current views on theoreticity is satisfactory or that Sneed's criterion is objectionable and should be replaced by a better one he may use *his* method of distinguishing theoretical terms from non-theoretical ones whenever this dichotomy crops up.

One additional word of clarification seems to be in order. The conceptual distinctions now to be made can also be considered as preparatory steps for a rational reconstruction of some important aspects of T. S. Kuhn's concepts of *normal science* and of *scientific revolution*. But it is definitively not the case that these distinctions are being made *in order to give Kuhn's work* a new interpretation; they are motivated quite independently. Only when the systematic exposition ends will we, so-to-speak as a side effect, sketch an interpretation of some aspects of what is called 'Kuhnianism' on the basis of the results obtained. This warning is intended only for those readers who may, by misunderstanding the present approach, be inclined to think that the following discussion emanates from a 'hermeneutic interpretation of Kuhn's writings'.

Let us first see why it would be inadequate to *identify* the theory T with a claim of kind (IV). A decision in favor of this identification would have the following consequences: If the range of intended applications of the theory would be changed, i.e., if $\mathbf{b}$ of (IV) would be increased or decreased, however slightly, we would have to say *that the theory itself had changed*. But what we actually would say in such a case is that *the range of application of the theory had changed while the theory itself remained constant*. Similarly, if a special law in one particular application would be replaced by another (or slightly improved or given up), this would have to count as a *change in the whole theory*. The same would hold true with respect to a change in the law-constraints. Again, such a way of speaking would be very odd indeed. We speak, e.g., of the Newtonians despite the fact that the scientists belonging to this group did not all agree on every particular hypothesis entertained by some of them. *Particular hypothetical laws may be changed while the theory remains constant.*

As every empirical hypothesis made on the basis of a theory of mathemathical physics is of form (IV), there seems to be only one possible approach which will account for the distinction between theories and their empirical claims. We must try namely, to separate the instable components from the relatively stable ones within (IV). We speak of the *relatively* stable ones instead of the *a priori* ones (or the *stable ones in an absolute sense* of the word), because the notion of stability is relative to a given theory. The stable ones are those, a change in which would cause us to say that the theory itself had changed.

The *relatively stable* components involved in (IV) are the following:[6] The set of *models* M, mirroring set-theoretically the fundamental law of the theory; the set of *possible models* M_p; the set of *partial possible models* M_{pp} and the general constraints C.[7] On the other hand, the *relatively instable* components are: the set of *special laws* L[8] and the set of *law-constraints* C_L.

Sneed has shown how these concepts can be used to define certain substructures of a theory. We shall follow him to some extent, mainly for two reasons: First, these concepts will be needed in the next two sections; secondly, a purely set theoretical analogue to (IV) having the shape of an *atomic proposition* will be given which will facilitate some formulations and which will further elucidate the concept of an empirical claim made with the help of a theory.

We can omit the explicit definition of the formal structure that a set M_p must have in order to function as a set of possible models for a theory. But the following feature of such an entity, called a *frame for a theory*, will be needed: M_p is a set of n-tupels consisting of one or several universes of individuals, followed by a sequence of non-theoretical functions being followed itself by a sequence of theoretical functions, each function having one of these universes as its domain. The function r, occurring within the next concept, is a function which maps every element of M_p to its 'corresponding' element in M_{pp} by 'cutting off' all, and only, the theoretical functions.

We shall say that K is a *structural core of a theory* or that $SC(K)$ iff K is a quintuple $\langle M_p, M_{pp}, r, M, C\rangle$ such that M_p is a frame for a theory, M_{pp} is the set of r-maps of elements of M_p, M is a subset of M_p and C is a set of constraints for M (in the sense defined below (III)).

Given a structural core K, *the class A of sets of possible applications* of a theory with this structural core can be defined by $A = \bar{\bar{R}}\,(Po(M) \cap C)$, with '$Po$' for the power set operation and $\bar{\bar{R}}$ being the function working 'two levels higher' than r, i.e., on classes of sets of elements of the domain of r, and having corresponding values. We can think of A as being the result of applying a function $\mathbb{A}$ on K, i.e., $A = \mathbb{A}\,(K)$. Obviously, A is the extension of a predicate obtained from (III) by substituting a new variable for '**b**'.

Furthermore, we shall say that E is an *expanded structural core of a theory* or $ES(E)$ iff E is an 8-tuple

$$\langle M_p, M_{pp}, r, M, C, L, C_L, \alpha\rangle$$

such that:

(1) the quintuple consisting of the first five members is the structural core for a theory;

(2) L is a class of subsets of M_p, i.e., L is the class of special laws of the theory;

(3) C_L is the set of special constraints or law-constraints of the theory; and

(4) α is the many-many-relation assigning every law to those possible applications, i.e., to those elements of M_{pp} in which these laws are supposed to hold.[9]

If $SC(K)$ then we call E an *expansion of* K, symbolically: $Ex(E, K)$ iff $ES(E)$ and K is idential with the quintuple of the first five members of K.

In analogy to the function $\mathbb{A}$, defined for structural cores as elements, one can give a somewhat more complicated definition of a function $\mathbb{A}_e$ applicable to *expansions of* structural cores of theories and yielding for each expansion E the class A^* of sets of possible applications: $A^* = \mathbb{A}_e(E)$.[10]

Suppose a scientist chooses at the time t the set I_t of elements of M_{pp} as the set of intended applications of his theory.

If E_t is the expansion of the theory used by him at t then *the empirical claim* to which our scientist is committed at t is the following *theory-statement* at t:

(V) $\quad I_t \in \mathbb{A}_e(E_t)$.

What is the relation between a theory-statement of this kind and a Ramsey-Sneed-sentence of form (IV)? The answer is very simple: If appropriate assignments are made then *statement* (V) *reproduces the content of* (IV) *in pure set-theoretical terms.* Of course, our present 't' has to be identified with the time index of which we said earlier that it ought to be added to (IV). Some hints concerning the assignments are: Our present M is to be taken as the extension of the former predicate S of which we said that it describes the mathematical structure of the theory. M_p is the class of possible models and M_{pp} is the class of partial possible models of that predicate. The class L of laws is to be taken as the class of the extensions of the predicates $S^1, \ldots, S^n$. Similar remarks hold for the general constraints and for the law-constraints. As far as the individual constant **b** of (IV) is concerned, we must think of it as designating our present entity I_t, and of $\mathbf{b}_1, \ldots, \mathbf{b}_n$ as designating suitable subsets of I_t.

These remarks conclude our sketch of the relations between the various structural components of a theory and the empirical claims made on the basis of these components. It should not be overlooked that no *formal* concept of a theory has thus far been used at any place. Every appearance of the term 'theory' was either an *intuitive* and therefore a *pre-systematic one*, or a contextual use intended to designate *another* concept like 'structural core' or 'expanded core'.

Sneed introduces in addition the concept of a *theory* as an ordered pair consisting of a structural core and the set of its intended applications. Unfortunately this second member makes Sneed's account platonistic and difficult to understand. Besides the present author, presumably other philosophers too will have some difficulties in understanding what kind of entity the set of 'true' applications of a given core is. In a more or less drastic departure from Sneed's procedure we shall introduce the concept of *availing oneself of a theory* without using a concept of *theory* at all. This will give us a more realistic basis for a logical reconstruction of the two *dynamic* aspects of scientific evolution which have been pointed out by T. S. Kuhn. Following this we shall, for several reasons, introduce a concept of a theory of mathematical physics which may be called non-platonistic or at least less platonistic than that of Sneed.

As is well known, the idea of a '*normal science*' in sense of Kuhn's has come under heavy attack from many philosophers. Perhaps the most severe criticism came from Popper. In his paper 'Normal Science and Its Dangers' Popper points out that a 'normal' scientist is "a person one ought to be sorry for" (p. 52) because he has as 'a victim of indoctrination' become a man incapable of critical thinking. He is a person who 'has been taught in the dogmatic spirit' and who himself teaches his students in the very same spirit. Therefore the possibility of its becoming normal is, according to Popper, a danger to science and even a danger to our civilization. It seems that a great many of philosophers have followed Popper in looking at these matters in the same or in a very similar way.

The present writer believes this picture of normal science is based on a total misunderstanding – as total as it can be. But it is understandable that Kuhn's work conjured this picture in the mind of its readers. At the same time it seems to us that the prevalence of this picture is something like a proof for the necessity of a *rational reconstruction* of the concept of normal science.

While historical examples plus socio-psychological analyses plus metaphors can not give us an understanding of this phenomenon *as a rational enterprise*, a logical reconstruction *can*.

The title of the next section was chosen with the particular dangers of 'normal science' in mind mentioned by Popper.

II. NORMAL SCIENCE WITHOUT DANGERS

The 2-place predicate '$Phys(I, K)$' shall mean: 'I is a set of physical systems with respect to K'. We shall leave the question open as to whether there are necessary and sufficient conditions for being a physical system. But in any case it is required of the set I, first, that it is a *subset of the second member of* K (i.e. of M_{pp}), and secondly, that any two domains of the elements of I be always *connected* by a finite sequence of domains of elements of I such that the intersection between each domain and its immediate successor is not empty.

We now define the concept '*L is a logical-empirical frame for a theory of mathematical physics*':

$$LEF(L) \text{ iff } \bigvee K \bigvee A\, [L = \langle K, A \rangle \wedge SC(K) \wedge A = \mathbb{A}(K)]\,.$$

Next we want to define what it means for a person (or for a group of persons) to avail himself (themselves) of a theory of mathematical physics or to use or to have such a theory. As already mentioned, Sneed's procedure amounts to something like this: He first introduces the concept of theory hereby using I as a platonic entity. In a second step he then introduces the concept which we are looking for. The most radical deviation from this platonism would be to define immediately the desired concept without first defining the concept of a theory. This we shall now try to do.

We use 'p' as a variable for persons (i.e. for the members of a scientific community), 't' as a variable for chronological time-intervals and 'E_t' as a variable for expanded structural cores used at t. In addition we shall use as undefined phrases the following: 'believes at t that' and 'has at t evidential support for'. 'p knows at t that X' is an abreviation for 'p believes at t that X and p has at t evidential support for X'.

(D1) *Avail* $_w(p, t, L)$ (to be read as 'in the weak sense p avails himself at t of a theory with the logical-empirical frame L') iff

$$\bigvee K \bigvee A \{[L = \langle K, A\rangle \wedge LEF(L)] \wedge \bigvee E_t [Ex(E_t, K) \wedge$$

p knows at t that

$$\bigvee I_t, Phys(I_t, K) \wedge I_t \in \mathbb{A}_e(E_t) \wedge$$

p believes at t that

$$\bigvee E^* (Ex(E^*, K) \wedge I_t \in \mathbb{A}_e(E^*) \wedge \mathbb{A}_e(E^*) \subseteq \mathbb{A}_e(E_t))^{11})$$

$\wedge$ p knows at t that

$$\bigwedge I' (Phys(I', K) \wedge I' \in \mathbb{A}_e(E_t)) \rightarrow I' \subseteq I_t)$$

$\wedge$ p knows at t that for all expansions E' of K known to him at t that

$$(I_t \in \mathbb{A}_e(E') \rightarrow \mathbb{A}_e(E_t) \subseteq \mathbb{A}_e(E'))]\}.$$

(Remember the meanings of A, $\mathbb{A}$, A^*, $\mathbb{A}_e$: A is the class of sets of possible applications of a theory having K as its structural core; the elements of A are sets of models satisfying all constraints; the function $\mathbb{A}$ has the value A for K as argument. The function $\mathbb{A}_e$ has the value A^* for the expansion E_t of K; therefore it is the class of sets of possible applications of this expanded core E_t.)

The last two members of the formula insure (1) that p has chosen among the possible candidates for the set of intended applications the largest set known to him to which the expanded core E_t applies, and (2) that on the other hand he has used the strongest expanded core which, according to his knowledge, is applicable to I_t.

No special symbol referring to a theory occurs within this formula. *The theory so to speak 'comes into existence' only by the existence of people who avail themselves of it.*

Now, we must look for a concept of availing oneself of a theory *in the strong sense*. This concept will be suggested as an explicatum for Kuhn's notion of *normal science*.

We have first to consider the concept of a paradigm. While Kuhn prefers – for reasons irrelevant to our purpose – to use this concept for *all* aspects of theory formation, we will use it only for an 'infinitesimal part' of these aspects, namely, for *the set of intended applications of a theory*.

This point is relevant because it will force us to deviate in another important respect from the traditional way of thinking about theories. When talking about the interpretation of a formal theory logicians use phrases like 'domain of individuals' or 'domain of application'. It is thereby supposed that the domain is given extensionally, i.e. that it is the extension of a known predicate. But is the range of application of an empirical theory *given extensionally*? While leaving open the question for empirical theories in general we can say that it is certainly not the *normal* case for a *physical* theory. Normally, the range of application of such a theory is given in a non-extensional way, i.e., by means of paradigmatic examples. Let us try to formulate the main features of this '*method of paradigmatic examples*' by using Wittgenstein's famous example of a game as a paradigm:

(1) The concept of a game is not introduced with the help of necessary and sufficient conditions for belonging to the set G of games. Instead, as a first step, a *proper subset* G_0 of G is introduced as a *minimal list* of games. The members of G_0 are given by a *finite enumeration*. They are the *paradigmatic cases* of games.

(2) It is then forbidden to remove an element of G_0 from the set G, i.e., we decide never to refuse to call an element of G_0 a game.

(3) The elements of G_0 may have a finite number of common characteristics. No matter whether they have or they have not – and in the case they have, whether we know them or not – these characteristics together form at most a necessary but *not a sufficient condition* for belonging to G.

(4) The sufficient condition for belonging to G contains an *irremediable vagueness*. In order, namely, to belong to the difference set $G - G_0$ an object must have a 'significant' number of properties in common with 'almost all' elements of G_0.

(5) We can even specify the sense in which this vagueness is irremediable: Although we can give *for every particular member* of $G - G_0$ a list of properties which this element has in common with almost all the elements of G_0, we can give *no finite list consisting of lists of properties* such that membership in G is guaranteed for an individual having all the characteristics of such a list.

Now let us take Newtonian physics. This seems to be a typical case where the method of paradigmatic examples applies. We would answer the question: 'What is the range of this theory?' by giving the class N_0 consisting of: the set containing the solar system and some subsystems of it (earth-moon, Jupiter – Jupiter-moons); the set of pendulums; the set of tides; the set consisting of the extension of 'being a free fall near the surface of the earth'.

In general, we shall call the set of paradigmatic examples of application of a theory I_0. This is always a set fixed from the beginning, i.e., from the time where the theory came into existence. By contrast, I_t is the set *believed at time t to be the range of application of the theory*. This set is *open* in the sense that from time $t-1$ to time t it may be increased by addition to I_{t-1} or decreased by removal from the set $I_{t-1}-I_0$.

The vagueness concerning membership in I_t-I_0 can be overcome by what would be called the *rule of autodetermination* of the range of application. Although at first glance it looks like a kind of autovertification, it is not. Roughly speaking, it says: "*Let the theory itself decide what belongs to this set*". (For a more detailed account of this rule vid. [*Theoriendynamik*], p. 224–231).

We have now reached a point where we can introduce a concept of availing oneself of a theory in the strong sense. The definition will be simplified by introducing the following abrogation: '$Par(p, t, I, L)$' for '$\bigvee K \bigvee A(L=\langle K, A\rangle \wedge SC(K) \wedge A=\mathbb{A}(K) \wedge p$ knows that $I \in \mathbb{A}(K) \wedge p$ chooses at t the set I as the paradigmatic set of application for every theory of mathematical physics with the logical-empirical frame L').

(D2) $Avail_{st}(p, t, L, L_0)$ (to be read as: '*in the strong sense p avails himself at t of a theory with the logical-empirical frame L and the paradigmatic set of application I_0*') iff

$$\bigvee K \bigvee A\{[L=\langle K, A\rangle \wedge LEF(L)] \wedge$$
$$\bigvee E_t(Ex(E_t, K) \wedge$$

p knows at t that

$$\bigvee I_t[Phys(I_t, K) \wedge I_0 \subseteq I_t \wedge I_t \in \mathbb{A}_e(E_t) \wedge \bigvee p_0 \bigvee t_0 \bigvee E_0$$
$$(Par(p_0, t_0, I_0, L) \wedge Ex(E_0, K) \wedge$$

p_0 knows at t_0 that

$$I_0 \in \mathbb{A}_e(E_0)) \wedge Par(p, t, I_0, L) \wedge$$

p knows at t that $I_0 \subseteqq I_t \wedge p$ knows at t that

$$\bigwedge I'(Phys(I', K) \wedge I' \in \mathbb{A}_e(E_t) \rightarrow I_0 \subseteqq I_t) \wedge p$$

knows at t that of all E' with $Ex(E', K)$ known to him at t that

$$(I_t \in \mathbb{A}_e(E') \rightarrow \mathbb{A}_e(E_t) \subseteqq \mathbb{A}_e(E'))])\}.$$

The decisive differences between the weaker and the stronger concept of using a theory of mathematical physics are the follwing ones:

(1) Only in the latter case is the historical origin of the theory made part of the concept of having a theory by mentioning the founder p_0 of the theory; (2) only in the stronger case is use made of the set I_0 of paradigmatic examples of applications introduced by the founder p_0 of the theory; (3) furthermore, the decision of p to 'take over' *this particular set* I_0 as the set of paradigms is incorporated into the definition.

One could opt for a procedure intermediate between the one just outlined and the one which was earlier called the Platonism of Sneed. It would consist, first, in introducing a less Platonistic concept of a theory and, secondly, in using this concept for a modification of (D1) and (D2). I will just sketch the basic ideas of this modification, leaving the technical details to the reader.

Let us first understand by a *potential theory* (of mathematical physics) a logical-empirical frame L which *can be filled in* by an appropriate class of physical systems, i.e., a logical-empirical frame L to which *there exists* a class I with $Phys(I, K)$, whereby K is the structural core of L and $I \in \mathbb{A}(K)$. A potential theory is called a *theory* T if, in addition, it can be expanded successfully in a non-trivial way, i.e., if

$$\bigvee E(Ex(E, K) \wedge E \neq \phi \wedge I \in \mathbb{A}_e(E)).$$

Again, you can use a concept of a theory either in the strong sense or in the weak sense depending on making the set I_0 of paradigmatic applications part of this concept or not. With '*Found* (p, T)' as short for 'p is the founder of the theory T' we get, i.e.: $Theory_{st}(T)$ ('T is a theory in the strong sense') iff

$$\bigvee K \bigvee A\{T = \langle K, A\rangle \wedge LEF(T) \wedge \bigvee I[Phys(I, K) \wedge$$
$$\wedge \bigvee p_0 \bigvee t_0 \bigvee I_0(Par(p_0, t_0, I_0, T) \wedge Found(p_0, T) \wedge$$
$$\wedge I_0 \subseteqq I) \wedge \bigvee E(Ex(E, K) \wedge E \neq \phi \wedge I \in \mathbb{A}_e(E))]\}.$$

The changes to be made in definitions (D1) and (D2) consist in replacing '*L*' by '*T*', where *T* is a theory in the weak sense or in the strong sense as the case may be. As we have now made the theory itself explicit we can use the definite article instead of the indefinite article when reading the predicates. E.g., we read $Avail_w(p, t, T)$ as '*p* avails himself at *t* of *the* theory *T*'.

Even if we do not change the original definition of having a theory, the concept of a theory may be useful for another purpose, e.g. to clarify some aspects of the 'Popperian' conception of science. Let us give just one example: If we use both classes of concepts, i. e., those of the original definitions (D1) and (D2) as well as the concepts of a theory, we can say that *p* avails himself of a theory *promisingly* if the logical-empirical frame *L* which he uses can be filled in to become a theory *T*. *p* avails himself of a theory *correctly* if the *I* which he uses in his beliefs is *identical with* one of the '*objective*' *I*'s needed to transform the logical-empirical *frame of* a theory into a *theory*.

Lakatos once pointed out that a scientific tragedy is possible consisting in the decrease of verisimilitude of a successfully better corroborated theory. If we take the concept of corroboration for granted but drop the metaphysical concept of verisimilitude we can try to explicate what Lakatos really meant in the following way: *p* avails himself at *t* of a theory *tragically* iff *p* avails himself at *t* of a corroborated theory but the logical-empirical frame which he uses cannot be filled out in such a way that it becomes a theory. We can re-enforce this by saying that *p* avails himself at *t* of a corroborated theory *very tragically* if *L* is not even a potential theory in the weak sense.

Kuhn has very often been called a *subjectivist* by his critics. What philosophers who maintain this *really mean* can perhaps be explicated with the help of the following predicate: A philosopher *x* is to be called a subjectivist (in the present context) iff *x* makes use of the concept of *having a theory* but refuses to use the concept of *a theory*. This is exactly the position already mentioned, according to which a theory comes into being only through the existence of persons who avail themselves of it. While there doesn't seem to be any objection in principal against this kind of 'subjectivism' we shall, for the discussion in (III), accept the 'objective' view, using the structuralistic concept of a theory. This decision is made only because the objective view seems to be a better starting basis for a clarification of some aspects of the problems of the immunity of theories and of the phenomenon of immediate supplanting of theories by rival ones.

In concluding this section let us emphasize the following points:

(1) To avail oneself of a theory in one of the senses suggested in no case means something like or similar to 'entertaining beliefs in particular statements' of 'accepting particular hypotheses'. *People belonging to one and the same scientific tradition or availing themselves of one and the same theory can at the same time accept different and even conflicting hypotheses.* Although all of them must agree in the belief that one and the same structural core K can successfully be expanded with respect to a class including I_0, they need not agree with respect to *which particular expansion E* will be successful.

(2) If we reconstruct the concept of a normal science in the way suggested, then we can say that *in the behaviour of a normal scientist there needn't be even a trace of irrationality.* Whatever beliefs he entertains, they can all be well-founded, and whatever hypotheses he uses, all of them can be 'well corroborated' whatever this means.

But for Popper and for his adherents scientific rationality is closely connected with such concepts as falsificability and vulnerability. The problems connected with these concept lead directly to the final section.

III. THEORY SUPPLANTING WITHOUT FALSIFICATION

In order to fix our ideas let us first agree that we use the 'objective' concept of a theory. Let us further suppose that a theory of testing (or a combination of a theory of corroboration or confirmation and a theory of testing) is at hand which, among other things, admits to talk about refutation or falsification of hypotheses. For many philosophers of science the following question is considered to be fundamental: *Is a theory falsifiable*? The correct answer to this has to be that strictly speaking this question is meaningless. The reason is simply that in our sense of the word *a theory is not that kind of entity of which one could reasonably say that it is falsified or refuted.* Therefore our problem reduces to the question of whether it would be advisable to *generalize* concepts like the concept of falsification in such a way that they not only apply to hypotheses but to theories as well.

The answer is negative. Let us dwell on this point for a while. For many critics of Kuhn, one of the most shocking aspects of his essay was the emphasis laid upon the immunity of a theory with respect to 'recalcitrant' empirical data. But actually a theory *is* empirically immune in several respects:

(1) First, suppose an empirical claim is made with the help of some theory T. This claim is an empirical hypothesis. (The hypothesis has the form of a Ramsey-Sneed-sentence, but we can forget this particular form for a moment.) Let us assume that this hypothesis is refuted. We can easily see that this refutation has no immediate impact upon the theory. All we can say is this: A person who made this particular empirical claim failed in his attempt to expand successfully the structural core of a theory. This of course does not prove that the core cannot be successfully expanded. *As the number of possible expansions of a given structural core is potentially infinite no given finite number of failures proves that the theory has to be given up.* There may be another expansion, as yet undiscovered, which, if used, would be successful. In particular in such cases where the theory has been successfully expanded in the past we will always blame first *the scientist having the theory*, and *not the theory itself*, in cases of failures. This is an obvious interpretation of Kuhn's remark that a scientist who in such a situation rejects his theory behaves like 'a poor carpenter who blames his tools' [12].

(2) There is a second immunity. It is *weaker* than the first one in being restricted in its range of application to elements of $I_t - I_0$ for every time t. But it is stronger than the first one in the following respect: Even if a whole generation of scientists failed in their attempts to apply the theory correctly to an element a of this set, and if in the end they unanimously come to the conclusion that *no expansion exists*, they are not forced to give up the theory. They can instead decide to apply the rule of autodetermination and to throw the system a out of the class $I_t - I_0$. So we see that this rule in it's range of application gives the theory a *complete immunity* even in case of *total failure*.

(3) The last point concerns the *fundamental law* occurring in the structural core of the theory. Isn't at least *this* law empirically refutable? It certainly is not *if* Sneed's conception of theoreticity turns out to be adequate: The fundamental law of a theory T necessarily contains T-theoretical quantities whose measurement is not possible in a T-indepen-

dant way. Therefore, in principle, in case of a conflict between this law and a measurement, we always have the option of *blaming the measurement and not the theory*. This, by the way, is the deeper reason for the irrefutability of the second law of Newton[13].

There certainly is a rationality gap in Kuhn's account of scientific revolutions. But all those philosophers who ask for a *'critical level'* at which a theory has to be given up, dislocalize this gap. *Such a critical level does not exist*. Recognizing this is not a matter of logical proof but of elementary psychological insight. Sneed, e.g., expresses this insight in the following way on the last page of his book: Just as a broken oar is better than none, we don't chuck a theory away until we have a better one.

Also this psychological truism preserves us from a false assessment of the rationality gap. It is of no help for the task of closing this gap once it is correctly localized.

The real problem is this: How can we differentiate between scientific changes *with* progress and scientific changes *without* progress? This question remains unanswered in Kuhn's account.[14] And the Kuhn-Feyerabend thesis of incommensurability seems to underline the unsolvability of this problem rather than to give a useful answer.

But upon closer inspection one easily realizes that this thesis of incommensurability *is restricted to a comparison of theories within the framework of the statement view of theories*. On p. 101 of [*Revolutions*], e.g., Kuhn argues that the derivation of Newtonian mechanics from relativistic dynamics as a limiting case is spurious because the fundamental concepts, like space, time and mass, have changed their meanings. Taking this for granted it still doesn't exclude saying that the first theory is *reducable* to the second one. The thesis of incommensurability would be compatible with the statement of reducibility if the notion of reduction used is based on a comparison of the accomplishments of the two theories, rather than on a comparison of the undefined and defined concepts of the theory, each theory being reconstructed as a class of sentences, and the mutual derivability of the theorems.

Interpreting Kuhn benevolently one could say that this is completely in accordance with his aims. As can be learned from the last pages of his book, what he really opposes is not the notion of rational scientific progress *as such, but rather the various teleological metaphysics* which are usually connected with the conception of rational progress. One such teleological conception is the Popperian notion of increasing verisimilitude.[15]

The way towards a reasonable concept of scientific progress which, on the one hand, is metaphysically neutral and which, on the other hand, by-passes Kuhn's difficulty of incommensurability was indicated in principle a long time ago by E. W. Adams. The basic idea is this: A theory T' must, in order to serve as a reducing theory for another theory T, satisfy two requirements. First, there must be a correspondence between the set M_{pp} of partial possible models of T and the set M'_{pp} of T', such that for each element x of M_{pp} there exists an element $x' \in M'_{pp}$. x and x' are 'the same physical objects' described in two different ways. Normally, the correspondence will be one many because T' will be able to differentiate where T will not. In other words: *to one and the same* state of affairs as described with the help of T, there will, as a rule, correspond several states of affairs, as described with the help of T'. Secondly, all successful explanations, predictions and other kinds of systematizations, obtainable with the help of T, can be 'reproduced' within T'. Translating this into the language of mathematical structures the condition amounts to the following:

(a) For any x, if there is an x' corresponding to it and having the mathematical structure of T', then x has the basic mathematical structure of T.

Within the conceptual framework of Sneed (a) has to be replaced by:

(b) If the set X' (of physical systems, i.e., of partial possible models) corresponds to a set X then $X' \in \mathbb{A}_e(E')$ only if $X \in \mathbb{A}_e(E)$.

Within (b) as opposed to (a), the following five additional aspects are taken into account: (1) the distinction between *theoretical* and *non-theoretical functions*, (2) single applications x and x' of a theory are replaced by *sets of* intended applications X and X', (3) the mathematical structure mentioned in (a) is replaced by an *expanded structural core* such that (4) cross-connections between members of X and of X' respectively may obtain via *constraints* and (5) in some of the elements of X and X' *special laws*, represented by restrictions of the fundamental law, may hold.

(b) is still not satisfactory as a basis for a definition of an adequate relation of reduction, mainly because the relation between the T-theoretical concepts and the T'-theoretical concepts is not yet taken into account. But this problem can be solved although it leads to some complications.[16]

Let us therefore take it for granted, first, that an adequate concept of reduction between expanded structural cores can be introduced, and secondly, that on the basis of this concept an adequate *reduction relation between theories* is definable. The rationality gap in Kuhn's account of scientific revolutions mentioned above can then easily be closed. If, in the course of a scientific revolution, a theory T_1 is supplanted by a theory T_2, this process exhibits a *scientific progress* only if T_1 is reducable to T_2 but T_2 is not reducible to T_1. If the radical departure from 'Platonism', consisting in accepting (D2) but abandoning the concept of a theory altogether, is favored, then this simple formulation has to be replaced by a longer one, using the reduction relation between *expanded cores* mentioned in (D2).

Reducibility, as well as irreducibility, may obtain whenever the two theories are incommensurable in the sense of Kuhn. Actually, the concept of incommensurability in this sense may be taken as a part of the very concept of scientific revolution. *A 'proper scientific revolution' exhibiting scientific progress consists in a theory T_1 being supplanted by a theory T_2 whereby* (1) *T_1 and T_2 are incommensurable and* (2) *T_1 is reducible to T_2 but not vice versa.* An apparent incompatibility between (1) and (2) would only arise by overlooking the fact that the relation of commensurability (and its negation) is to be defined within the framework of the statement view, while the various concepts of reducibility are part of the structuralist view of theories. There is no objection against using these notions *within one and the same statement,* as long as the different genealogy of the two families of concepts is not forgotten.

One may further require that the progress be *mirrored epistemically.* Roughly speaking, this would mean that the transition from T_1 to T_2, besides *being* progress, is *known to be progress* by the persons who avail themselves of the new theory T_2. This additional aspect can be incorporated into the concept of scientific progress by accepting a requirement of the following kind: (3) *There are successful expansions of the structural core of T_2,* i.e., *expansions known to be supported by observational data to which there don't exist corresponding successful expansions of the structural core of T_1.* It seems to us that Lakatos when he introduced the somewhat misleading expression 'sophisticated falsification' really had in mind this *epistemic superiority* of a supplanting theory in the course of scientific progress, perhaps in addition to an attempt to close the rationality gap in Kuhn's account on the same line as we did, namely by means of a concept of *reduction* of theories.[17]

NOTES

1 For details concerning the following sentences suggested as reproducing the empirical claims of a theory vid. Sneed, [*Mathematical Physics*], p. 42ff, or Stegmüller, [*Theoriendynamik*], p. 65ff.

2 It should be noted that our use of the word 'empirical' is an informal one. It only means that people whom we call empirical scientists don't get involved in the problem of theoretical functions when testing the truth of (II).

3 For a precise definition vid. [*Theoriendynamik*], p. 84.

4 Some, or even all, of the law-constraints are allowed to be empty, i.e., to be true tautologically.

5 It should not be overlooked that the elements of an intended application are not simply domains of individuals but rather *domains of individuals plus non-theoretical functions*.

6 From now on only (informal) set theoretic concepts will be used. We shall henceforth omit indices referring either to an intuitive entity like a theory in the presystematic sense or to a linguistic entity such as a predicate expressing a mathematical structure.

7 The reason for including the general constraints, i.e., those 'cross-combining' *all* intended applications, may be exemplified by the Newtonian concept of *mass*: Of a person, originally called a Newtonian, who decided to use a *non-extensive* mass function, thereby changing a general constraint, we would certainly say that he has exchanged the Newtonian *theory* for a new one and not just that he replaced a particular hypothesis *within* the Newtonian theory by another one.

8 This is the set having as elements the extensions of the predicates occuring in (IV) formed from 'S' with the help of an upper index.

9 A formal definition of α is given in [*Theoriendynamik*], on p. 131. The definition given by Sneed at the top of p. 180 of his work doesn't seem to be quite correct.

10 The technical definition of this function $\mathbb{A}_e$ would correspond to definition (D35) on p. 181 in Sneed's work. A slightly different definition to this is given in [*Theoriendynamik*] on p. 133.

11 This member expresses what could be called *the belief in progress within normal science*, i.e., *the belief in scientific progress without revolutions*.

12 [*Revolutions*], p. 79, 80.

13 For a detailed analysis of the epistemological status of this law vid. Sneed, [*Mathematical Physics*], p. 150–153.

14 Vid. Kuhn, [*Revolutions*], p. 166: "Revolutions close with a total victory for one of the two opposing camps. Will that group ever say that the result of its victory has been something less than progress?" If Kuhn should believe that this is the last word to be said about progress in science, then he can hardly claim that 'progress' in science is more rational than any change in the field of politics.

15 This notion is a *teleological* one because it characterizes the state of scientific

progress by means of *distance from truth* as the *final aim* of science. It is a *metaphysical* one because, whatever the exact definition of this distance may amount to, we'll certainly never be able to use it as a means of evaluating a suggested hypothesis.

[16] For details vid. Sneed, [*Mathematical Physics*], p. 223ff. For a simplified version vid. Stegmüller, [*Theoriendynamik*], p. 148–151. For readers of Sneed's book we mention that the text is mutilated on the pages 229 and 230.

[17] The important new concept in the recent writings of Lakatos is this concept of sophisticated falsification and *not* his concept of a research program. Contrary to what Lakatos says, a research program is *not* a sequence of theories, but rather a sequence of *empirical claims* made on the basis of *one and the same theory*. It can, therefore, best be considered as a subcase of what Kuhn calls normal science, including all kinds of progress within one and the same theory which are not accompanied by setbacks (while 'normal science' includes *all* kinds of changes of a theory, progressions as well as setbacks). By contrast, the concept of *sophisticated falsification* is introduced *as a relation between theories*. For a proof of the claim made in the text vid. [*Theoriendynamik*], p. 259f. If this claim is correct it would have been better if Lakatos, instead of saying '*T_1 is falsified by T_2*', had used a phrase like '*T_1 is surpassed by T_2*'. Surpassing may be understood in such a way as to include both reduction and 'excess corroboration', or epistemic superiority.

BIBLIOGRAPHY

Diederich, W. (ed.): *Theorien der Wissenschaftsgeschichte. Beiträge zur diachronischen Wissenschaftstheorie*, Frankfurt a.Main 1974.

Feigl, H.: 'The 'Orthodox' View of Theories: Remarks in Defense as well as Critique', in M. Radner and S. Winokur (eds.), *Minnesota Studies in the Philosophy of Science*, Vol. IV: *Analyses of Theories and Methods of Physics and Psychology*, Minneapolis 1970, 3–16.

Feigl, H.: 'Research Programmes and Induction', *Boston Studies in the Philosophy of Science*, Vol. VIII (1973), 147–150.

Feyerabend, P. K.: 'Das Problem der Existenz theoretischer Entitäten', in E. Topitsch (ed.), *Probleme der Wissenschaftstheorie. Festschrift für Victor Kraft*, Wien 1960, 35–72.

Feyerabend, P. K.: 'Problems of Empiricism', in R. G. Colodny (ed.), *Beyond the Edge of Certainty. Essays in Contemporary Science and Philosophy*, Englewood Cliffs 1965, 145-260.

Feyerabend, P. K.: 'Problems of Empiricism, Part II', in R. G. Colodny (ed.), *The Nature and Function of Scientific Theory: Essays in Contemporary Science and Philosophy*, Pittsburgh 1969, 275-353.

Feyerabend, P. K.: 'Consolations for the Specialist', in I. Lakatos, and A. Musgrave (eds.), *Criticism and the Growth of Knowledge*, Cambridge 1970, 197–230.

Feyerabend, P. K.: 'Against Method', in M. Radner, and S. Winokur (eds.), *Minnesota Studies in the Philosophy of Science*, Vol. IV: *Analyses of Theories and Methods of Physics and Psychology*, Minneapolis 1970, 17–130.

Hanson, N. R.: *Patterns of Discovery*, Cambridge 1958.

Hempel. C. G.: 'On the 'Standard Conception' of Scientific Theories', in M. Radner, and S. Winokur (eds.), *Minnesota Studies in the Philosophy of Science*, Vol. IV: *Analyses of Theories and Methods of Physics and Psychology*, Minneapolis 1970, 142–163.

Hempel, C. G.: 'The Meaning of Theoretical Terms: A Critique of the Standard Empiricist Construal', in P. Suppes, L. Henkin, A. Joja and G. C. Moisil (eds.), *Logic, Methodology and Philosophy of Science* IV. *Proceedings of the* 1971 *International Congress*, Bukarest 1971, Amsterdam (forthcoming).
Hübner, K.: Review of T. S. Kuhn, *The Structure of Scientific Revolutions*, Philosophische Rundschau, Jahrg. 15 (1968), 185–195.
Koertge, N.: 'For and Against Method', Discussion of P. Feyerabend's [Against], *The British Journal for the Philosophy of Science*, Vol. 23 (1972), 274–285.
Koertge, N.: 'Inter-Theoretic Criticism and the Growth of Science', in *Boston Studies in the Philosophy of Science*, Vol. VIII (1972), 160–173.
Kordig, C. R.: *The Justification of Scientific Change*, Dordrecht 1971.
Krüger, L., *Die systematische Bedeutung wissenschaftlicher Revolutionen. Pro und Contra Thomas Kuhn*, in: Diederich, W. (ed.), Theorien der Wissenschaftsgeschichte, Frankfurt a.Main 1974, 210–246.
Kuhn, T. S.: *The Copernican Revolution*, New York 1957.
Kuhn, T. S.: [Revolutions] *The Structure of Scientific Revolutions*, second enlarged ed. Chicago 1970. German translation of the first ed. by K. Simon: *Die Struktur wissenschaftlicher Revolutionen*, Frankfurt a. Main 1967.
Kuhn, T. S.: 'Logic of Discovery or Psychology of Research?" in I. Lakatos, and A. Musgrave (eds.), *Criticism and the Growth of Knowledge*, Cambridge 1970, 1–23.
Kuhn, T. S.: 'Reflections on My Critics', in I. Lakatos and A. Musgrave (eds.), *Criticism and the Growth of Knowledge*, Cambridge 1970, 231–278.
Kuhn, T. S.: 'Notes on Lakatos', in *Boston Studies in the Philosophy of Science*, Vol. VIII (1972), 137–146.
Lakatos, I.: [Research Programmes] 'Falsification and the Methodology of Scientific Research Programmes', in I. Lakatos and A. Musgrave (eds.), *Criticism and the Growth of Knowledge*, Cambridge 1970, 91–195.
Lakatos, I.: 'History of Science and Its Rational Reconstruction', in *Boston Studies in the Philosophy of Science*, Vol. VIII (1972), 91–136.
Lakatos, I.: 'Replies to Critics', in *Boston Studies in the Philosophy of Science*, Vol. VIII (1972), 174–182.
Masterman, M.: 'The Nature of a Paradigm', in I. Lakatos, and A. Musgrave (eds.), *Criticism and the Growth of Knowledge*, Cambridge 1970, 59–89.
McKinsey, J. C. C., Sugar, A. C., and Suppes, P. C.: 'Axiomatic Foundations of Classical Particle Mechanics', *Journal of Rational Mechanics and Analysis*, Vol. II (1953), 253–272.
Popper, K. R.: *The Logic of Scientific Discovery*, London 1959. German translation by L. Walentik, *Logik der Forschung*, fifth ed., Tübingen 1973.
Popper, K. R.: *Conjectures and Refutations*, third ed., London 1969.
Popper, K. R.: *Objective Knowledge. An Evolutionary Approach*, Oxford 1972.
Popper, K. R.: [Dangers] 'Normal Science and Its Dangers', in I. Lakatos and A. Musgrave (eds.), *Criticism and the Growth of Knowledge*, Cambridge 1970, 51–58.
Przełecki, M.: 'A Set Theoretic Versus a Model Theoretic Approach to the Logical Structure of Physical Theories'. Some Comments on J. Sneed's *The Logical Structure of Mathematical Physics*, Studia Logica 1974, 91–112.
Putnam, H.: 'What Theories are Not', in E. Nagel, P. Suppes, and A. Tarski (eds.) *Logic, Methodology and Philosophy of Science*, Stanford 1962, 240–251.
Ramsey, F. P.: 'Theories', in *The Foundations of Mathematics*, second ed., Littlefield, N. J. 1960, 212–236.

Scheffler, I.: *Science and Subjectivity*, New York 1967.
Scheffler, I.: 'Vision and Revolution: A Postscript on Kuhn', *Philosophy of Science*, Vol. 39 (1972), 366–374.
Shapere, D.: Discussion of T. S. Kuhn, *The Structure of Scientific Revolutions*, *Philosophical Review*, Vol. 73 (1964), 383–394.
Shapere, D.: 'Meaning and Scientific Change', in R. G. Colodny (ed.), *Mind and Cosmos*, Pittsburgh 1966, 41–85.
Simon, H. A.: 'The Axioms of Newtonian Mechanics', *Philosophical Magazine*, Vol. 38 (1947), 88–95.
Simon, H. A.: 'The Axiomatization of Classical Mechanics', *Philosophy of Science*, Vol. 21 (1954), 340–343.
Simon, H. A.: 'The Axiomatization of Physical Theories', *Philosophy of Science*, Vol. 37 (1970), 16–27.
Smart, J. J.: 'Science, History and Methodology', Discussion of I. Lakatos, Research Programmes and History, *The British Journal for the Philosophy of Science*, Vol. 23 (1972), 266–274.
Sneed, J. D.: [Mathematical Physics] *The Logical Structure of Mathematical Physics*, Dordrecht 1971.
Stegmüller, W.: *Probleme und Resultate der Wissenschaftstheorie und Analytischen Philosophie*, Vol. II: *Theorie und Erfahrung*, Berlin-Heidelberg-New York 1970.
Stegmüller, W.: 'Das Problem der Induktion: Hume's Herausforderung und moderne Antworten', in H. Lenk (ed.), *Neue Aspekte der Wissenschaftstheorie*, Braunschweig 1971, 13–74. Appears in translation as Chapter 4 of this book.
Stegmüller, W.: *Probleme und Resultate der Wissenschaftstheorie und Analytischen Philosophie*, Vol. IV: *Personelle und Statistische Wahrscheinlichkeit*. First half volume: *Personelle Wahrscheinlichkeit und rationale Entscheidung*. Second half volume: *Statistisches Schließen – Statistische Begründung – Statistische Analyse*, Berlin-Heidelberg-New York 1973.
Stegmüller, W.: [Theoriendynamik] *Probleme und Resultate der Wissenschaftstheorie und Analytischen Philosophie*, Vol. II: *Theorie und Erfahrung*. Second half volume: *Theorienstrukturen und Theoriendynamik*, Berlin-Heidelberg-New York 1973.
Stegmüller, W.: 'Theoriendynamik und logisches Verständnis', in: W. Diederich (ed.), *Theorien der Wissenschaftsgeschichte*, Frankfurt a. Main 1974, 167–209. Appears in translation as Chapter 6 of this book.
Stegmüller, W.: *Hauptströmungen der Gegenwartsphilosophie*, fifth ed. Stuttgart 1975, 2d Vol., Chapter V.
Watkins, J.: 'Against 'Normal Science'', in I. Lakatos and A. Musgrave (eds.), *Criticism and the Growth of Knowledge*, Cambridge 1970, 25–37.

CHAPTER 8

LANGUAGE AND LOGIC

1. PREFACE

It has been claimed by many of today's logicians that logical-epistemological investigations can reach clear and precise results only if the object of study is a linguistic system constructed according to precise rules. Due to the vagueness pervading it, ordinary language is unable to satisfy this condition. According to this view, it must therefore be replaced by a formalized language or a series of formalized languages to be constructed on the basis of certain explicitly formulated rules. When one speaks of the vagueness of ordinary language what comes immediately to mind is so-called equivocation, i.e., the multiple meanings an expression may take; e.g. the expression 'bark' may mean respectively (1) the outer covering of trees, (2) the kind of sound omitted by dogs, or (3) a type of sailing ship. Such ambiguities, however, are trivial, for one can without difficulty gather from the respective context exactly which of the several meanings of that word is intended. Hence it would be absurd to justify the demand for a more precise logical language by pointing to ambiguous expressions such as 'bark'. But, there are still other reasons for using a symbolic language to pursue logical studies, the main one being the possibility of achieving greater perspicuity and economy of expression. Just as mathematics would have made but little progress without resorting to the appropriate mathematics symbols, so logic cannot be expected to arrive at significant results if denied the use of symbolic language. Were we not permitted to resort to algebraic symbols, even a simple math statement like: '$(a + b)^2 = a^2 + 2ab + b^2$' would commit us to the rather complicated expression: the square of the sum of any two numbers is the same as the sum of the square of the first, plus the product of the first and second times two, plus the square of the second'. In an analogous way, statements of an even more complicated structure would, as a whole, require such a complicated formulation in ordinary language that a logical analysis would become troublesome and time-consuming unless this formulation be replaced by a more transparent one allowing free recourse to symbols.

For the moment, however, let's concentrate exclusively on the objection of vagueness which is quite legitimately raised against ordinary language. Contrary to the above example, this objection must obviously be supported by non-trivial cases. In what follows I will cite a few such non-trivial cases. It is absolutely essential to clear them up since any misunderstanding about them might lead to grave philosophical mistakes, namely, either to the omission of justifiable questions or, as is even more often the case, to the formulation of misleading questions in the face of which we are left only the choice of giving no answer at all or simply a meaningless one.[1]

2. THE FUNCTIONS OF 'IS'

One of the most important words in our language is the word 'is'. It is likewise one of the most philosophically dangerous words. The reason for this is that it has a plethora of totally different functions on the one hand, while, on the other hand, occasioning the formulation of the basic ontological problem, the so-called problem of Being. Thus, by glossing over these several functions we have often been led astray. Consider the following cases: the theist claims 'God *is*'; the teacher of geography utters in the course of his lesson the sentence: 'Managua *IS* the capital of Nicaragua', and afterwards upon being questioned he states 'Matagapla *IS* a town'; the teacher of natural history tells his students 'the whale *is* a mammal'; in an elementary math class the following expression comes up '7+2 *is* 9'; the proud mother brags about her son 'John *is* intelligent'; a father teaches his son new colour words and while doing so points and says 'this *is* ocher'; in the course of a discussion a person responds to another's statement with the words 'so it *IS*'. Let's therefore, begin to sort out clearly the various meanings of 'is'.

(1) In the first example we have an existential sentence, since the same sentence can obviously be restated equally well with the words 'God exists' or 'there is a God'. It is not always possible to formulate (a positive or negative) existential sentence by using the word 'is'. This can only be done in cases where the position of the grammatical subject is occupied by a name or a so-called description.[2] 'God exists' as well as 'Jupiter does not exist' are both examples of the first kind since 'God' and 'Jupiter' are individual designators which function as names; both of the following sentences: 'the first person to climb Mt. Everest exists' and 'the first person to climb the moon mountain[3] Longomontanus does not exist' are examples of the second kind, since both of the expressions 'the first person to climb Mt. Everest' and 'the first person to climb the lunar mountain Longomontanus' assume the form of individual

descriptions. One speaks in such cases of particular existential sentences. These do not at all represent the normal type of existential assertion. Ordinarily such an assertion takes the form of a (positive or negative) general existential statement: 'Flying fish exist', 'Sea-serpents do not exist'. Here it is asserted of objects characterized solely along class lines, like 'to be a flying fish' or 'to be a sea-serpent', that they exist or do not exist. By force of a convention, a positive general existential statement will be considered true even if just a single object satisfies the condition expressed in the predicate. 'Men taller than two and a half meters exist' will be considered true even if there is only one such man. It is thus not advisable to employ a term like 'some' in the formulation, as has been the case in traditional logic, e.g., 'some fish fly'; for this term tends to suggest that there must be a plurality, albeit indefinite, of cases which satisfy the predicate in order to make the entire statement true. That the word 'is' can not be used to formulate such general existential assertions is simply due to the fact that the grammatical subjects are in the plural while 'is', on the other hand, represents the singular case. This reason is obviously trivial; the plural of 'is' is 'are'. Consequently, instead of formulating them as above, we may construe the statements as 'there are flying fish' or, respectively, 'there are no sea-serpents'.

On account of the many other functions still to be considered in which the words 'is', 'are' (and of course also 'am') are used it is best we construct all sorts of positive as well as negative existential assertions, singular as well as general, without resorting to 'is' or 'are'. But even the other versions may be misleading, particularly those in which the word 'exists' comes up. The reason for this is the following: in our language we have at our disposal three kinds of tools for talking about the properties of an object, viz., adjectives (red, ugly), nouns (man, horse), and intransitive verbs (runs, flies). This break-down is obviously accidental and accordingly no such distinction is even made in symbolic language-systems, where all predications are expressed in exactly the same way. More cause for concern is the fact that in language, words having quite a different function assume at times one of these grammatical forms. One of them is the word 'exist'. It is an intransitive verb. Looked at superficially, it leads one to believe that it expresses a property as do most other intransitive verbs. Here is where the views according to which 'Being' is a predicate originate, which already Kant had quite rightly rejected. Both of the following statements: 'Frogs quack' and 'Frogs exist' have the same grammatical structure in our ordinary language, and consequently we are strongly tempted to speculate not only about the quacking of frogs but also about the existence of frogs. As a matter of fact, however, it is only in the former statement, and not in the latter, that we are dealing with two predicate expressions. If 'x' is a variable for any object whatsoever, then we might exhibit the two predicates appearing in the first statement by means of the following linguistic expression 'x is a frog' and 'x quacks'. The whole statement would then read 'given any object x, if x is a frog, then x quacks'. The second statement, on the contrary, can by no means be construed in a comparable way, viz., 'given any object x, if x is a frog, then x exists'; it must, instead, be rendered by 'there are frogs', i.e., 'there are objects x such that x is a frog'. Thus it becomes clear that only the predicate 'frog' appears in the existential assertion. Assertions of existence are so extremely important in everyday life as well as in science that logicians have introduced a special symbol for the expression 'there is an object x'; viz., '(Ex)'. By resorting to this symbol, the second statement would then be written '(Ex) (x is a frog)'. The fact that we have only *one* predicate expression here is made clear by the mode of expression.

But would one not try to interpret existence statements in such a way that this existence or Being is a property? It must indeed be a most general property: everything which we say exists, would have this property. N. Hartmann is, in fact, a contemporary representative of just such a point of view. Being is for him that which identically recurs in everything that exists.[4] Being is, therefore, taken to be the most general attribute: it is so all-embracing that nothing whatsoever can escape it. The predicate 'red' for example holds true only of red things, but everything that is not red escapes it; the predicate 'Being', on the contrary, would hold true of everything whatsoever. Consequently, the word 'Being' would be a name of something. Everything to which we refer to by means of a name and about which we can then speak is, however, counted as an existent. And so Being would itself be an existent. But since all existents are supposed to possess the property of Being, then there must obviously also be a Being of Being, and in endless succession a Being of Being of Being, a Being of Being of Being of Being, ... etc.[5] One can hardly escape this consequence if one begins to speak of Being as the most general property of everything that exists. Yet another difficulty follows from this interpretation, viz., if I say of some object or other that it possesses a certain property, I thereby implicitly presuppose that the object exists when I refer to it by means of a name or in some other way. As a result, a positive singular existential assertion would become a tautological claim; for with the word 'exists' the object designated 'so and so' in the statement 'The so and so exists' would be explicitly ascribed the very property which had already been attributed to it by the 'so and so' in the first part of the statement. A negative singular statement, on the other hand, would represent a contradiction; for, obviously, I cannot ascribe a property to a thing in the first half of the statement and then go on to deny it in the second part of the statement. Even if the interpretation that Being designates a general property were discarded, an air of paradox would still surround expressions such as 'The God Jupiter does not exist' or 'the square circle does not exist'. Later on we will again discuss how to cope with this apparent contradiction.

So it is a faulty grammar that occasions us to speak of the 'Being of the existent'. Nor is language less deficient when it expresses negative existential statements via predicates. We may not only say 'Aristotle is wise' and 'greyhounds are fast', but also 'The King is dead' and 'sea-serpents are fictitious'; from all this there arises the absurd inclination to talk not only of the wise Aristotle and fast greyhounds, but also of the dead King and fictitious sea-serpents as some special sort of objects. Here, we must nevertheless concede that through such formulations language expresses more than would be possible through simple negative existential statements. 'Unicorns are fictitious' does not simply mean 'there are no unicorns' but more than that. What is conveyed by it may perhaps be put roughly as follows: 'we can use the word "unicorn" as a meaningful word of our language, we can imagine unicorns, paint unicorns, and even believe that they exist; nevertheless, there exist no unicorns'. Some will perhaps feel inclined to make a last ditch effort at rescuing the theory of 'existence is a property' by arguing as follows: sure enough, sea-serpents do not exist in the real world of space and time, but sea-serpents do exist, however, as *unactualized possibilities*. Later we also want to come back to this thesis.[6] For the moment we are still confronted with the task of pointing out the various other functions of 'is'.

(2) In 'Managua is the capital of Nicaragua' the 'is' stands merely for identity and in this context we may replace it by the sign '=' and so obtain 'Managua = the capital of Nicaragua'. It has often been claimed that this concept of identity is so elementary that it could not be explained any further. Any such pseudo-explanation would only replace the predicate 'is identical with' by a synonym, as is, for example, the case when two objects are said to be identical with one another if and only if they really are one and the same thing. If there is nevertheless a philosophical problem in connection with this concept, it has nothing whatsoever to do with the concept itself but rather with its possible use. One might speak of a downright paradox of the theory of identity: it might be expressed in the following way: every statement according to which a thing is identical with itself must be true in a trivial sense and every statement in which it is asserted that a thing is identical

with another is false. The whole theory of identity seems, consequently, to collapse into two classes of uninteresting claims: a class of trivial truths and a class of falsehoods. How is it then at all possible that such a concept can play a role in science and in everyday life, and that textbooks of logic contain a separate chapter with the title 'theory of identity'? The answer is as simple as it is significant:[7] were our language perfect in the sense that for every object, we would have at our disposal one and only one designation, so that in every case we were able to make reference to a thing solely by means of a simple name, then this concept of identity would actually turn out to be completely useless. For the only truths we would then be able to reach with the help of such a concept would be expressions entirely devoid of content, expressions of the form 'Leibniz = Leibniz', 'Vienna = Vienna', etc. from which we would obtain no information whatsoever. Such a language would, however, be radically different from ours. We can designate one and the same person via the labels 'Aristotle' and 'the teacher of Alexander the Great', 'Cicero' and 'Marcus Tullius', and the same is true also of '4^3' and '59 + 5' or '15 degrees Celsius' and 'The highest temperature registered in Innsbruck on June 2, 1955'. Evidently it is a significant advantage of our language that it does not possess the 'perfection' just cited, for it would otherwise render such expressions impossible since there would then obtain a unique correlation between things and their designations. Thus the necessity of using the concept of identity is not due to ontological considerations, but rather to a linguistic peculiarity of our language. This, though, must not be misunderstood and taken to mean that identity is a relation between linguistic expressions. On the contrary, it is the objects which are identified; but in the statement of identity two names or other labels are linked by means of the symbol '=' and the identity sentence then says that these two expressions really designate the same object. The non-trivial cases of such assertions are marked off by the fact that a mere analysis of the meaning of the expressions in such statements does not suffice to determine the truth of the identity statement. The above examples are precisely of such a kind. Two additional examples would be astronomy's claim 'the Morning Star = the Evening Star' or the biological truth 'the class of creatures with a heart = the class of creatures with kidneys'.

(3) In 'Matagalpa is a city' the 'is' functions quite differently than in 'Managua is the capital of Nicaragua'. This last statement may, as we have already seen, be rephrased by means of the identity symbol, that is, 'Managua = the capital of Nicaragua'. Were one to apply the same sort of rephrasing to the former statement as well one would arrive at absurd consequences. Identity possesses, namely, the so-called property of transitivity; i.e., if an object *a*

is identical with a second object *b* and this object *b* is in turn identical with a third object *c*, then *a* must also be identical with *c*. Now, it is not just the statement 'Matagalpa is a city' that holds *T* but also the statement 'Vienna is a city'. On account of the transitivity just mentioned, the restatement of both of these true sentences with the help of '=', namely, 'Matagalpa = city' and 'Vienna = city', would yield the conclusion 'Vienna = Matagalpa'; in other words, the assertion that the city of Vienna is identical with the city of Matagalpa, something which, according to present-day geography, surely does not accord with the facts.

Quite a few possibilities still remain open for an adequate interpretation of the statement in question. Deciding between these various possibilities is no purely linguistic matter but depends upon the kind of ontology one is willing to accept. What precisely the expression 'to accept an ontology' means will become completely clear only later. For now, it should suffice to say that the recognition of certain objects and/or types of objects presupposes an ontology in which these objects or types are counted among the existing objects. This is especially important in connection with the question of abstract objects. He who is of the opinion that there are, in addition to particular objects in space and time, also such things as numbers, mathematical functions, properties, classes, and the like, presupposes an ontology which is called Platonistic, since classes, numbers, etc. are not concrete objects. A fundamental concept here is the concept of a class or set. It can be shown that many other kinds of abstract objects, in particular all mathematical objects such as functions, numbers, and relations, are reducible to this class or set concept. Thus whoever acknowledges not just concrete objects, but also classes of them, reveals his Platonistic bent. Due to the conclusion between the concept of a class and the concept of a concrete whole, aggregate or heap, this point is sometimes overlooked. In contrast to a concrete whole, there need be no real connection between the things which are collected into a class. I can compile a class of three elements of which the first is a mountain on the moon, the second a cave in the Himalayan mountains and the third Alexander the Great. It must, of course, be admitted that the possibility of constructing such odd classes offers as yet no cogent grounds for speaking here of an abstract object. For even if normally a real connection is required if a concrete thing is meant, this is, however, not necessary. One might grant that a concrete object consists of 'bits' randomly distributed in a spatio-temporal world. As a matter of fact, even in physics, for example, one speaks of the atom as an object although the electrons are extremely distant from the protons in relation to their size. But where is one to draw the line between the admissible and inadmissible degree of 'splitting' and what degree of homogeneity need obtain between the bits so as to warrant still speaking of one and the same concrete thing? To set such limits would obviously be a purely arbitrary matter. Why not, therefore, stipulate that the mountain on the moon, the cave, and Alexander the Great be part of one and the same concrete whole? If such an interpretation is permitted, then we have escaped Platonism.

But now the difference emerges in yet another guise. One may ascribe or deny to a concrete heap of stones the very same properties that apply to the stones themselves, but not, however, to the class of these stones. The heap has a certain diameter, a particular weight, and a closed three-dimensional spatial surface inside of which the entire heap is contained. But all of this does not hold true for the class of stones. The difference becomes completely clear as soon as we correlate different classes to one and the same concrete whole; for instance, a particular individual organism may be correlated to the class of its cells as well as to the class of molecules of which it is composed. The concrete whole of these cells is identical with the concrete whole of molecules. The two classes, however, are different; for the class of cells contains, say, a few million elements, the class of molecules a few billions. That the two classes differ from one another is shown, therefore, by their different numerical value. This example ought not to be misunderstood as meaning that we have thereby shown the necessity of positing the existence of classes. Rather, it simply means that *if* one is at all disposed to accept classes, *then* he must necessarily distinguish them from concrete aggregates and furthermore admit that different classes might correspond to one and the same aggregate. The Nominalist is unwilling to make such a concession for he is of the opinion that two objects are distinguished from one another only in so far as their content differs. He, therefore, simply refuses to acknowledge that in addition to the concrete whole of elements there are also classes of these elements. This does not at all depend, of course, on the choice of the expression 'class'. With it the Nominalist can attempt to designate what we have called the concrete whole or aggregate. Whether the word is understood in this way or in a Platonistic sense can only be determined by seeing how it is used. If the expression 'class' is employed in such a way that the class of cells of an organism is identified with the class of molecules of this same organism, then we have the 'aggregate interpretation'. If, on the other hand, these two classes are distinguished from one another on the ground that they contain a different number of elements, then we have the abstract interpretation.

Yet another reason why the Platonistic character of the class concept failed to be recognized in traditional philosophy may be seen in the fact that, as a rule, the Platonistic standpoint has been illustrated by adjectives employed as nouns or by appending the end syllable 'hood' ('ness') to a noun. Thus it was said, for example that within a Platonistic world-view one accepts the existence not only of blue things, but also of blueness, the existence not only of horses, but of horsehood as well. But obviously it is completely indifferent whether I speak of blueness or of the class of blue things, and of horsehood or of the class of horses.[8] In each case one proceeds, via a predicate that makes sense only for concrete individuals, to a new abstract essence. Whether this transition is effected by appending the end syllable 'hood' to the predicate expression or by prefixing the words 'class of' is of no significance.

Let's now suppose that the recognition of classes is not viewed as suspect. We might then interpret the above 'is' statement as a class membership relation. This relation will be represented as in math by the epsilon symbol 'ϵ'; '$\alpha \epsilon K$' means, therefore, that α is an element of K. We then interpret all property words as names of distinct classes: 'green' denotes the class of green objects, 'eagle' the class of eagles, and 'city' the class of cities. 'Matagalpa is a city', according to this interpretation, actually says 'Matagalpa ϵ city', i.e., 'Matagalpa is an element of the class of cities'. A great many everyday as well as scientific 'is sentences' are amenable to this kind of interpretation: 'Fritz is a winter sportsman', 'Aristotle is wise', 'the sky is blue', when translated become: 'Fritz ϵ winter sportsman', 'Aristotle ϵ wise', 'the sky ϵ blue'.

But what if one is not willing to espouse Platonism, that is, is not willing to interpret property words as *names* of abstract objects? Would such statements then become meaningless? The fact that they are indispensible in everyday as well as in scientific discourse would constitute an indirect proof for the validity of Platonism. Such a conclusion would, however, be premature. One may, without contradiction, take the following position: the only linguistic units to have a meaning are statements. Single expressions when torn from their contexts do not by themselves mean anything but are merely incomplete linguistic symbols which only acquire meaning to the extent that they can be used to form statements which are meaningful by themselves. This holds true especially for all predicate expressions. A predicate such as 'white' has, therefore, no meaning as an isolated linguistic symbol; in particular, it is not the name of an abstract essence – whiteness – or of the class of white things. Yet even according to this interpretation the symbol 'white' is still quite useful. To recognize this we must proceed from a certain simple statement containing this predicate, for example, 'the snow is white'. By deleting 'the snow' we obtain the sentential fragment 'is white' which has one empty place that may be filled in by some arbitrary symbol, say '*x*', and thus obtain '*x* is white'. '*x*' is a variable for it holds the place free for the designation of any object whatever. Complexes such as '*x* is white', '*x* is a city', '*x* is a man' are also called open sentences. Open sentences are neither true nor false; they become so as soon as they become genuine statements. These can be formed either by substituting a specific designation of an object for the variable, or by prefixing an 'all' or 'there is' to the complex, thus forming a universal or existential sentence (e.g., 'there are things *x* such that *x* is a man', in other words 'there are men'). The Nominalist who refuses to acknowledge abstract objects can always by such means interpret predicate expressions not as names of abstract objects but as open sentences which he then regards as mere sentential fragments to be turned into genuine statements by performing certain operations on them. Thus he need not admit into his world anything but concrete things. In contradistinction to the Platonistic interpretation, the 'is' does not represent a relation either (class membership relation or thing property relation) but is just a mere fragment of a fragment, for it makes its appearance as an incomplete symbol in incomplete expressions of the form '*x* is white'.

But 'is' may also be interpreted as 'has the property' so that 'α is *B*' comes to mean 'α has the property *B*' whereby '*B*' is construed as the name of a property. Again properties are not concrete objects, and consequently conceiving property words as *names of* properties leads us once more right back into Platonism. Nevertheless it is not the same Platonism we encountered before but in a certain sense a richer one. Consider the empirical claim that presumably all and only those creatures with a heart also possess kidneys. Let's regard this as an established fact; in such a case, the class of creatures with a heart is identical with the class of creatures with kidneys. Thus, if both of the compound expressions 'creature with heart' and 'creature with kidneys' are construed as class names, the identity sentence 'creature with heart = creature with kidneys' holds true. If, on the contrary, they are construed as designations of properties – let's call it the 'property interpretation' – then, since the property of being a creature with a heart is different from the property of being a creature with kidneys, obviously 'creature with heart = creature with kidneys' holds true. If 'α' is the name of some object or other, then within the framework of class interpretation both of the statements '$\alpha \in$ creature with heart' and '$\alpha \in$ creature with kidneys' have the same import whereas 'α is a creature with a heart' and 'α is a creature with kidneys' do not represent statements of equal import under the property interpretation. It generally holds true that one and the same class can be determined by different properties while, on the contrary, one and the same property can never be determined by different classes of objects. The addition of classes, just like the admission of properties, to the universe of existing things leads, indeed, to a Platonistic ontology; this latter, however, will contain a bigger store of objects than the former on account of the different conditions of identity holding between classes and properties just mentioned. Since the class belonging to a property is also called the extension of this property, while the different properties that correspond to one and the same class are considered their intensions, one might, therefore, distinguish between an extensional and an intensional Platonism. Consequently we have three possible interpretations of the predicating 'is':

(a) 'is' represents an incomplete linguistic symbol occurring in sentences as well as sentential schemata. Sentential schemata are open sentences with an individual variable and can be turned into meaningful statements in two different ways: by substituting an individual name for the variable or by prefixing an 'all' or 'there is' (Nominalistic Interpretation).

(b) The predicate expressions occurring in the predications are class names, and 'is' expresses accordingly the class membership relation (extensional Platonism).

(c) Predicates are names of properties, and 'is' in a predication expresses accordingly the relation between a thing and the property which that thing possesses (intensional Platonism).

(4) How about the statement 'the whale is a mammal'? It would be totally mistaken to claim that under the class interpretation this statement must be put on a par with the sentence 'Matagalpa is a city' that is, with 'Matagalpa ϵ city' and so require that a faithful translation of it read: 'the whale ϵ Mammal'. 'Matagalpa' is the name of an individual object, while 'the whale', on the contrary, is not a name of something individual. Hence within the framework of class interpretation the statement is equivalent to saying 'the class of whales is a subclass of the class of mammals'. In such a case it is, therefore, not the relation between an element and the corresponding class that is conveyed by 'is' but rather the relation between subclass and the corresponding class. In math it is usual to symbolize the relation between a subclass and the class embracing it by means of the symbol '$\subset$'; in other words, 'the class A is a subclass of the class B' becomes '$A \subset B$'. The relations of element to class and subclass to class must not be confused with one another, not even if within the class membership relation the element should itself turn out to be a class. The things which belong to a subclass of a class obviously also belong to the class itself. Therefore, we may assign to all the

objects of which the predicate determining the subclass can be predicated the predicate determining the entire class as well. If it can be justifiably asserted of an object that it is a whale, then it must also hold that it is a mammal. Hence the adequate translation of 'the whole is a mammal' should read: 'whale $\subset$ mammal'. If, on the other hand, a class A is an element of a second class B, the elements of class A are not elements of B but simply elements of an element of B. In doubtful cases this can serve as a criterion for deciding whether a certain class is an element of a second class or merely a particular subclass of this second class. Must we, for example, construe the class of Anabaptists as an element of the class of the Christian sects or as a subclass of the class of the Christian sects? Consider a single Anabaptist. Can one say of him that he is a Christian sect? Of course not. Therefore the class of Anabaptists is not a subclass of the class of Christian sects, in which case the predication we have just negated would have to be possible, but an element of the class of Christian sects along with all the other elements represented by the class of Mormons, the class of Baptists, etc.[9]

We have so far interpreted this new function of 'is' set-theoretically. But a class interpretation means Platonism, even if of an extensional sort. Now, does not at least this function of 'is' exclude other interpretations? No, it does not. Even here we can in principle escape Platonism, for the assertion that there obtains a relation between a subclass and a class of concrete things can always be replaced by an equivalent universal statement in which the 'all' ranges solely over concrete things. So the above statement, for example, may also be rendered by 'everything that is a whale is a mammal', and this is a formulation that is reconcilable with Nominalism if only we construe 'is a whale' and 'is a mammal' once again as incomplete linguistic symbols.

None of the functions of 'is' examined up to now commits us, at the risk of impoverishing our use of language, to accepting a particular ontology. But since they are all, from a logical point of view, essential functions of this little word, its ontological neutrality is thus shown.

(5) Both of the cases that still remain to be examined are trivial. One of them concerns statements of the form: 'so it is'. The 'is' represents here a linguistic means of expressing agreement. Such a phrase obviously says the same as 'I think so too', 'exactly what I think', 'that I admit', and the like. Depending on the linguistic situation either the subjective component, (the agreement of opinion) or the objective component (the truth of what is said) can be emphasized. In this last case the phrase 'so it is' can also be construed as 'this statement is right (true)', so that what we have is simply an abbreviated form of a truth predication.

(6) The case of learning colour words can be resolved even more quickly. 'This is ocher' is simply a different version of the statement 'people call this ocher' or 'this is called ocher'. Once again, 'is' does not have a logical function of its own at all, but merely serves as an abbreviation for a statement which would otherwise contain more words or at least more syllables or sounds.

We have thus acquired a sufficient casuistry to enable us to arrange the various different is-statements. Both of the other examples cited at the beginning can quite easily be accommodated. In '7 plus 2 is 9' the 'is' reflects an identity so that an adequate reading of it must be '7 plus 2 = 9'; according to the class interpretation 'Henry is intelligent' represents 'Henry ϵ intelligent', etc.

By way of conclusion I should like to add a remark about the plural of 'is', viz., 'are'. This word makes its appearance whenever a plurality of objects is involved. We have here once more the source of an ambiguity. The predication may involve each individual object or the entire class of objects. *Quine* offers as an example the following two statements: 'the apostles are pious, and 'the apostles are twelve'. [10] The former is intended to affirm that each single Apostle is pious; in the latter, however, it is not claimed that each single apostle is twelve. 'Twelve' must not be taken to denote a property of concrete things but a property of classes. All the classes which contain exactly 12 elements have this property in common. The class which contains just the continents has the property 5, etc. Numbers can thus be construed as class properties. Since each property determines a class, numbers can be construed as classes of classes: 12 is the class of all classes that contain 12 things, etc. This conception leads to the logical construction of the concept of number. The apparent circle in the formulation just given is of course avoided there. The number 12 can, for example, be more precisely defined as the class of all those classes which after the subtraction of one element (from each) contain 11 things. What 'substraction of one element' means can be very easily defined, and thus one finally arrives by means of recursion at the number 0 which, in turn, receives a direct logical definition, viz. the class whose only element is the empty class.

3. 'ALL', 'SOMETHING' AND 'NOTHING'

How must we interpret statements that contain one of these three words? One is first inclined to think that these expressions function in much the same way as names; for in a statement they may appear at exactly the same place as do names. We may form the true statements

'Alexander is big and smart',

'Caesar is identical with himself',

as well as the false statement

The moon is colder than $-273°$ Celsius';

likewise we can construct the three true sentences

'Something is big and smart',

'Everything is identical with itself' and

'Nothing is colder than $-273°$ Celsius'.

Here the words 'something', 'everything' and 'nothing' appear at precisely the same place where a name or an individual description occurred in the first three statements; we might thus feel inclined to represent these three expressions by the three letters '*a*' for 'all', '*s*' for 'something', and '*n*' for 'nothing'. Such an approach, however, leads us immediately into absurdities.

Let's consider once again the sentence

(1) 'Alexander is big and smart'.

The name 'Alexander' can here be distributed across the 'and'; for both predicates are indeed predicated of Alexander. Thus statement (1) says the same thing as the following statement:

(2) 'Alexander is big and Alexander is smart'.

The statement

(3) 'something is big and smart',

however, surely does not mean the same as

(4) 'something is big and something is smart'.

Consequently, 'something' cannot be replaced by the constant symbol '*s*', for otherwise we would be forced to assert not only the logical equivalence of (1) and (2), but, analogously, of (3) and (4) as well; that is of '*s* is big and smart' and '*s* is big and *s* is smart'. That no such equivalence obtains in this latter case can be immediately seen if we insert the predicate 'round' for 'big' and the predicate 'square' for 'smart'; for the sentence

(5) 'something is round and square'

is not just false, but downright contradictory; while, on the other hand, the sentence

(6) 'something is round and something is square'

is true, since there exist round as well as square objects. And so it is obvious that because of their different truth-values, the two statements (5) and (6) cannot be logically equivalent.

Exactly the same holds for the expressions 'all' and 'nothing'. 'Nothing is round and square' is a true statement, whereas 'Nothing is round and nothing is square' is false. Furthermore, the word 'nothing' cannot possibly represent a constant that refers to something. From this alone we can see the absurdity that attaches to philosophical systems which employ the word 'nothing' as a noun, place the definite article in front of it, and speak of 'The nothing' as an object in its own right. To do this is simply to succumb to a faulty form of expression of our everyday language. If the kind of interpretation employed by such philosophies were possible, then we should be able to distribute the word 'nothing' – just like any other designation of an object – across the 'and' without changing the truth-value of the statement. The word 'nothing' is a faulty, because misleading, means of forming the negation of an existential statement; and the word 'something' is a not unobjectionable means of formulating an affirmative existential sentence.

'Something is round and square' abbreviates 'there is something which is round and square'.

If one negates this statement, there results a statement that may be more completely rendered as 'it is not the case that there is something that is round and square'. And for the complex expression 'it is not the case that there is something that' we substitute the abbreviating symbol 'nothing', so that we now have 'nothing is round and square'.

Since we human beings tend to think of ourselves as more important than anything else, we use special words such as 'somebody' and 'nobody' to construct affirmative and negative existential statements where members of the species homo sapiens are involved. Here once again these expressions do not function as names. We could, of course, employ 'nobody' jokingly as a name in order to say something that should really be expressed differently. And this, then, is the one positive aspect that our language possesses precisely because of logically faulty grammar: we can use it to formulate jokes which would not be possible in a logically precise language. Thus, for example, someone who takes a rather pessimistic view about the course of economic developments might say:

> 'nobody is about to claim the boom is over' and then add
> 'I am this nobody'. This, of course, is supposed to mean that
> 'I am the only one who realizes that ...'.

There is, to be sure, a technical concept that could be called 'the nothing'. Just as a mathematician includes the number 0 among the whole numbers, so as to simplify and round off his theoretical statements, it likewise proves useful in set theory to introduce a class that contains no element: the empty class. Such a class might be introduced via the defining condition that it contains as elements precisely those things which are not identical with themselves. Since there are no such things, it follows that the class is empty. Someone might then be tempted to christen the empty class 'the Nothing' since there is nothing in it. If it is clearly understood that only the object just described is meant then there is nothing objectionable in such a manner of speaking; for in the context of such a theory, the empty class is a certain particular object about which statements can be made just like the other math objects. Even here, though, we must proceed with caution. The definite article 'the' signals that we are dealing with just one object. There are, however, systems of set theory, as for example all those based on so-called type-theory, for which there exists not just one empty class, but infinitely many different empty classes, viz. one for each type. But then we can no longer speak of *the* nothing, since we have here infinitely many 'Nothings'.

Let's finally take another look at 'all'. As we have seen, this word can also occupy the position of grammatical subject. Hence we may still be tempted to believe that 'all' designates some object or other. To realize that this cannot possibly be the case, let's note that proper names, like other object designations, may be distributed across 'and' as well as across 'or'. If on the basis of Jack's poor marks his teacher comes to the conclusion

'Jack is stupid or lazy', this is tantamount to saying

'Jack is stupid or Jack is lazy'. Now, the statement

'everything is green or not green'

is surely true, for it represents nothing else but the principle of the excluded middle as applied to the concrete predicate 'green'. The statement

'everything is green or everything is not green',

on the contrary, says something entirely different, in fact something false; for it asserts that either every object whatsoever must be green or that there are no green objects at all. This example shows that 'all', too, behaves quite differently from a name.

Our aim in this section was simply to arrive at the negative result that the words 'something' 'all', and 'nothing', to which we may also add 'somebody' and 'nobody', are not names that designate something. The job that these words really perform will become clear at the end of the next section.

'I', 'YOU', 'HE', 'SHE', 'IT'

We come now to a very important point. Pronouns fulfill two entirely different functions in everyday language; some of them, however, are limited to only one of these functions.

If a hundred people utter the sentence

'Australia is a continent',

they would all be saying the same thing; they would be ascribing a certain property to one and the same object. If these one hundred persons were, on the other hand to say

'I am hungry',

they would all be saying something quite different, although they are uttering exactly the same sentence. The reason for this is to be sought in the word 'i' for, unlike the name 'Australia' its reference varies according to the verbal context. To fully explain the situation we must recognize the fact that linguistic objects such as 'word' 'sentence' 'expression' 'sign', etc. are ambiguous. If I write down 'red' and after a while I once again write down 'red', then we might say either that I have written down the same word twice, or that I have jotted down two words that look alike and are very similar to the following word: 'red'. What is meant by a word in this latter case is obviously a completely concrete phenomenon that can be exactly located in space and time. A word in its written form has, as a rule, a much longer temporal span than a word in its acoustic form, since, ordinarily, written or printed matter enjoys a longer lifespan than the sounds streaming out of my mouth.

Let's speak here of the occurrence of a word, sign, expression, or sentence. If, on the contrary, one says that the same word has been written down twice, then this implies that what is meant by a word is not a concrete phenomenon but rather something general and abstract, a Platonic essence. If we once again take extensional Platonism as our basis, we may say that a word is a class of word-occurrences which stand in a certain similarity relationship to one another. The same goes, of course, for signs, sentences, and other expressions construed as Platonic essences. For these classes let's retain the expressions 'word', 'sign', etc. It is clear that within Nominalism, the existence of signs, words, and sentences in this sense has to be denied. Let's say that the single word-occurrences belonging to one and the same word (in a Platonic sense) are copies of any single specimen whatever, or briefly that they are copies of this word. This last formulation, though, must not be taken literally, since individual things cannot be copies of a Platonic essence; otherwise, in analogy to Aristotle's 'third man' argument against Plato, a comparable argument about the 'third word' could be employed here. Thus, the first 'red' above is a copy of the second, the second a copy of the first, both are copies of a word-occurrence 'red' printed somewhere, and all of them together we call copies *of the* word 'red'.

Let's go back to the word 'I'. We are dealing here with a special case of a so-called indicator word, i.e. of an expression whose reference can be ascertained only by taking the concrete linguistic context into account. The exact definition of an indicator word reads: an indicator is a word every single copy of which names something different. Strictly speaking, this applies only to the word 'I' as well as to other expressions that relate to a person in the capacity of speaker, e.g. 'mine'. [11] If, for example, 10,000 persons say 'I' they are referring to 10,000 different things and if a billion persons say 'I' they are referring to a billion different things. With respect to the word 'you' the case is quite different for several persons can address one and the same person with the word 'you'. Similarly, a group of persons may refer to the same thing when using 'him' or 'her'. Hence the definition of the concept of an indicator must be liberalized in such a way that the different copies of the word may, but need not, designate something different. At this point a further problem crops up, namely, that one proper name can also designate different persons. This, though, is not of much consequence. Surely there exists more than one person with the same 'John Smith' or 'Joe Miller', but it is quite possible that they could all have different names just as, for example, the numbers in the Arabic numerical system are all given different designations. But as long as this is not the case, we must also regard the proper names in current use as indicators. In contradistinction to names, any such revision regarding words like 'I' 'you' 'he', etc. is unthinkable. To remove the 'potential ambiguity' that attaches to them would be tantamount to destroying their linguistic function.

Besides these personal indicators, as we may call them, there are also spatial and temporal indicators like 'here', 'there', 'now', 'yesterday', etc. The place and time at which they are uttered are just as essential here as was the person of the speaker in the former case. 'I' always designates the speaker (i.e., 'I' designates that person who in a particular situation utters the sound 'I'), 'you' designates the person whom the speaker is addressing, 'now', depending on the circumstances, the time or time-interval [12] during which the expression in question is uttered, etc. In order to determine the referent we sometimes need an additional gesture on the part of the speaker as in the case of 'over there'.

These remarks about indicators throw a new light on the frequently advocated thesis: 'only sentences can be true or false'. A sentence here is understood not as a concrete sentence-occurrence, but rather as an abstract object, so that 'Caesar was a Roman general' and 'Caesar was a Roman general' are not regarded as two sentences but as one and the same sentence written down twice. When applied to our everyday language such a thesis turns out to be untenable. Consider the sentence 'he does not feel well today'. Is this sentence true or false? The question, obviously, does not make any sense. Only when the sentence is uttered by a particular person in a particular situation does it make any sense to pose such a question and then the answer will very often be 'true' and very often 'false'. If we want to call such an utterance of a sentence under certain circumstances a statement, we then have to say that it is not sentences but only statements, i.e., sentences uttered by particular persons at a particular time, which are true or false. Only in a language that contains no indicator words can the thesis, according to which statements must be either true or false, be justifiably extended to sentences. Hence, when indicator words play no part, the two expressions 'statement' and 'sentence' can be used synonymously.

'He', 'she', 'it' can also be used as indicator words, just like 'I' and 'you', but they need not be. Consider the following statements:

(1) 'my sister has traveled to Munich; *she* will remain there a week'

and

(2) 'Given any number: *it* is smaller than 0, or *it* is equal to 0, or *it* is greater than 0,

which, in effect, is an elaboration of the statement

(2′) 'Every number is smaller than, equal to, or greater than 0'.

In sentence (1) 'she' is an indicator word, and the person meant depends on who uttered the sentence; but when it is uttered, 'she' refers to something quite concrete; not so in the second example. The 'it' represents a so-called variable. This can best be demonstrated by resorting to Quine's technique.[13] If one replaces 'or' with the symbol 'v' the three symbols '$<$' '$>$' and '$=$' are taken in their ordinary sense, and excess linguistic baggage is excluded, we arrive at the following shorter version of (2):

(3) 'every number [(it $<$ 0) v (it $=$ 0) v (it $>$ 0)].

What statement (2) says about 0 holds also for every other number, that is, the following *statement* is true:

(4) 'whatever number one may choose, every number is greater than, equal to, or smaller than it',

or, since 'whatever' means the same as 'for every', briefly

(5) 'every number [every number is greater than, equal to, or smaller than it]'

The part of statement (5) enclosed in brackets differs from (2′), and consequently also from (2), only in virtue of the fact that in the place of '0' the word 'it' appears. It, therefore, seems plausible to rewrite this part, namely,

(6) 'every number is greater than, equal to, or smaller than it' in a manner analogous to the transformation of (2) into (3). From (6) we then get:

(7) 'every Number [(it $<$ it) v (it = it) v (it $>$ it)]'

and from (5) we subsequently obtain:

(8) 'every number [every number [(it $<$ it) v (it = it) v (it $>$ it)]]'

This formulation, however, is useless since it does not let us know to which of the two 'every number' expressions each particular 'it' refers to. The flaw can nevertheless be remedied by affixing numerical indices in such a way that each 'every' and each 'it' that belong together have the same index. Statement (5) would thus assume the following form:

(9) 'every_1 number [every number is greater than, equal to, or smaller than it_1]'.

Here the portion enclosed in brackets can once again be written as:

(10) 'every_2 number [($\text{it}_2 < \text{it}_1$) v ($\text{it}_2 = \text{it}_1$) v ($\text{it}_2 > \text{it}_1$)]'.

As a final version of (4) we consequently get in place of the unusable formulation (8) the following sentence:

(11) 'every_1 number [every_2 number [$\text{it}_2 < \text{it}_1$) v ($\text{it}_2 = \text{it}_1$) v ($\text{it}_2 > \text{it}_1$)]].'

These subscripts correspond in everyday language to 'initially' and 'subsequently', or respectively 'the former' and 'the latter'. Thus in everyday language (11) would read something like: 'whatever number we may *initially* choose, it will be the case that, whatever number we subsequently choose, this *latter* is smaller than, equal to, or greater than the *former*'.

Employing pronouns with subscripts is not very practical, although such a method suits the interpretation of everyday language particularly well in case we have more than two pronouns, for then we need to speak of the first, second, third, etc. in order to make ourselves understood. It is more convenient to simply take different letters like 'x', 'y', 'z' in place of the different pronouns and to use the same letter enclosed within parentheses in place of 'every'. Statement (3) thus acquires the following more transparent form:

(12) '(y) number [($y < 0$) v ($y = 0$) v ($y > 0$)]'

0 and (11), in turn, becomes:

(13) '(x) number [(y) number [($y < x$) v ($y = x$) v ($y > x$)]]'.

The expression '(x) number' may be read 'for all numbers x'. The letters ('x', 'y' ... are names of arbitrary numbers, that is, they are number variables. The word 'number' behind '(x)' or '(y)' indicates that the variables are to range solely over numbers. One might, therefore, call this word a 'scope indicator'. It behooves us to make yet another simplification which will result in the elimination of scope indicators. For statements that hold universally such a scope indicator is not necessary at all. 'Everything is identical with itself should read

(14) $(x)(x = x)$,

i.e., 'for every x, it holds that $x = x$'. One can now convert the preceding formulas into the form of statement (14) by simply inserting behind the prefix '(x)', '(y)' an if-then-sentence whose if-component explicitly states the restriction to the desired domain. Statement (12) should then read:

(15) '(y) [if y is a number, then $y < 0) \vee (y = 0) \vee (y > 0)$].

A statement of the form 'if ... then – – –' is usually abbreviated by means of the symbol '→' to '... → – – –'. So statement (13) would then attain the following final form:

(16) '(x) $\lfloor x$ is a number → (y) $\lfloor y$ is a number → $((y < x) \vee) (y = x) \vee (y > x))]]$'

The prefix '(x)' and '(y)' are called 'universal quantifiers' and the variable appearing in them, the quantification variable. Had we started with an existential statement, we would have obtained the existential quantifier '$(\mathrm{E}x)$' already mentioned. Following the quantifier is an open sentence which contains in one or more places the same variable as the quantifier. We then say that these variables are bound by the quantifier.

These bound variables are nothing but pronouns serving the second of the two functions that we discussed, while the quantifiers correspond to the words 'all' or 'every' and 'something' or 'there is'. The word 'nothing' is the means with which ordinary language negates a statement beginning with an existential quantifier. In order to formulate 'nothing is more beautiful than Apollo', we first write 'there is something more beautiful than Apollo', in other words; '$(\mathrm{E}x)$ (x is more beautiful than Apollo)', and we then negate the whole expression. If we use the symbol '$\neg$' as our sign of negation, we then obtain '$\neg$ $(\mathrm{E}x)$ (x is more beautiful than Apollo)'. What corresponds to 'nothing' in this formulation is the combination '$\neg$ $(\mathrm{E}x)$'. In this connection it is impotant to point out two things:

(1) the quantifiers are the tools by means of which we form existential and universal statements;

(2) the pronouns occurring within such existential and universal statements are bound variables.

If one wishes to find out whether in a certain linguistic complex the pronouns 'he', 'she', 'it' occur as indicators in the sense described earlier or as variables, one needs to ascertain what they refer back to; if they refer to an individual object like 'Jack' or 'my sister', then we are dealing with indicator words; if, on the other hand, they refer to 'each' or 'all' [14] or 'something', when we are dealing with variables.

Bound variables play an important role in connection with the question of ontology. We have seen that the predicates we use do not commit us to any particular ontology. In order to be able to apply the predicate 'red' meaningfully, one needs not believe in redness or in the class of red things as some kind of entity. Since expressions such as 'not', 'and', 'or' etc. surely do not involve any ontological presuppositions, and since concrete individual designations (as we will later have occasion to see) could all be eliminated in favor of predicates and quantifiers, one might well conclude that *language in general is ontologically neutral*. This, however, would be a mistake. The neutrality ceases the moment quantification with bound variables comes into play. If someone says 'there are numbers of such and such a kind', 'there are classes of things which ...', or 'for any class whatever it holds that ...' he thereby lets us know that among the values of his variables he counts not just concrete objects but also abstract objects like classes, numbers, and the like: in other words, espouses at the very least an extensional Platonism. Thus, if one wishes to find out, on the basis of the language someone employs whether that person is a Platonist or a Nominalist, he should not look at the predicates which are used but must, instead, study the kind of variables (or pronouns in their second capacity) that occur in his language; if there occur only variables whose values are concrete individuals, then we have Nominalism; if, on the other hand, he also admits variables ranging over classes, attributes, relations, functions, numbers etc., then we have a case of Platonism. But even a predicate like 'x belongs to certain classes K which in turn satisfy a condition G', which sounds 'horribly Platonistic' to nominalistic ears, can quite readily be incorporated into a nominalistic system if we simply construe the whole expression as a single predicate and ascribe to the particular words in the complex just as little meaning when isolated as to the single letters in a word. The Nominalist, like the Platonist, can also afford to make a statement such as 'beauty is revered'; he simply has to add that he does not regard the word 'beauty' as the name of an abstract entity but that the entire proposition functions for him merely as an abbreviation for the longer sentence 'all revere beautiful objects', or something of the sort, in which abstract names no longer crop up. The Platonist can, therefore, draw the following inference from the above statement: '$(\mathrm{E}x)$ (x is revered)', in other words, 'there are objects x such that x is revered', the Nominalist, on the other hand, is not in a position to derive such a statement; for such derivation would require that he also counts an object such as beauty among the objects over which his variables range. This demonstrates once more that it is not the predicates but solely the bound variables which are relevant for the question of ontological differences.

As conceived here the 'Platonism-Nominalism' dichotomy represents a complete disjunction: recognition or non-recognition of abstract objects, i.e., their admission or non-admission to the domain of variables. What is usually meant by 'conceptualism' is a position midway between Nominalism and Platonism: according to it there are abstract objects, but 'only in the mind'. When we try to render this metaphorical description more precise, it becomes clear that we are not dealing with a position between Nominalism and Platonism, but rather with a special kind of Platonism. It demands that abstract objects, since they are human inventions, satisfy certain principles of construction. This is the point of view of Constructionism which has found expression for example in intuitionist mathematics, whereas classical math represented an unlimited Platonism with respect to the concept of class or set. It was assumed there that all sets exist 'of themselves', and that one could then pick from this fixed totality any particular set whatever by stipulating any conditions one wished. These assumptions led to the famous paradox of set theory, which in turn shattered the unlimited Platonism of classical math. But the revisions forced upon us as a result of this situation by no means lead us out of Platonism into a nominalistic construction of math; even the systems with the greatest restrictions in comparison to classical math remained within the framework of constructive Platonism. A Nominalistic construction of math has not only never been tried, but there are, moreover, no signs that any such attempt could ever succeed were it to do away completely with the fundamental concept of a class.

The concept of a variable enables us to expand our earlier remarks about the concept of identity in an important respect. There we were contending that 'is', taken in the sense of identity, hence ' = ', connects two names or descriptions, a circumstance which, according to what we have earlier ascertained, is due, in all non-trivial cases, to the fact that our language contains an overabundance of designations. The ' = ' can also be flanked on either side by bound variables. We are actually permitted to use as many variables in statements as we wish, over which we then quantify. Their number depends solely on the complexity of the statements and on the length of the relations[15] used in the statement. Different variables can, moreover, refer to the same as well as to different objects. Should one wish to explicitly stipulate that two variables refer to the same thing, the identity sign is available for this purpose;

and if, on the contrary, one wishes to exclude the possibility that the variables refer to the same objects, one need only insert a component consisting of the sign ' = ' flanked by the two variables and negate this whole expression. Thus a statement such as 'there is at most one giant diamond' would be formulated in the following way: '(x) (y) [(x is a giant diamond and y is a giant diamond) $\rightarrow x = y$]' and the statement: 'there are at least two different things' is translated as '$(\mathrm{E}x)$ $(\mathrm{E}y)$ (xy)'.

5. 'NOT', 'AND', 'OR', 'IF... THEN – – –'

The words we have just written down, to which we may add still others, serve an important function within language. These expressions obviously do not designate anything. It would, therefore, be pointless to look for an objective referent of 'not', 'or', etc. The function of these words consists, rather, in showing us how the truth-value ('true' or 'false') of the statement formed with their help depends on the truth-value of its constituent parts. Hence, besides being called 'logical constants' they are also commonly referred to as 'truth-functions'. If 'p' is any statement whatever, then 'not p' is uniquely determined by the fact that it is false when 'p' is true, and true in case 'p' is false. A conjunction consisting of 'p' and 'q' is true only if both components are true. For a disjunction the situation is no longer unambiguous; one must state whether it is the inclusive or the exclusive 'or' that is intended. In the former case the disjunction is true when both of its components are true, whereas in the latter case such a circumstance would render it false. But the case where one makes use of an exclusive 'or' must not be confused with the case where the two components exclude one another. In this case it is not possible to reach a decision as to which 'or' has been used. When the mathematician stipulates that the symbol '$\leq$' is to mean 'smaller *or* equal to and adds nothing further, we are not then warranted in condemning him for having omitted to state whether in this definition he is using the inclusive or exclusive 'or'; such a distinction would here be pointless. We can only distinguish between the two sorts of 'or' when both cases are simultaneously possible, a possibility which, however, does not obtain here, since a number cannot both be smaller and equal to another number. So '$a \leq b$' is not a case of an exclusive 'or', but instead a neutral case. Similarly, in the above subordinate clause 'whether in this definition he is using the inclusive or the exclusive "or" ' the one 'or' not within quotation marks is neutral. The exclusive 'or', on the other hand, comes up in the statement of a father who, for example, upon being asked by his child for permission to go swimming in the afternoon and to the movie at night, refuses by saying 'you either go swimming in the afternoon or to the movie at night'. Even more delicate is the case of 'If ...then – –'. The logician is not disposed to leave open any 'truth-gaps', so that a statement of the form 'if *p* then *q*' must always be either true or false whenever both components '*p*' and '*q*' assume a truth-value. This does not conform entirely with ordinary usage; for in everyday life we only judge as true or false an if-then statement in which '*p*' is true; and indeed according to whether the '*q*' is likewise true or false. If, on the contrary, '*p*' is not true, then, as a rule, we consider such a statement void, so that the question of its truth or falsity fails to arise. In Logic, however, an if-then statement is in this case for reasons of convenience taken to be true. It would be extremely impractical not to assign a truth-value to every compound statement constructed by means of 'not', 'or' 'and' and 'if-then' for every distribution of truth-values to the single sentential components. A general definition of logical validity, logical falsehood, etc. would otherwise be considerably more difficult.

While in a logical system one symbol is employed for every truth-function, in everyday language there are often many different words that express the same truth-function. Thus, for example, words such as 'but', 'nevertheless', 'on the contrary', 'while' (taken in a non-temporal sense), 'as well as' perform much the same job as 'and'. They do, however, differ from one another in their rhetorical function in that at times they emphasize contrast, at times the common core is stressed. Instead of 'John remained here, *and* Frank left', we may prefer to say 'John remained here, *but* Frank, (*nevertheless, on the contrary*, etc.) left'; instead of 'John left and Frank left' we may prefer 'John as well as Frank left'. What all these variations have in common is that the entire statement becomes true only if both of its sentential components are true. The task of logical analysis here is to extract the truth-functional kernel from the various rhetorical flourishes of the above examples as well as many others.

It must however, be expressly emphasized that the fact that many compound statements built up from simpler statements have a truth-functional character does not warrant inferring that all compound statements are truth-functions. Compare, for instance, the following two statements:

(1) 'there was a landside in the night and on the following morning the water was contaminated' and

(2), 'because there was a landslide in the night, the water was contaminated on the following day'

Statement (1) is surely correct in case both of the components bound by 'and' are true. Statement (2), on the other hand, need not be true even in such a case. With 'because' we want to express more than just a truth-functional dependence, namely, a causal relation in the present case. Should (1) be true we would consider (2) false if there turns out to be a different cause for the contamination of the water. Consequently, a causal statement is not amenable to a logical analysis within the context of a theory of truth-functions. It is the indifference of a statement of form (1) to the question of an 'inner connection between the facts described via the sentential components' that renders possible its description in terms of truth-functions.

To the logical constants mentioned above still others may be added, among which, however, 'if and only if' alone is of any practical value. It can be shown that all these other logical constants may be reduced to the ones we have cited above. Thus, for example, '*p* if and only if *q*' has the same meaning as 'if *p*, then *q*, and if *q*, then *p*'. This as well as all the other cases can be tested by means of the so-called truth-table: one compiles all the possible combinations of 'true' and 'false' of the components and ascertains that both compounds get the same truth-values. With the help of such a method it can also be shown that an even further reduction may be undertaken; for example., 'not' along with 'and' suffice, since '*p* or *q*' is logically equivalent to 'not (not-*p* and not-*q*)' and 'if *p* then *q*' is logically equivalent to 'not-*p* or *q*', if we are willing to accept the above convention for the case where the protasis '*p*' is false. Parenthetically, it may be noted that even a reduction to a single constant such as 'neither ... nor – – –' is possible.

6. LOGICAL TRUTH

How are statements 'which are true on purely logical grounds' to be distinguished from all the rest? We have now at our disposal all the means to answer such a question, at least in principle. Let's first group together the logical constants mentioned in the last section along with the individual variables and the existential and universal quantifiers under the heading 'logical expressions'. All expressions different from them we call 'descriptive'. To this latter group belong all the predicate expressions as well as, at least provisionally,[16] the proper names and definite descriptions ('the author of Wallenstein'). In a Platonistic ontology we might say that the descriptive expressions are those which, in contrast to the logical ones, 'designate something objectively real'. We know, however, that predicate constants can be employed even in the context of a nominalistic ontology without thereby having to ascribe to them the function of naming or designating something. Thus such a characterization would involve limiting ourselves in advance to a particular ontology, something which is unnecessary. Since all the logical expressions can be explicitly listed, we may distinguish the descriptive expressions in a negative way as being those which are not logical.

We then distinguish, following Quine, between an essential and an inessential occurrence of a word in a sentence. A word occurs essentially in a statement whenever it is possible to change the truth-value of the statement by replacing the word with another assuming, of course, that such a substitution still yields a statement that makes sense. Should this prove impossible we then speak of an inessential occurrence of a word in a sentence.

(1) 'Vienna is a city' is a true statement.

Substituting 'Australia' for 'Vienna' results in the falsehood:

(2) 'Australia is a city'.

Here, therefore, 'Vienna' occurs essentially in (1). 'City' likewise occurs essentially in (1) since 'Vienna is a mountain' is false. Consider, on the other hand, the following statement:

(3) 'John is stupid or John is not stupid'.

Here the name 'John' surely occurs inessentially, for if we replace 'John' by the name of an object for which it makes sense to apply the predicate 'stupid', then it is once again true of this object (or person) that it (he, she) be stupid or not. The predicate 'stupid' likewise occurs inessentially, for no matter what predicate we substitute for 'stupid', as long as it makes any sense at all when applied to the individual John, it must be true of John or not; and in fact this is exactly what is expressed by the sentence that results from substituting in (3). The logical truths are now distinguished as those special cases of true statements in which only the logical expressions occur essentially. Statement (3) exemplifies precisely such a truth; for the only two descriptive expressions appearing in (3) are 'John' and 'stupid' and, as we have just seen, they occur inessentially in (3). Every statement of the form:

(4) '... is – – –or...is not – – –'

is true, as long as for '... ' and ' – – –' a substitution is made that preserves meaning. Statement (4) may be thought of as the 'logical skeleton' of statement (3). It is exactly this logical skeleton that determines 'true' be the truth-value of statement (3), and on the basis of these notions this is supposed to hold for all logical truths: it is always solely on the logical skeleton that the truth-value of the statement depends.

Statement (3) is a simple case of a logical truth in which only logical constants but not quantifiers occur essentially. Logical truth is here reducible to the concept of truth-functional validity. We obtain an even larger class of logical truths as soon as we bring in all the statements in which quantifiers occur essentially. A case in point is the following sentence:

(5) 'If all murderers are despised and Brutus is a murderer, then Brutus will be despised'.

The three descriptive expressions of this sentence: 'Brutus', 'murderer', and 'is despised' all occur inessentially. The truth-value of (5) may not be changed by substituting for these expressions others which might be meaningfully inserted at the appropriate place in the sentence. Substituting, say 'Caesar' for 'Brutus' and 'is mortal' for 'is despised' and 'dog' for 'murderers' we get:

(6) 'If all dogs are mortal and Caesar is a dog, then Caesar is mortal',

that is, a true statement once again. We have here a special case of a 'quantificational validity'. Among other things the task of Logic is to develop a method that will enable us to sort out the logical truths from the class of all meaningful statements. We succeed in both cases but the techniques are of entirely different kinds. For truth-functional validity we can resort to a purely mechanical testing procedure, for example, the truth-table method we have already mentioned. To pick out the valid statements of quantification, however, we must proceed axiomatically: certain statements, true solely on the basis of their truth-functional and quantificational structure, are taken as axioms and all the rest are derived from them via logical deduction. Thanks to the investigations of *K. Gödel*, we know that it is possible to set up axiomatic systems that allow us to derive all and only the quantificationally valid statements. As regards the question of whether a particular statement is a logical truth in this wider sense, we have, however, no mechanical decision procedure at our disposal. On the basis of another theorem, proved by the American logician *A. Church*, we even know that such a mechanical decision procedure cannot exist, that is, is logically impossible.

7. 'THE'

Expressions which begin with the definite article are called descriptions. At first it seems as if their function might be described in the following way: a particular object is characterized by means of a predicate that it alone satisfies instead of by a proper name; the definite article has the job of linguistically registering the fact that one and only one object satisfies the predicate. Thus one might speak of *the* discoverer of the north pole, of *the* (present) queen of England, of *the* dagger with which Caesar was murdered, for the predicates 'x discovered the north pole', 'x is now queen of England', and 'x is a dagger and Caesar was murdered with x' are each satisfied by only one object.

A problem arises the moment we try to form a singular negative existential statement whose grammatical subject is a description, e.g., 'the present king of France does not exist', 'the square circle does not exist'. These and many other analogous statements might be true but, nevertheless, they cannot be construed as denying the existence of certain objects, objects such as the 'present king of France' or 'square circle'. If there are such objects, then they exist, and all such statements represent logical contradictions. We are grappling here with the old problem of the 'existence of the non-existent'. As a first attempt at a solution we might introduce the hypothesis of the existence of unrealized possibilities, i.e., the very same hypothesis that we mentioned earlier in our last ditch effort at rescuing the theory according to which existence is a property. Thus to say that the present king of France does not exist means that he is an unactualized possibility. This theory, according to which one may ascribe existence not just to actual things but also to possible things, leads to numerous problems. Is the possible gray cat on that mat the same cat as the possible white cat on that same mat, or are they different possible cats? How many possible cats are then lying on that mat? Are there more possible gray than white cats among them? Under the assumption of possible things, such questions and many others wait in vain for an answer! An answer which would, in any case, turn out to be purely arbitrary since we have no criteria on hand to reach such decisions. As concerns the sentence 'the square circle does not exist', even the theory of unactualized possibilities would not suffice since a square circle is not only not real, it is simply impossible. We must, therefore, consider even unactualized impossibilities as existing, in which case the theory can easily be shown to be contradictory,or declare a predicate like 'square circle' to be meaningless. But to regard contradictions as meaningless leads us into a series of still further untenable consequences. One of them is that all the logical truths would likewise have to be considered meaningless since the negation of a meaningful statement is also meaningful and all contradictory sentences can be obtained by negating logical truths.[17]

B. Russell in his theory of descriptions has shown us the way out of these difficulties; a description must not be interpreted as a designation of a particular object, but must, instead, be regarded as an incomplete linguistic symbol. A theory of descriptions has, therefore, the task of showing how descriptions may be eliminated from statements in which they occur, i.e., how contexts containing descriptions may be converted into ones which no longer contain any such descriptions, without, however, changing their meaning in the course of the transformation. To explain this theory we will confine ourselves to the following two illustrations: the context is either a simple case of predication or an assertion of existence. The former case may be illustrated by the statement

(1) 'The discoverer of the north Pole was a Norwegian'.

According to *Russell* (1) is to be transformed into:

(2) 'Someone (more exactly: something) discovered the North Pole and was a Norwegian and nobody (nothing) else discovered the North Pole'.

In (2) there appears, in fact, no longer any description. Upon applying the *Russellian* analysis, the existential assertion

(3) 'The author of the Magic Mountain exists'

would read as follows:

(4) 'Someone (something) wrote the Magic Mountain and nobody (nothing else wrote the Magic Mountain'.

Analogously, the translation of a negative existential assertion like

(5) 'The discoverer of the cause of cancer does not exist'

may be formulated as follows:

(6) 'Either there is nobody (nothing) who discovered the cause of cancer or more than one person discovered the cause of cancer'.

These examples should have made sufficiently clear what is meant by saying that a description is an incomplete linguistic symbol: what is claimed is that such a symbol considered by itself alone does not name anything but only acquires meaning when it is inserted in a more inclusive context. That it makes sense *only within a context* is shown by the fact that after a full analysis it ceases to play the role of grammatical subject. And so the puzzle about the existence of the non-existent, so far as descriptions are concerned, is resolved; the puzzle arose only because a description was taken to be an independent linguistic expression that named something or other.

What of the case where someone, alluding to the war-god of the Greeks says:

(7) 'Ares does not exist'?

The word 'Ares' is a name and not a description and so the *Russellian* theory is not applicable to it; as a result, the whole existence – non-existence puzzle crops up once again. *Quine* has here pointed the way out. The procedure consists very simply in transforming names into descriptions and then eliminating these descriptions in accord with *Russell's* theory. In example (7), the transformation succeeds rather easily, for we can simply substitute the description 'the war-god of the Greeks' for the name 'Ares' and thus obtain the statement

(8) 'the war-god of the Greeks does not exist'.

In other cases, however, we still have no other choice but to interpret the original proper name as a predicate that holds true of one object; in other words, to replace the idea 'Name of such and such' by the concept 'Predicate applicable exclusively to such and such'. If the atheist wants to say:

(9) 'God does not exist',

he must, therefore, proceed in such a way that 'God' is interpreted not as a name but as a predicate, i.e. 'x is God', and from it form the description 'the one x such that x is God' and insert it into (9) in place of the name 'God'. Otherwise statement (9) would represent a contradiction. The corresponding theistic statement reads:

(10) 'The one x such that x is God, exists'.

And this, according to the *Russellian* analysis is equivalent to

(11) 'There is an x such that x is God and nothing else is God'.

All these considerations have demonstrated two things:

(1) The problem of the existence of the non-existent is a pseudo-problem; and so all those philosophical attempts which espouse unactualized possibilities, unrealized impossibilities, or the meaninglessness of contradictory statements lose their point.

(2) Descriptions and names are, strictly speaking, superfluous. Both of them can always be eliminated from the context if only the language in question possesses suitable predicates and logical expressions. Thus, a language lacking designations for objects needs not be any poorer than one possessing them.

8. 'IT IS POSSIBLE THAT ...', 'IT IS NECESSARY THAT ...'

In certain contexts we sometimes use the nouns 'possibility' and 'necessity'; e.g., 'there is the possibility of frost in the next few days', 'the necessity of centralizing currency'. To speak in some such way predisposes one to prematurely give ontological weight to the concepts of possibility and impossibility, i.e., to speak of possible things and to construe the possibility or impossibility of something being so and so as a property of the respective object. We have just seen that the assumption of possible objects originates from still other motives and likewise that such an assumption leads also to quite undesirable consequences. Let's resume here once more our train of thought and scrutinize more closely the role of these expressions in our language.

It must first be observed that all such modal expressions exhibit a great variety of different uses. When someone claims that the presence of life on a certain planet is biologically impossible or that the existence of an absolutely rigid body is physically impossible, he thereby presupposes the correctness of an empirical scientific hypothesis. 'Biologically impossible' is tantamount to saying 'impossible according to current knowledge about organic substances'; 'physically impossible' means 'impossible according to current physical theories'. But today's valid theories may turn out to be false tomorrow, for no scientific hypothesis can be said to have been proved once and for all. Consequently, all such expressions are only right if the validity of certain statements is presupposed. If these latter are discarded, the former must likewise follow suit. An absolutely rigid body or a velocity greater than that of light is 'mechanically possible' if possibility is here construed in the sense of classical mechanics and 'mechanically impossible' if we refer to relativistic mechanics. *Today* such things would be said to be mechanically impossible since at present we have no reason to consider relativity theory false, while the principles of classical mechanics do not coincide with our experience.

It is the view of many philosophers that there is a use for these modal expressions which remains unaffected by the change in scientific theories. Such a use occurs when possibility is taken in the strict sense of logical possibility and necessity is likewise understood in the strict sense of logical necessity. In what follows we will take this strict sense as our basis. We are at first inclined to consider expressions such as 'it is possible that ...' and 'it is necessary that ...' as logical operators in much the same way as, say negation or conjunction represent logical operators. If, '*p*' is any statement whatever, then just as we can form the negation '$\neg p$', we might also take '*Np*' and '*Mp*' for 'it is necessary that *p*' and 'it is possible that *p*' respectively. However, such modal operators manifest characteristic differences vis-à-vis the logical constants.

Let's begin with the *Fregean* distinction between the direct and indirect occurrence of a word in a sentence. [18] For clarity's sake let's for the moment confine ourselves to the case where this word is a name, but let's not here eliminate the name via the method we have previously described. If a statement deals with an object, it is obviously indifferent what word we use in designating this object; the truth-value of the statement does not depend on the form of the word. In such a case, it is said that the word occurs *directly*. Should the truth-value of the statement depend also on the form of the word, we then speak of an *indirect* occurrence of the word in the statement. What is the criterion for determining whether a word occurs directly or indirectly in a statement? As we will have occasion to see, such a determination is often not at all easy and so it is, at the very least, premature to rely here solely on intuitions. *Frege* has provided us with an answer that is both clear and simple. The word in question must obey the laws of identity if it is to occur directly. This means that if one speaks about an object *a* and in so doing employs the word '*A*' to designate this object, then, if '*B*' is another designation of *a*, the word '*A*' may be replaced in this statement by '*B*' without affecting the truth-value of the statement. The reason for choosing such a criterion is obvious. The statement '$A = B$' holds by virtue of our presupposition; i.e., the object *A* (the object designated by '*A*') is identical with the object *B* (the object designated by '*B*'. If in a statement one then speaks about this object itself, it must obviously be indifferent whether this object is designated by means of '*A*' or '*B*'. Thus the word 'Vienna' for example, occurs directly in the statement 'Vienna has nearly two million inhabitants'. Why? Because the identity 'Vienna = the capital of Austria' holds so that the right-hand side of this identity statement may be substituted in the above sentence for 'Vienna' yielding the equivalent statement 'the capital of Austria has nearly two million inhabitants'.

We have a simple case of an indirect occurrence of a word in a sentence when a statement is made about this word itself as is indicated in writing by the use of quotation marks. For example in ' "Aristotle" consists of 9 letters' we have an indirect occurrence of 'Aristotle' since substituting by virtue of the true identity 'Aristotle = the teacher of Alexander the Great' leads to the false statement ' "The teacher of Alexander the Great" consists of 9 letters', for here the number of letters is actually more than double the number asserted. This example, however, is trivial since it is immediately clear in this case that one is not making an assertion about the man Aristotle but rather about the word 'Aristotle'.

Less obvious is the case of an utterance that begins with the words 'Frank believes that ...'. In the statement

(1) 'Frank believes that Managua is in Argentina'

does the word 'Managua' occur directly or indirectly? Let's suppose that statement (1) is true and let's subject it to the Fregean test. The identity sentence 'Managua = the capital of Nicaragua' is true. Substituting one designation for the other in (1) results in the statement

(2) 'Frank believes that the capital of Nicaragua is in Argentina',

and this is a false statement assuming Frank is not so utterly ignorant about geography (as to think, say, that Argentina is a continent). And so the test turns out to be negative; 'Managua' does not occur directly in this belief sentence. We would have arrived at that same result if, instead of 'believes that ...', we had chosen expressions such as 'knows that ...' 'asserts that ...' 'is afraid that ...' 'doubts that ...', and the like. The result is somewhat surprising here because we have first a statement in which a name occurs directly and this direct occurrence changes into an indirect one as soon as expressions such as 'believes that ...' 'asserts that ...' etc. are placed in front of it. Quine calls such contexts 'referentially opaque'.

It is now easy to show that modal contexts too are referentially opaque. *Quine* presents two rather lucid examples.[19] Both of the following statements are true:

(3) 'it is necessary that there are creatures on the evening star if there are creatures on the evening star'

and

(4) 'it is possible that the number of planets is less than seven'.

With respect to the claim that (4) is true, we must remember that the expression 'possible' is taken here to mean 'logically possible'; and in fact, it is surely not logically precluded that less than 7 planets rotate around the sun. Now, both of the following identity statements hold true:

(5) 'the evening star = the morning star' and

(6) 'the number of planets = nine'.

By applying the *Fregean* test to (3) and (4) we get the following two sentences:

(7) 'it is necessary that there be creatures on the evening star if there are creatures on the morning star' and

(8) 'it is possible that nine is less than seven'.

The falsity of (8) can immediately be seen; the falsity of (7) can just as readily be seen if we just bear in mind that 'necessary' means here once again 'logically necessary' and that a purely logical investigation would obviously not suffice to determine whether there must be creatures on the evening star in case there are creatures on the morning star. One needs at the very least to learn from astronomy that the evening star is in fact identical with the morning star.

As *Quine* points out, we have yet another criterion available for deciding whether a word occurs directly in a statement. It consists in observing what happens when one makes an existential generalization. From 'Harry is intelligent' it follows that 'something is intelligent', in other words, '(Ex) (x is intelligent)' and from 'Aristotle is wise' it follows that 'something is wise', i.e., '(*Ex*) (*x* is wise)'. Such an inference is justified on the grounds that what is true of an object mentioned by name must surely also be true of something. It becomes apparent that in the case of an indirect occurrence of a word such an existential inference cannot be drawn. Let's consider the obvious case in which a statement is made about a word. From ' "Aristotle" consists of 9 letters' can one infer '(*Ex*) ("*x*" consists of 9 letters)'? The statement we have just now written down consists of the false sentence: ' "*x*" consists of 9 letters', which is equivalent to the equally false sentence: 'the 24th letter of the alphabet consists of 9 letters' in front of which an existential quantifier '*Ex*' has been placed, that lacks an object. This quantifier lacks an object because in the expression that follows it the variable '*x*' does not occur at all; what occurs is just the constant name ' "*x*" ' of this variable (observe: this last printed sign is a name of that constant name. Whenever we want to speak *about* something, we must always use a name for it. If I want to speak about the name of a variable, I must use a name for the name of this variable).

Can one from statement (1) infer the following statement: '(*Ex*) (Frank believes that *x* lies in Argentina)', i.e., the statement

(9) 'there is something such that Frank believes that it lies in Argentina'?

What is this *x* then supposed to be? Managua, i.e., the capital of Nicaragua, (for both of them are surely one and the same)? To accept this would involve us in a contradiction with the fact that statement (2) is false.

A similar difficulty appears should we wish to apply existential generalization to (3) and (4). We would then obtain the following two statements:

(10) '(*Ex*) (it is necessary that there be creatures on *x*, if there are creatures on the evening star)' and

(11) '(*Ex*) (it is possible that *x* is less than seven)'.

What is that object that must of necessity have creatures on it should there be creatures on the evening star? Is *x* the evening star, i.e., the morning star (since once again the two of them are surely identical)? Such a supposition stands clearly in contradiction with the falseness of statement (7). Analogously one may ask what object it is that is supposed to be possibly less than 7: say the number of planets, i.e., nine (since the number of planets is indeed nine)? Such a claim would contradict the fact that (8) is a false statement.

From this and the earlier observation, we must conclude with *Quine* that names in a statement beginning with the words 'it is possible that ...' or 'it is necessary that ...' do not occur directly. And this, in turn, means nothing else but that 'is necessarily so and so' as well as 'is possibly so and so' cannot be properites of the objects themselves but depend, instead, on how we relate linguistically to the objects. It must here be emphasized, though, that the above statements (10) and (11) are not to be confused with those in which the existential generalization appears behind the expressions 'it is possible that ...' and 'it is necessary that ...'. The following example may illustrate the difference: if in my bookcase there is room for twenty identically thick volumes of a certain periodical, yet I want to fit in twenty-one such volumes, then it becomes necessary that a volume be left out; there is, however, no one specific volume of which we may say that it must necessarily be left out.

Thus, it turns out that an existential generalization in a modal context leads to a result that was not intended. Throughout the argument we still made use of names, however. But, as *Quine* points out, [20] this makes no difference. For we may characterize one and the same number which is greater than seven in various ways, some of which have as a necessary consequence the statement that this number is greater than seven, while others on the contrary do not have such a necessary consequence. The same number nine, for example, is defined by

(12) 'there are exactly x planets'

as well as by

(13) '$(x = 3 \times \sqrt{x})$ and $(x \neq 0)$'.

(13) yields as a necessary conclusion '$x > 7$', but from (12) no such necessary consequence results. From all this it becomes apparent that 'to be necessarily greater than seven' is not a property that can be predicated of a number x. In the present case the necessity rests on the special way of characterizing the said number by means of (13) instead of through method (12).

We might have included all of these observations in the earlier section dealing with the functions of 'is'; for in the context '... is possible', '... is necessary' a new function of 'is' comes to light.

The final comments we have made point up once again the importance of investigating the logic of language. The conclusions we have reached render questionable the modal ontologies in which possibility and necessity appear as 'modes of Being'. But even all of modal *logic* becomes questionable, a field which, according to the view of many contemporary logicians is supposed to represent an important addition to the rest of the logical disciplines. The mutual substitution of identicals for one another and existential generalization constitute such elementary logical operations that it might seem highly questionable whether a logic can be constructed in which one cannot make unlimited use of these two operations. Attempts have been made to remedy this flaw by adopting an intensional logic in place of an extensional logic; in place of concrete objects designated by names there appear what *Frege* has called an 'individual concept' as the intension of a name, and in the place of classes attributes serve as the intensions of predicate expressions. Two names may designate the same thing and yet have different individual concepts for their intensions, and similarly two open sentences which determine the same class may manifest different attributes in their intensions. When it is thus required of the identity calculus that in order for two expressions to be substituted for one another they must not only designate the same thing (have the same extension) but also have the same intension, and, furthermore, that the individual variables of the language range not over objects but over intensions, the above defects do not arise. The concept of intension, however, is just as problematic as the concept of synonymy and analyticity. These three concepts can be shown to belong to one and the same problem complex. This complex, however, is so difficult and so full of ramifications that a discussion of it cannot be included in this chapter.

NOTES

[1] The subjects discussed in the following sections are to a certain extent scattered in text-books of modern logic. Some of the equivocations dealt with were already known to Aristotle and the Scholastics. Most of the inspiration for my observations comes from the logical and philosophical works of Prof. *Willard van Orman Quine*.

[2] In a description, a predicate expression appears together with the definite article ('the author of Wallenstein' 'the queen of England'. 'the book with the greatest number of editions in the year 1954'). The definite article expresses the fact that the predicate is satisfied by one and only one object. We will later come back to this kind of description.

[3] What is meant is a mountain on the moon and not a single elevation of the so-called Moon-mountains of South America.

[4] 'One may take the fundamental question about existence simply as the question about Being; for this is obviously that which is identical in the multiplicity of existing things'. In '*Towards a Foundation of Ontology*', Berlin 1935, p. 41.

[5] For a more exact discussion of these questions cf. my book: '*Metaphysics, Knowledge, and Scepticism*'.

[6] As regards the question of unactualized possibilities cf. '*Metaphysics, Knowledge, and Scepticism*', p. 73.

[7] A more detailed treatment of this point can be found in *W. Quine's*: '*Methods of Logic*', New York 1950, p. 208.

[8] This is not entirely the same, albeit for a reason that is without significance as regards the issue of Platonism. The conditions of identity for both need not be the same. The class of men is identical with the class of featherless bipeds, yet the property of being a man is not identical with the property of being a featherless biped. Abstract objects, however, are present in both cases and this alone is essential for now.

[9] To experts of modern logic. I would like to emphasize that I am not unaware of the

existence of axiomatic systems of set theory in which certain objects may at the same time be both elements and subclasses of other classes.

[10] *Mathematical Logic*, Cambridge, Mass., 1951, p. 237.

[11] Whether even this word is used as an indicator word in the strict sense of the word may depend on external circumstances such as, for example, the system of law. Insofar as there is common property in a country, two different persons may justifiably call one and the same object 'my house'.

[12] The temporal interval may in certain circumstances be very long. 'In earlier times one used an impractical number-system for counting; *now*, one uses the Arabic number-system.' 'Now' means here the same as 'since so and so many centuries'.

[13] *Mathematical Logic*, p. 65.

[14] The distinction between the plural 'all' and the singular 'each' is from a logical point of view of no significance.

[15] By the length of a relation we here mean the number of variable-places which must be mentioned in an explicit rendering of the relation. So, for example, the relation expressed by the verb 'pay' has length 4, since the explicit reading of this relation 'x pays y sum z for object u' contains 4 different variables.

[16] In the next section we will see that names and definite descriptions are superfluous.

[17] For additional arguments against such a claim cf. my book '*Metaphysics, Knowledge, and Scepticism*', p. 77.

[18] Frege, Gottlob, 'On Sense and Nominatum', *Readings in Philosophical Analysis*, p. 85 (ed. by H. Feigl and W. Sellars), Appleton-Century, New York, 1949.

[19] 'Reference and Modality' in: *From a Logical Point of View*, Cambridge, Mass., 1953, p. 143.

[20] *Ibid.*, p. 149.

CHAPTER 9

REMARKS ON THE COMPLETENESS OF LOGICAL SYSTEMS RELATIVE TO THE VALIDITY-CONCEPTS OF P. LORENZEN AND K. LORENZ[1]

1. The so-called semantics of elementary logic (predicate logic of first order) has some peculiarities which may be considered as disadvantages, at least if looked at from a certain point of view. First of all, it makes use of a very strong set-theoretical apparatus which is highly non-constructive. Strict constructivism may not be obtainable for a semantic foundation of logic; but even if one does not subscribe to constructivism one should expect that a weaker apparatus would be sufficient to define logical validity or logical implication on the elementary level. Secondly, this set-theoretical approach is restricted to classical logic and can therefore not be used, e.g. to define a concept of validity for intuitionistic logic or other logical systems differing from the classical one. This fact will not be considered as a drawback by those for whom classical logic is the only 'real' logic. On the other hand 'classicists' as well as 'intuitionists' should welcome an account of logic with the help of which different logical systems can be compared on the basis of semantical concepts alone – an account in which the deviations of logical systems from each other would be mirrored by different concepts of validity. Thirdly there are two characteristics of this semantics based upon the Bolzano-Tarski approach which in various contexts have been the main points of attack in the arguments of intuitionists and constructivists against this approach (which are mistakenly thought to be arguments against classical *logic*): (a) the procedure of introducing logical connectives as truth-functions tacitly presupposes that every meaningful sentence is either true or false (true-false-alternative). In view of such unproved and unrefuted sentences as 'there is at least one odd perfect number' one can reasonably doubt whether this assumption is correct. Namely if one decides to identify in mathematical contexts 'true' with 'provable' and 'false' with 'refutable' it is certainly not justified. And if one does not accept this identification then if one doesn't want to destroy the meaning of 'true' altogether it seems hardly possible to do without some kind of 'ontological hypothesis' about the pre-existence of numbers or other kinds of mathematical entities; but the best that can be said about

Reprinted from the Notre Dame Journal of Formal Logic 5, No. 2 (*April* 1964) *with permission*

such a hypothesis is that it is in need of a further justification. Contrary to a widespread belief the meaningfulness of sentences does not always rest upon the true-false-alternative. With respect to the given example the thesis of its meaningfulness can be based on the fact that – using an innocuous counterfactual – it is known what would be accepted as a *proof* of it. (b) The definition of validity contains a universal quantifier ranging over all non-empty universes. The inclusion of infinite universes is essential. A person to whom the concept of a closed infinite totality does not make sense would interpret the quantifier 'for all non-empty universes' in the definition of validity as 'for all non-empty *finite* universes' and thereby get a different logic. In this indirect way the concept of a closed infinite set enters into the definition of logical validity. One could say that all the philosophers of the past who rejected the possibility of actual infinity could either not have accepted this concept of validity or would necessarily have misinterpreted it in the way just indicated.

2. P. Lorenzen's recent account of logical connectives and quantifiers given in [2] and [3] can best be interpreted as a new kind of semantics as has been done in [1] by K. Lorenz. This semantics differs in some essential respects from the Bolzano-Tarski approach: First, the two objections (a) and (b) can not be made any more because it is free from the true-false-alternative and the concept of infinite set does not enter into definition of validity. Secondly, it turned out to be more flexible than the set-theoretical approach as this method makes it possible to define validity for different logical systems, especially for classical *and* intuitionistic logic (though this feature apparently is not quite in accordance with Lorenzen's original intention). As far as the important question of constructivity is concerned this point will briefly be discussed later. Anticipating the result of this discussion we can say that it is not constructive in the strict sense. But allowing the use of a comparative instead of a classificatory concept of constructivity, it seems to be more constructive and the technical apparatus needed seems to be weaker than concept formations used within the set-theoretical approach.

Technically speaking Lorenzen's approach differs from the usual one by the use of concepts which belong to the theory of games instead of concepts that belong to set theory. We therefore distinguish this type of semantics – the *game-theoretical semantics* – from the *set-theoretical semantics* of the Bolzano-Tarski approach. A few remarks about the term 'semantics' seem to be in order here. First this semantics does not 'abstract from' the users of the language. An account for which this holds true is sometimes called 'pragmatics' rather than 'semantics.' If the motivation for this distinction is based on the assumption that every explicit reference to the users of a language must make the investigation in question an empirical one (R. Carnap, *Introduction to Semantics*, § 4 and 5, especially p. 13), it would be wrong in the present case. This simply follows from the fact that the reference made does not differ from the reference to the players in the mathematical theory of games, which is obviously not an empirical science. Secondly the occurrence of terms like 'designates,' 'names,' 'denotes,' 'refers to' etc. among the primitives is sometimes considered as a criterion for what properly should be called 'semantics;' but the game-theoretical semantics does not contain such terms. Here it may be sufficient to notice that all the terms quoted are applicable only to descriptive signs. What is at stake within formal logic is the meaning-assignment to logical signs so that we can abstract from the question what the meanings of descriptive terms consist in and what these terms refer to. But of course in case there should be other and more cogent reasons for not using the name 'semantics' to describe the game-theoretical interpretation of logical signs and the theory erected upon this interpretation, no objections should be made against exchanging this word for a better one. Perhaps one should not take too seriously the question of what can be properly called 'semantics'. The use of this term, which was originally intended to designate the theory of meanings (read: *intensions*) for a *purely referential* theory like the Bolzano-Tarski approach to logic is highly artificial anyway. The expression *'mengentheoretische Pradikatenlogik'* ('set-theoretical predicate logic'), as used in Hilbert-Bernays' *Grundlagen der Mathematik*, was a better term insofar as it clearly says what kind of tools are used.

3. The main part of this paper will consist of a detailed completeness proof of intuitionistic logic relative to the game-theoretical definition of validity. This logic was chosen for the proof because it is the strongest and presumably the most interesting among those logical systems for which no intuitively satisfactory concept of validity had *previously been* defined. At the end some hints will be given as to how this method can be used to prove the completeness of three other logical systems including the classical one. In many details we will avail ourselves of the explications and technical improvements of Lorenzen's original characterization of the new approach which are due to K. Lorenz (vid. [1]). We especially accept from the thesis of K. Lorenz the following items: the way of characterizing the asymmetry between the two players considered, the concept of (open and closed) round, the explicit formulation of a rule which corresponds to what is here called 'structural

rule,' the concept of the reduced tableau and the *gentzen*-like calculus (with minor modifications). What is new in this proof is the systematic use of *tree-constructions*. Apart from the fact that this method makes a quasi-constructive proof of the completeness and soundness of certain calculi possible it will have some further advantages: it generally facilitates the application of game-theory to logic; it makes easier the comparison with other investigations of intuitionistic logic in which trees play an essential role; it finally establishes a link between fundamental concepts of logic and of Brouwer's set theory ('finitary spread,' 'choice sequence'). The branches of the trees to be considered will represent choice sequences in the most literal sense of the word. The construction used will therefore help to answer the question about the degree of constructivity of the concepts involved.

4. For the sake of illustration the type of games to be considered will be characterized by using some elementary set-theoretical terms: We have two players, called W (White) and B (Black), a set M of positions (each of which in the logical application will be represented by a tableau) and a rule R which formally is a two-placed relation obtaining between positions. If xRy for positions x and y we say that x has been transformed into y by a permissible move. M is subdivided into two exclusive domains: the domain (of moves of) W and the domain of B, called M_W and M_B. Using the terminology of K. Lorenz we further require that R be compatible with this subdivision in the sense that a pair $x; y$ belongs to R iff x and y respectively belong to different subdomains (intuitively speaking no player is allowed to make two moves in succession). R will usually be a many-many relation. If xRy then x is called an R-predecessor of y and y an R-successor of x. If to a given x there is no z such that xRz (i.e. no R-successor of x is defined) then x is called an end-position.

We distinguish between a *game* as a type and a 'concrete performance' of a game or a *tournament*. In a tournament either B or W has to produce the initial position of the tournament in the zero-step. Because of the asymmetry between B and W introduced below the class of tournaments of a type of game thereby splits up into two proper sub-classes. If an initial position x after a finite number of moves (each made in accordance with R) is transformed into an end-position e which is an element of M_B then W has won the tournament (because this means that the next move would be up to B but B is not allowed to make a move by the rule of the game). W wins *only* in this case. If e belongs to the domain of W then B has won. There is no necessity that an end-position must be reached in a finite number of steps. Such a tournament formally of infinite length could be considered as a typical candidate for a draw. But no draw shall be admitted in the games considered. Rather in such a situation it is stipulated that *B* has won. This introduces the first asymmetry between the two players: *B* not only wins by reaching an end-position favourable to him in a finite number of steps but as well by preventing *W* from reaching such an end-position favourable to *W*.

5. Now we come to the application to logic. The following logical signs are used: $\wedge$, $\vee$, $\neg$, $\rightarrow$, $\bigwedge$, $\bigvee$. Within the metalanguage we use Greek capitals to designate formulas, small Greek letters to designate individual variables, '*a*' (without or with subscript) to designate individual constants (i.c.) taken from a potentially infinite list of such constants and '*p*' to designate prime formulas. The latter are either propositional letters or predicate letters with an appropriate number of individual variables or constants attached. Only closed formulas (i.e. formulas without free individual variables) will be considered.

Lorenzen's basic idea can be described like this: The meanings of logical signs are not determined with the help of truth-conditions but by a precise description of their function in language-games of a special sort, called *dialogue-games*; more exactly: *the meaning of a logical sign is determined by specifying how sentences (formulas) containing it as the principal logical sign after having been presented by one player (the 'proponent') may be attacked by the counter-player (the 'opponent') and defended against this attack by the first player.*

The dialogue-games are special kinds of games falling under the abstract schema described above. The names 'proponent' (*P*) and 'opponent' (*O*) shall be used not to designate special players but only to characterize a momentary situation in the game with respect to any of the two players (this use is different from Lorenzen's who usually calls that player 'proponent' whom we name 'global validity-proponent' and 'opponent' the counter-player of this one): whoever attacks a move of this counter-player is *in this function* opponent and whoever presents either the very first formula or another formula in a move attacked later is *in this function* proponent.[2] The player who in the zero-step sets forth a formula is called the *global proponent* and his counter-player the *global opponent*. If the global proponent is identical with *W* we call him the *(global) validity-proponent* because he will represent the validity-claim with respect to the formula having been set forth in the zero-step; *B* is in this case called the *(global) validity-opponent*. On the other hand *B* in the role of the global proponent represents the satisfiability-claim and is to be called the *(global) satisfiability-proponent* and *W* in this situation the *(global) satisfiability-opponent.*

The *moves* of the game are of two kinds: (1) setting forth closed formulas and (2) making challenges: ? (dubito), $\overset{?}{l}$ (dubito left), $\overset{?}{r}$ (dubito right), $\overset{?}{a}$ (dubito for *a*) (*a* is an i.c.).

The *rule* **R** consists of three parts: the logical rule **L**, the basic rule **B** and the structural rule **S**.

L is so-to-speak the core of the game-rule. Suppose the proponent has set forth the formula Φ. **L** prescribes which attacks are permissible and what defence moves are possible against these attacks: (1) if Φ is $\Phi_1 \wedge \Phi_2$ then the opponent can choose between the two moves $\overset{?}{l}$ and $\overset{?}{r}$. In the first case the only possible defence consists in setting forth Φ_1 and in the second case in setting forth Φ_2; (2) if Φ is $\Phi_1 \vee \Phi_2$ then the only possible attack is ?; *P* can defend by his own free choice by setting forth Φ_1 or Φ_2; (3) if Φ is $\neg\Phi_1$ then the only possible attack consists in setting forth Φ_1. No defence is possible (i.e. *P* can make only other kinds of counter-moves if they are permitted by the rules, e.g. to attack Φ_1); (4) if Φ is $\Phi_1 \rightarrow \Phi_2$ then the only possible attack consists in setting forth Φ_1 and the only possible defence-move of *P* consists in setting forth Φ_2 (but *P* can make other moves if they are allowed by the rules; these rules allow in all cases to choose an attack against the Φ_1 of *O* instead of defending against his attack); (5) if Φ is $\Lambda\alpha\Phi_1$ then *O* can choose between infinitely many possible attacks: the attack move consists in $\overset{?}{a}$ whereby the i.c. *a* is picked out by *O* according to his own free choice. The only possible defence reaction of *P* is Φ_1 $\binom{\alpha}{a}$[3]; (6) if Φ is $V\alpha\Phi_1$ then the attack consists in the move ?. The defence is Φ_1 $\binom{\alpha}{a}$ whereby this time *P* can arbitrarily choose *a* from the potentially infinite list of i.c.

The basic rule **B** imposes upon *W* restrictions in the use of (closed) prime formulas within attack- or defence-moves: *W* is allowed to use a prime formula in such a move only if the same prime formula has been set forth in a previous move by *B*. There is no restriction in the use of prime formulas for *B*. It goes without saying that prime formulas may never be attacked within a dialogue.

Before formulating the last part of the game-rule it is necessary to characterize the formal representation of dialogues and positions. Taking a word from Beth this representation is made with the help of tableaux. By a *tableau* we understand a diagram in which the expressions designating moves are inserted. It consists of a *B-column* on the left and a *W-column* on the right. The dialogue is subdivided into *rounds* each represented by one line of the tableau. The rounds are counted (without explicit numeration) starting on top of the diagram, the upper-most round being called the zero-round. The first move presenting the *initial formula* of the dialogue *opens* the zero round which will never be closed. In the following steps an attack always *opens* a new round (following the last round which contains a symbol for a move) and a defence against the attack *closes* the same round. The latter can happen only if a defence is possible (which is not the case if the attack was made against a ¬-formula). We sometimes say that an attack is made against a formula or against a round meaning that it is made against a move consisting of setting forth this formula or a move in that round. As attack moves can be made not only against formulas in the immediately preceding round but against formulas in earlier rounds as well, the attack move is to be accompanied by a number indicating the round against which the attack was made. This numeration has the further purpose of telling us for each closed round occurring in a tableau which of the two moves in this line is the attack (with number attached) and which is the defence (without number). If one wants to use a single tableau to read off the whole course of a dialogue then in addition to the first use of numbers a second numeration indicating the steps is to be used (as in the general case a player is allowed to 'jump back' to close an earlier round). But this numeration is not necessary. From a formal point of view one can identify a position in a concrete dialogue D reached after move m has been made with that part of the tableau depicting D which was obtained in the momen the symbol designating m had been inserted.

The structural rule **S** specifies the circumstances and the number of times attacks and defences can be made (the logical rule doesn't say anything about this): (1) B may attack *once* (and only once) by means of an attack move in a round k a formula of the W-column occurring in a round i if $k > i$; (2) W may attack *an arbitrary number of times* a formula of the B-column occurring in a round i in case the attack is made in a round k with $k > i$; (3) B as well as W may defend a formula against an attack made in round i by a defence move made in the same round (thereby closing round i) if all rounds $k > i$ containing moves are closed (this part of the rule requires especially that for the closure of open rounds a certain order has to be observed so that later open rounds have to be closed before the earlier ones (if at all); a further consequence of this part of the rule will be discussed later).

We can now define: The *rule* **R** of the game is *the logical rule* **L** *restricted and regulated in application by the basic rule and the structural rule.* The name 'structural rule' was used for the third part of **R** because it determines the structure of the dialogue-game as intuitionistic, classical etc. If it is formulated in the way described above then it turns out that we get the intuitionistic logic.

(**L** and **B** have been explicitly formulated by P. Lorenzen; **S** constitutes what K. Lorenz called 'special rule', **L** is his 'general rule' and **B** what is called the supplement to the general rule).

Win and *loss* are defined as in the abstract case: W has won a dialogue iff after a finite number of moves a position was reached (formally represented by a tableau X) which is in the domain of B but for which no R-successor is defined (B can make no further move). In all the other cases B wins.

A player p_i has chosen a *strategy* S with respect to an initial formula Φ iff for each possible move of his counter-player (i.e. for each corresponding tableau in the domain of p_i) the R-successor is uniquely determined in advance, the zero-move consisting of setting forth the formula Φ. p_i can either be identical with the player who has set forth this initial formula or can be different from him. Formally speaking such a strategy is a function of higher order which for every X in the domain of p_i uniquely determines an R-successor whereby the first X contains the formula in question only. The concept of a strategy could be introduced in a completely general way (i.e. without reference to a special formula) but for the applications needed the relativised concept will do.

We sometimes use the symbol '$X(\Phi)$' to designate a tableau whose initial formula is Φ (this symbol is ambiguous as it does not tell whether the formula appears on the right or on the left upper corner of the tableau, i.e. whether it has been set forth by W or by B in the zero-move). Similarly we use '$D(\Phi)$' to designate a dialogue starting from this formula. A strategy S (with respect to the initial formula Φ), chosen by player W, is called a *W-win-strategy* for the initial position (which may be either in the domain of B or in that of W) iff W by making his moves in accordance with S wins every dialogue $D(\Phi)$ beginning with this initial position, i.e. he reaches in a finite number of moves an end position $X(\Phi)$ favourable for him (in the domain of B), no matter what moves B chooses for the tableaux $X(\Phi)$ in M_B. Similarly a strategy S (with respect to an initial formula) chosen by player B is a *B-win-strategy* for the initial position iff B wins every dialogue starting from this initial position in case he makes all his moves as prescribed by S. It should be kept in mind that in these definitions of win-strategies the asymmetry between B and W comes into play: that B wins every dialogue by choosing S does *not* mean that he reaches in every case an end position favourable for him in a finite number of steps (as it would be the case for W in place of B) but that he succeeds by reacting according to S in preventing W

from winning. In this case only some of the dialogues will end after a finite number of steps whereas the others will formally be of infinite length. The latter will be the normal case because if one single formula appears on the *B*-column that may be attacked by *W* in accordance with **L** and **B** this attack may be repeated by him an arbitrary number of times according to part (2) of the structural rule.

Validity and invalidity can now be introduced thus:

Df_1. Φ is *valid* $=_{\mathrm{Df}}$ there exists a *W*-win-strategy for the initial position *produced by W* in setting forth Φ.

Df_2. Φ is *invalid* $=_{\mathrm{Df}}$ there exists a *W*-win-strategy for the initial position *produced by B* in setting forth Φ.

Both concepts are reduced to *W*-win-strategies: in the first case *W* successfully defends his validity claim for the formula he has set forth in the zero-move; in the second case *W* successfully refutes the satisfiability claim of *B* for the formula *B* has set forth in the zero-move. The dual concepts of satisfiability and rejectability which we shall not need in what follows could be introduced by reading in Df_2 and Df_1 '*B*-win-strategy' instead of '*W*-win-strategy.'

It is not immediately clear in what relation these concepts stand to their analogues within set-theoretical semantics of classical logic. It turns out that they are the intuitionistic counterparts of these concepts (if the structural rule is chosen in the way it has been formulated).

In each concrete application an assertion of the form 'Φ is valid' or 'Φ is invalid' has to be used in the effective sense: a *W*-win-strategy of the kind required can effectively be given. Formally a win-strategy too can be represented by a tableau, making use in an obvious way of Beth's construction of subtableaux: A diagram representing a *W*-win-strategy must take into account *all* possible moves of *B* if permitted by the rules. The same procedure can be used to show that no *W*-win-strategy exists: here a fixed *B*-strategy is represented by a diagram taking into account all possible choices of *W* and showing that in no case *W* reaches an end position favourable for him.

Remark 5.1. Using the concept of the *closure* of a tableau a calculus based upon the game-rules alone could be introduced in an analogous way to that chosen by Beth for the classical case with the help of his concept of a closed semantic tableau.

The following examples are used for illustration:

B		*W*
		¬¬(*p* ∨ ¬*p*)
¬(*p* ∨ ¬*p*)	*0*	*1* *p* ∨ ¬*p*
?	*2*	¬*p*
p	*3*	
		1 *p* ∨ ¬*p*
?	*5*	*p*

The numbers indicate the rounds attacked. All the rounds before the last (closed) round that are open could not have been closed because they all stem from an attack against a ¬-formula. It is essential for the win of *W* that he can (in round 5) repeat an earlier attack (made in round 2) against the formula in round 1 of the *B*-column: after his first counter-attack made in round 2 he lost the part of the dialogue ending with the *B*-attack in round 4 because *B* used a prime formula for this attack; it is exactly this prime formula which *W* can use after his second attack against the formula in round 1 to defend the formula needed for this attack. *B* never has a choice between different moves. So the tableau can not only be used to represent a concrete dialogue ending with win for *W*. It can be taken as formally representing a win-strategy for *W*. For this use the tableau is to be interpreted as a *schema* covering infinitely many cases differing from each other with respect to the prime formula which here remains arbitrary (whereas within its use to depict a concrete dialogue *p* designates a particular prime formula or atomic sentence).

This example at the same time illustrates the fact that the last move of *W* leading to win for him must *always* consist in 'taking over' a prime formula from the *B*-column in order to make a permissible defence-move or a permissible attack-move. As long as *W* uses a complex formula in one of his moves it can be attacked by *B* within the next move and if *W* uses a challenge it can be answered by *B* because for *B* there is no restriction upon the use of formulas.

It is clear that no analogous *W*-win-strategy for the case *p* ∨ ¬*p* exists: here *W* can defend against the challenge of *B* only by setting forth ¬*p* and has lost as soon as this formula is attacked by *B*. This is one of the few cases where *B* reaches an endposition favourable for him in a finite number of steps.

B			W
			$\bigvee\alpha\neg\Phi(\alpha)\to\neg\bigwedge\alpha\Phi(\alpha)$
$\bigvee\alpha\neg\Phi(\alpha)$	*0*		$\neg\bigwedge\alpha\Phi(\alpha)$
$\bigwedge\alpha\Phi(\alpha)$	*1*		
$\neg\Phi(a)$		*1*	?
$\Phi(a)$		*2*	$\underset{a}{?}$
		3	$\Phi(a)$

In this example Φ is supposed to be a prime formula. Again the tableau can be used not only to represent a concrete dialogue with win for *W* but a schema representing a *W*-win-strategy because for *B* there is always only one possible type of move. It is true that this time *B* can choose the i.c. in his defence move in round 3 in infinitely many different ways; *W* will win in all cases if he only chooses the same i.c. (in round 4) for his attack against the universal formula in round 2. So the schema-interpretation of the tableau this time not only covers all possible prime formulas taken as Φ but all possible i.c.'s taken as the *a* as well.

In the case of the present formula *W* gets a win-strategy as well if he slightly changes the order of moves made by him: for his second move he can decide to make a counter-attack instead of defending against *B*'s first attack. This case illustrates what it means to 'jump back' and close an earlier open round (if the later rounds are closed). We therefore depict this alternative too, this time – following K. Lorenz – using an additional numbering on the outer borders to designate the order of moves:

	B			*W*	
				$\bigvee\alpha\neg\Phi(\alpha)\to\neg\bigwedge\alpha\Phi(\alpha)$	*0.*
1.	$\bigvee\alpha\neg\Phi(\alpha)$	*0*		$\neg\bigwedge\Phi(\alpha)$	*4.*
3.	$\neg\Phi(a)$		*1*	?	*2.*
5.	$\bigwedge\alpha\,\Phi(a)$	*1*			
7.	$\Phi(a)$		*3*	$\underset{a}{?}$	*6.*
			2	$\Phi(a)$	*8.*

Of course most cases are not as simple as the two mentioned: As soon as there exist for *B* different types of reactions they have all to be taken into account either by constructing a tableau with nested subtableaux or by constructing a set of separate tableaux.

We now give a simple negative example which at the same time illustrates the method of subtableaux:

B			W		
			$\neg\Lambda\alpha\Phi(\alpha) \rightarrow V\alpha\neg\Phi(\alpha)$		
$\neg\Lambda\alpha\Phi(\alpha)$ *0*			$V\alpha\neg\Phi(\alpha)$		
? *1*			$\neg\Phi(a)$		*1* $\Lambda\alpha\Phi(\alpha)$
$\Phi(a)$ *2*		$?_d$ *2*		*1* $\Lambda\alpha\Phi(\alpha)$	*loss*
	$?_c$ *3*		*1* $\Lambda\alpha\Phi(\alpha)$	*loss*	
$?_b\,(b \neq a)$ *4*			*loss*		

Here again Φ is supposed to be a prime formula. To each left (right) subcolumn of the W-column there corresponds a left (right) subcolumn of the B-column; the same holds for each subcolumn etc. The first subdivision arises from the fact that W after the first attack of B can choose between defending (by setting forth $V\alpha\neg\Phi(\alpha)$) or counter-attacking (by setting forth $\Lambda\alpha\Phi(\alpha)$). In the latter case he loses as soon as attacked by B (he can not make good later for the omitted defence against B's first attack without violating the structural rule as there are rounds left open below the first round in which the defence-move would have to be made). In the former case where W chooses defence after the first attack of B the left subtableau again splits up as soon as B has made his attack against $V\alpha\neg\Phi(\alpha)$ because now W can either choose to defend against this attack (by taking an a and setting forth $\neg\Phi(a)$) or to counter-attack B's formula $\neg\Lambda\alpha\Phi(\alpha)$ etc. *W loses in all cases.* As the tableau takes into account all possible moves of W there cannot exist a W-win-strategy and therefore the formula in question is not valid under the definition given. In the leftmost case B has to make sure that in his last attack against W's $\Lambda\alpha\Phi(\alpha)$ he chooses an i.c. *different* from that one chosen by W before (in his defence-move $\neg\Phi(a)$). This shows that 'silly reactions' of B may lead to a win of W even if there exists no W-win-*strategy*. In the same way W may lose a dialogue about a *valid* formula because he chooses a wrong strategy. This of course was to be expected: If the application of the game-rules would be mechanical we would have an effective decision procedure contradicting the recursive unsolvability of quantification theory.

The schema-interpretation of the tableau used to prove the non-validity of the formula in our last example requires an additional consideration: In none of the cases B reaches a win-position after a finite number of steps because in principle W can repeat (in all 3 cases) his attack against the formula $\neg \bigwedge \alpha \Phi(\alpha)$ of the B-column an arbitrary number of times. But W can never win as long as B answers again and again in the way described in the tableau. Therefore this is a situation where B wins because he can prevent W from winning in a finite number of steps. All the dialogues are formally of infinite length. The words 'loss' inserted within the subcolumns of the W-column have to be interpreted in this sense.

If for the moment we take it for granted that the concept of validity defined coincides with intuitionistic validity then this example illustrates how the method of subtableaux (usually to be combined with an additional consideration of the kind just described) can be used to show the intuitionistic unprovability of certain formulas. This procedure is in most cases simpler than the other known methods.

In case the method is to be used to represent a fixed B-strategy (as in our last example) or a fixed W-strategy there is another item to be mentioned: Whenever that player all of whose moves have to be taken into account attacks a $\bigwedge$-formula or defends a $\bigvee$-formula he can choose the i.c. in infinitely many ways. Therefore strictly speaking we would get an infinite number of subtableaux (in our example in round 2 of the leftmost case). But it can easily be seen that this situation reduces to a finite number of possibilities consisting of 2 classes: the one class contains the choices of an i.c. already occurring in the tableau before that move; and the other class contains the choices of a *new* i.c. In the latter case only one arbitrary new i.c. has to be taken into consideration.

For the completeness proof no use will be made of the method of subtableaux. Rather the different dialogues emerging from a certain initial position will be represented as separate branches of a tree formally depicting a strategy chosen by one of the two players.

Remark 5.2. Special attention should be paid to the *threefold asymmetry* between B and W: the first is mirrored by the basic rule which introduces a difference in handling *prime formulas*; the second is given by the structural rule which allows only *W the repetition of attacks*; the third follows from the difference in the definition of 'win' and 'loss' for B and W.

Remark 5.3. The concepts of open and closed round as introduced by K. Lorenz and the precise formulation of the operations of opening and closing rounds is essential. It can be shown that the original presentation of the game-theory as given by P. Lorenzen which does not make use of this concept leads to inadequate results. One could e.g. challenge Lorenzen's claim that his formulation gives the intuitionistic logic by the following counter-example (*W*-win-strategy for double negation elimination):[4]

B	*W*
	$\neg\neg p \to p$
$\neg\neg p$	$\neg p$
p	p

Here attacks and counter-attacks as well as defences are inserted without distinction of rounds and use is made only of the fact that *W* can first decide to counter-attack $\neg\neg p$ and later to defend his original formula by using the p that has been set forth by *B* in his last attack. Using the methods of rounds this case is to be represented in the following way:

B	*W*
	$\neg\neg p \to p$
$\neg\neg p$ *0*	
	1 $\neg p$
p *2*	

This time *W* loses; the use of p to close round 1 would violate part 3) of **S** because there are later open rounds 2 and 3 which can not be closed but which had to be closed before a closure of round 1 were allowed.

Remark 5.4. From the point of view of adequacy the question naturally arises whether an intuitive justification can be given for the rules of the (intuitionistic) logic-game. Here a distinction has to be made between the structural rule and the other rules.

As far as the structural rule is concerned the answer is negative. The best one can do, e.g., with respect to part (2) of **S** is to bring forward certain plausibility arguments: *W* can 'increase his knowledge' in the course of a dialogue because of new information he gets by the prime formulas set forth by *B*. As has already been shown in the first example it may happen that *W* is successful in his second attack against a formula of *B* because *B*'s reaction to his first (unsuccessful) attack provides *W* with the formula needed.

But of course considerations of this kind do not justify this rule as necessary. If it is dropped one gets other logical systems. Furthermore there is no intuitive justification at all for *not allowing W* a *repetition of defences* as well.

As has been shown by K. Lorenz the admission of defence-repetition produces the classical logic-game. Therefore there seems to be no possibility to mark out on the game-theoretical basis the intuitionistic logic as the 'effective' or 'real' logic against the classical one.

So it has to be admitted that the structural rule contains an element of arbitrariness. But it is exactly this element of arbitrariness which makes the game-theoretical semantics more flexible than the usual one so that it can be used to define validity-concepts for *different* systems of logic.

With respect to the other rules an intuitive justification can be given though a somewhat more complex consideration seems to be needed than suggested by the remarks of P. Lorenzen. As far as **L** is concerned one can agree that in case of $\wedge$, $\vee$ and V the rules are in accordance with intuitionistic ideas proper: It has been suggested by intuitionists that for the meaning-assignment to logical signs the concept of *truth* has to be replaced by the concept of *proof*. E.g. a $\wedge$-sentence is to be considered as proved if both $\wedge$-members are proved or a V-sentence is to be considered as proved if an object is 'effectively given' and the sentence proved for this object. The parts (1), (2) and (6) of the logical rule of the game can be considered as a translation of this idea into the language of game-theory (with additions to be made similar to those for the other cases below). In the case of the other 3 logical signs Lorenzen's game-theoretical interpretation (parts (3), (4) and (5) of **L**) gives a generalization of this approach. We take $\rightarrow$-formulas as an example to discuss the intuitive justification in these cases.

Suppose *W* as global proponent has presented the initial formula $\Phi_1 \rightarrow \Phi_2$. *B* can attack setting forth Φ_1. *W* has a choice between counter-attack and defence. Suppose he chooses the first and succeeds, i.e. he wins the 'attack-dialogue' against Φ_1. As *B* is the representant of the satisfiability claim *W* has thereby shown the unsatisfiability of Φ_1. It is in sufficient accordance with the common usage of '*D*' to say in such a case that $\Phi_1 \rightarrow \Phi_2$ has been established as valid: This part of the rule **L** (4) amounts to the acceptance of the '*ex falso quodlibet*' for the definition of '$\rightarrow$' (therefore it is not possible on this basis to introduce a validity concept for minimallogic, at least not without changing the logical rule). Suppose *W* chooses the second alternative and wins the 'defence-game' about the Φ_2. He has thereby shown that no counterexample for Φ_2 can be constructed *if* the satisfiability of Φ_1 is taken for granted. This again is in accordance with the intended meaning.

The situation is different if *B* is the global proponent who presents this formula in the first step. He claims only satisfiability and succeeds in 'proving' this if he is able to show either the non-validity of Φ_1 (by constructing a counterexample against *W*'s attack) or the satisfiability of Φ_2 in case Φ_1 is granted as valid. Again this is in accordance with the presystematic meaning. But it shows that a *different* kind of intuitive justification has to be given for the game-rule L(4) depending on whether *W* or *B* presents the $\rightarrow$-formula in the zero-step. The situation is even slightly more complicated because for *W* (though not for *B*) it does make a difference whether the $\rightarrow$-formula is presented in the first step or later: if later, then *W*'s validity-claim is relative to certain 'parameters' entering in this claim, namely the prime formulas that have been set forth before by *B*. Speaking in terms of sentences instead of in terms of formulas we can put it this way: *W* in this case does not claim validity outright but only validity on the assumption that certain elementary sentences are proved. The reasoning needed to justify the other parts of the logical rule are analogous.

The intuitive motivation for the *basic rule* is obvious: *W* as representant of the validity-claim (as global proponent) or invalidity-claim (as global opponent) cannot be allowed to base this claim on the assumption of special formulas (sentences) whereas *B* in the dual position of a representant of the satisfiability- or rejectability-claim can do this.

For the definition of 'win' and 'loss' we have a straightforward justification too: The validity-claim can be accepted as established if this has been done in a finite number of steps.

So the only 'intuitive gap' lies in the structural rule. It should not be overlooked that part (3) of this rule contains more than a precise description of the order in which the open rounds have to be closed and thereby another kind of 'intuitive gap': As a round opened by an attack against a $\neg$-formula can never be closed this part (3) bars all preceding open rounds from ever being closed. The example $\neg\neg p \rightarrow p$ of remark 5.3 is an illustration of this point. This stipulation can hardly be justified in a different way than by pointing out that only by accepting it can one get a 'reasonable' logic-game.

The artificiality in the structural rule is the price which has to be paid to get a more flexible concept of logical truth that is applicable to different logical systems and at the same time independent from a certain problematic basic assumption mentioned in the beginning.

Stretching the idea of 'how to determine the meanings of logical signs' somewhat more, one could think of using the introduction-elimination-rules of a system of natural deduction as an alternative semantical approach as well. The artificiality in this case would consist in the well-known 'structural restrictions' needed to prevent the rules from producing nonsense. What makes the game-theoretical approach more interesting are the connections it brings about between logic and another field of mathematical research and the fruitful applications to various classes of problems like the question of constructivity, intuitionistic unprovability and perhaps even consistency.

Remark 5.5. With respect to the definition of validity given the question arises whether the reference made within this definition to *all possible moves of B* (consistent with the rules) introduces a non-constructive element. Using Brouwer's terminology one can say that we have here *a universal quantifier ranging over free choice sequences*. A dialogue emerging from a given initial position on the basis of a fixed *W*-win-strategy consists of a sequence of arbitrary choices made by *B* restricted by the 'spread law' **R**. We can not enter here into a discussion of the basically philosophical question of constructivity. All we can say is this: *if* two things are admitted, namely (a) that a *comparative* concept of constructivity should be given preference over a classificatory one, and (b) that the concept of a *free choice sequence is more constructive* than the concept of an *arbitrary set*, then the game-theoretical concept of validity (and analogously of invalidity etc.) is more constructive than the corresponding concept of the Bolzano-Tarski-approach.[5]

Quite apart from this question the following proof may be called *quasi-constructive* because it shows how a given *W*-win-strategy ('given' either by a system of nested subtableaux or by a strategy-tree to be described later) can be transformed effectively in a derivation within a suitable calculus.

6. We now come to the formulation of a calculus of intuitionistic quantification theory. This calculus, called S_{int}, is apart from the symbolism and a minor detail identical with that given by K. Lorenz in [1], p. 102 ff. We use the following signs: $\mathfrak{a}$; $\mathscr{B}$... are variables of the metalanguage designating arbitrary sequences of formulas. The symbol Γ will be used to designate either the empty formula or expressions of the type $[\Phi]$ with a (non-empty) formula inside. Expressions of this latter kind will sometimes be called *bracket-expressions* or *improper formulas.* $\Phi(\substack{\alpha \\ a})$ designates the result of substituting the i.c. *a* for the free occurrences of the variable α in Φ. The arrow $\Rightarrow$ is used to communicate rules of derivation. The semicolon; is used to separate premisses in the rules. The signs of the *object language* consist of the usual logical apparatus plus the following additional symbols: $*$, '**A**' (always with two formulas as indices, e.g. $\mathbf{A}_{\Phi_1\,,\,\Phi_2}$), the comma ',' and the two brackets '[' and ']'. As before '*a*' is always used to designate an i.c. (analogously '*b*', '*c*' etc.) and '*p*' stands for an arbitrary prime formula.

The formula expressions of the calculus are of the type $\mathfrak{a} * \Phi$ or $\mathfrak{a} * \Gamma$, called *tableau-sequents*. The first type could be called a *B*-tableau-sequent and the second a *W*-tableau-sequent. The star $*$ is called the sequent-symbol, the sequence of formulas preceding it in a sequent is called the antecedent and the (proper or improper) formula following it the succedent.

The axiom schema as well as the rules are to be applied irrespective of the order of the formulas in the antecedents (this stipulation can be rendered precise with the help of the concept of 'cognate,' comp. S.C. Kleene, IM, p. 480).

Axiom schema: $\mathcal{A}, p * p$

Rules:

(1) (a) $\mathcal{A} * [\Phi];\ \mathcal{A} * [\Psi] \Rightarrow \mathcal{A} * \Phi \wedge \Psi$

(b) $\mathcal{A} * [\mathsf{A}_{\Phi,\Psi}] \Rightarrow \mathcal{A} * \Phi \vee \Psi$

(c) $\mathcal{A}, \Phi * [\Psi] \Rightarrow \mathcal{A} * \Phi \rightarrow \Psi$

(d) $\mathcal{A}, \Phi * \Rightarrow \mathcal{A} * \neg\Phi$

(2) (a) $\mathcal{A} * [\Phi\,(\tfrac{\alpha}{a})] \Rightarrow \mathcal{A} * \Lambda\alpha\Phi$

(b) $\mathcal{A} * [\Phi] \Rightarrow \mathcal{A} * \mathrm{V}\alpha\Phi$

(3) (a) $\mathcal{A}, \Phi \wedge \Psi, \Phi * \Gamma \Rightarrow \mathcal{A}, \Phi \wedge \Psi * \Gamma$

$\mathcal{A}, \Phi \wedge \Psi, \Psi * \Gamma \Rightarrow \mathcal{A}, \Phi \wedge \Psi * \Gamma$

(b) $\mathcal{A}, \Phi \vee \Psi, \Phi * \Gamma;\ \mathcal{A}, \Phi \vee \Psi, \Psi * \Gamma \Rightarrow \mathcal{A}, \Phi \vee \Psi * \Gamma$

(c) $\mathcal{A}, \Phi \rightarrow \Psi, \Psi * \Gamma;\ \mathcal{A}, \Phi \rightarrow \Psi * \Phi \Rightarrow \mathcal{A}, \Phi \rightarrow \Psi * \Gamma$

(d) $\mathcal{A}, \neg\Phi * \Phi \Rightarrow \mathcal{A}, \neg\Phi * \Gamma$

(4) (a) $\mathcal{A}, \Lambda\alpha\Phi, \Phi\,(\tfrac{\alpha}{a}) * \Gamma \Rightarrow \mathcal{A}, \Lambda\alpha\Phi * \Gamma$

(b) $\mathcal{A}, \mathrm{V}\alpha\Phi, \Phi\,(\tfrac{\alpha}{a}) * \Gamma \Rightarrow \mathcal{A}, \mathrm{V}\alpha\Phi * \Gamma$

(5) (a) $\mathcal{A} * \Phi \Rightarrow \mathcal{A} * [\Phi]$

(b) $\mathcal{A} * \Phi \Rightarrow \mathcal{A} * [\mathsf{A}_{\Phi,\Psi}]$

$\mathcal{A} * \Psi \Rightarrow \mathcal{A} * [\mathsf{A}_{\Phi,\Psi}]$

(c) $\mathcal{A} * \Phi\,(\tfrac{\alpha}{a}) \Rightarrow \mathcal{A} * [\Phi]$

In the rules (2) (a) and (4) (b) the i.c. *a must not occur in the sequent* which is the *conclusion* of that rule.

It has been proved in [1] that (a calculus immediately seen to be equivalent with) S_{int} is equivalent with Kleene's intuitionistic calculus $G3$ (IM, p. 480) in the sense that $*\Phi$ ($\Phi*$) is derivable in S_{int} if $\to \Phi$ ($\Phi\to$) is derivable in $G3$ ('$\to$' being the sequent-symbol of $G3$). As $G3$ is equivalent in the well-known way with a formulation of intuitionistic quantification theory (e.g. with Heyting's or Kleene's) it is sufficient to prove the following:

THEOREM 1. *If Φ is valid in the sense of Df_1 then the expression $*\Phi$ is derivable in S_{int}.*

Proof: (I) As a preparatory step we choose a slightly different way of representing dialogues: Instead of inserting all (symbols for) moves into one and the same tableau we split the tableau up in a linear sequence of tableaux. The first tableau of this sequence contains the formula having been set forth in the zero-step only (in our case: it contains nothing besides the formula Φ in the right upper corner). Each of the other tableaux contains all the expressions occurring in its immediate predecessor plus the symbol for the next move. This sequence can be of finite or of infinite length. The elements of this sequence depict the momentary subsequent positions of the whole dialogue. Every sequence of this kind therefore represents a concrete dialogue.

We think of this sequence as written in a vertical order, starting at the bottom.

(II) Next we represent strategies with respect to a certain initial position by *trees*. Trees representing W-win-strategies will be transformed by successive steps into proof trees within S_{int}.[6]

A *strategy-tree* (**S.T.**) associated with a certain initial position (and thereby with the formula occurring in this position) can be of one of the following 4 types:[7]

(1) A *Black-White-Strategy-Tree* (**BWS.T.**): This is the degenerate case where both of B and W have chosen a fixed strategy. From these choices a concrete dialogue emerges. We can therefore identify a **BWS.T.** with a sequence described in (I).

(2) An *Open-Strategy-Tree* (**OS.T.**): Here neither B nor W has chosen a fixed strategy. The tree has therefore to represent all possible moves and counter-moves. The *origin* consists of the tableau containing the initial formula (on the right or on the left corner). To each tableau T we add as *immediate upper tableau* (i.u.t.) all those tableaux which are R-successors of T (the positions of the dialogues hereby being identified with the tableaux as their formal representants). If there are several i.u.t. T_i of T we arrange them

on the basis of a lexicographical ordering of the expressions representing the new move in T_i.

By a *branch* of this tree we understand a sequence of tableaux beginning with the origin and containing to each given tableau exactly one of the i.u.t. Each branch represents one possible dialogue starting from the given initial position and each such dialogue is represented by one branch.

In general, an **OS.T.** will be infinite for two different reasons: It will contain some *branches of infinite length* (if to each T on that branch an R-successor is defined and therefore the dialogue represented by it has no end position). It will be remembered that such a branch expresses a loss for W (rather than a draw). Furthermore it will contain *infinite bifurcations* whenever a Λ-formula is attacked or a V-formula is defended because the i.c. used for this move can be chosen in infinitely many different ways.

(3) A *Black-Strategy-Tree* (**BS.T.**) is a tree differing from that one mentioned in (2) in this respect: for all tableaux in M_B the i.u.t. is uniquely determined by the strategy chosen.

(4) A *White-Strategy-Tree* (**WS.T.**) is to be constructed similar to that in (3). Here the i.u.t. of a $T_i \in M_W$ is uniquely determined.

A **BS.T.** as well as a **WS.T.** can exhibit the same twofold infinity as an **OS.T.** with the difference that this time the infinite bifurcation can only arise when the counter-player (i.e. the player who has not chosen a fixed strategy) makes the attacks or defences mentioned.

If a branch of a tree is of finite length the uppermost tableau is called *peak-tableau*. It represents an end position favourable for one of the two players. Every tree is subdivided into *levels*; to each level a natural number is assigned as *rank*, the origin having the rank *0* and the i.u.t. of a tableau of rank n belonging to the level with rank $n + 1$.

For the proof we suppose that the origin consists of a tableau containing Φ only in the right upper corner. If W has a win-strategy for this initial position the corresponding **WS.T.** becomes a *White-Win-Strategy-Tree* (**W_WS.T.**). According to the definition of 'win' for White this player wins every dialogue in finitely many steps no matter what moves are made by B. The **W_WS.T.** has therefore only branches of finite length and for all peak-tableaux T_i: $T_i \in M_B$. We call this tree $Tr(\Phi)$. The number of tableaux lying on the branch of greatest length is called *the order* of W's win-strategy represented by that tree. It is the smallest number n that can be given at the beginning of the dialogue such that W will win after at most n steps. This concept is not necessary for the following proof; it rather serves to get an additional result.

Remark 6.1. The tree-representation may be used as a tool towards a clarification of the question of constructivity. Branches of a strategy-tree represent free choice sequences. In case of an **OS.T.** the choices are made alternatingly by both players; in case of a **BS.T.** or **WS.T.** the choices are made by the counter-player. Suppose now the following numbering has been introduced: a Gödelnumbering *gn* of formulas, an assignment of rank-numbers to the tree and an additional number-representation of the results of the choices made by the players so that the free choice sequences become number theoretic functions (this e.g. can be done with the help of an additional Gödelization of the reduced tableaux introduced below which replace the original tableaux in the tree). We consider a statement of the form that a dialogue originating from an initial formula set forth by W and developing on the basis of a fixed W strategy S and a set of free choices made by B reaches an end position favourable for W after n steps. Under the numbering we get a 3-placed relation between a number theoretic choice sequence α, a rank number $2y + 1$ and a *gn* x of the formula in question. As it is effectively decidable whether a dialogue has at a certain moment reached an end position which means win for W we get a *recursive relation* $R(\alpha, y, x)$ between a number-theoretic function and two numbers. The statement that the strategy S chosen by W is a win-strategy for the formula in question means the same as: there exists to every choice sequence produced by the moves of B (relative to the fixed S) a step-number n such that after n steps a win-position is reached for W. In terms of the numbering this becomes: $\bigwedge \alpha \bigvee y R(\alpha, y, x)$ with R recursive.[8] If the phrase 'there exists a W win-strategy ...' is interpreted in the non-constructive way then the statement that the formula with Gödelnumber x is valid becomes even more involved, namely: $\bigvee F \bigwedge \alpha \bigvee y R(F, \alpha, y, x)$ whereby F represents the function called 'strategy'. The analogous representation of effective satisfiability would be more complicated, namely: $\bigwedge \alpha (\bigvee y R(\alpha, y, x) \vee \bigwedge z N(\alpha, z, x))$. This is due to the fact that dialogues without end position are part of the B-win-strategy.

(III) We now replace all the tableaux on the $\mathbf{W_W S.T.}$ $Tr(\Phi)$ by their so called reductions (introduced in [1]). Roughly speaking a reduced tableau $\overline{T}$ is obtained from a tableau by eliminating from T everything that is irrelevant for the further course of the dialogue and inserting in the open rounds symbols to designate the possible defence-moves in these rounds. More exactly $\overline{T}$ is obtained from T by the following operations:

(a) cancel all numbers indicating moves or rounds; (b) cancel all challenges (a challenge can never be attacked); (c) cancel all formulas of the W-column that have already been attacked (they can not be attacked any more);

(d) insert the following special symbols d in the open rounds; let m be an arbitrary move, m' an attack against m and m'' a possible defence of m against m' (m'' always occurs in the same round as m'): If m' is an attack against a $\wedge$, $\rightarrow$ or $\bigwedge$- formula then m'' is uniquely determined and d shall be the expression $[m'']$. If m' is an attack against a $\neg$-formula then d is the expression [ ]. If m is a $\vee$-formula $\Phi \vee \Psi$ then d is $[\mathbf{A}_{\Phi,\Psi}]$ ('**A**' for 'alternative'). If m is the $\bigvee$-formula $\bigvee \alpha \Phi$ then d is the same as $[\Phi]$ (so if the existential quantifier was not vacuous, the formula within the bracket contains the free variable α);

(We call [ ] the empty bracket expression. As in the case of the calculus we call every sequence of symbols beginning and ending with brackets an improper formula or a bracket expression. We use $\Gamma\#$ in the same sense as Γ but this time including the empty bracket (so $\Gamma\#$ is *either* the empty formula *or* a bracket expression with a proper formula inside *or* the empty bracket).) (e) replace the horizontal line on top of the tableau by an arrow pointing to the left if $T \in M_B$ and to the right if $T \in M_W$; (f) arbitrary permutations of proper formulas and of proper formulas with bracket expressions are allowed as long as the order of bracket expressions among themselves is maintained (this holds for both columns).

By requirement (e) the domain of moves is made explicit. This is necessary in case the difference in the number of open rounds on the two columns (which difference is always *0* or *1*!) is *0* because in this case one cannot find out by the structure of a reduced tableau in whose domain it lies if it is not explicitly indicated. The restriction in (f) with respect to the order of bracket expressions is necessary because this order symbolizes the order of open rounds (which is essential in view of the structural rule). To get a certain kind of uniqueness in the representation we decide always to 'push' the bracket expressions to the end of the reduced tableau so that they follow all proper formulas.

The reduction of the tableau on p. 251, used to exemplify the W-win-strategy for a quantificational formula, looks like this:

$$
\begin{array}{r|l}
\multicolumn{2}{l}{\longleftarrow} \\
\bigvee \alpha \neg \Phi(\alpha) & \\
\bigwedge \alpha \;\; \Phi(\alpha) & \\
\neg \Phi(a) & \Phi(a) \\
\Phi(a) & [\quad]
\end{array}
$$

By the procedure described in (III) $Tr(\Phi)$ has been transformed into another tree $Tr^*(\Phi)$ which consists instead of tableaux of their corresponding reductions. In the subsequent discussions we shall retain the original designations like 'i.u.t.' referring by them to the modified tree *Tr**.

We now extend the use of the concept of win-strategy: First we speak of a *W*-win-strategy for a tableau, meaning that *W* in following that strategy will certainly win if the dialogue starts at a position represented by the given tableau. Secondly we even speak of a win-strategy for a *reduced* tableau. The latter way of talking is justified because if *W* has a win-strategy for a tableau *T* (whose reduction therefore is $\bar{T}$) then obviously this same strategy is a win-strategy for all the other tableaux with the same reduction $\bar{T}$ as well: these other tableaux differ from the given one only with respect to items that are irrelevant for the further course of the dialogue.

(IV) By a *deduction string* of a tableau-sequent *t* in S_{int} we understand a (finite or infinite) sequence of tableau-sequents t_1, t_2, ... such that *t* is the first one and for each i, t_{i+1} is one of the premisses of t_i for an application of one of the rules of S_{int}. If there is a last tableau-sequent in the string it is called the *peak-tableau-sequent* of that string. The number of tableau-sequents occurring in a string with finitely many tableaux is called the *length* of that string. By a *deduction tree* of a tableau-sequent *t* in S_{int} we understand an assemblage of deduction strings of *t* which together form a deduction of *t* within S_{int}. If all deduction strings are of finite length then we call the tree a *finite* deduction tree. The peak-tableau-sequent of the strings which compose this tree are called the *premises* of that deduction tree. If all the premises of a finite deduction tree are axioms then the tree is called a *proof tree* of *t*. The length of the longest deduction string in a proof tree of *t* is called the *order of the* (S_{int}-) *proof of t*.

We shall show that the modified $\mathbf{W_W S.T.}$ $Tr^*(\Phi)$ of the valid formula Φ can by successive steps be transformed into a proof tree of the tableau-sequent $*\Phi$ in S_{int}. We shall get the further result that the order of the proof of $*\Phi$ is not greater than the order of the win-strategy of Φ which was used in the construction of the $\mathbf{W_W S.T.}$ of Φ.

The tree *Tr** will be modified into a new tree whose reduced tableaux are of a very simple type: If the reduced tableau is in the domain of *B* then in the new tree it will always be of this type:

(A) $\overleftarrow{\quad\quad a} \;\rceil\; \Psi$

If the reduced tableau is in the domain of *W* then in the new tree it will always be of this type:

(B) $a \;\lceil\; \overrightarrow{\Gamma\#\quad\quad}$

Hereby $\mathfrak{a}$ is in both cases a (possibly empty) column consisting of *proper* formulas only (i.e. no bracket expression occurs in it), Ψ in (A) is one single proper formula and $\Gamma\#$ in (B) is to be interpreted in the way described described above (p. 262). We call this new tree Tr^s or more exactly $Tr^s(\Phi)$ ('s' for 'simplified'). It will turn out that it differs from a proof tree in S_{int} only in symbolism (namely the vertical line and the arrow in the reduced tableaux has to be replaced by the sequent-symbol* and the columns of formulas by rows containing the same formulas).

The modifications to be made on Tr^* start at the origin of the tree. Step by step the modifications are carried through to the higher levels of the tree. But we immediately consider the two general cases that a given reduced tableau T either is an element of M_B or an element of M_W.

Case 1: $T \in M_B$. Then this reduced tableau is of type (A) described above. This is certainly true for the initial position (with $\mathfrak{a}$ empty) because the origin of Tr consisted of the tableau $\overline{\quad|}\ \Phi$ which has in Tr^* the reduction $\overleftarrow{\quad|}\ \Phi$

For the other cases this assertion about the structure of the reduced tableaux is part of the proof.

So we can assume that T is:

(a) $\overleftarrow{\quad \mathfrak{a} \quad|}\ \Psi$

We distinguish two subcases.

Subcase 1.1: The principal logical sign of Ψ is one of the 5 signs $\wedge, \vee, \rightarrow, \neg, \mathrm{V}$.[9] In these cases we leave the reduced immediate upper tableaux of (a) unchanged. So e.g. if Ψ is the same as $\Psi_1 \wedge \Psi_2$ then the next level of the tree contains the two reductions:

(C_1) $\quad \mathfrak{a}\ \overrightarrow{|\ [\Psi_1]\quad}$ $\qquad\qquad \mathfrak{a}\ \overrightarrow{|\ [\Psi_2]\quad}$

To see that this is true one has to remember that on the next level the reductions of the tableaux depicting *all possible* moves of B must appear; but B in the situation described by (a) can only attack the $\wedge$-formula on the right by means of $\overset{?}{l}$ or $\overset{?}{r}$ so that we get the two reductions of (C_1) (B can not choose to defend because there is no bracket expression on the left column representing a possible B-defence and he cannot choose another attack because there is no other formula on the right column which he could attack besides the one mentioned in (a)).

Similarly if Ψ is $\Psi_1 \vee \Psi_2$ the i.u.t. of (a) is:

(C_2) $\quad \mathfrak{a}\ \overrightarrow{|\ [A_{\Psi_1,\Psi_2}]\quad}$

If Ψ is $\Psi_1 \to \Psi_2$ the i.u.t. of (a) is:

$$(C_3)\quad \begin{array}{c|l} & \longrightarrow \\ a & \\ \Psi_1 & [\Psi_2] \end{array}$$

If Ψ is $\neg\Psi_1$ the i.u.t. of (a) is:

$$(C_4)\quad \begin{array}{c|l} & \longrightarrow \\ a & \\ \Psi_1 & [\ \ ] \end{array}$$

If Ψ is $\bigvee\alpha\Psi_1$ then the i.u.t. of (a) is:

$$(C_5)\quad \begin{array}{c|l} & \longrightarrow \\ a & [\Psi_1] \end{array}$$

(throwing a glance at the mapping of reduced tableaux to tableau-sequents below the reader can immediately see that we have got applications of the 4 rules (1) of S_{int} and of (2)(b)).

Subcase 1.2: If Ψ is $\bigwedge\alpha\Psi_1$ then the situation is different because the original tree *Tr* as well as the modified tree *Tr** contain an infinite bifurcation at this node, as *B* in his next move can attack the universal formula in infinitely many different ways. This bifurcation is removed with the help of the following:

LEMMA 1. Suppose *W* has chosen a fixed strategy *S*. Suppose further that in the dialogue to which this *S* is applied a (position represented by a) tableau *T* is reached whose reduction *T* is:

$$\text{(i)}\quad \begin{array}{r|l} \longleftarrow & \\ a & \bigwedge\alpha\Sigma \end{array}$$

Then *S* is a *W*-win-strategy for *T* iff it is a *W*-win-strategy for:

$$\text{(ii)}\quad \begin{array}{c|l} & \longrightarrow \\ a & [\Sigma(\tfrac{\alpha}{a})] \end{array}$$

whereby *a* is an i.c. not occurring in (i).

Proof: *S* is a *W*-win-strategy for (i) iff it is one for all *R*-successors of it. As (ii) is one of these one has only to show that *S* is a *W*-win-strategy for (i) if it is one for (ii). This simply follows from the fact that the infinitely many possible choices of individual constants in *B*'s attack $\overset{?}{a}$ against the formula $\bigwedge\alpha\Sigma$ can be represented by *one single choice* of 'the worst kind for *W*', namely of one i.c. that has not yet occurred: *If B* chooses another i.c. not occurring in (i) then we get a system of dialogues isomorphic to those starting with the position whose reduction is (i) (namely differing from these dialogues with respect to one i.c. only and therefore all ending with a win-position for *W* as well). If *B* ('is so silly to') choose(s) an i.c. which already occurs in (i) then the same holds. The only difference to the former case is this: it may happen that W can win quicker than he could before (if the i.c. occurs within a prime formula of the B-column in (i) which can be used for a move leading to win for W). This at the same time shows that the implication of the Lemma from (ii) to (i) would not hold if the additional requirement in (ii) concerning the i.c. were omitted.

Going back to our tree-construction we now decide to replace all the infinitely many reduced immediate upper tableaux of (a) by the reduced tableau:

$$(C_6) \qquad \mathfrak{a} \,\Big|\, [\Psi_1(\tfrac{\alpha}{c})] \rightarrow$$

whereby c is the alphabetically first i.c. not occurring in the given reduction (a).

Together with the elimination of all the other i.u.t. of (a) *all subtrees having them as origins are eliminated as well*. By Lemma 1 the new tree represents a win-strategy of W iff the old tree represents such a win-strategy. As the tree has only been trimmed and nothing added, the order of the win-strategy has not been increased by this manipulation.

(Under the mapping mentioned before we now get an application of the rule (2)(a) of S_{int}).

Case 2: $T \in M_W$. Then the reduced tableau T is of type (B). This holds for the situation after the first step as shown by the 6 cases (C_1) to (C_6). That it holds for the other cases as well is part of the proof. So we assume that T which may occur on a level with rank number r is:

$$\text{(b)} \qquad \mathfrak{a} \,\Big|\, \Gamma\# \rightarrow$$

(the $\Gamma\#$ instead of Γ is to be used because of the cases (C_4)).

This case is different in principle from case 1 in the following respect: A strategy chosen by W is a win-strategy for a position in the domain of B if it is a win-strategy for *all* R-successors of that position. This was the general situation in case 1. On the other hand such a W-strategy is a win-strategy for a position in W's domain if it is a win-strategy for *at least one* R-successor of that position (because now it is up to W to make the proper choice). This is the situation of case 2.

If the position is like that described in (b) two classes of possibilities have to be taken into consideration: The given W-strategy can either prescribe *defence* for the next move (of course only if the symbol in the W-column of (b) expresses a possible defence that can be realized) or it can prescribe *attack* against one of the formulas occuring in the W-column of (b). As the tree represents a fixed strategy chosen by W only one special case of these possibilities applies (i.e. the i.u.t. of the given one is uniquely determined).

Subcase 2.1: The W-strategy S prescribes *defence*. Then the tree is left unchanged. So if the $\Gamma\#$ in (b) is of kind $[\Sigma]$ and Σ does not contain a free variable then the i.u.t. in level with rank $r+1$ is: $\overleftarrow{\boldsymbol{a}\;}|\,\Sigma$. If $\Gamma\#$ is $[\mathsf{A}_{\Sigma_1,\Sigma_2}]$ then the i.u.t. is either $\overleftarrow{\boldsymbol{a}\;}|\,\Sigma_1$ or $\overleftarrow{\boldsymbol{a}\;}|\,\Sigma_2$ (depending on what S prescribes). If $\Gamma\#$ is $[\Sigma]$ with a free variable α in Σ then the i.u.t. is $\overleftarrow{\boldsymbol{a}\;}|\,\Sigma(\genfrac{}{}{0pt}{}{\alpha}{a})$ [10] (if the previous B-attack was made against a V-formula with vacuous quantifier so that the quantification variable does not occur within the formula itself, then the first case applies here too). *All the tableaux on level with rank r + 1 are now of kind* (A).

Subcase 2.2: The strategy chosen by W prescribes *attack* against one of the formulas of $\boldsymbol{a}$. Again 4 subcases have to be distinguished.

Subcase 2.2.1: S prescribes attack against a $\wedge$-, $\vee$- or Λ-formula. Then we eliminate the immediate upper tableaux on the level $r+1$ but leave the (reduced) tableaux on level $r+2$ unchanged. If e.g. S prescribes an attack against a formula $\Sigma_1 \wedge \Sigma_2$ then the i.u.t. of (b) is

$$\text{either } (x) \quad \overleftarrow{\begin{array}{c|c} \boldsymbol{a}' & \\ \Sigma_1 \wedge \Sigma_2 & \Gamma\# \\ [\Sigma_1] & \end{array}} \qquad \text{or } (y) \quad \overleftarrow{\begin{array}{c|c} \boldsymbol{a}' & \\ \Sigma_1 \wedge \Sigma_2 & \Gamma\# \\ [\Sigma_2] & \end{array}}$$

$\boldsymbol{a}'$ being the column of formulas of $\boldsymbol{a}$ different from $\Sigma_1 \wedge \Sigma_2$ (and empty after the first move). In this situation the only move B can make is to realize the possible defence designated by the bracket-expression on the left column. Therefore there is respectively only one i.u.t. of (x) or (y), namely

$$\text{either } (C_7) \quad \overrightarrow{\begin{array}{c|c} \boldsymbol{a}' & \\ \Sigma_1 \wedge \Sigma_2 & \Gamma\# \\ \Sigma_1 & \end{array}} \qquad \text{or } (C'_7) \quad \overrightarrow{\begin{array}{c|c} \boldsymbol{a}' & \\ \Sigma_1 \wedge \Sigma_2 & \Gamma\# \\ \Sigma_2 & \end{array}}$$

S is a W-win-strategy for the former tableaux iff it is one for the latter. Therefore the elimination of the reduced tableau (x) or (y) of level $r+1$ does not do any harm; it just removes an unnecessary intermediate member from the modified W-win-strategy-tree.

If S prescribes an attack against a formula $\Sigma_1 \vee \Sigma_2$ then the i.u.t. of (b) is

$$\overleftarrow{\begin{array}{c|c} \boldsymbol{a}' & \\ \Sigma_1 \vee \Sigma_2 & \\ [\mathsf{A}_{\Sigma_1,\Sigma_2}] & \Gamma\# \end{array}}$$

which is now being eliminated so that only its *two* i.u.t. on level $r+2$ are retained, namely

$$(C_8)\quad \begin{array}{c} \mathfrak{a}' \\ \Sigma_1 \vee \Sigma_2 \\ \Sigma_1 \end{array} \left| \begin{array}{c} \longrightarrow \\ \Gamma\# \\ \end{array} \right. \qquad \text{and } (C'_8)\quad \begin{array}{c} \mathfrak{a}' \\ \Sigma_1 \vee \Sigma_2 \\ \Sigma_2 \end{array} \left| \begin{array}{c} \longrightarrow \\ \Gamma\# \\ \end{array} \right.$$

The justification is the same as before.

If finally S prescribes an attack against a formula $\Lambda\alpha\Sigma$ then we get by the same elimination procedure as immediate upper tableau of (b) on level $r+2$

$$(C_9)\quad \begin{array}{c} \mathfrak{a}' \\ \Lambda\alpha\Sigma \\ \Sigma(\tfrac{\alpha}{a}) \end{array} \left| \begin{array}{c} \longrightarrow \\ \Gamma\# \\ \end{array} \right.$$

whereby the i.c. a is determined by W's attack.

Nothing has been changed with respect to the given win-strategy; but some branches of the strategy-tree have become shorter.

(Under the final mapping applications of the rules, (3) (a), (b) and (4)(a) of S_{int} have been obtained).

Subcase 2.2.2: S prescribes to attack a formula $\mathrm{V}\alpha\Sigma$ of the column $\mathfrak{a}$ in (b). On this node the tree again exhibits an infinite bifurcation because on level $r+2$ there appear the reductions of the tableaux representing the defence moves of B for all possible choices of individual constants. The following modifications are now made on the tree: First, the i.u.t. of (b) on level $r+1$, namely:

$$\begin{array}{c} \longleftarrow \\ \mathfrak{a}' \\ \mathrm{V}\alpha\Sigma \\ [\Sigma] \end{array} \left| \begin{array}{c} \\ \Gamma\# \\ \end{array} \right.$$

is eliminated. Secondly all the i.u.t. of this one on level $r+2$ are eliminated except:

$$(C_{10})\quad \begin{array}{c} \mathfrak{a}' \\ \mathrm{V}\alpha\Sigma \\ \Sigma(\tfrac{\alpha}{c}) \end{array} \left| \begin{array}{c} \longrightarrow \\ \Gamma\# \\ \end{array} \right.$$

whereby c is the alphabetically first i.c. not occurring in the given reduction (b). Thirdly of course all the subtrees having the eliminated reduced tableaux of level $r+2$ as origins are abolished too.

The elimination on level $r+1$ is justified as before. The justification for the second and third elimination step is based on the following:

LEMMA 2: Suppose in a dialogue a position is reached whose corresponding reduction is:

$$\text{(i)} \quad \boldsymbol{a} \;\Big|\; \overrightarrow{\Gamma\#}$$

Suppose further that W has chosen a strategy S which prescribes attack against a formula of the B-column $\boldsymbol{a}$ which is of the kind $\mathsf{V}\alpha\Sigma$. Then S is a W-win-strategy for (i) iff it is a W-win-strategy for

$$\text{(ii)} \quad \begin{array}{c|l} \boldsymbol{a} & \overrightarrow{\Gamma\#} \\ \Sigma\binom{\alpha}{a} & \end{array}$$

whereby a is an i.c. not occurring in (i).

Proof: By the assumption made on S this strategy is a W-win-strategy for (i) iff it is one for the uniquely determined successor of (i)), namely

$$\text{(i')} \quad \begin{array}{c|l} \overleftarrow{\boldsymbol{a}} & \\ {[\Sigma]} & \Gamma\# \end{array}$$

It now has only to be observed that B can in this situation make no other kind of move than to defend. The proof from this point on is the same as in Lemma 1: all possible defence-moves of B can be represented by a single one which is 'of the worst kind' for W.

Because of this Lemma the tree trimmed by the procedures of this subcase still represents a full W-win-strategy for the given position. As in the former 3 cases the present modification only shortens certain branches of the tree without elongating others.

(Under the final mapping this case becomes an application of rule (4)(b)).

Remark 6.2. The procedures leading to (C_6) and (C_{10}) have the effect of removing the two kinds of infinite bifurcations from the tree. The elimination of the reduced tableaux on level $r + l$ in the last four cases prevent the reduced tableaux from having a more complicated structure than those of type (A) and (B).

Subcase 2.2.3: S prescribes an attack against a formula $\Sigma_1 \rightarrow \Sigma_2$ of the column $\boldsymbol{a}$ in (b). The i.u.t. on level $r + 1$ therefore is

$$\text{(x)} \quad \begin{array}{c|l} \overleftarrow{\boldsymbol{a}'} & \\ \Sigma_1 \rightarrow \Sigma_2 & \Sigma_1 \\ {[\Sigma_2]} & \Gamma\# \end{array}$$

This again is a reduced tableau of an unwanted type having proper and improper formulas on both sides. This time a proper replacement is made on the tree (and not only a trimming as before) based on the following:

LEMMA 3: Suppose in a dialogue a position is reached whose reduction is:

$$\text{(i)}\quad \mathfrak{a} \;\;\Big|\; \overrightarrow{\;\Gamma\#\;}$$

Suppose further W has chosen a strategy S which prescribes attack against a formula $\Sigma_1 \to \Sigma_2$ occurring within $\mathfrak{a}$ on the B-column. Then S is a W-win-strategy for (i) iff it is a W-win-strategy for

$$\text{(ii)}\quad \overleftarrow{\begin{array}{c} \mathfrak{a}' \\ \Sigma_1 \to \Sigma_2 \end{array}} \;\Big|\; \Sigma_1 \qquad \text{and for (iii)}\quad \begin{array}{c} \mathfrak{a}' \\ \Sigma_1 \to \Sigma_2 \\ \Sigma_2 \end{array} \;\Big|\; \overrightarrow{\;\Gamma\#\;}$$

The orders which S has as a win-strategy of (ii) and (iii) are each smaller than the order of S as a win-strategy for (i).

Proof: By presupposition S is a W-win-strategy for (i) iff it is one for the R-successor of (i) (uniquely determined by S), i.e. for

$$\text{(i}'\text{)}\quad \overleftarrow{\begin{array}{c} \mathfrak{a}' \\ \Sigma_1 \to \Sigma_2 \\ [\Sigma_2] \end{array}} \;\Bigg|\; \begin{array}{c} \Sigma_1 \\ \Gamma\# \end{array}$$

It is therefore sufficient to relate (i′) with (ii) and (iii). In the situation described by (i′) B has the choice between a counter-attack against the formula Σ_1 or a defence by setting forth Σ_2. It is stated in this Lemma that these two cases can be treated *separately* so that W's strategy is a win-strategy for the original case iff it is one for each of these two cases.

(1) Suppose S is a W-win-strategy for (ii) and (iii). Then S is a W-win-strategy for (i′) as well. For if B in case (i′) should decide to attack Σ_1 then W's strategy is the same as in case (ii) so that B cannot prevent W from winning (by the assumption made on (ii)) as long as B continues this 'counter-attack dialogue' about the formula Σ_1. The additional improper formula $\Gamma\#$ on the right in (i′) cannot be attacked by B and therefore does not increase his chances of winning. If B decides in case (i′) to defend by setting forth Σ_2 again he can not prevent W from winning (by the assumption made on (iii)) as long as he continues this 'defence-dialogue.' Now in general B will make use of *both* possibilities (counter-attacking *and* defending). But still he cannot prevent W from winning as long as W reacts in the one situation as determined by S for (ii) and in the other situation as determined by S for (iii). B cannot benefit by combining both possibilities because for B there does not exist an 'increase of information' obtained in the course of the dialogue (for this reason it would *not* be possible to 'split up' a dialogue about a $\to$-formula

asserted by W in the way described in Lemma 3, because W could win the complex dialogue consisting of two part-dialogues each of which he would lose separately).

(2) Suppose S is a W-win-strategy for (i′). Then it certainly is one for (iii) as well. S, being a W-win-strategy for (i′), it must be one for *all* R-successors of (i′), especially for that one in which B has decided to defend in the next move by setting forth Σ_2. The reduction of this position differs from (iii) only by containing the additional formula Σ_1 on the right column. But this formula gives B an additional possibility of counter-attacking. So if W has a win-strategy in this case then a fortiori he has one for (iii).

Furthermore S under this assumption is a W-win-strategy for (ii) as well. This time the fact has to be used that S is a W-win-strategy for the successor of (i′) characterized by an attack of B against Σ_1. The additional possibility (if it is one) for W described by $\Gamma\#$ in (i′) is only an apparent one that can not be used by W as long as B continues his attack-dialogue against Σ_1: By setting forth Σ_1 W has opened a new round which must first be closed before W can make use of the possible defence $\Gamma\#$ which is already mentioned in (i) and therefore must go back to an *earlier* open round. So the fact that W has a win-strategy for (i′) can in this case not be based on $\Gamma\#$ (here for the first time within the completeness-proof the regulation about closing open rounds comes into play).

As in a situation described by (i′) B can always try out both possibilities open to him (whereas in each of the cases (ii) and (iii) he has only one possibility), the order of S as a W-win-strategy for (i′) is certainly greater than the order of S as a W-win-strategy of (ii) and as a W-win-strategy of (iii).

Going back to Subcase 2.2.3 we now replace the reduced tableau (x) and the subtree originating in it by the two reduced tableaux

$$(C_{11})\quad \begin{array}{c|c} \multicolumn{2}{c}{\longleftarrow} \\ a' & \\ \Sigma_1 \to \Sigma_2 & \Sigma_1 \end{array} \qquad \text{and} \qquad (C'_{11})\quad \begin{array}{c|c} \multicolumn{2}{c}{\longrightarrow} \\ a' & \\ \Sigma_1 \to \Sigma_2 & \Sigma\# \\ \Sigma_2 & \end{array}$$

and the two (shorter) trees representing W-win-strategies for them. That this can always be done has been shown in Lemma 3. Special attention should be paid to the fact that (C_{11}) contains a proper formula on the right (therefore the arrow goes to the left) and (C'_{11}) contains an improper formula on the right (so that the arrow goes to the right too).

(Under the final mapping this has become an application of rule (3) (c) of S_{int}).

Subcase 2.2.4: S prescribes a W-attack against a formula $\neg\Sigma$ of the B-column in (b). The i.u.t. of (b) on level $r + 1$ is

$$\text{(y)}\quad \begin{array}{c|c} \overleftarrow{\;a'\;} & \\ \neg\Sigma & \Sigma \\ [\;\;] & \Gamma\# \end{array}$$

The simplification of the tableau is this time based on the following:

LEMMA 4: Suppose in a given dialogue a position is reached whose reduction is

$$\text{(i)}\quad a \,\big|\, \overrightarrow{\;\Gamma\#\;}$$

Suppose further W has chosen a strategy S which prescribes attack against a formula $\neg\Sigma$ on the B-column. Then S is a W-win-strategy for (i) iff it is a W-win-strategy for

$$\text{(ii)}\quad \begin{array}{c|c} \overleftarrow{\;a'\;} & \\ \neg\Sigma & \Sigma \end{array}$$

Proof: The R-successor of (i) is under the assumption made

$$\text{(i')}\quad \begin{array}{c|c} \overleftarrow{\;a'\;} & \\ \neg\Sigma & \Sigma \\ [\;\;] & \Gamma\# \end{array}$$

So it is sufficient to relate (i') and (ii) by an iff-sentence. If S is a W-win-strategy for (ii) then it is one for (i') too because the empty bracket represents no additional possibility for B whereas the $\Gamma\#$ on the right in (i') may perhaps represent an additional defence-possibility for W (but as it will turn out immediately this additional possibility is a spurious one).

If S is a W-win-strategy for (i') then it is one for (ii) as well: First the omission of $\Gamma\#$ in (ii) does not hurt. By attacking a $\neg$-formula W has opened a round *which can never be closed.* On the other hand $\Gamma\#$ already occurs in (i) and therefore can represent a possible defence (if at all) coming from an earlier open round only. Therefore W-s win-strategy for (i') must be independent of it so that it need not be mentioned at all. Second the omission of the empty bracket in (ii) does not make a difference either because there is no bracket symbol above it (but it *would* make a difference if on the B-column there were symbols for possible defences coming from earlier open rounds whose realization is barred by [ ], but admitted after removal of this barrier; however besides [ ] there appear proper formulas on the B-column in (i') only). This again shows the importance of part (3) of the structural rule.

With the help of Lemma 4 the reduced tableau (y) is replaced by

$$(C_{12})\qquad \begin{array}{c|c} \overleftarrow{\quad \boldsymbol{a}' \quad} & \\ \neg\Sigma & \Sigma \end{array}$$

and the tree originating in (y) by the tree which represents *W*'s win-strategy for (C_{12}). Actually the only modification to be made with respect to the other members of the tree consists in eliminating the same 2 items of (y) that have been cancelled from (C_{12}). Especially the order of the win-strategy has not been increased.

All the reduced tableaux obtained from applying the modifications in subcase 2.2 *are either of type* (A) *or of type* (B). So in every case we can apply the same procedures described in case 1 and case 2 again and again. After a finite number of steps the construction must come to an end, because by presupposition all the branches of the tree *Tr*(Φ) and therefore of *Tr**(Φ) are of finite length and the modifications to be made lead to branches of the same or a smaller length. Apart from the symbols used the resulting tree $Tr^s(\Phi)$ has become a *proof tree* of S_{int}. To get such a tree in the symbolism of this calculus one has only to perform the following mappings:

(1) replace all *B*-tableaux $\overleftarrow{\boldsymbol{a}\quad}\big|\ \Psi$ by $\boldsymbol{a} * \Psi$

(2) replace all *W*-tableaux (a) $\boldsymbol{a}\big|\overrightarrow{\ [\Psi]\ }$ by $\boldsymbol{a} * [\Psi]$

(b) $\boldsymbol{a}\big|\overrightarrow{\ [A_{\Psi_1, \Psi_2}]\ }$ by $\boldsymbol{a} * [A_{\Psi_1, \Psi_2}]$

(c) $\boldsymbol{a}\big|\overrightarrow{\ [\ ]\ }$ by $\boldsymbol{a} *$

Hereby the $\boldsymbol{a}$ in the tableau-sequent is an (arbitrary) linear arrangement of the same formulas occurring within the column of the reduced tableau which is called $\boldsymbol{a}$ too.

The cases described in (C_1) – (C_6) have become applications of the rules (1) and (2); the situations dealt with in subcase 2.1 have become applications of the rules (5); and the cases described in (C_7) – (C_{12}) have become applications of the rules (3) and (4). The reduced peak tableaux – representing win-positions for *W* – are in the domain of *B* and therefore of type (A). The formula on the right must be a prime formula which must occur somewhere in the column of the left. This shows that the reduced peak-tableaux under the final mapping have become tableau-sequents falling under the axiom schema of S_{int}.

We have got the additional

COROLLARY: Suppose Φ is valid and the W-win-strategy for Φ is given (by means of a **W$_W$S.T.** or a system of nested subtableaux each of which is closed) then a proof of $*\Phi$ can effectively be constructed such that the order of this proof is not greater than the order of the given win-strategy.

INVALIDITY AND SOUNDNESS: S_{int} at the same time provides a proof-procedure for invalidity: *If* Φ *is invalid then the tableau-sequent* Φ^* *is provable in* S_{int}.

The proof follows immediately from that of theorem 1 and the definition of invalidity (the latter meaning W-win-strategy for an initial position of kind: Φ | with reduced tableau: $\overleftarrow{\Phi}$ |, finally mapped on Φ^*).

THEOREM 2: (Soundness of S_{int}) *If* $*\Phi$ (Φ^*) *is provable in* S_{int} *then* Φ *is valid (invalid).*

The proof is obvious: Tableau-sequents with a proper formula behind the $*$ are mapped on reduced B-tableaux (with arrow to the left) and tableau-sequents with an improper formula behind the $*$ are mapped on reduced W-tableaux. In each application of rule (1)(d) the empty space behind the $*$ has to be filled in with [ ]. The rules of S_{int} are interpreted in this sense: 'if there is a W-win-strategy for a tableau whose reductions stand before the $\Rightarrow$ then the same holds for the tableau behind the $\Rightarrow$'. This apparently holds in all cases and especially – because of the iff-character of the four Lemmas – for the rules (2)(a), (3)(c) and (d), (4)(b). Finally, axioms are mapped on reductions of tableaux representing end-positions with win for W. From these facts the theorem follows.

7. *Classical logic*. As has been shown by K. Lorenz other logical systems are obtained by changing that part of the rule which we called 'structural rule,' leaving the logical rule and the basic rule unchanged. The classical logic game is obtained by permitting W (and *only* him) besides the repetition of attacks the *repetition of defences* as well. As in the intuitionistic logic-game defence moves can be made only in order to close an open round, this change in the structural rule requires the introduction of a new type of rounds which are *opened* by defence moves (therefore called *defence rounds* by K. Lorenz in distinction to the 'attack-rounds') and always remain open *for B* in the further course of the dialogue. No additional requirement for such openings of new rounds are made (analogous to those for *closing* rounds by defences). W is

allowed to open the same kind of defence rounds an arbitrary number of times.

With this modified rule of the game the concept of validity can be defined in literally the same way as before (the same holds for the other 'semantical' concepts). It turns out that this concept coincides with classical validity. This can be shown by proving the soundness and completeness of a calculus S_{cl} formally equivalent to the classical version of *G3*. It is somewhat surprising that the completeness proof given in 6. can be carried over *literally* to the classical case. As we do not presuppose that the reader is familiar with the thesis of K. Lorenz some indications will be made how to get S_{cl} from S_{int}. The reader can then carry out the proof without difficulty.

The only change that has to be made in S_{int} is to insert in some of the rules names for arbitrary sequences of bracket-expressions. With $\mathcal{L}$ as a symbol designating such sequences (possibly empty) we make the following changes: in the axiom schema insert $\mathcal{L}$ between the $*$ and the p of the succedent; in rules (1), (2) and (5) add an $\mathcal{L}$ immediately behind the $*$; in rules (3) and (4) replace the Γ by $\mathcal{L}$ (and in the premise of rule (3)(d) insert $\mathcal{L}$ immediately behind the $*$).

Reduced tableaux are introduced in an analogous way as before; the only change that has to be made is this: in the *B*-column only those possible defences have to be introduced which come from open rounds following the last defence round. No such restriction holds for the *W*-column (for *W* a defence round is not an open round).

The reduced tableaux used in the completeness- and soundness proof will differ from the reductions of type (A) and (B) above (p. 263) by containing *both* additional bracket expressions on the right column. This is due to the fact that the strategy chosen by *W* may tell him, for certain positions in his domain, to open a new defence round instead of making use of a possible defence coming from an earlier attack-round (thereby leaving possible defences in earlier attack-rounds in the stage of mere possibilities). As in the intuitionistic case the tree has to be left unchanged whenever the strategy chosen by *W* prescribes defence (no matter what *type* of defence).

8. Non-intuitionistic subsystems of classical logic. As shown in [1] other logical systems are obtained by modifying the structural rule in other respects. One gets the ***anti-intuitionistic logic*** if one accepts the principle of defence repetition for *W* (like in classical logic) but forbids attack repetitions for *W*. If complete symmetry is introduced between *B* and *W* as far as the structural rule goes (by allowing both of them to make one attack and one defence only) then the *strict logic* is obtained, which is a sublogic of the intuitionistic as well as of the anti-intuitionistic logic. Systems similar to S_{int} and S_{cl} – formally equivalent with *gentzen*-like calculi of sequents in the strict sense – can be constructed in an obvious manner: the rules for the strict logic calculus S_{st} are the same as that for S_{int} except for not containing the formula with the logical sign in the premises of rules (3) and (4). And the rules of the anti-intuitionistic calculus S_{ai} are obtained from those of S_{cl} by exactly the same change of the rules (3) and (4).

The completeness- and soundness proof by means of tree-construction carries over to S_{st} and S_{ai}. The only modification to be made concerns the analogon to Lemma 3 (p. 270 f.). Using the symbolism of that Lemma we get the following change (whereby for S_{ai} in addition the one bracket expression in (i), (iii) and (i′) has to be replaced by a column of such expressions and in (ii) the same column to be inserted on the right side below the proper formula Σ_1):

In (i′), (ii) and (iii) the →-formula has to be cancelled from the left (it can not be attacked a second time).

Furthermore the column $\mathfrak{a}'$ of formulas occurring in (i′) has to be subdivided exhaustively into two mutually exclusive subclasses $\mathfrak{a}'_1$ and $\mathfrak{a}'_2$ such that one of them ($\mathfrak{a}'_1$ say) occurs on the left in (ii) and the other on the left in (iii). What remains to be proved is this: If *W*'s strategy is a win-strategy for the (modified) reduced tableau (i′) then it is one for the two reduced tableaux (ii) and (iii) – both modified in the two respects mentioned – as well. Suppose *B* decides in case (i′) only to attack Σ_1. Then by assumption *W* has a win-strategy for this case. In order to succeed *W* will normally need some attacks against proper formulas of the *B*-column $\mathfrak{a}'$. We call them $\mathfrak{a}'_1$ and take them as the *B*-column for (ii). But *W* must by assumption be able to win in case (i′) even if *B* later decides to set forth Σ_2 in a defence move. For this case *W* will again in the normal case need some attacks against formulas of the *B*-column. But they must *all be different* from those formulas of the *B*-column that have been attacked in order to win the part-dialogue beginning with *B*'s attack against Σ_1 (i.e. they must be different from $\mathfrak{a}'_1$). This justifies the subdivision of formulas in two exclusive classes within (ii) and (iii). If there are formulas on the left column in (i′) which *W* does not need to attack in order to win with certainty, then these formulas can arbitrarily be assigned to the one or to the other subclass, e.g. to the second calling it $\mathfrak{a}'_2$ and using it in (iii) on the left.

NOTES

[1] This paper was originally intended to be part of a philosophical article from which it had to be separated because of its technical character. The philosophical remarks in the introductory section are not elaborated and serve only the purpose of facilitating a better understanding of the following parts (by contrast and comparison). The paper is selfcontained. No previous knowledge of the works of P. Lorenzen and K. Lorenz is presupposed.

[2] So a player can be opponent and proponent even with respect to one and the same move, depending on whether we relate this move to a previous or to a later move of his counter-player.

[3] This is the result of substituting a for the free occurrences of α in Φ_1.

[4] This simple negative example was brought to my attention by Mr. W. Essler, Munich.

[5] We shall come back to the more technical aspect of this question in the course of the completeness proof.

[6] I should like to emphasize that the following tree-construction was suggested to me by the two Lemmas 6 (p. 72ff.) and 9 (p. 99ff.) in [1]. On the other hand only this tree-construction seems to make the completeness- (and soundness-) property of S_{int} explicit and at the same time simplifies the treatment by reducing what has to be proved to four critical cases dealt with in Lemma 1 to Lemma 4 below. The construction may therefore be considered as a completion and elaboration of the validity- and soundness-claim made in that thesis.

[7] In the following section a more precise description of trees could be given. As it would not affect the proof we do without it. The reader who is interested in a precise characterization can easily obtain it from the material available in the literature.

[8] Because of this fact the game-theoretical concept of validity can also be related to the theory of constructive ordinals (vide S.C. Kleene: On the forms of the predicates in the theory of constructive ordinals (second paper); *American Journ. of Math.* 77, No. 3, especially Theorem I, p. 417).

[9] In the initial position Ψ must have logical signs because W cannot use a prime formula in his first move. If Ψ is a prime formula in a later position then (a) is the reduction of a peak tableau at which the process stops.

[10] The i.c. a is determined by S.

BIBLIOGRAPHY

[1] K. Lorenz, *Arithmetik und Logik als Spiele*. Doctorial thesis, Kiel 1961.

[2] P. Lorenzen, Ein dialogisches Konstruktivitätskriterium; in: Infinistic Methods, *Proc. of the Symp. on Found. of Math.*, Warsaw 1959.

[3] P. Lorenzen, *Metamathematik*, Mannheim 1962.

BIBLIOGRAPHY OF WORKS
BY WOLFGANG STEGMÜLLER

IN ENGLISH

Books:

[1] *Main Currents in Contemporary German, British and American Philosophy*, Dordrecht-Holland 1969. This is an English translation of the 4th edition of [26].

[2] *The Structures and Dynamics of Theories*, New York 1976. This is an English translation of [23].

Articles in Scientific Periodicals:

[3] 'Remarks on the Completeness of Logical Systems Relative to the Validity-Concepts of P. Lorenzen and K. Lorenz', *Notre Dame Journal of Formal Logic* 5 (1964), 81 – 112. Reprinted as Chapter 9, Vol. II, of these *Collected Papers*.

[4] 'Carnap's Normative Theory of Inductive Probability', in P. Suppes *et al.* (eds.), *Logic, Methodology and Philosophy of Science* IV, Amsterdam 1973, pp. 501 – 513. Reprinted as Chapter 5, Vol. II, of these *Collected Papers*.

[5] 'Personal Probability, Rational Decision and Statistical Probability', *Methodology and Science* 7 (1974), 1 – 24.

[6] 'Structures and Dynamics of Theories. Some Reflections on J.D. Sneed and T.S. Kuhn', *Erkenntnis* 9 (1975), 75 – 100. Reprinted as Chapter 7, Vol. II, of these *Collected Papers*.

[7] 'Accidental ("Non-Substantial") Theory Change and Theory Dislodgement: To What Extent Logic Can Contribute to a Better Understanding of Certain Phenomena in the Dynamics of Theories', *Erkenntnis* 10 (1976), 147 – 178.

[8] 'On the Interrelations between Ethics and Other Fields of Philosophy and Science', *Erkenntnis* 11 (1977), 55 – 80.

[9] 'A Combined Approach to the Dynamics of Theories. How to Improve Historical Interpretations of Theory Change by Applying Set Theoretical Structures', to appear in *Theory and Decision* (1977).

Review Article:

[10] R. Carnap, *Der logische Aufbau der Welt* and *Scheinprobleme in der Philosophie, Journal of Symbolic Logic* 32 (1967) 509 – 514.

Short Reviews:

[11] A. Church, Symposium on 'Ontological Commitment', *Journal of Symbolic Logic* 24 (1959), 266 – 267.

[12] I. Scheffler, *Inscriptionalism and Indirect Quotation, Journal of Symbolic Logic* 24 (1959), 267.

IN GERMAN

Books:

[13] *Das Wahrheitsproblem und die Idee der Semantik*, Vienna 1957; 3rd ed., 1977.

[14] *Unvollständigkeit und Unentscheidbarkeit*, Vienna 1959; 3rd revised ed., 1973.

[15] *Glauben, Wissen und Erkennen. Das Universalienproblem einst und jetzt* (Collection of articles [36], [37], and [39]), Vol. 44 of the Libelli Series, Darmstadt 1965.

[16] *Der Phänomenalismus und seine Schwierigkeiten. Sprache und Logik* (Collection of articles [35] and [40]), Vol. 139 of the Libelli Series, Darmstadt 1969.

[17] *Aufsätze zur Wissenschaftstheorie* (Collection of articles [42], [43], [45] and [59]), Vol. 245 of the Libelli Series, Darmstadt 1970.

[18] *Aufsätze zu Kant und Wittgenstein* (Collection of articles [48], [49] and [50]), Vol. 191 of the Libelli Series, Darmstadt 1970, 3rd ed. 1974.

[19] *Das Problem der Induktion: Humes Herausforderung und moderne Antworten. Der sogenannte Zirkel des Verstehens* (Collection of articles [54] and [56]), Darmstadt 1974.

[20] *Metaphysik – Skepsis – Wissenschaft*, 2nd revised and enlarged ed., Berlin-Heidelberg-New York 1969. The 1st ed. was published in Vienna 1954 under the title *Metaphysik – Wissenschaft – Skepsis*.

[21] *Probleme und Resultate der Wissenschaftstheorie und Analytischen Philosophie*. Vol. I: *Wissenschaftliche Erklärung und Begründung*, Berlin-Heidelberg-New York 1969. This book has also been published as a five volume study-edition – Part 1: *Das ABC der modernen Logik und Semantik. Der Begriff der Erklärung und seine Spielarten*; Part 2: *Erklärung, Voraussage, Retrodiktion. Diskrete Zustandssysteme. Das ontologische Problem der Erklärung. Naturgesetze und irreale Konditionalsätze*; Part 3: *Historische, psychologische und rationale Erklärung. Kausalitätsprobleme. Determinismus und Indeterminismus*; Part 4: *Teleologie, Funktionalanalyse und Selbstregulation*; Part 5: *Statistische Erklärungen. Deduktiv-nomologische Erklärungen in präzisen Modellsprachen. Offene Probleme.*

[22] *Probleme und Resultate der Wissenschaftstheorie und Analytischen Philosophie*. Vol. II: *Theorie und Erfahrung*; Sub-volume 1: *Begriffsformen, Wissenschaftssprache, Empirische Signifikanz und Theoretische Terme*, Berlin-Heidelberg-New York 1970. This book has also been published as a three volume study-edition – Part A: *Erfahrung, Festsetzung, Hypothese und Einfachheit in der wissenschaftlichen Begriffs- und Theorienbildung*; Part B: *Wissenschaftssprache, Signifikanz und theoretische Begriffe*; Part C: *Beobachtungssprache, theoretische Sprache und die partielle Deutung von Theorien.*

[23] *Probleme und Resultate der Wissenschaftstheorie und Analytischen Philosophie*. Vol. II: *Theorie und Erfahrung*; Sub-volume 2: *Theorienstrukturen und Theoriendynamik*, Berlin-Heidelberg-New York 1973. This book has also been published as a two volume study-edition – Part D: *Logische Analyse der Struktur ausgereifter physikalischer Theorien. 'Non-statement view' von Theorien*; Part E: *Theoriendynamik. Normale Wissenschaft und wissenschaftliche Revolutionen. Methodologie der Forschungsprogramme oder epistemologische Anarchie*?

[24] *Probleme und Resultate der Wissenschaftstheorie und Analytischen Philosophie.*

Vol. IV: *Personelle und Statistische Wahrscheinlichkeit*; Sub-volume 1: *Personelle Wahrscheinlichkeit und Rationale Entscheidung*, Berlin-Heidelberg-New York 1973. This book has also been published as a three volume study-edition – Part A: *Aufgaben und Ziele der Wissenschaftstheorie. Induktion. Das ABC der modernen Wahrscheinlichkeitstheorie und Statistik*; Part B: *Entscheidungslogik (rationale Entscheidungstheorie)*; Part C: *Carnap II: Normative Theorie des induktiven Räsonierens.*

[25] *Probleme und Resultate der Wissenschaftstheorie und Analytischen Philosophie.* Vol. IV: *Personelle und Statistische Wahrscheinlichkeit*; Sub-volume 2: *Statistisches Schliessen – Statistische Begründung – Statistische Analyse*, Berlin-Heidelberg-New York 1973. This book has also been published as a two volume study-edition – Part D: *'Jenseits von Popper und Carnap': Die logischen Grundlagen des statistischen Schliessens*; Part E: *Statistische Begründung. Statistische Analyse. Das Repräsentationstheorem von de Finetti. Metrisierung qualitativer Wahrscheinlichkeitsfelder.*

[26] *Hauptströmungen der Gegenwartsphilosophie*, 6th enlarged ed. in 2 volumes, Stuttgart 1976.

Collaboration:

[27] With Rudolf Carnap on *Induktive Logik und Wahrscheinlichkeit*, Vienna 1959.

Articles in Scientific Periodicals:

[28] 'Der Wahrheitsbegriff in der gegenwärtigen Erkenntnislehre', *Die Pyramide* (1952) March, 46 – 49.

[29] 'Die neuere Erkenntnistheorie und die exakten Wissenschaften', *Die Pyramide* (1952) April.

[30] 'Der Evidenzbegriff in der formalisierten Logik und Mathematik', *Wiener Zeitschrift für Philosophie, Psychologie und Pädagogik* 4 (1953), 289 – 296.

[31] 'Bemerkungen zum Wahrscheinlichkeitsproblem', *Studium Generale* 6 (1953), 563 – 593.

[32] 'Der Begriff der synthetischen Urteile a priori und die moderne Logik', *Zeitschrift für philosophische Forschung* 8 (1954), 535 – 563.

[33] 'Ethik und Wirtschaftspolitik', *Besinnung* (Zeitschrift für Fragen der Ethik) 3 (1955), 1 – 12.

[34] 'Die Antinomien und ihre Behandlung', *Innsbrucker Beiträge zur Kulturwissenschaft* 3 (1955), 27 – 40.

[35] 'Sprache und Logik', *Studium Generale* 9 (1956), 57 – 77. Translated into English for Vol. II of these *Collected Papers*, Chapter 8.

[36] 'Das Universalienproblem einst und jetzt' (Part 1), *Archiv für Philosophie* 6 (1956), 192 – 225. Translated into English for Vol. 1 of these *Collected Papers*, Chapter 1.

[37] 'Glauben, Wissen und Erkennen', *Zeitschrift für philosophische Forschung* 10 (1956), 509 – 549.

[38] 'Ontologie und Analytizität', *Studia Philosophica* 16 (1957), 191 – 223. Translated into English for Vol. I of these *Collected Papers*. Chapter 5.

[39] 'Das Universalienproblem einst und jetzt' (Part 2), *Archiv für Philosophie* 7 (1957), 45 – 81. Translated into English for Vol. 1 of these *Collected Papers*, Chapter 1.

[40] 'Der Phänomenalismus und seine Schwierigkeiten', *Archiv für Philosophie* 8 (1958), 36 – 100. Translated into English for Vol. 1 of these *Collected Papers*, Chapter 4.

[41] 'Carnaps Auffassung der induktiven Logik', in R. Carnap and W. Stegmüller, *Induktive Logik und Wahrscheinlichkeit*, Vienna 1959, pp. 1 – 11.

[42] 'Das Problem der Kausalität', in E. Topitsch (ed.), *Probleme der Wissenschaftstheorie: Festschrift für Victor Kraft*, Vienna 1960, pp. 171 – 190. Translated into English for Vol. II of these *Collected Papers*, Chapter 2.

[43] 'Einige Beiträge zum Problem der Teleologie und der Analyse von Systemen mit zielgerichteter Organisation', *Synthese* 13 (1961), 5 – 40.

[44] 'Die Äquivalenz des klassischen und intuitionistischen Ableitungsbegriffs im Gentzen-Quine-Kalkül und in Kleene's Kalkül H', *Archiv für mathematische Logik und Grundlagenforschung* 8 (1965), 3 – 27.

[45] 'Erklärung, Voraussage, wissenschaftliche Systematisierung und nicht-erklärende Information' (German-English), *Ratio* 8 (1966), 1 – 22. English version reprinted as Chapter 3, Vol. II, of these *Collected Papers*.

[46] 'Einheit und Problematik der wissenschaftlichen Welterkenntnis', lecture held on the occasion of the 494th Munich University Founders' Day on 2 July 1966, Munich University Speeches, New Series, Issue 41, 1966.

[47] 'Der Begriff des Naturgesetzes', *Studium Generale* 19 (1966), 649 – 657.

[48] 'Eine modelltheoretische Präzisierung der Wittgensteinschen Bildtheorie', *Notre Dame Journal of Formal Logic* 7 (1966), 181 – 195. Translated for Vol. I of these *Collected Papers*, Chapter 3.

[49] 'Gedanken über eine mögliche Rekonstruktion von Kants Metaphysik der Erfahrung. Part I: Kants Rätsel der Erfahrungserkenntnis' (German-English), *Ratio* 9 (1967), 1 – 30. English version reprinted as Part I of Chapter 2, Vol. I, of these *Collected Papers*.

[50] 'Gedanken über eine mögliche Rekonstruktion von Kants Metaphysik der Erfahrung. Part II: Die Struktur des progressiven Argumentes' (German-English), *Ratio* 10 (1968), 1 – 31. English version reprinted as Part II of Chapter 2, Vol. I, of these *Collected Papers*.

[51] 'Die Ergebnisse der Erkenntnistheorie', in L. Reinisch (ed.), *Grenzen der Erkenntnis*, Freiburg 1969, pp. 11 – 30.

[52] 'Wissenschaft und Erklärung', *Zeitschrift für allgemeine Wissenschaftstheorie* 1 (1970), 252 – 263.

[53] 'Das Problem der Kausalität', in L. Krüger (ed.), *Erkenntnisproblem der Naturwissenschaften*, Köln-Berlin 1970, pp. 156 – 173. (Reprint of [39].)

[54] 'Das Problem der Induktion: Humes Herausforderung und moderne Antworten', in H. Lenk (ed.), *Neue Aspekte der Wissenschaftstheorie*, Braunschweig 1971, pp. 13 – 74. Translated into English for Vol. II of these *Collected Papers*, Chapter 4.

[55] 'Rudolf Carnap: Induktive Wahrscheinlichkeit', in J. Speck (ed.), *Grundprobleme der grossen Philosophen*, Philosophie der Gegenwart I, Göttingen 1972, pp. 45 – 97.

[56] 'Der sogenannte Zirkel des Verstehens', in K. Hübner and A. Menne (eds.), *Natur und Geschichte* (Proceedings of the 10th German Congress for Philosophy held at

Kiel, 8-12 October 1972), Hamburg 1973, pp. 21 – 45. Translated into English for Vol. II of these *Collected Papers*, Chapter 1.

[57] 'Theoriendynamik und logisches Verständnis', in W. Diederich, *Beiträge zur diachronischen Wissenschaftstheorie*, Frankfurt/M. 1974, pp. 167 – 209. Translated into English for Vol. II of these *Collected Papers*, Chapter 6.

[58] Introduction to *Das Universalienproblem*, Darmstadt 1977. (Cf. [60].)

Contributions to Collections:

[59] 'Eine Axiomatisierung der Mengenlehre', in M. Käsbauer and F. v. Kutschera (eds.), *Logik und Logikkalkül: Festschrift für Wilhelm Britzelmayr*, Freiburg 1962, pp. 57 – 103.

[60] As editor of *Das Universalienproblem*, Darmstadt 1977.

Contribution to Encyclopedia:

[61] The article 'Wissenschaftstheorie' in the Fischer-Lexicon *Philosophie*, 1958.

Review Articles:

[62] 'Die Ontologie und Anthropologie von P. Häberlin', *Zeitschrift für Philosophische Forschung* 2 (1947).

[63] N. Goodman, *The Structure of Appearance, Philosophische Rundschau* 5 (1957).

[64] W.V.O. Quine, *From a Logical Point of View, Philosophische Rundschau* 5 (1957).

[65] A. Pap, *Analytische Erkenntnistheorie, Philosophische Rundschau* 6 (1958).

[66] 'Conditio irrealis, Naturgesetze, Dispositionen und Induktion' (on N. Goodman's *Fact, Fiction and Forecast), Kant-Studien* 5 (1958-9).

[67] P. Lorenzen, *Einführung in die operative Logik und Mathematik, Philosophische Rundschau* 6 (1958-9).

[68] M. Davis, *Computability and Unsolvability, Ratio* 3 (1960).

[69] K. Schütte, *Beweistheorie, Ratio* 3 (1960).

[70] E. Stenius, *Wittgenstein's Tractatus, Philosophische Rundschau* 13 (1965).

[71] L. Wittgenstein, *Bemerkungen über die Grundlagen der Mathematik, Philosophische Rundschau* 13 (1965).

Reviews:

[72] R. Carnap, *Formalization of Logic, Philosophischer Literaturanzeiger* 4 (1952).

[73] R. Carnap, *Introduction to Semantics, Zeitschrift für philosophische Forschung* 5 (1951).

[74] R. Carnap, *Logical Foundations of Probability, Philosophischer Literaturanzeiger* 4 (1952).

[75] P. Häberlin, *Philosophia perennis, Philosophischer Literaturanzeiger* 6 (1954).

[76] W.V.O. Quine, *Methods of Logic, Philosophische Rundschau* 5 (1957).

[77] W.V.O. Quine, *Mathematical Logic, Philosophische Rundschau* 5 (1957).

[78] J.B. Rosser, *Logic for Mathematicians, Philosophische Rundschau* 5 (1957).

[79] S.C. Kleene, *Introduction to Metamathematics, Philosophische Rundschau* 5 (1957).

[80] F.B. Fitch, *Symbolic Logic, Philosophische Rundschau* 5 (1957).

[81] Hao Wang and R. McNaughton, *Les systèmes axiomatiques de la théorie des ensembles, Philosophische Rundschau* 5 (1957).

[82] W. Ackermann, *Solvable Cases of the Decision Problem, Philosophische Rundschau* 6 (1958).

[83] A. Robinson, *Complete Theories, Philosophische Rundschau* 6 (1958).

[84] I.M. Copi, *Symbolic Logic, Philosophische Rundschau* 9 (1961).

[85] A. Church, *Introduction to Mathematical Logic, Philosophische Rundschau* 9 (1961).

[86] A.A. Fraenkel and Y. Bar-Hillel, *Foundations of Set Theory, Kant-Studien* 54 (1963).

[87] P. Bernays and A.A. Fraenkel, *Axiomatic Set Theory, Kant-Studien* 54 (1963).

[88] E.W. Beth, *The Foundations of Mathematics, Kant Studien* 54 (1963).

[89] H. Hermes, *Aufzählbarkeit, Entscheidbarkeit, Berechenbarkeit, Kant-Studien* 54 (1963).

[90] *Philosophy and Analysis. A Selection of Articles Published in* Analysis *between 1933-1940 and 1947-1953* (short review), *Philosophische Rundschau* **12** (1964).

INDEX OF NAMES

SYNTHESE LIBRARY

Monographs on Epistemology, Logic, Methodology,
Philosophy of Science, Sociology of Science and of Knowledge, and on the
Mathematical Methods of Social and Behavioral Sciences

1. J. M. Bocheński, *A Precis of Mathematical Logic.* 1959, X + 100 pp.
2. P. L. Guiraud, *Problèmes et méthodes de la statistique linguistique.* 1960, VI + 146 pp.
3. Hans Freudenthal (ed.), *The Concept and the Role of the Model in Mathematics and Natural and Social Sciences, Proceedings of a Colloquium held at Utrecht, The Netherlands, January 1960.* 1961, VI + 194 pp.
4. Evert W. Beth, *Formal Methods. An Introduction to Symbolic Logic and the Study of Effective Operations in Arithmetic and Logic.* 1962, XIV + 170 pp.
5. B. H. Kazemier and D. Vuysje (eds.), *Logic and Language. Studies Dedicated to Professor Rudolf Carnap on the Occasion of His Seventieth Birthday.* 1962, VI + 256 pp.
6. Marx W. Wartofsky (ed.), *Proceedings of the Boston Colloquium for the Philosophy of Science, 1961-1962,* Boston Studies in the Philosophy of Science (ed. by Robert S. Cohen and Marx W. Wartofsky), Volume I. 1973, VIII + 212 pp.
7. A. A. Zinov'ev, *Philosophical Problems of Many-Valued Logic.* 1963, XIV + 155 pp.
8. Georges Gurvitch, *The Spectrum of Social Time.* 1964, XXVI + 152 pp.
9. Paul Lorenzen, *Formal Logic.* 1965, VIII + 123 pp.
10. Robert S. Cohen and Marx W. Wartofsky (eds.), *In Honor of Philipp Frank,* Boston Studies in the Philosophy of Science (ed. by Robert S. Cohen and Marx W. Wartofsky), Volume II. 1965, XXXIV + 475 pp.
11. Evert W. Beth, *Mathematical Thought. An Introduction to the Philosophy of Mathematics.* 1965, XII + 208 pp.
12. Evert W. Beth and Jean Piaget, *Mathematical Epistemology and Psychology.* 1966, XII + 326 pp.
13. Guido Küng, *Ontology and the Logistic Analysis of Language. An Enquiry into the Contemporary Views on Universals.* 1967, XI + 210 pp.
14. Robert S. Cohen and Marx W. Wartofsky (eds.), *Proceedings of the Boston Colloquium for the Philosophy of Science 1964-1966, in Memory of Norwood Russell Hanson,* Boston Studies in the Philosophy of Science (ed. by Robert S. Cohen and Marx W. Wartofsky), Volume III. 1967, XLIX + 489 pp.

15. C. D. Broad, *Induction, Probability, and Causation. Selected Papers.* 1968, XI + 296 pp.
16. Günther Patzig, *Aristotle's Theory of the Syllogism. A Logical-Philosophical Study of Book A of the Prior Analytics.* 1968, XVII + 215 pp.
17. Nicholas Rescher, *Topics in Philosophical Logic.* 1968, XIV + 347 pp.
18. Robert S. Cohen and Marx W. Wartofsky (eds.), *Proceedings of the Boston Colloquium for the Philosophy of Science 1966-1968*, Boston Studies in the Philosophy of Science (ed. by Robert S. Cohen and Marx W. Wartofsky), Volume IV. 1969, VIII + 537 pp.
19. Robert S. Cohen and Marx W. Wartofsky (eds.), *Proceedings of the Boston Colloquium for the Philosophy of Science 1966-1968*, Boston Studies in the Philosophy of Science (ed. by Robert S. Cohen and Marx W. Wartofsky), Volume V. 1969, VIII + 482 pp.
20. J.W. Davis, D. J. Hockney, and W. K. Wilson (eds.), *Philosophical Logic.* 1969, VIII + 277 pp.
21. D. Davidson and J. Hintikka (eds.), *Words and Objections: Essays on the Work of W. V. Quine.* 1969, VIII + 366 pp.
22. Patrick Suppes, *Studies in the Methodology and Foundations of Science. Selected Papers from 1911 to 1969*, XII + 473 pp.
23. Jaakko Hintikka, *Models for Modalities. Selected Essays.* 1969, IX + 220 pp.
24. Nicholas Rescher *et al.* (eds.), *Essays in Honor of Carl G. Hempel. A Tribute on the Occasion of His Sixty-Fifth Birthday.* 1969, VII + 272 pp.
25. P. V. Tavanec (ed.), *Problems of the Logic of Scientific Knowledge.* 1969, XII + 429 pp.
26. Marshall Swain (ed.), *Induction, Acceptance, and Rational Belief.* 1970, VII + 232 pp.
27. Robert S. Cohen and Raymond J. Seeger (eds.), *Ernst Mach: Physicist and Philosopher*, Boston Studies in the Philosophy of Science (ed. by Robert S. Cohen and Marx W. Wartofsky), Volume VI. 1970, VIII + 295 pp.
28. Jaakko Hintikka and Patrick Suppes, *Information and Inference.* 1970, X + 336 pp.
29. Karel Lambert, *Philosophical Problems in Logic. Some Recent Developments.* 1970, VII + 176 pp.
30. Rolf A. Eberle, *Nominalistic Systems.* 1970, IX + 217 pp.
31. Paul Weingartner and Gerhard Zecha (eds.), *Induction, Physics, and Ethics: Proceedings and Discussions of the 1968 Salzburg Colloquium in the Philosophy of Science.* 1970, X + 382 pp.
32. Evert W. Beth, *Aspects of Modern Logic.* 1970, XI + 176 pp.
33. Risto Hilpinen (ed.), *Deontic Logic: Introductory and Systematic Readings.* 1971, VII + 182 pp.
34. Jean-Louis Krivine, *Introduction to Axiomatic Set Theory.* 1971, VII + 98 pp.
35. Joseph D. Sneed, *The Logical Structure of Mathematical Physics.* 1971, XV + 311 pp.
36. Carl R. Kordig, *The Justification of Scientific Change.* 1971, XIV + 119 pp.
37. Milič Čapek, *Bergson and Modern Physics*, Boston Studies in the Philosophy of Science (ed. by Robert S. Cohen and Marx W. Wartofsky), Volume VII. 1971, XV + 414 pp.

38. Norwood Russell Hanson, *What I Do Not Believe, and Other Essays* (ed. by Stephen Toulmin and Harry Woolf). 1971, XII + 390 pp.
39. Roger C. Buck and Robert S. Cohen (eds.), *PSA 1970. In Memory of Rudolf Carnap*, Boston Studies in the Philosophy of Science (ed. by Robert S. Cohen and Marx W. Wartofsky), Volume VIII. 1971, LXVI + 615 pp. Also available as paperback.
40. Donald Davidson and Gilbert Harman (eds.), *Semantics of Natural Language.* 1972, X + 769 pp. Also available as paperback.
41. Yehoshua Bar-Hillel (ed.), *Pragmatics of Natural Languages.* 1971, VII + 231 pp.
42. Sören Stenlund, *Combinators, λ-Terms and Proof Theory.* 1972, 184 pp.
43. Martin Strauss, *Modern Physics and Its Philosophy. Selected Papers in the Logic, History, and Philosophy of Science.* 1972, X + 297 pp.
44. Mario Bunge, *Method, Model and Matter.* 1973, VII + 196 pp.
45. Mario Bunge, *Philosophy of Physics.* 1973, IX + 248 pp.
46. A. A. Zinov'ev, *Foundations of the Logical Theory of Scientific Knowledge (Complex Logic)*, Boston Studies in the Philosophy of Science (ed. by Robert S. Cohen and Marx W. Wartofsky), Volume IX. Revised and enlarged English edition with an appendix, by G. A. Smirnov, E. A. Sidorenka, A. M. Fedina, and L. A. Bobrova. 1973, XXII + 301 pp. Also available as paperback.
47. Ladislav Tondl, *Scientific Procedures*, Boston Studies in the Philosophy of Science (ed. by Robert S. Cohen and Marx W. Wartofsky), Volume X. 1973, XII + 268 pp. Also available as paperback.
48. Norwood Russell Hanson, *Constellations and Conjectures* (ed. by Willard C. Humphreys, Jr.). 1973, X + 282 pp.
49. K. J. J. Hintikka, J. M. E. Moravcsik, and P. Suppes (eds.), *Approaches to Natural Language. Proceedings of the 1970 Stanford Workshop on Grammar and Semantics.* 1973, VIII + 526 pp. Also available as paperback.
50. Mario Bunge (ed.), *Exact Philosophy – Problems, Tools, and Goals.* 1973, X + 214 pp.
51. Radu J. Bogdan and Ilkka Niiniluoto (eds.), *Logic, Language, and Probability. A Selection of Papers Contributed to Sections IV, VI, and XI of the Fourth International Congress for Logic, Methodology, and Philosophy of Science, Bucharest, September 1971.* 1973, X + 323 pp.
52. Glenn Pearce and Patrick Maynard (eds.), *Conceptual Chance.* 1973, XII + 282 pp.
53. Ilkka Niiniluoto and Raimo Tuomela, *Theoretical Concepts and Hypothetico-Inductive Inference.* 1973, VII + 264 pp.
54. Roland Fraïssé, *Course of Mathematical Logic* – Volume 1: *Relation and Logical Formula.* 1973, XVI + 186 pp. Also available as paperback.
55. Adolf Grünbaum, *Philosophical Problems of Space and Time.* Second, enlarged edition, Boston Studies in the Philosophy of Science (ed. by Robert S. Cohen and Marx W. Wartofsky), Volume XII. 1973, XXIII + 884 pp. Also available as paperback.
56. Patrick Suppes (ed.), *Space, Time, and Geometry.* 1973, XI + 424 pp.
57. Hans Kelsen, *Essays in Legal and Moral Philosophy*, selected and introduced by Ota Weinberger. 1973, XXVIII + 300 pp.
58. R. J. Seeger and Robert S. Cohen (eds.), *Philosophical Foundations of Science. Proceedings of an AAAS Program, 1969*, Boston Studies in the Philosophy of

Science (ed. by Robert S. Cohen and Marx W. Wartofsky), Volume XI. 1974, X + 545 pp. Also available as paperback.

59. Robert S. Cohen and Marx W. Wartofsky (eds.), *Logical and Epistemological Studies in Contemporary Physics,* Boston Studies in the Philosophy of Science (ed. by Robert S. Cohen and Marx W. Wartofsky), Volume XIII. 1973, VIII + 462 pp. Also available as paperback.
60. Robert S. Cohen and Marx W. Wartofsky (eds.), *Methodological and Historical Essays in the Natural and Social Sciences. Proceedings of the Boston Colloquium for the Philosophy of Science, 1969-1972,* Boston Studies in the Philosophy of Science (ed. by Robert S. Cohen and Marx W. Wartofsky), Volume XIV. 1974, VIII + 405 pp. Also available as paperback.
61. Robert S. Cohen, J. J. Stachel and Marx W. Wartofsky (eds.), *For Dirk Struik. Scientific, Historical and Political Essays in Honor of Dirk J. Struik,* Boston Studies in the Philosophy of Science (ed. by Robert S. Cohen and Marx W. Wartofsky), Volume XV. 1974, XXVII + 652 pp. Also available as paperback.
62. Kazimierz Ajdukiewicz, *Pragmatic Logic,* transl. from the Polish by Olgierd Wojtasiewicz. (1974, XV + 460 pp.
63. Sören Stenlund (ed.), *Logical Theory and Semantic Analysis. Essays Dedicated to Stig Kanger on His Fiftieth Birthday.* 1974, V + 217 pp.
64. Kenneth F. Schaffner and Robert S. Cohen (eds.), *Proceedings of the 1972 Biennial Meeting, Philosophy of Science Association,* Boston Studies in the Philosophy of Science (ed. by Robert S. Cohen and Marx W. Wartofsky), Volume XX. 1974, IX + 444 pp. Also available as paperback.
65. Henry E. Kyburg, Jr., *The Logical Foundations of Statistical Inference.* 1974, IX + 421 pp.
66. Marjorie Grene, *The Understanding of Nature: Essays in the Philosophy of Biology,* Boston Studies in the Philosophy of Science (ed. by Robert S. Cohen and Marx W. Wartofsky), Volume XXIII. 1974, XII + 360 pp. Also available as paperback.
67. Jan M. Broekman, *Structuralism: Moscow, Prague, Paris.* 1974, IX + 117 pp.
68. Norman Geschwind, *Selected Papers on Language and the Brain,* Boston Studies in the Philosophy of Science (ed. by Robert S. Cohen and Marx W. Wartofsky), Volume XVI. 1974, XII + 549 pp. Also available as paperback.
69. Roland Fraïssé, *Course of Mathematical Logic* – Volume 2: *Model Theory.* 1974, XIX + 192 pp.
70. Andrzej Grzegorczyk, *An Outline of Mathematical Logic. Fundamental Results and Notions Explained with All Details.* 1974, X + 596 pp.
71. Franz von Kutschera, *Philosophy of Language.* 1975, VII + 305 pp.
72. Juha Manninen and Raimo Tuomela (eds.), *Essays on Explanation and Understanding. Studies in the Foundations of Humanities and Social Sciences.* 1976, VII + 440 pp.
73. Jaakko Hintikka (ed.), *Rudolf Carnap, Logical Empiricist. Materials and Perspectives.* 1975, LXVIII + 400 pp.
74. Milič Čapek (ed.), *The Concepts of Space and Time. Their Structure and Their Development,* Boston Studies in the Philosophy of Science (ed. by Robert S. Cohen and Marx W. Wartofsky), Volume XXII. 1976, LVI + 570 pp. Also available as paperback.

75. Jaakko Hintikka and Unto Remes, *The Method of Analysis. Its Geometrical Origin and Its General Significance*, Boston Studies in the Philosophy of Science (ed. by Robert S. Cohen and Marx W. Wartofsky), Volume XXV. 1974, XVIII + 144 pp. Also available as paperback.
76. John Emery Murdoch and Edith Dudley Sylla, *The Cultural Context of Medieval Learning. Proceedings of the First International Colloquium on Philosophy, Science, and Theology in the Middle Ages – September 1973*, Boston Studies in the Philosophy of Science (ed. by Robert S. Cohen and Marx W. Wartofsky), Volume XXVI. 1975, X + 566 pp. Also available as paperback.
77. Stefan Amsterdamski, *Between Experience and Metaphysics. Philosophical Problems of the Evolution of Science*, Boston Studies in the Philosophy of Science (ed. by Robert S. Cohen and Marx W. Wartofsky), Volume XXXV. 1975, XVIII + 193 pp. Also available as paperback.
78. Patrick Suppes (ed.), *Logic and Probability in Quantum Mechanics.* 1976, XV + 541 pp.
79. H. von Helmholtz, *Epistemological Writings.* (A New Selection Based upon the 1921 Volume edited by Paul Hertz and Moritz Schlick, Newly Translated and Edited by R. S. Cohen and Y. Elkana), Boston Studies in the Philosophy of Science, Volume XXXVII. 1977 (forthcoming).
80. Joseph Agassi, *Science in Flux*, Boston Studies in the Philosophy of Science (ed. by Robert S. Cohen and Marx W. Wartofsky), Volume XXVIII. 1975, XXVI + 553 pp. Also available as paperback.
81. Sandra G. Harding (ed.), *Can Theories Be Refuted? Essays on the Duhem-Quine Thesis.* 1976, XXI + 318 pp. Also available as paperback.
82. Stefan Nowak, *Methodology of Sociological Research: General Problems.* 1977, XVIII + 504 pp. (forthcoming).
83. Jean Piaget, Jean-Blaise Grize, Alina Szeminska, and Vinh Bang, *Epistemology and Psychology of Functions.* 1977 (forthcoming).
84. Marjorie Grene and Everett Mendelsohn (eds.), *Topics in the Philosophy of Biology*, Boston Studies in the Philosophy of Science (ed. by Robert S. Cohen and Marx W. Wartofsky), Volume XXVII. 1976, XIII + 454 pp. Also available as paperback.
85. E. Fischbein, *The Intuitive Sources of Probabilistic Thinking in Children.* 1975, XIII + 204 pp.
86. Ernest W. Adams, *The Logic of Conditionals. An Application of Probability to Deductive Logic.* 1975, XIII + 156 pp.
87. Marian Przełęcki and Ryszard Wójcicki (eds.), *Twenty-Five Years of Logical Methodology in Poland.* 1977, VIII + 803 pp. (forthcoming).
88. J. Topolski, *The Methodology of History.* 1976, X + 673 pp. (forthcoming).
89. A. Kasher (ed.), *Language in Focus: Foundations, Methods and Systems. Essays Dedicated to Yehoshua Bar-Hillel*, Boston Studies in the Philosophy of Science (ed. by Robert S. Cohen and Marx W. Wartofsky), Volume XLIII. 1976, XXVIII + 679 pp. Also available as paperback.
90. Jaakko Hintikka, *The Intentions of Intentionality and Other New Models for Modalities.* 1975, XVIII + 262 pp. Also available as paperback.
91. Wolfgang Stegmüller, *Collected Papers on Epistemology, Philosophy of Science and History of Philosophy*, 2 Volumes, 1977 (forthcoming).

92. Dov M. Gabbay, *Investigations in Modal and Tense Logics with Applications to Problems in Philosophy and Linguistics.* 1976, XI + 306 pp.

93. Radu J. Bogdan, *Local Induction.* 1976, XIV + 340 pp.

94. Stefan Nowak, *Understanding and Prediction: Essays in the Methodology of Social and Behavioral Theories.* 1976, XIX + 482 pp.

95. Peter Mittelstaedt, *Philosophical Problems of Modern Physics,* Boston Studies in the Philosophy of Science (ed. by Robert S. Cohen and Marx W. Wartofsky), Volume XVIII. 1976, X + 211 pp. Also available as paperback.

96. Gerald Holton and William Blanpied (eds.), *Science and Its Public: The Changing Relationship,* Boston Studies in the Philosophy of Science (ed. by Robert S. Cohen and Marx W. Wartofsky), Volume XXXIII. 1976, XXV + 289 pp. Also available as paperback.

97. Myles Brand and Douglas Walton (eds.), *Action Theory. Proceedings of the Winnipeg Conference on Human Action, Held at Winnipeg, Manitoba, Canada, 9-11 May 1975.* 1976, VI + 345 pp.

98. Risto Hilpinen, *Knowledge and Rational Belief.* 1978 (forthcoming).

99. R. S. Cohen, P. K. Feyerabend, and M. W. Wartofsky (eds.), *Essays in Memory of Imre Lakatos,* Boston Studies in the Philosophy of Science (ed. by Robert S. Cohen and Marx W. Wartofsky), Volume XXXIX. 1976, XI + 762 pp. Also available as paperback.

100. R. S. Cohen and J. Stachel (eds.), *Leon Rosenfeld, Selected Papers.* Boston Studies in the Philosophy of Science (ed. by Robert S. Cohen and Marx W. Wartofsky), Volume XXI. 1977 (forthcoming).

101. R. S. Cohen, C. A. Hooker, A. C. Michalos, and J. W. van Evra (eds.), *PSA 1974: Proceedings of the 1974 Biennial Meeting of the Philosophy of Science Association,* Boston Studies in the Philosophy of Science (ed. by Robert S. Cohen and Marx W. Wartofsky), Volume XXXII. 1976, XIII + 734 pp. Also available as paperback.

102. Yehuda Fried and Joseph Agassi, *Paranoia: A Study in Diagnosis,* Boston Studies in the Philosophy of Science (ed. by Robert S. Cohen and Marx W. Wartofsky), Volume L. 1976, XV + 212 pp. Also available as paperback.

103. Marian Przełęcki, Klemens Szaniawski, and Ryszard Wójcicki (eds.), *Formal Methods in the Methodology of Empirical Sciences.* 1976, 455 pp.

104. John M. Vickers, *Belief and Probability.* 1976, VIII + 202 pp.

105. Kurt H. Wolff, *Surrender and Catch: Experience and Inquiry Today,* Boston Studies in the Philosophy of Science (ed. by Robert S. Cohen and Marx W. Wartofsky), Volume LI. 1976, XII + 410 pp. Also available as paperback.

106. Karel Kosík, *Dialectics of the Concrete,* Boston Studies in the Philosophy of Science (ed. by Robert S. Cohen and Marx W. Wartofsky), Volume LII. 1976, VIII + 158 pp. Also available as paperback.

107. Nelson Goodman, *The Structure of Appearance,* Boston Studies in the Philosophy of Science (ed. by Robert S. Cohen and Marx W. Wartofsky), Volume L. 1977 (forthcoming).

108. Jerzy Giedymin (ed.), *Kazimierz Ajdukiewicz: Scientific World-Perspective and Other Essays, 1930-1963.* 1977 (forthcoming).

109. Robert L. Causey, *Unity of Science.* 1977, VIII + 180 pp. + indices (forthcoming).

110. Richard Grandy, *Advanced Logic for Applications.* 1977 (forthcoming).

111. Robert P. McArthur, *Tense Logic*. 1976, VII + 84 pp.
112. Lars Lindahl, *Position and Change: A Study in Law and Logic*. 1977, IX + 299 pp.
113. Raimo Tuomela, *Dispositions*. 1977 (forthcoming).
114. Herbert A. Simon, *Models of Discovery and Other Topics in the Methods of Science*, Boston Studies in the Philosophy of Science (ed. by Robert S. Cohen and Marx W. Wartofsky), Volume LIV. 1977 (forthcoming).
115. Roger D. Rosenkrantz, *Inference, Method and Decision*. 1977 (forthcoming).
116. Raimo Tuomela, *Human Action and Its Explanation. A Study on the Philosophical Foundations of Psychology*. 1977 (forthcoming).
117. Morris Lazerowitz, *The Language of Philosophy*, Boston Studies in the Philosophy of Science (ed. by Robert S. Cohen and Marx W. Wartofsky), Volume LV. 1977 (forthcoming).
118. Tran Duc Thao, *Origins of Language and Consciousness*, Boston Studies in the Philosophy of Science (ed. by Robert S. Cohen and Marx. W. Wartofsky), Volume LVI. 1977 (forthcoming).

SYNTHESE HISTORICAL LIBRARY

Texts and Studies
in the History of Logic and Philosophy

Editors:

1. M. T. Beonio-Brocchieri Fumagalli, *The Logic of Abelard.* Translated from the Italian. 1969, IX + 101 pp.
2. Gottfried Wilhelm Leibnitz, *Philosophical Papers and Letters.* A selection translated and edited, with an introduction, by Leroy E. Loemker. 1969, XII + 736 pp.
3. Ernst Mally, *Logische Schriften,* ed. by Karl Wolf and Paul Weingartner. 1971, X + 340 pp.
4. Lewis White Beck (ed.), *Proceedings of the Third International Kant Congress.* 1972, XI + 718 pp.
5. Bernard Bolzano, *Theory of Science,* ed. by Jan Berg. 1973, XV + 398 pp.
6. J. M. E. Moravcsik (ed.), *Patterns in Plato's Thought. Papers Arising Out of the 1971 West Coast Greek Philosophy Conference.* 1973, VIII + 212 pp.
7. Nabil Shehaby, *The Propositional Logic of Avicenna: A Translation from al-Shifā: al-Qiyās,* with Introduction, Commentary and Glossary. 1973, XIII + 296 pp.
8. Desmond Paul Henry, *Commentary on De Grammatico: The Historical-Logical Dimensions of a Dialogue of St. Anselm's.* 1974, IX + 345 pp.
9. John Corcoran, *Ancient Logic and Its Modern Interpretations.* 1974, X + 208 pp.
10. E. M. Barth, *The Logic of the Articles in Traditional Philosophy.* 1974, XXVII + 533 pp.
11. Jaakko Hintikka, *Knowledge and the Known. Historical Perspectives in Epistemology.* 1974, XII + 243 pp.
12. E. J. Ashworth, *Language and Logic in the Post-Medieval Period.* 1974, XIII + 304 pp.
13. Aristotle, *The Nicomachean Ethics.* Translated with Commentaries and Glossary by Hypocrates G. Apostle. 1975, XXI + 372 pp.
14. R. M. Dancy, *Sense and Contradiction: A Study in Aristotle.* 1975, XII + 184 pp.
15. Wilbur Richard Knorr, *The Evolution of the Euclidean Elements. A Study of the Theory of Incommensurable Magnitudes and Its Significance for Early Greek Geometry.* 1975, IX + 374 pp.
16. Augustine, *De Dialectica.* Translated with Introduction and Notes by B. Darrell Jackson. 1975, XI + 151 pp.

Made in the USA
Las Vegas, NV
14 November 2024

11642946R00175